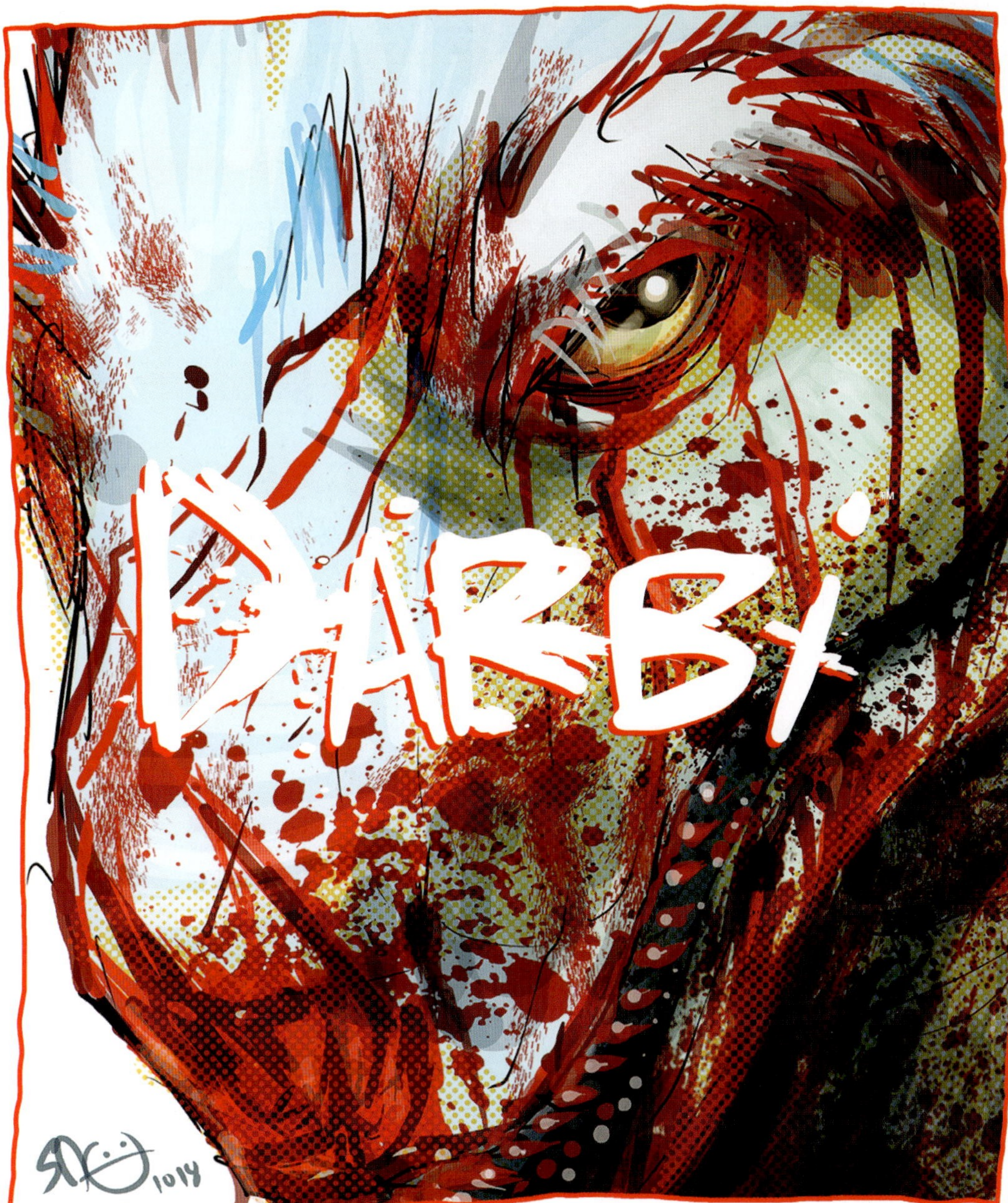
DARBI™

BY

SHERARD JACKSON

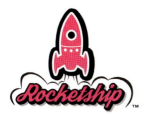

Rocketship Entertainment, LLC

Tom Akel, CEO & Publisher
Rob Feldman, CTO
Jeanmarie McNeely, CFO
Brandon Freeberg, Dir. of Campaign Mgmt.
Phil Smith, Art Director
Jed Keith, Social Media

DARBI VOLUME 1
ISBN SOFTCOVER: 978-1-952126-17-8
ISBN HARDCOVER: 978-1-952126-18-5
ISBN BLOODED EDITION: 978-1-952126-58-1
First printing. June 2021. Published by Rocketship Entertainment, LLC. 136 Westbury Ct., Doylestown, PA 18901. Contains material orginally published online as "Darbi" on the LINE Webtoon app. Printed in China.

rocketshipent.com

DARBI originally published digitally at WEBTOON

EVERYTHING HATES YOU
PG. 3

BLOODED
PG. 39

CRETACEOUS BOOGALOO
PG. 103

EVERYTHING HATES YOU

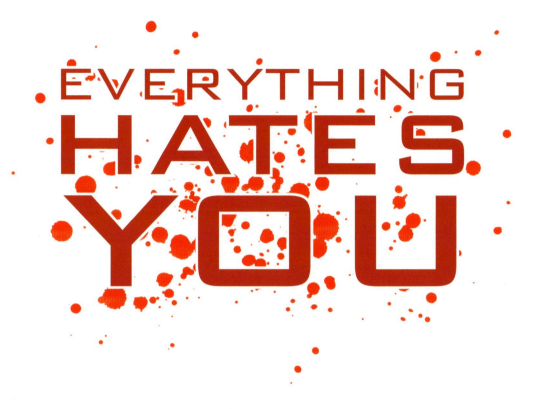

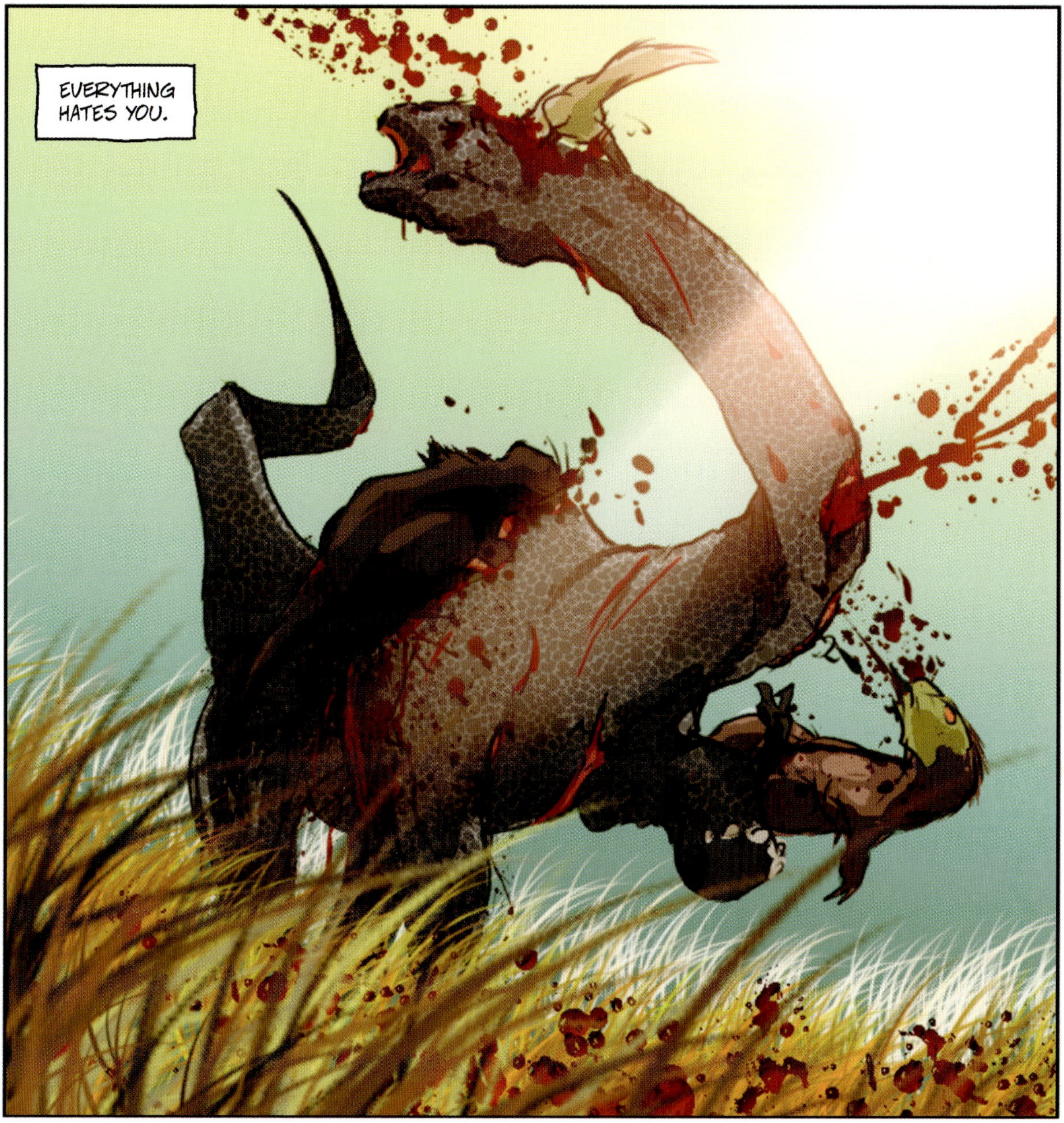
EVERYTHING HATES YOU.
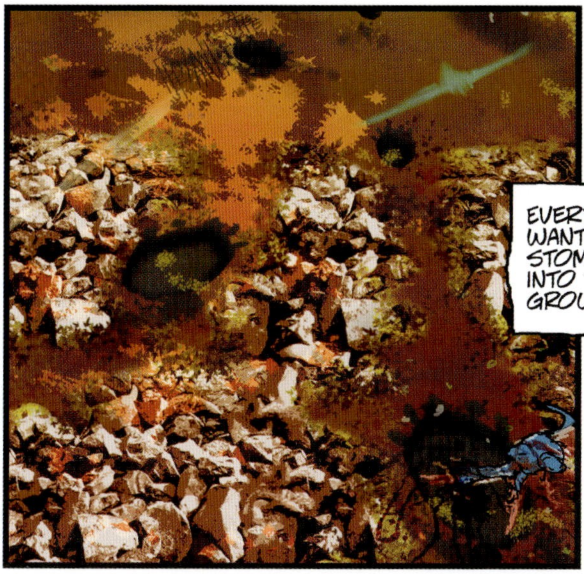
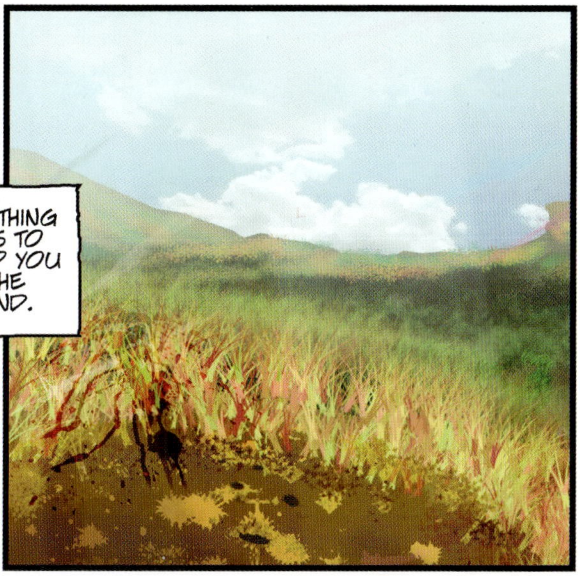
EVERYTHING WANTS TO STOMP YOU INTO THE GROUND.

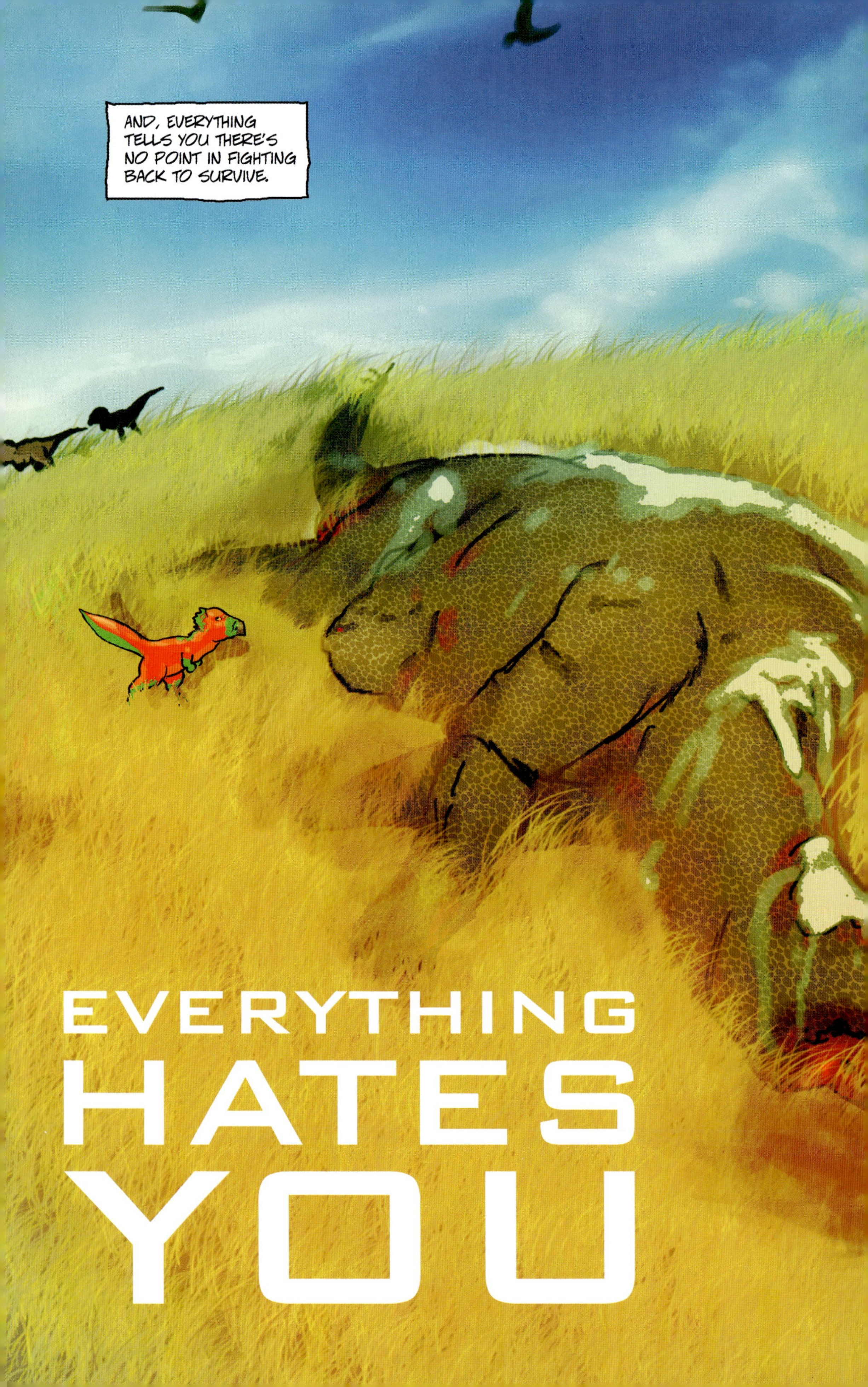
AND, EVERYTHING TELLS YOU THERE'S NO POINT IN FIGHTING BACK TO SURVIVE.
EVERYTHING HATES YOU

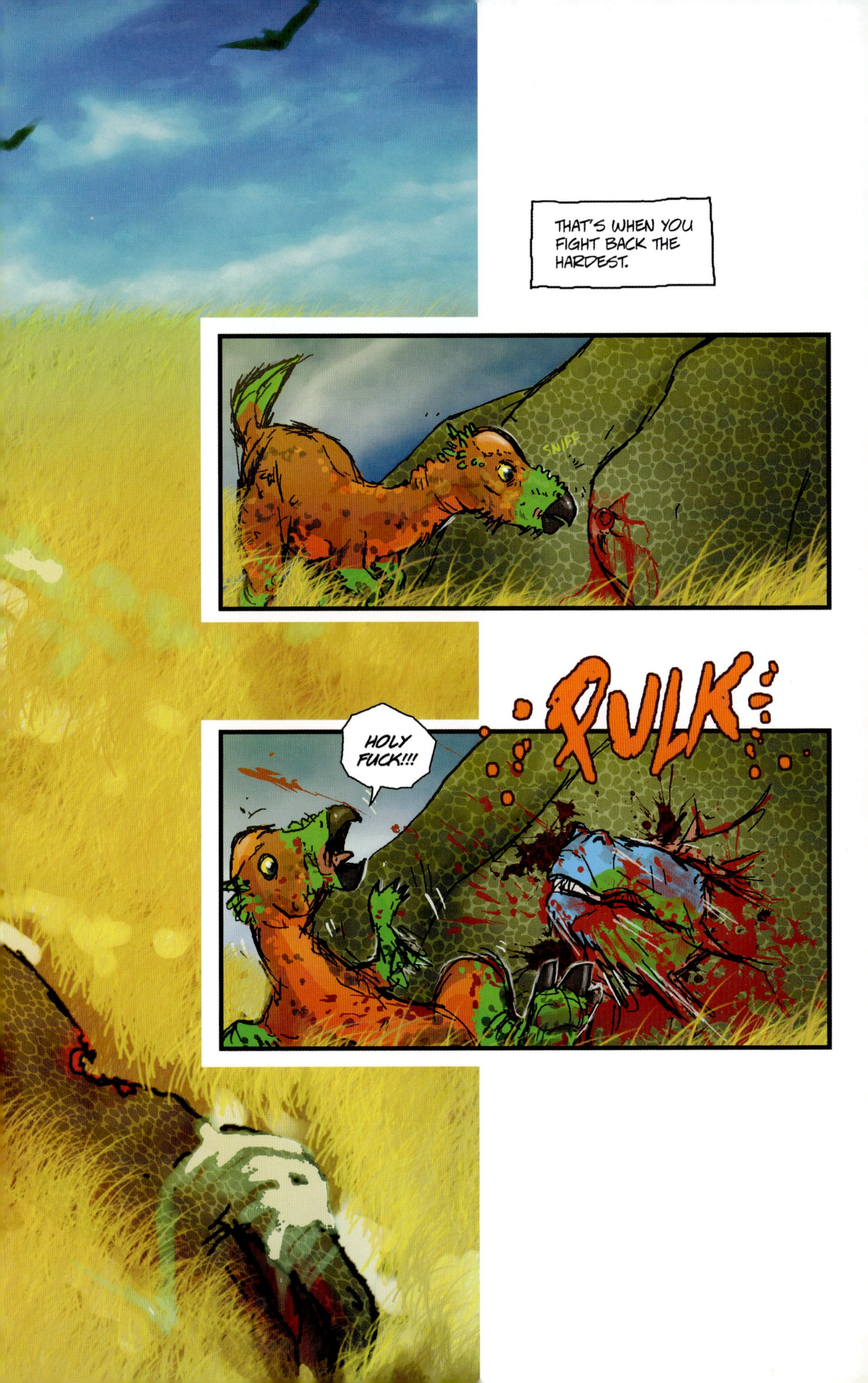
THAT'S WHEN YOU FIGHT BACK THE HARDEST.
SNIFF.
PULK
HOLY FUCK!!!

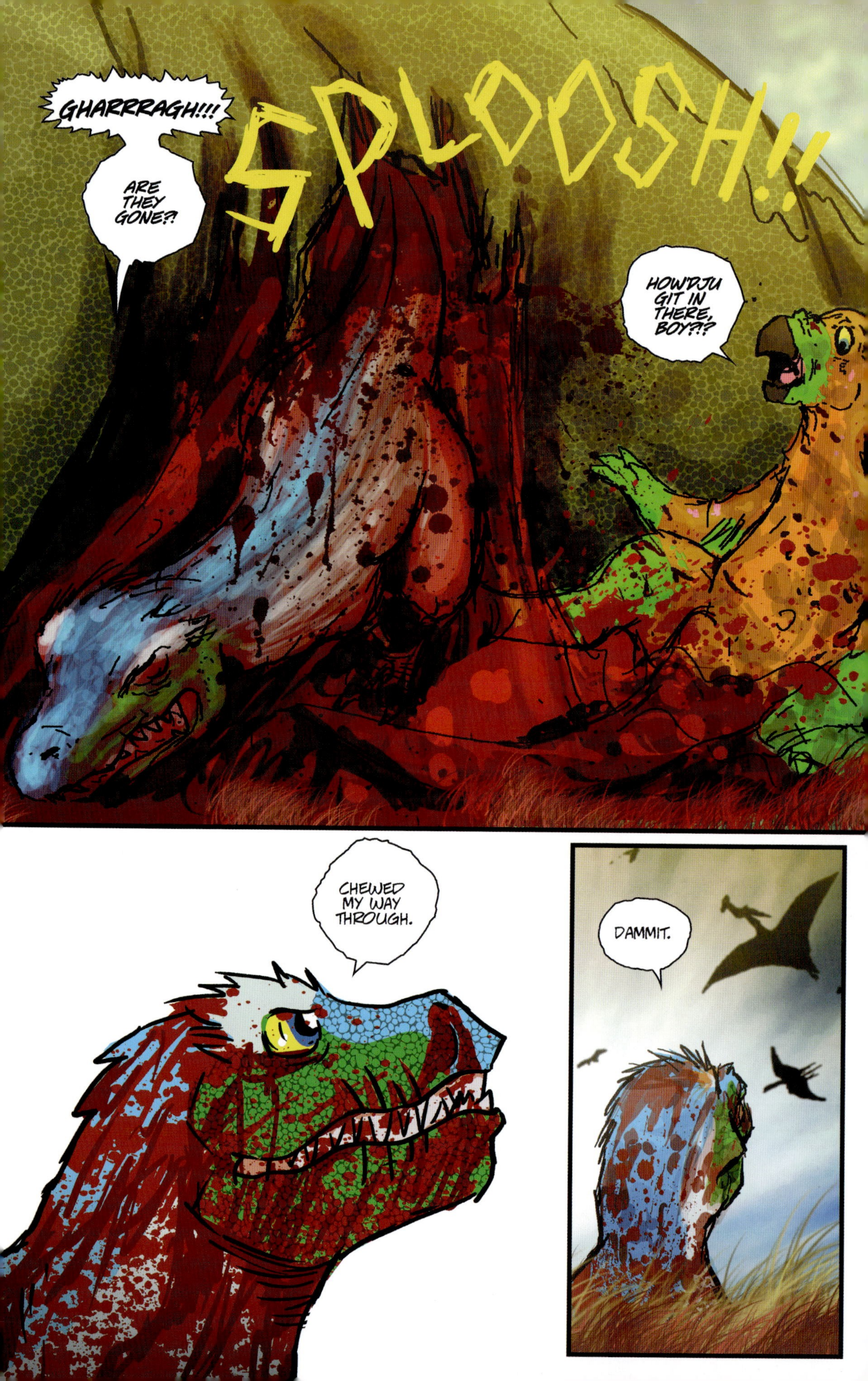
GHARRRAGH!!!
SPLOOSH!!
ARE THEY GONE?!
HOW'DJU GIT IN THERE, BOY?!?
CHEWED MY WAY THROUGH.
DAMMIT.

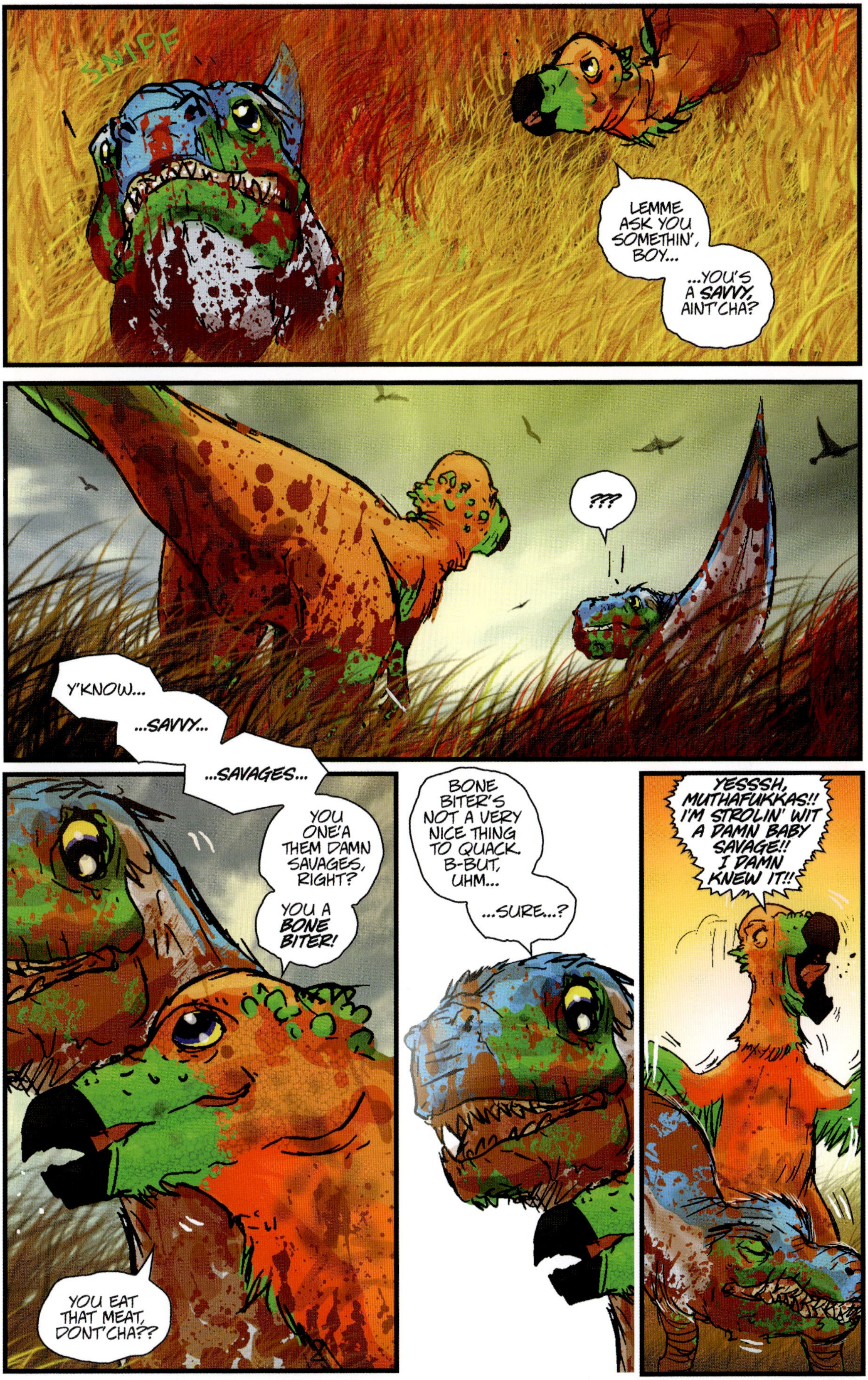
SNIFF
LEMME ASK YOU SOMETHIN', BOY...
...YOU'S A SAVVY, AINT'CHA?
???
Y'KNOW...
...SAVVY...
...SAVAGES...
YOU ONE'A THEM DAMN SAVAGES, RIGHT?
YOU A BONE BITER!
YOU EAT THAT MEAT, DONT'CHA??
BONE BITER'S NOT A VERY NICE THING TO QUACK. B-BUT, UHM...
...SURE...?
YESSSH, MUTHAFUKKAS!! I'M STROLIN' WIT A DAMN BABY SAVAGE!! I DAMN KNEW IT!!

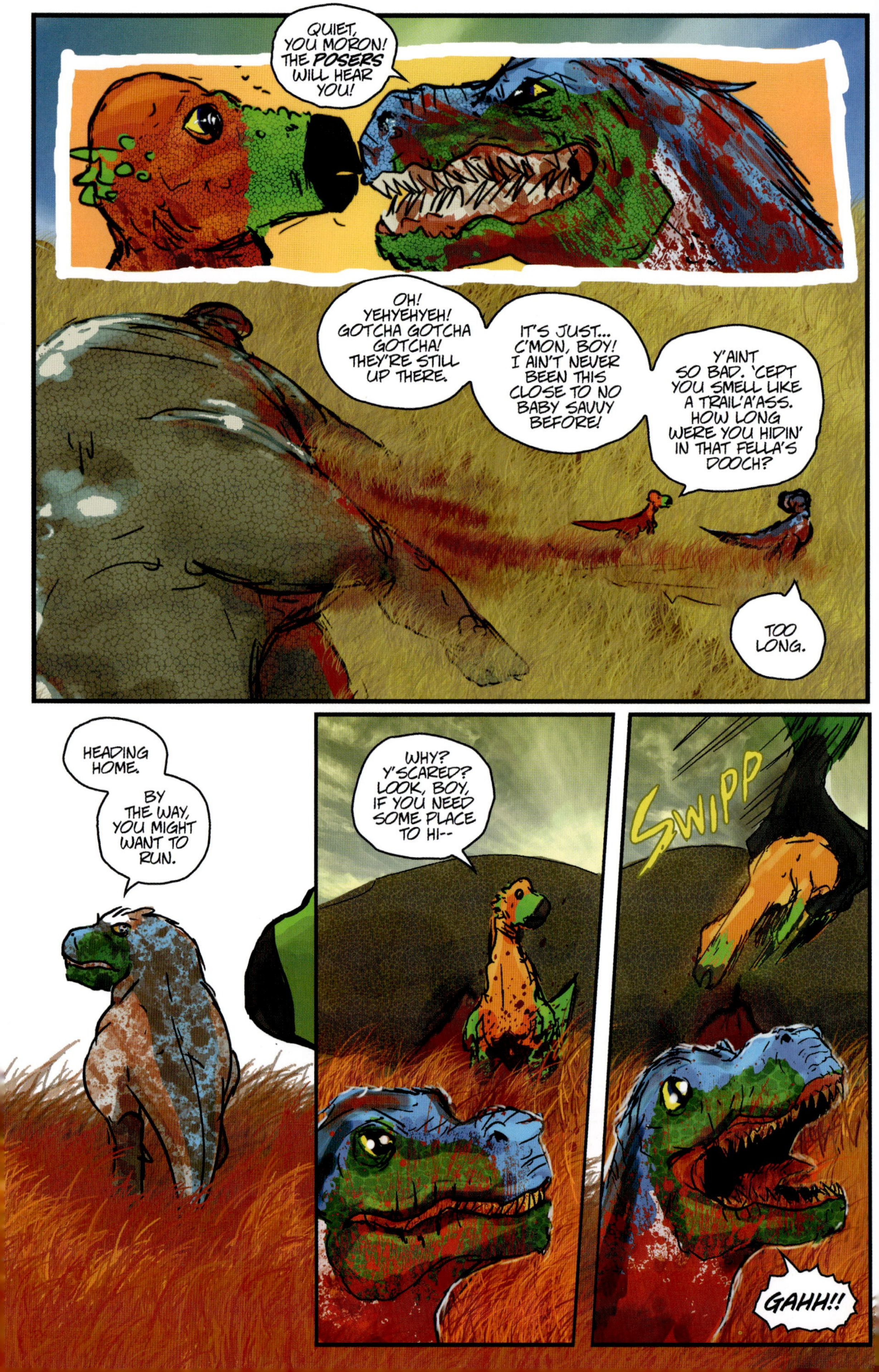
QUIET, YOU MORON! THE **POSERS** WILL HEAR YOU!
OH! YEHYEHYEH! GOTCHA GOTCHA GOTCHA! THEY'RE STILL UP THERE.
IT'S JUST... C'MON, BOY! I AIN'T NEVER BEEN THIS CLOSE TO NO BABY SAVVY BEFORE!
Y'AINT SO BAD. 'CEPT YOU SMELL LIKE A TRAIL'A'ASS. HOW LONG WERE YOU HIDIN' IN THAT FELLA'S DOOCH?
TOO LONG.
HEADING HOME.
BY THE WAY, YOU MIGHT WANT TO RUN.
WHY? Y'SCARED? LOOK, BOY, IF YOU NEED SOME PLACE TO HI--
SWIPP
GAHH!!

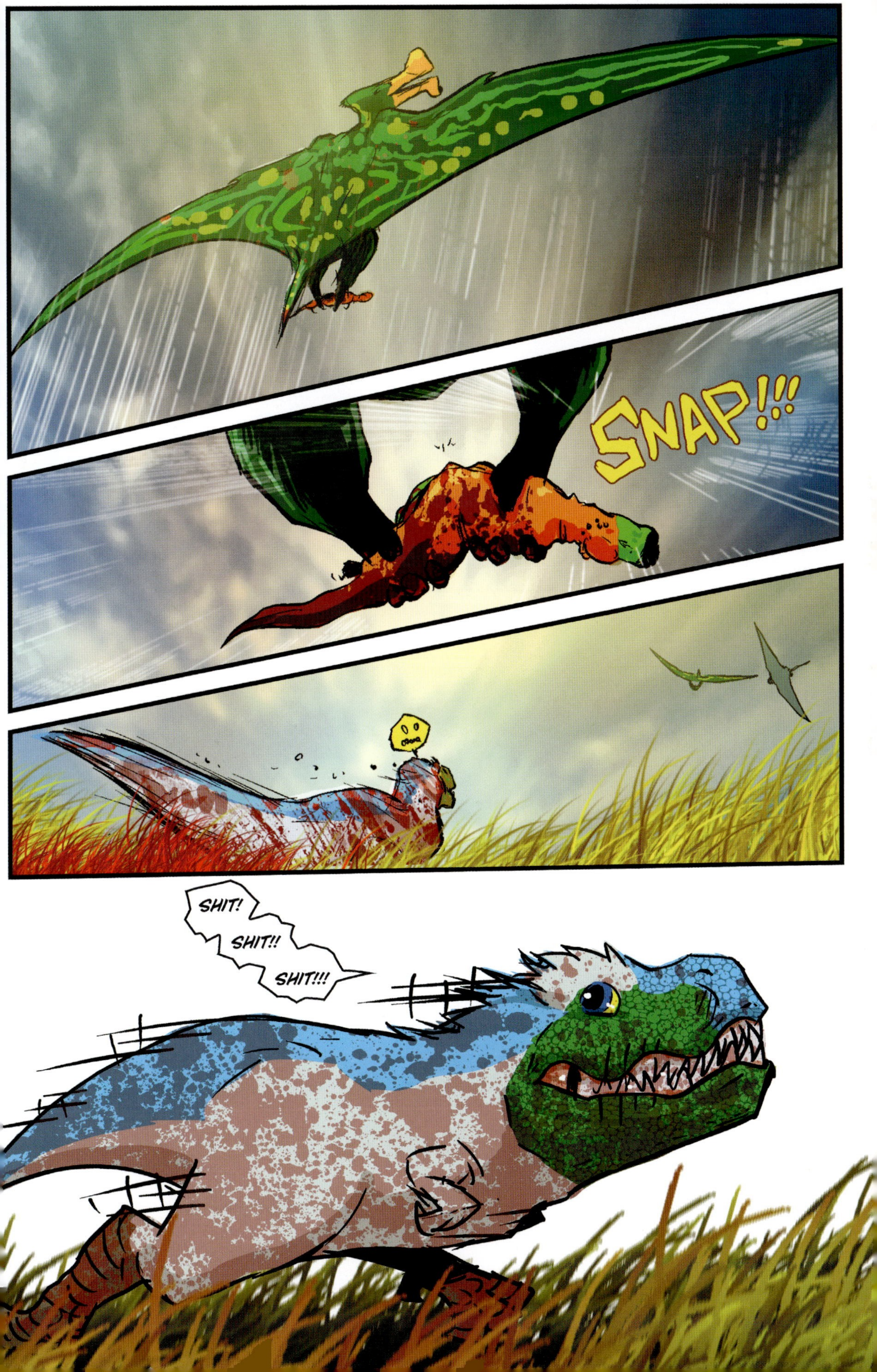
SNAP!!!
SHIT!
SHIT!!
SHIT!!!

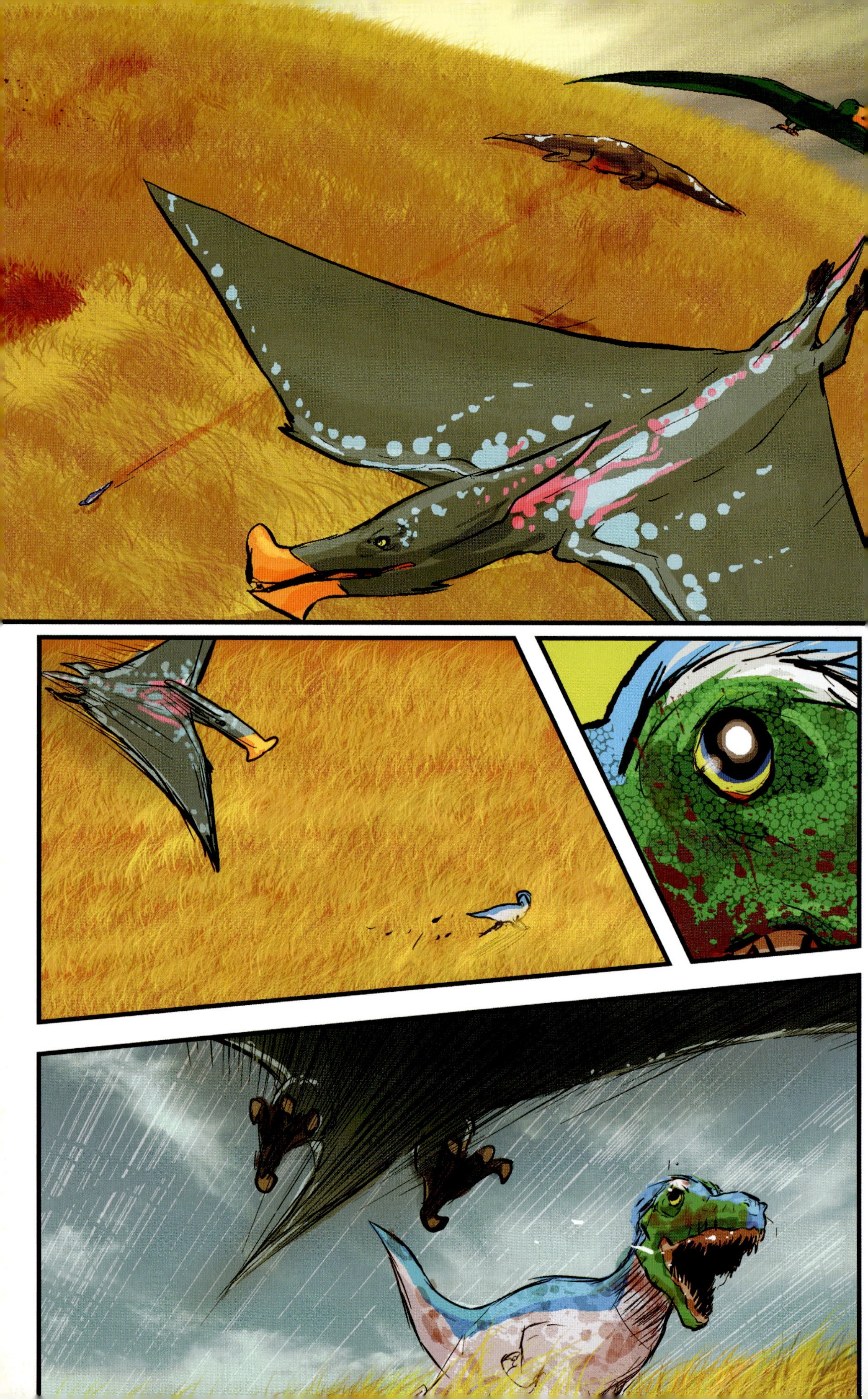

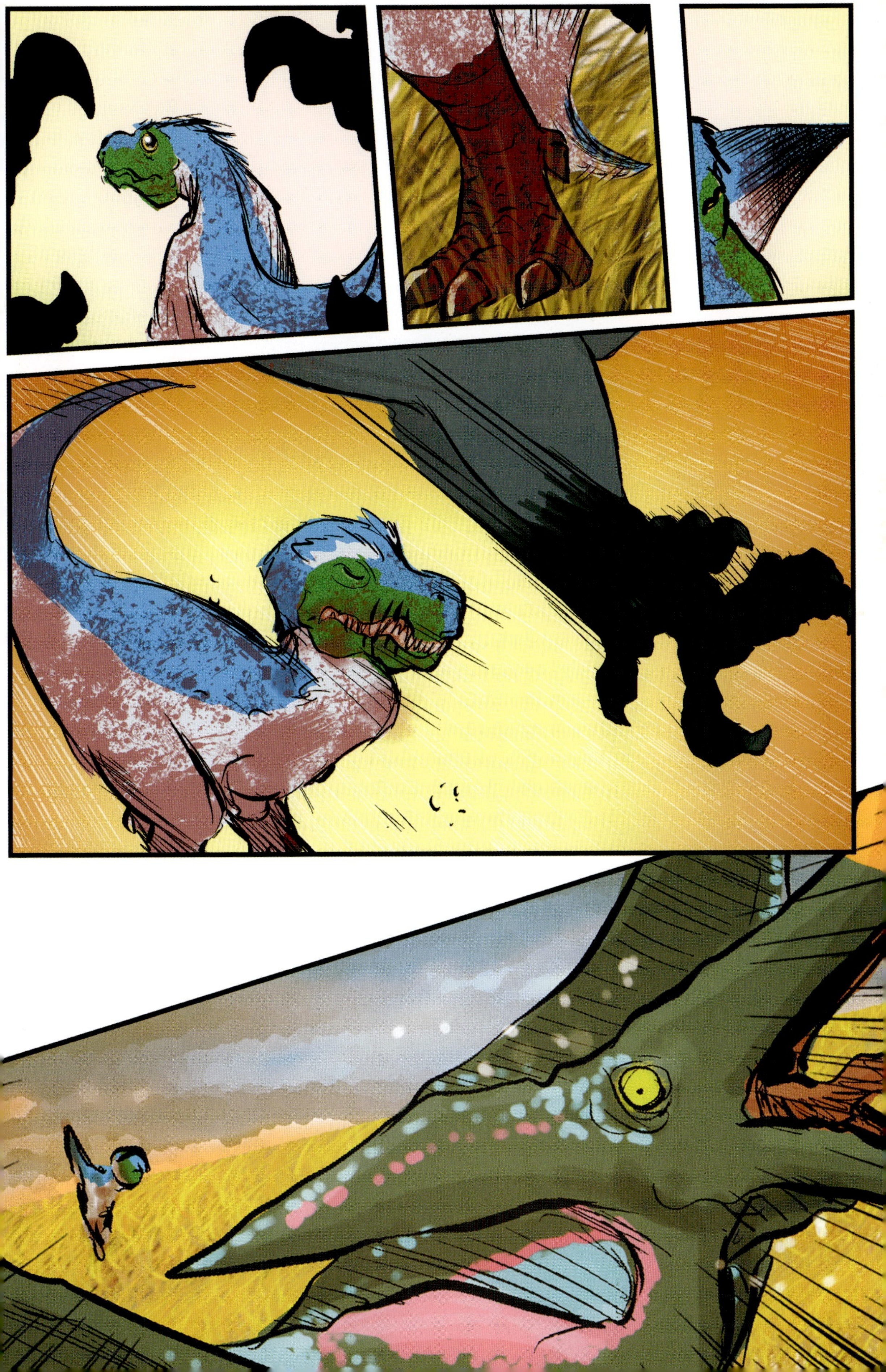

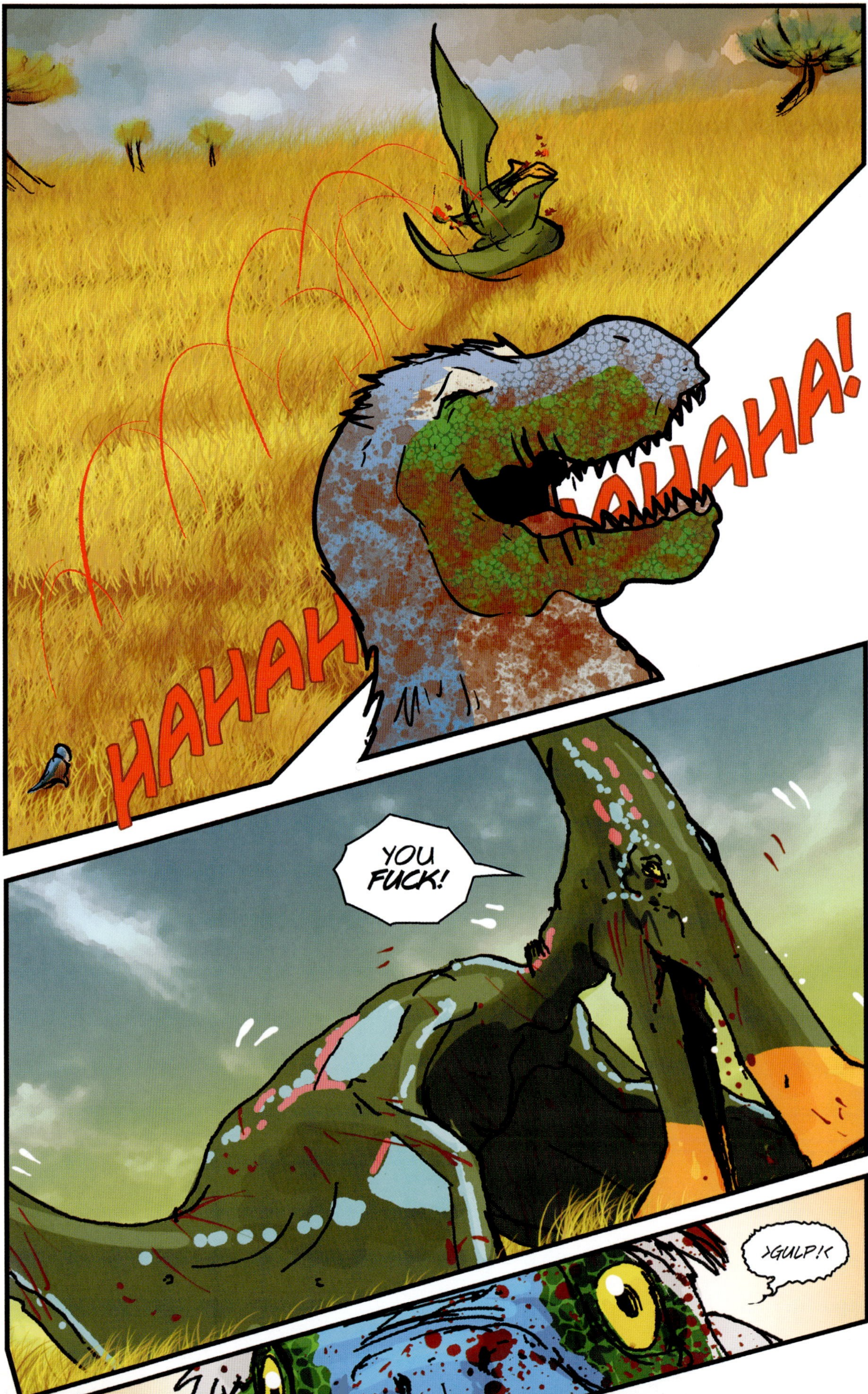
HAHAHAHAHAHA!
YOU FUCK!
>GULP!<

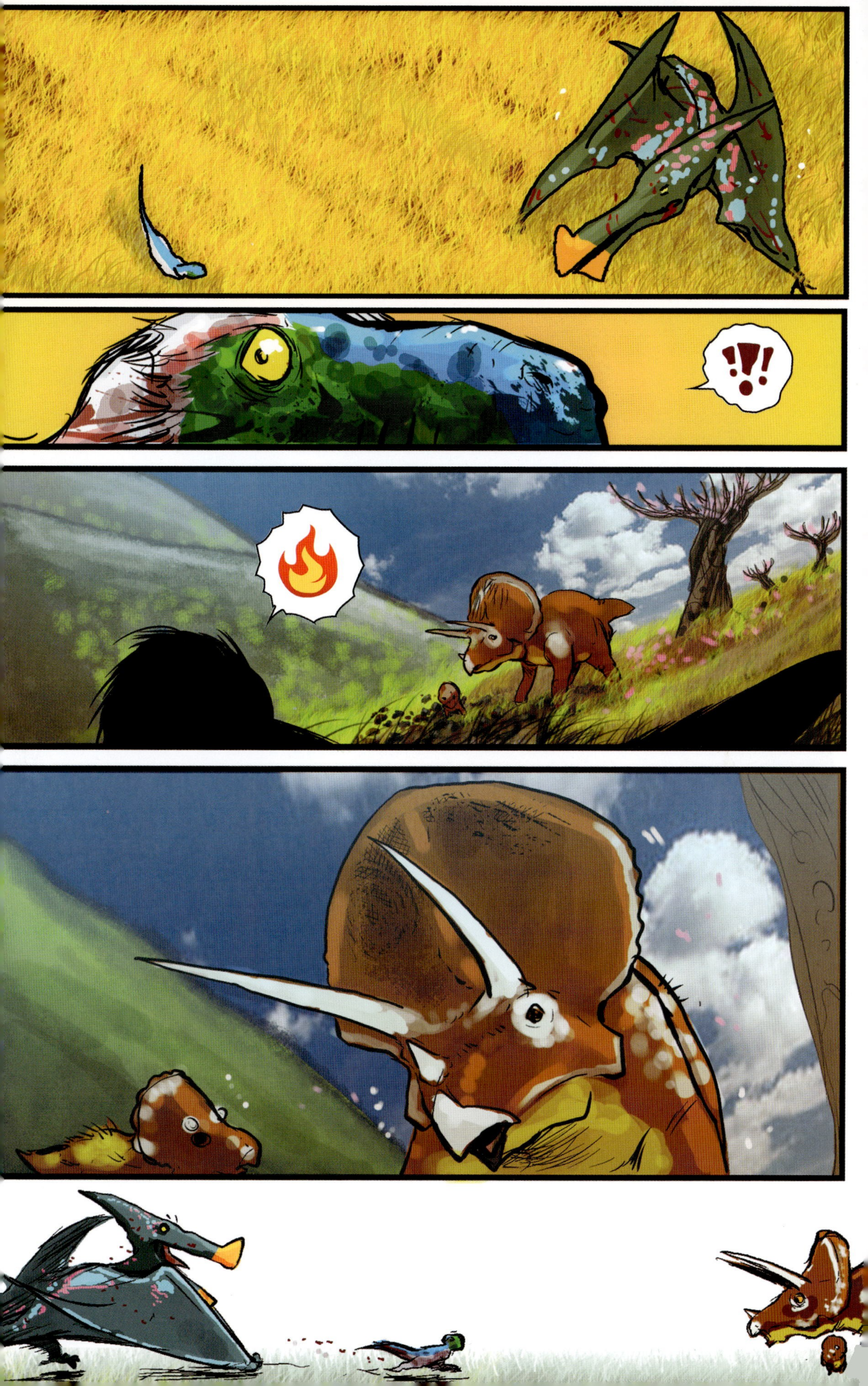
!!!

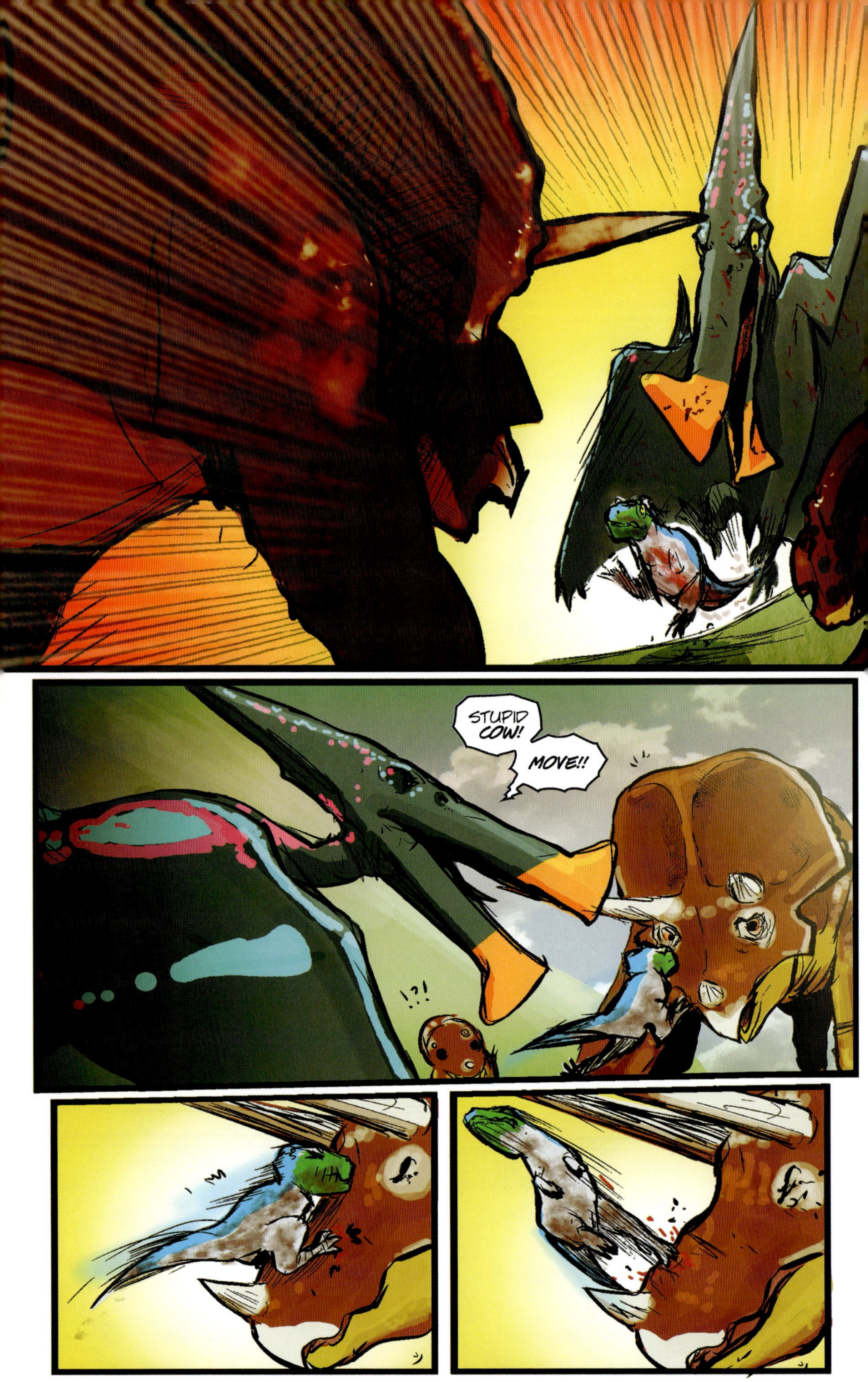
STUPID COW!
MOVE!!
!?!

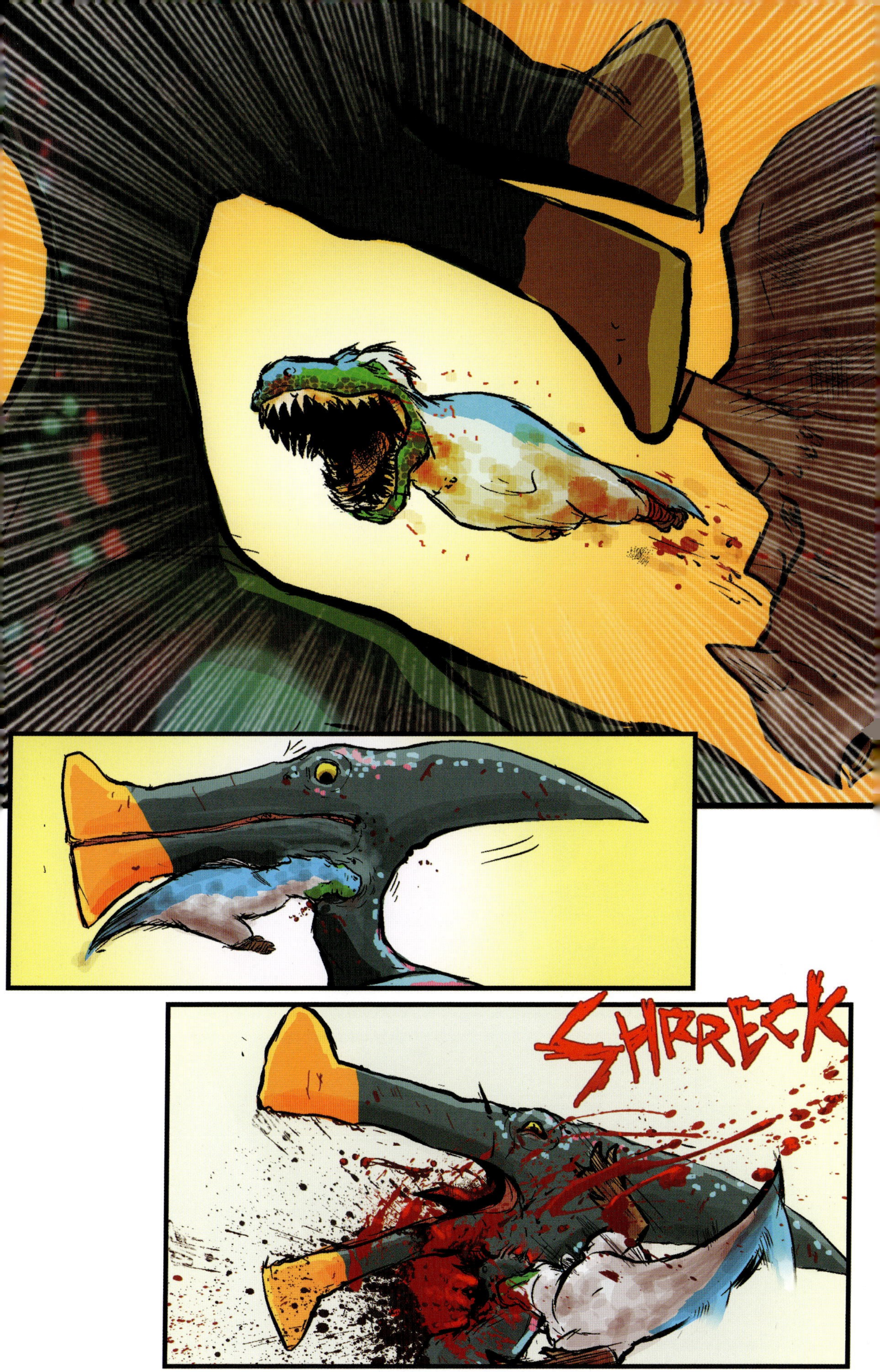
SHRRECK

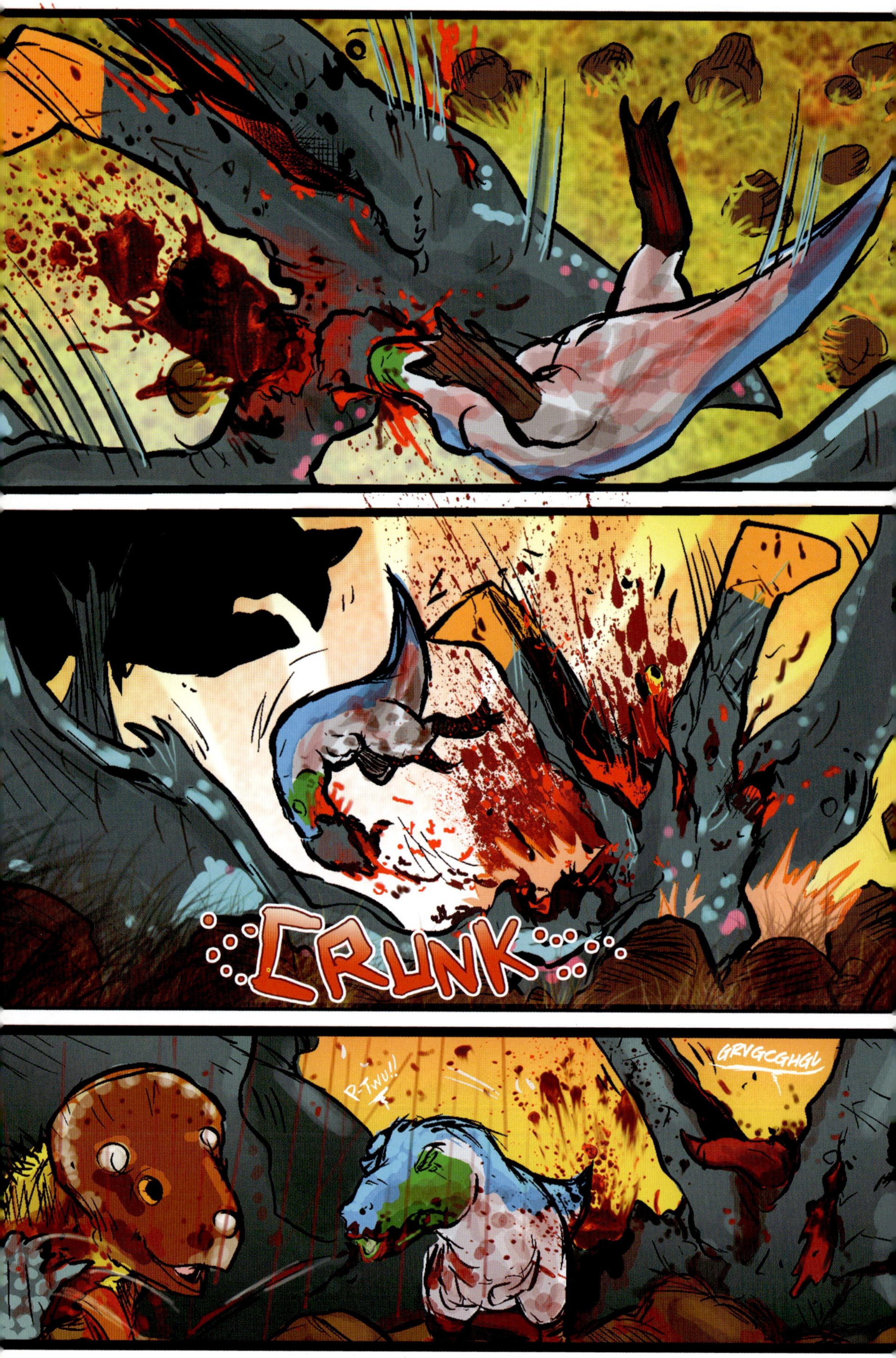
CRUNK
P-TWU!!
GRVGCGHGL

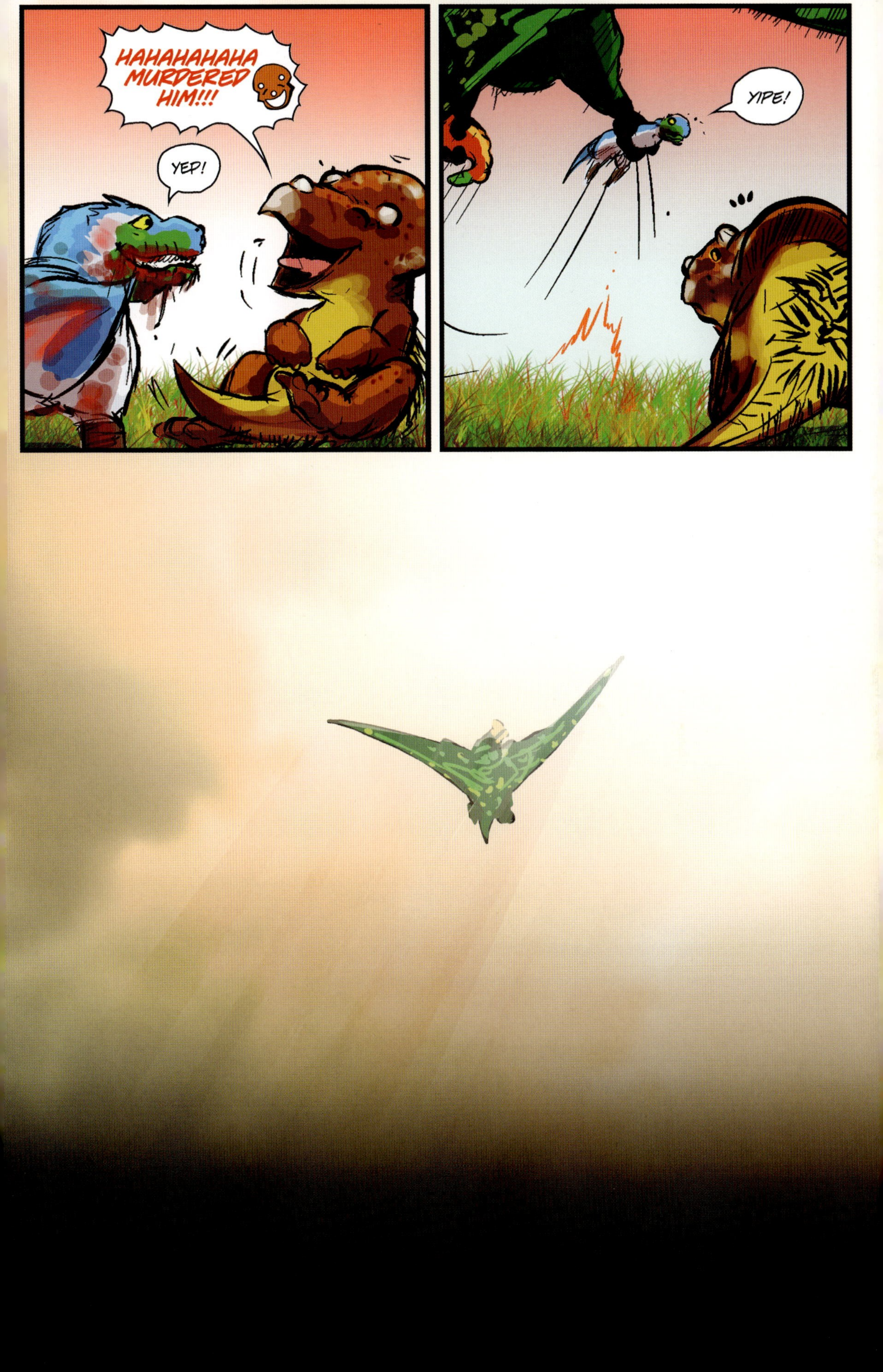
HAHAHAHAHA MURDERED HIM!!!
YEP!
YIPE!

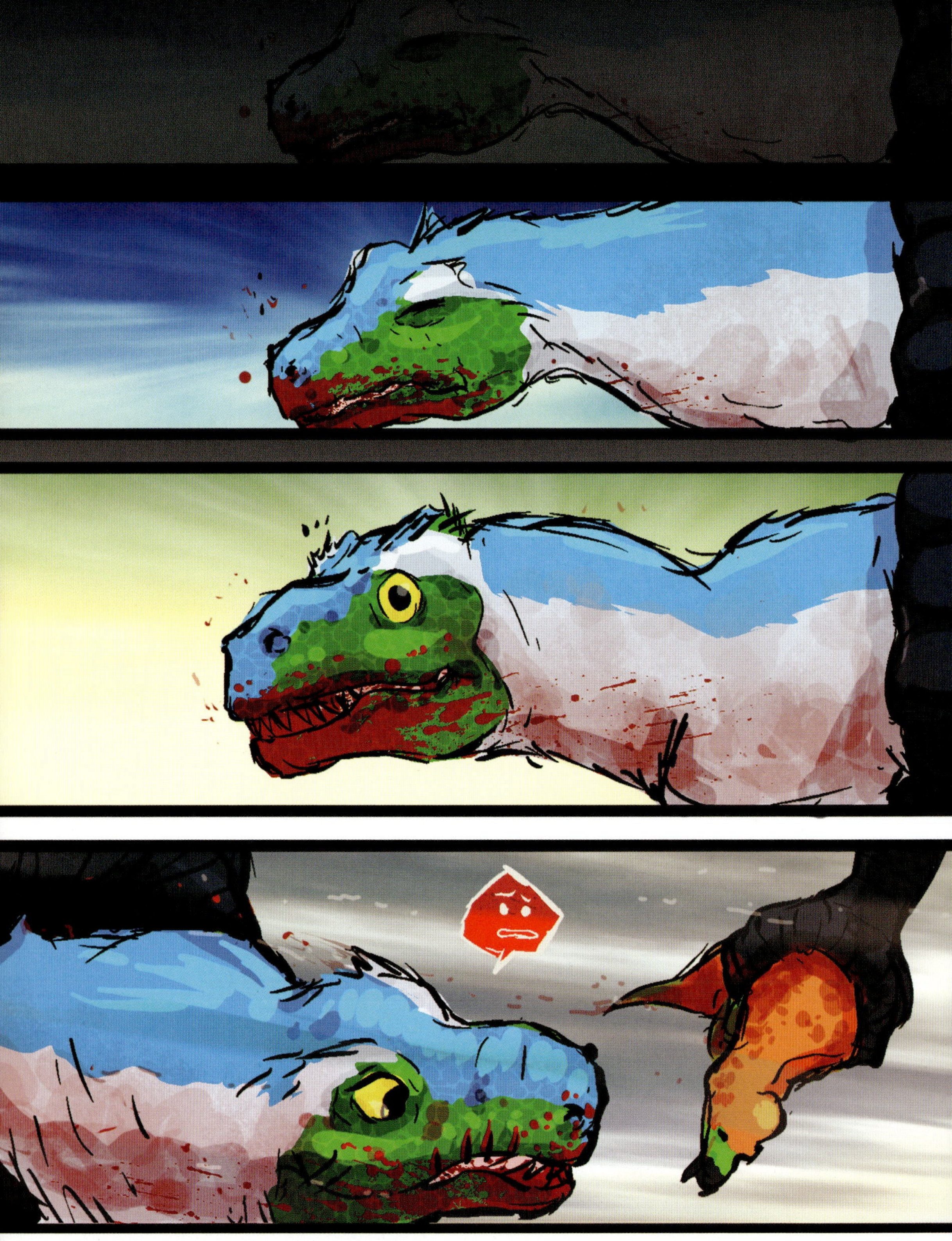

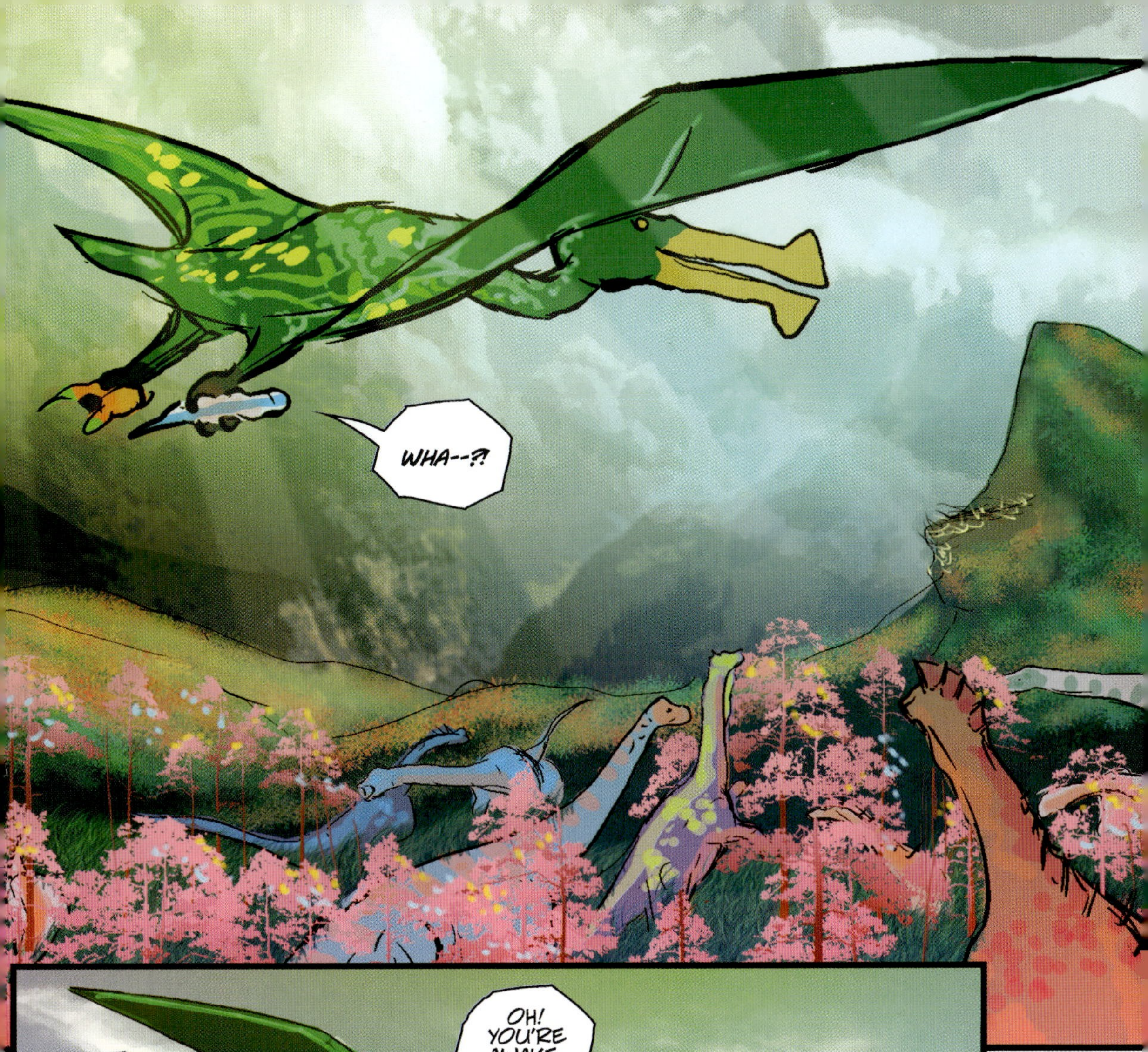
WHA--?!

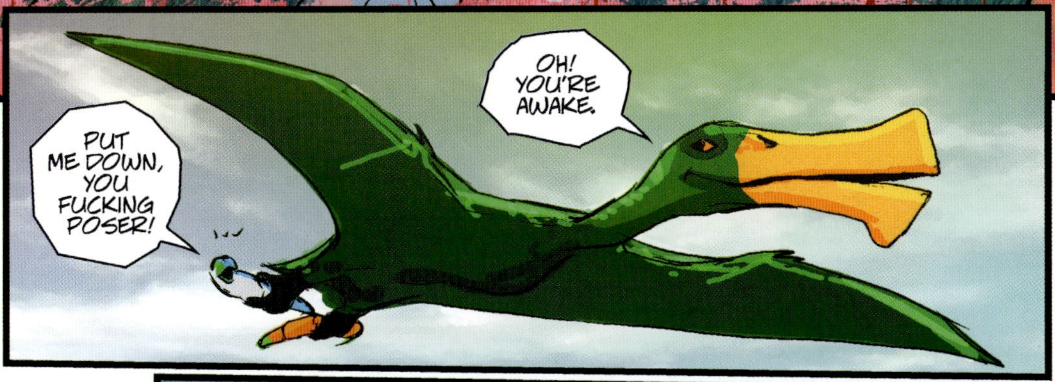
OH! YOU'RE AWAKE.
PUT ME DOWN, YOU FUCKING POSER!

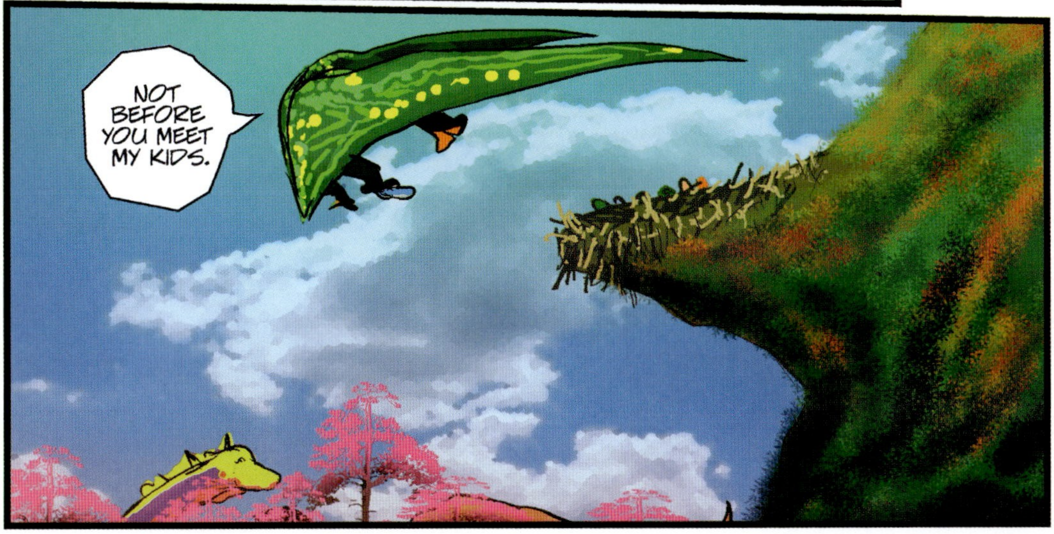
NOT BEFORE YOU MEET MY KIDS.

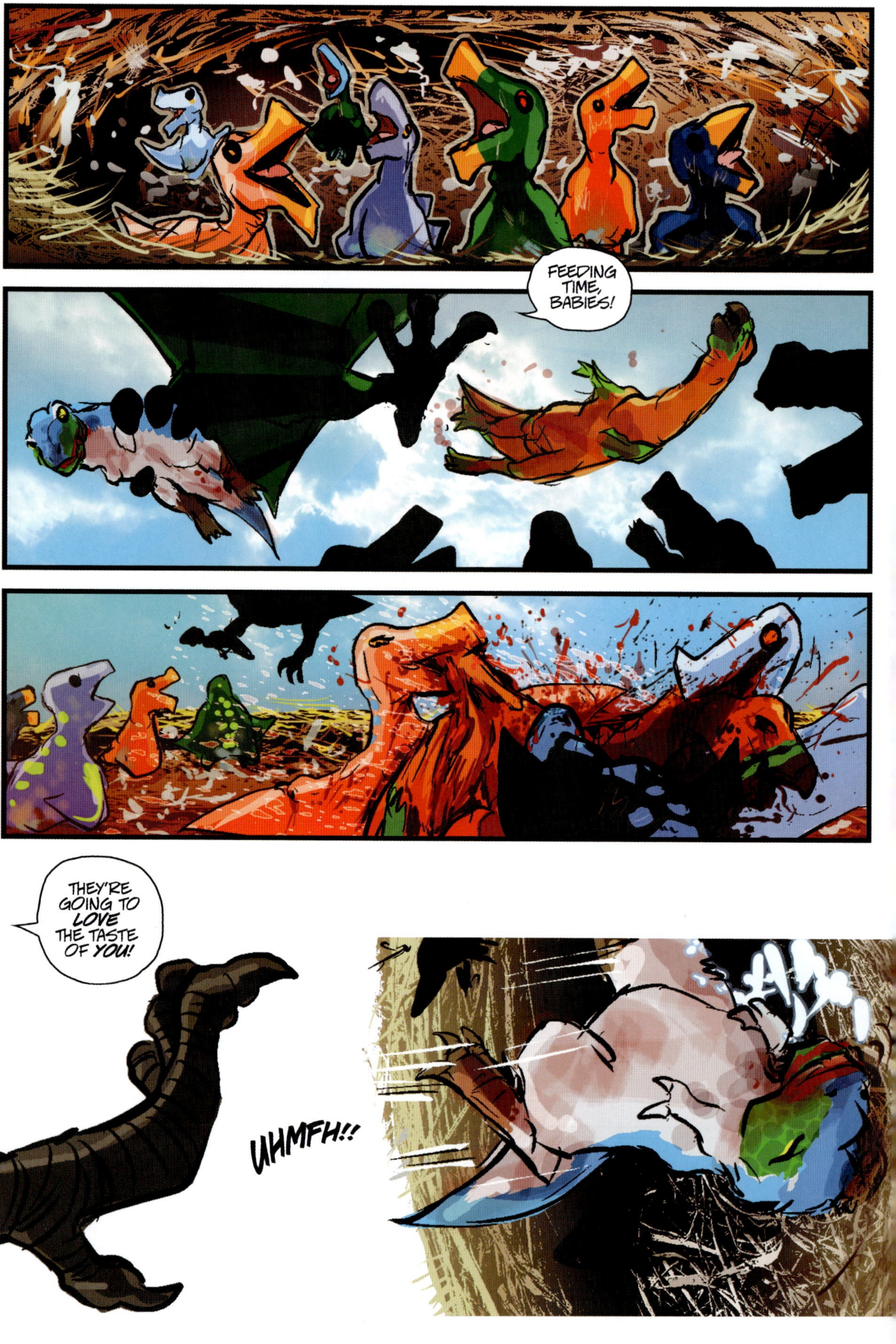
FEEDING TIME, BABIES!
THEY'RE GOING TO *LOVE* THE TASTE OF *YOU!*
UHMFH!!

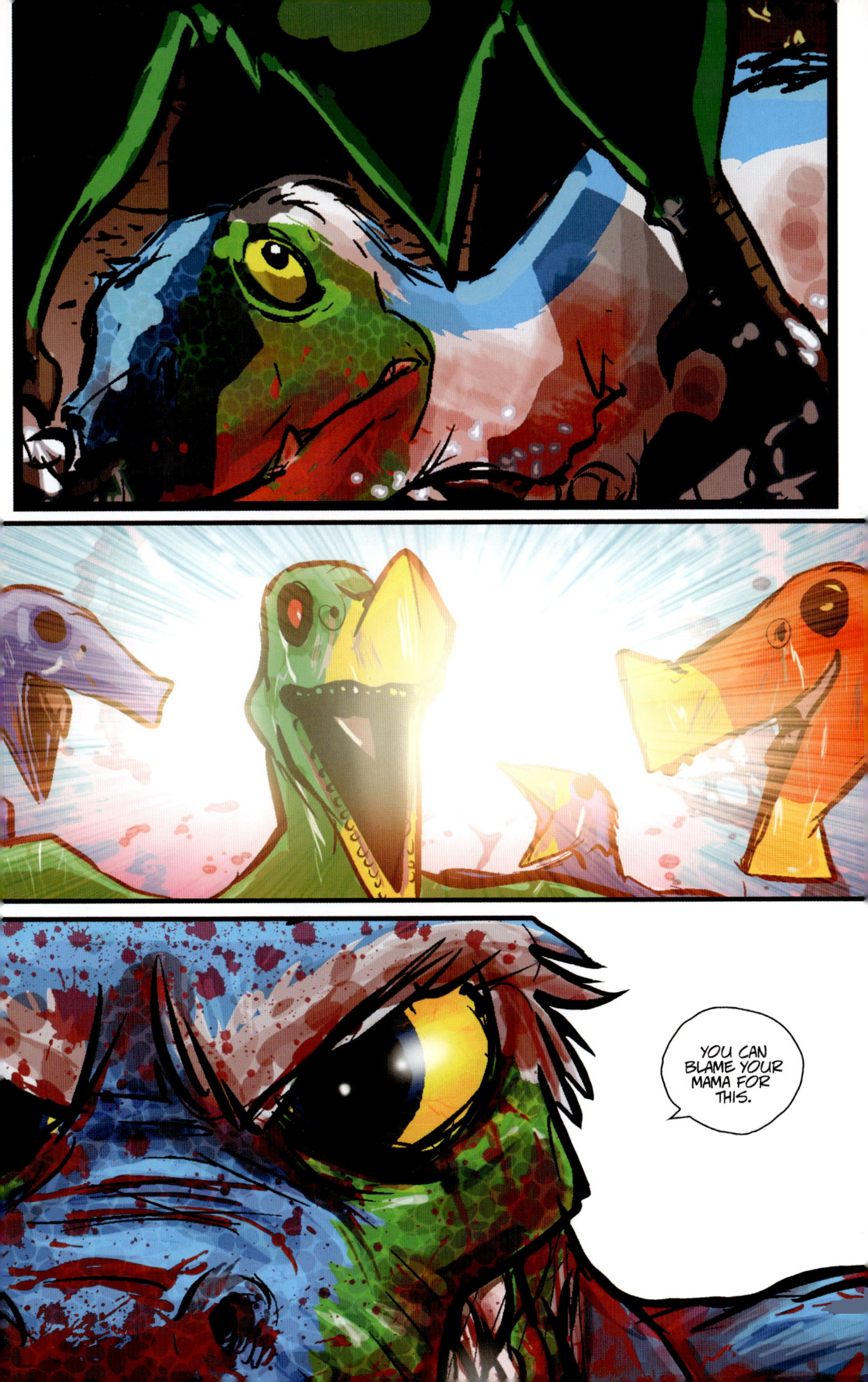
YOU CAN BLAME YOUR MAMA FOR THIS.

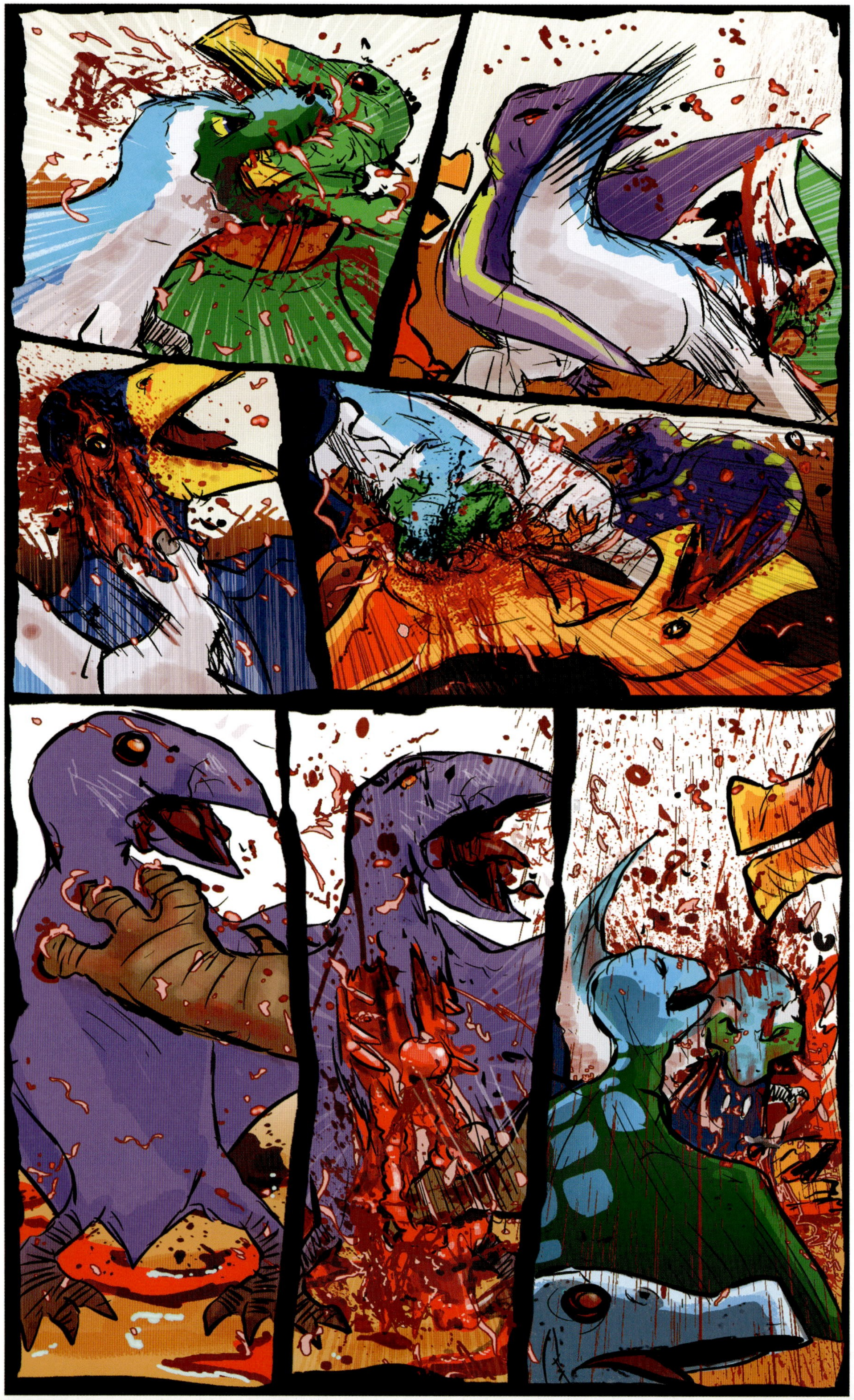

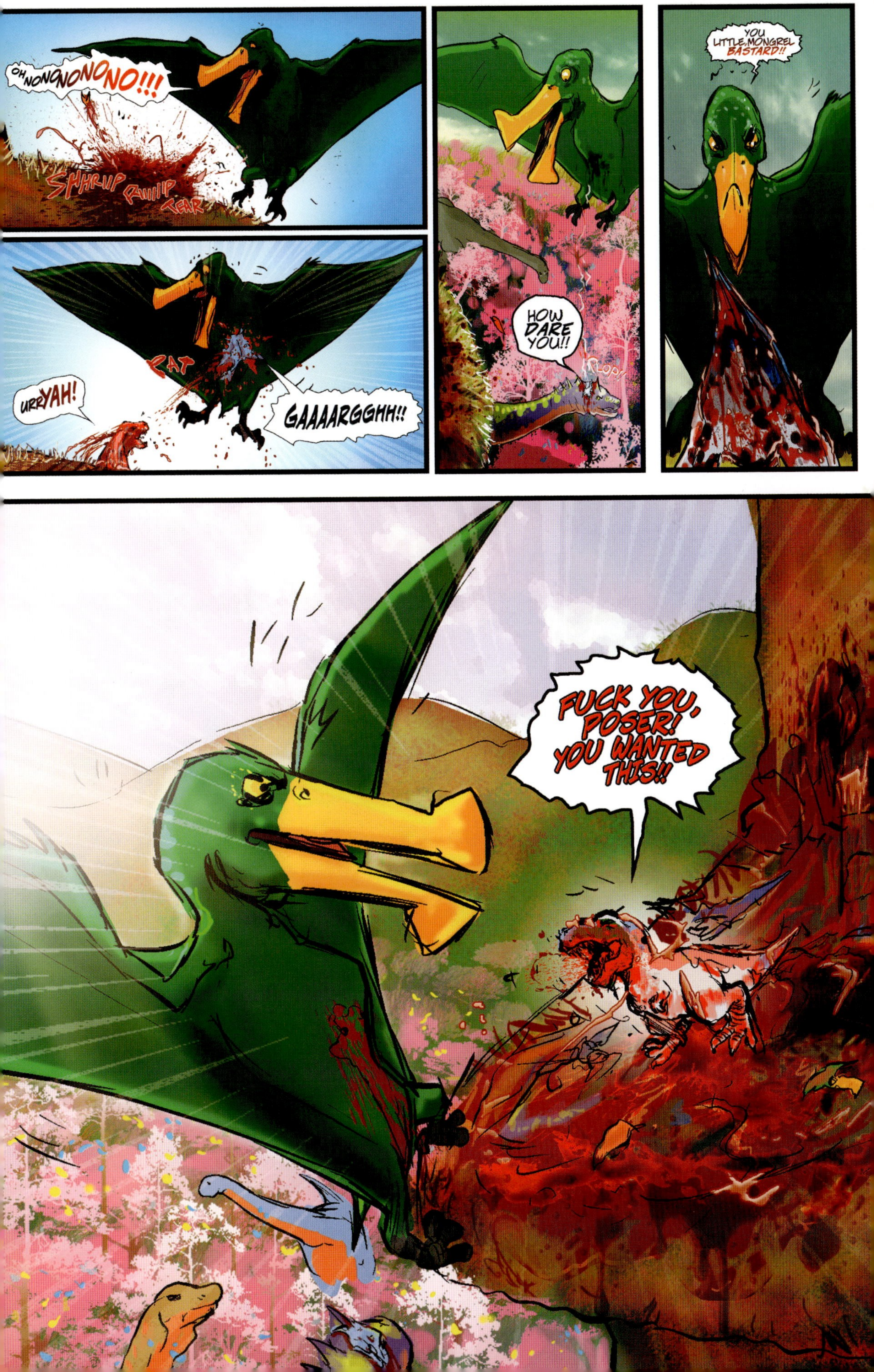
OH NONONONONONO!!!
SHHRIIP RIIIIP TEAR
PAT
URRYAH!
GAAAARGGHH!!
HOW DARE YOU!!
PLOP!!
YOU LITTLE MONGREL BASTARD!!
FUCK YOU, POSER! YOU WANTED THIS!!

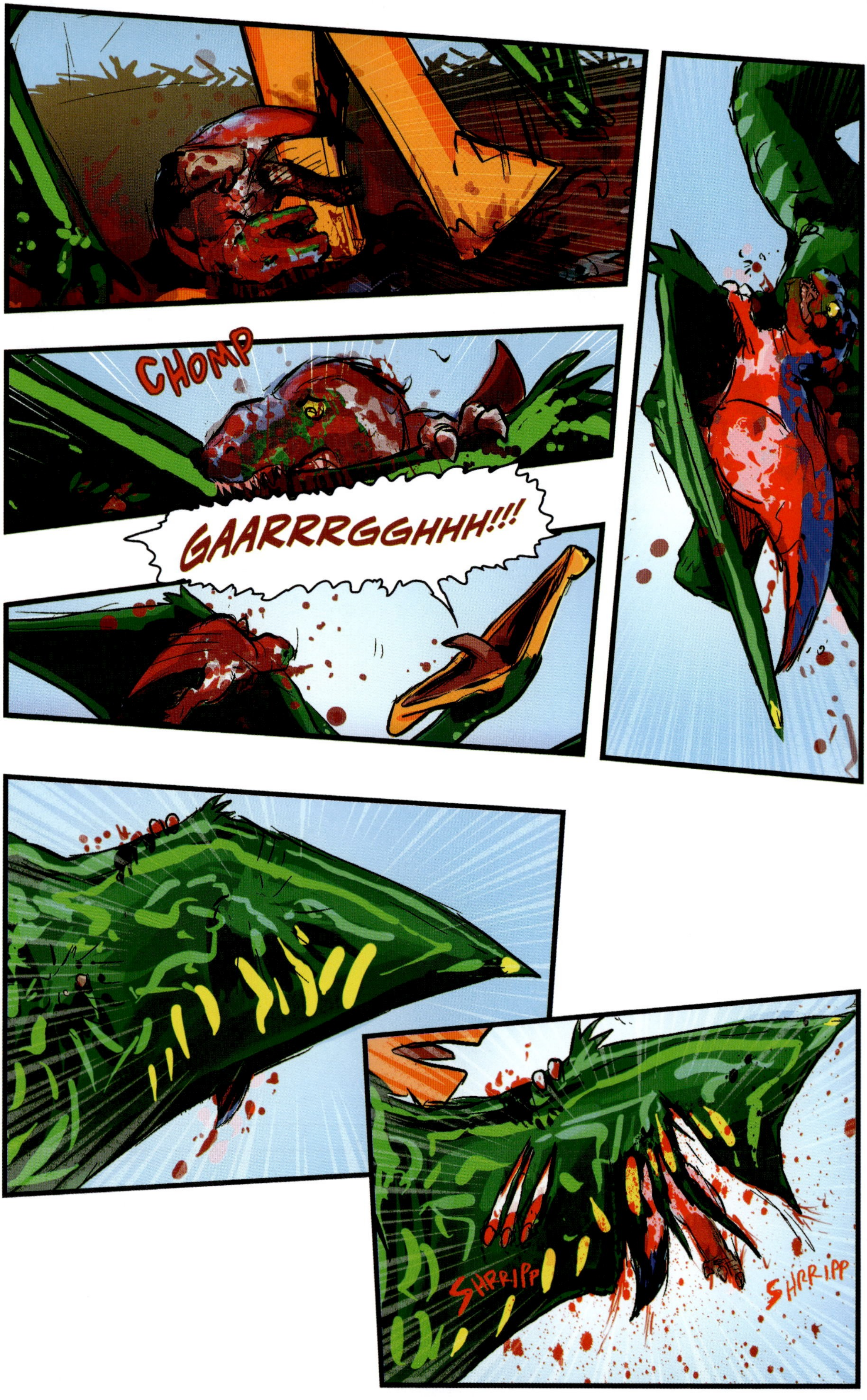
CHOMP
GAARRRGGHHH!!!
SHRRIPP
SHRRIPP

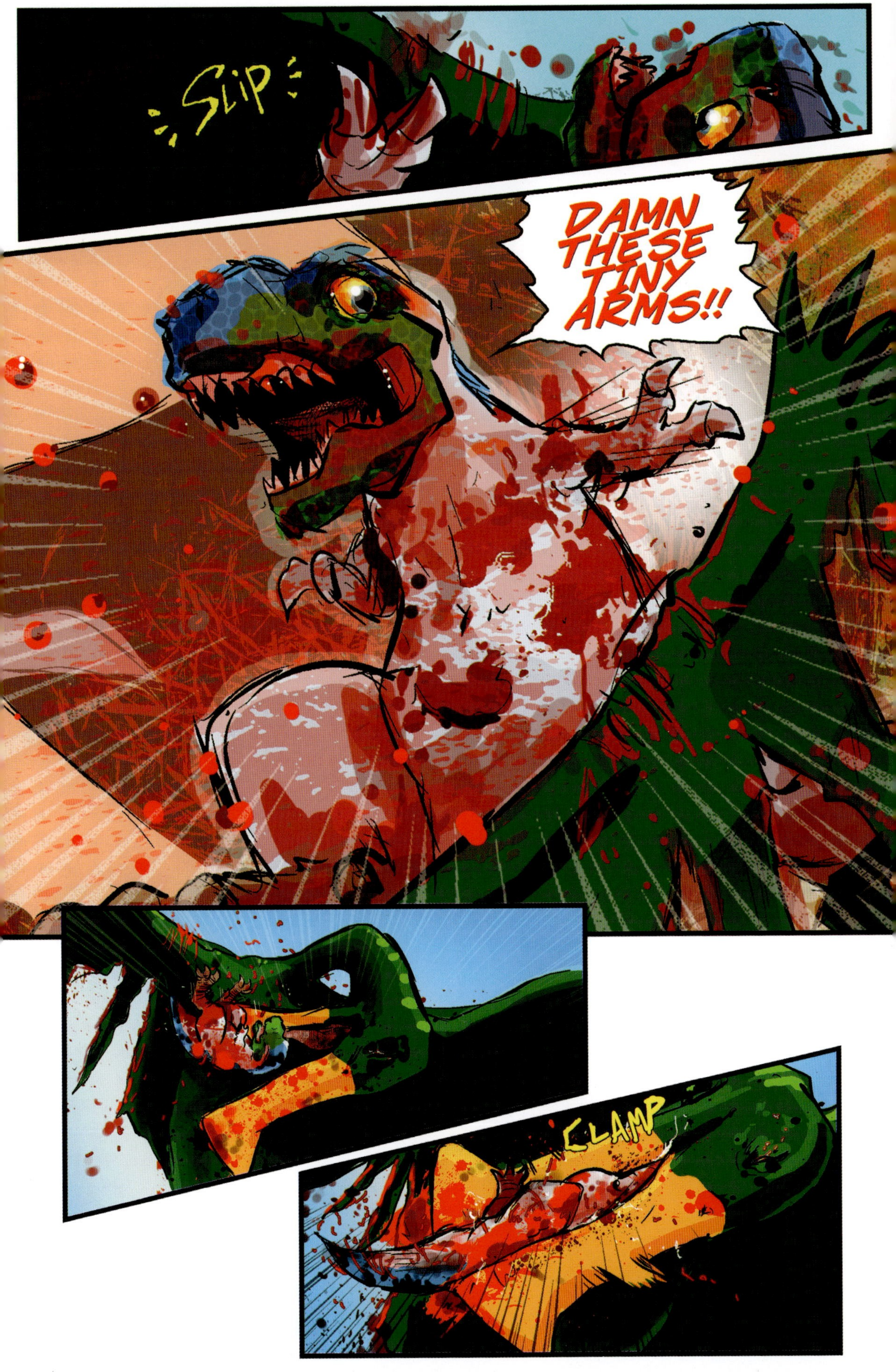
SLIP
DAMN THESE TINY ARMS!!
CLAMP

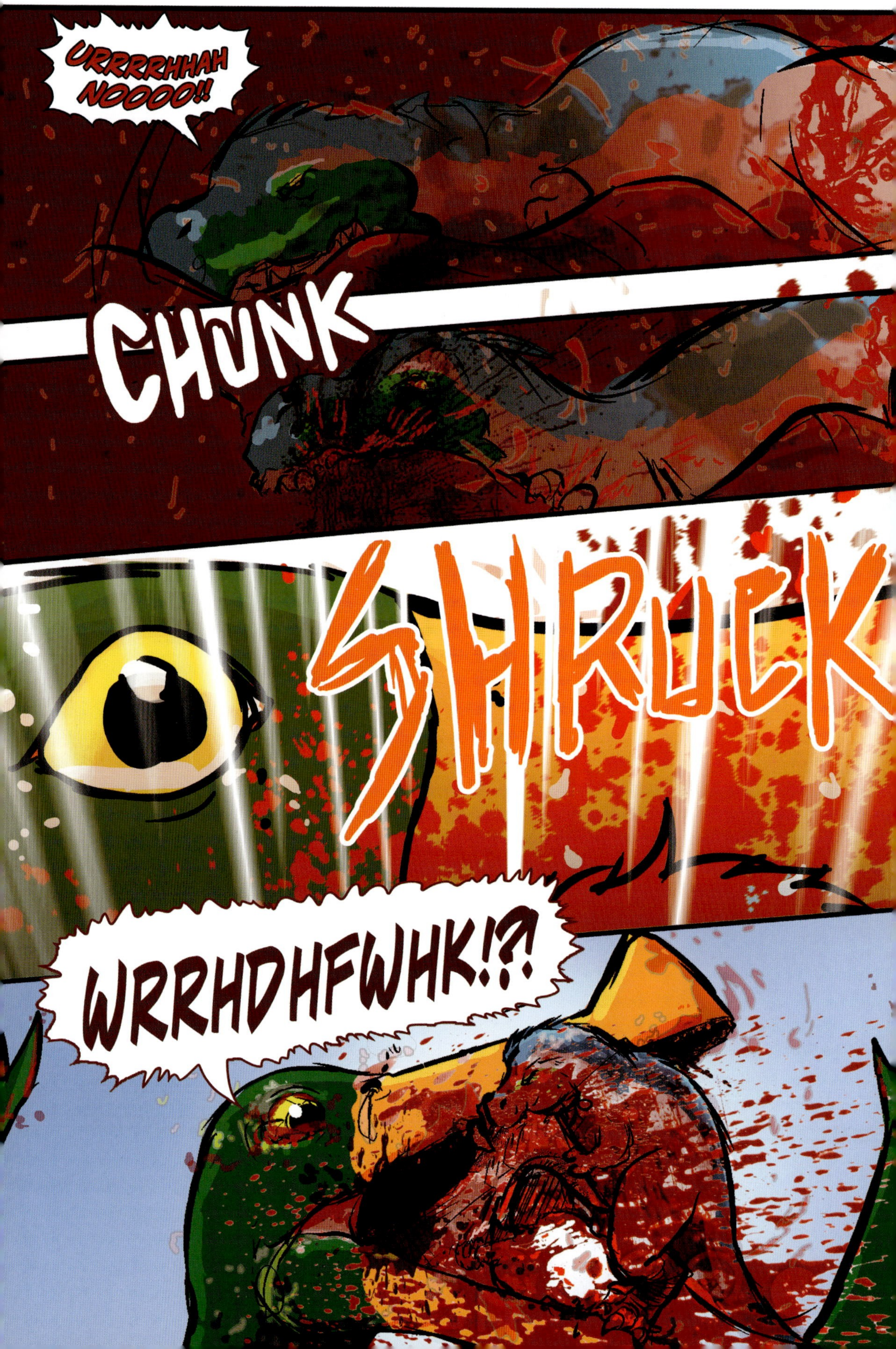
URRRRHHAH NOOOO!!
CHUNK
SHRUCK
WRRHDHFWHK!?!

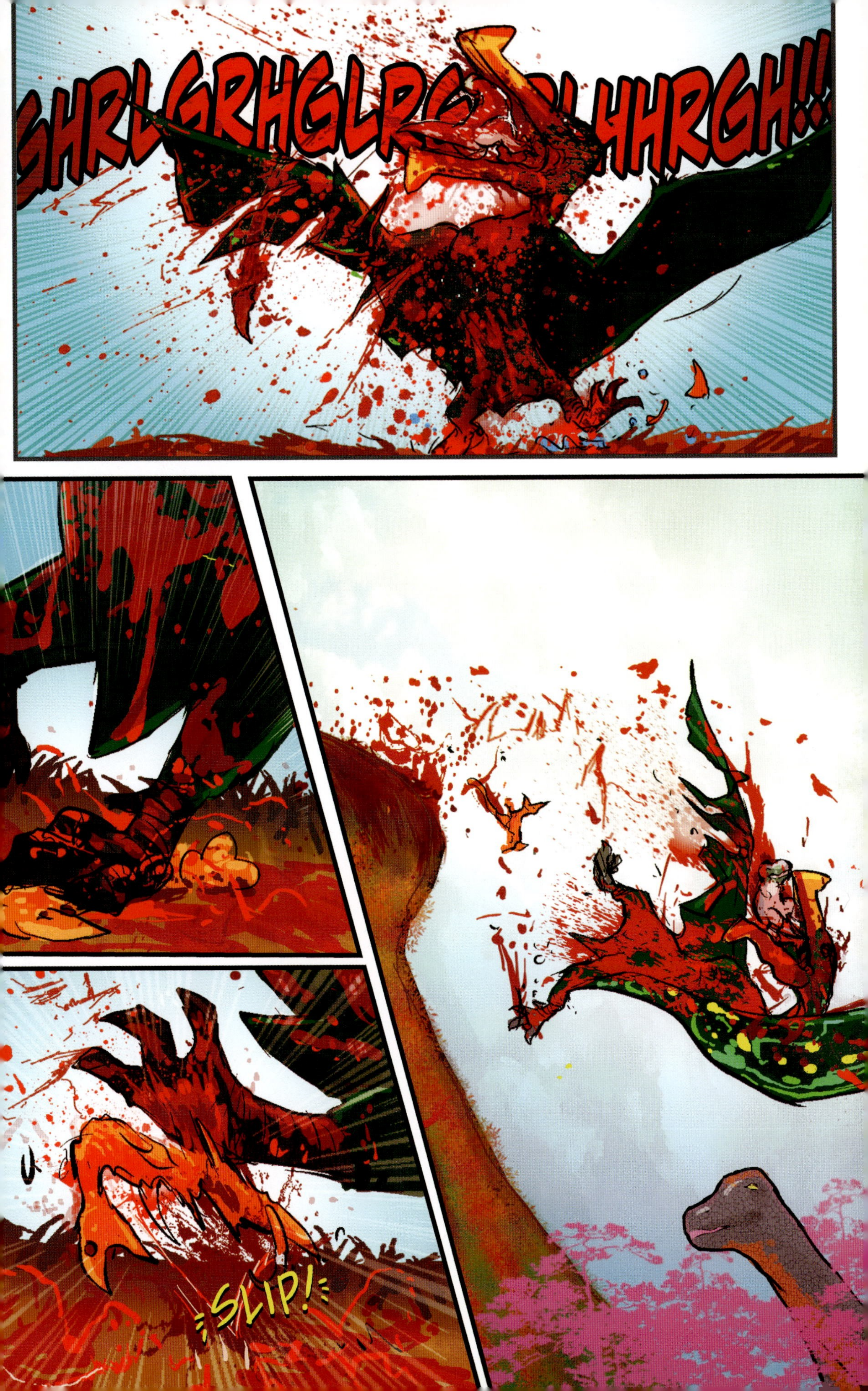
GHRLGRHGLR LHHRGH!!
SLIP!

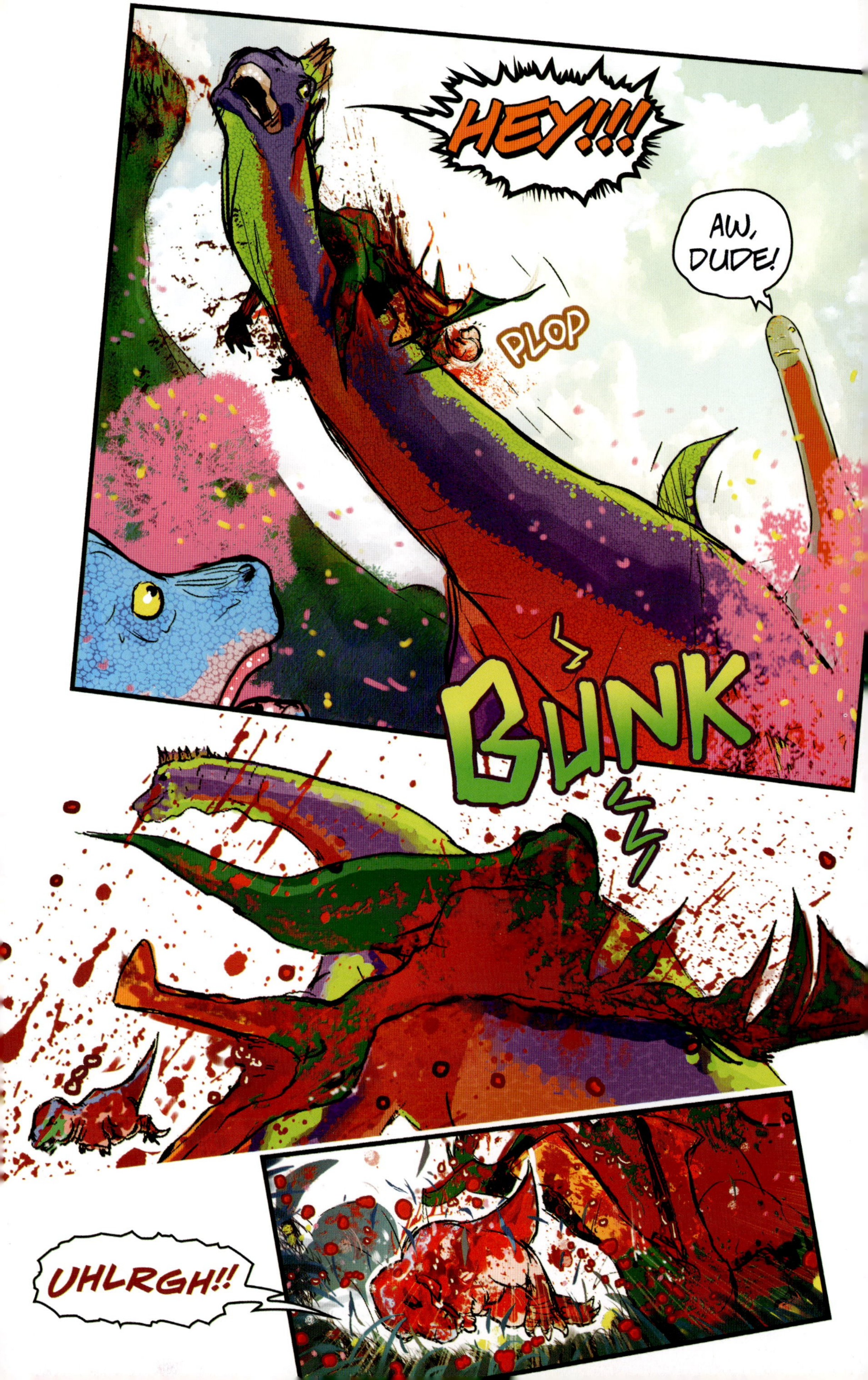
HEY!!!
AW, DUDE!
PLOP
BLINK
UHLRGH!!

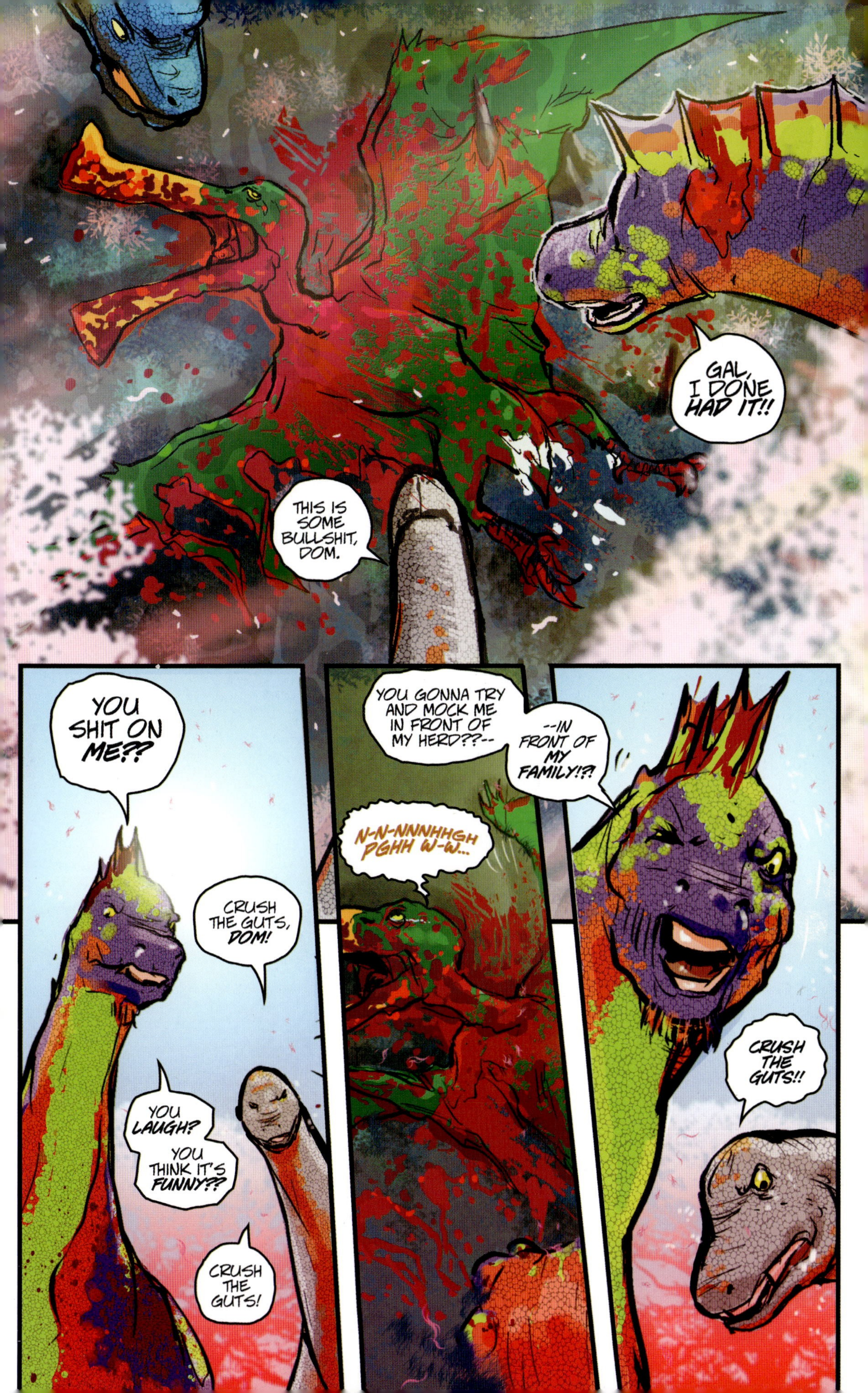
GAL, I DONE HAD IT!!
THIS IS SOME BULLSHIT, DOM.
YOU SHIT ON ME??
CRUSH THE GUTS, DOM!
YOU LAUGH?
YOU THINK IT'S FUNNY??
CRUSH THE GUTS!
YOU GONNA TRY AND MOCK ME IN FRONT OF MY HERD??--
--IN FRONT OF MY FAMILY!?!
N-N-NNNHHGH PGHH W-W...
CRUSH THE GUTS!!

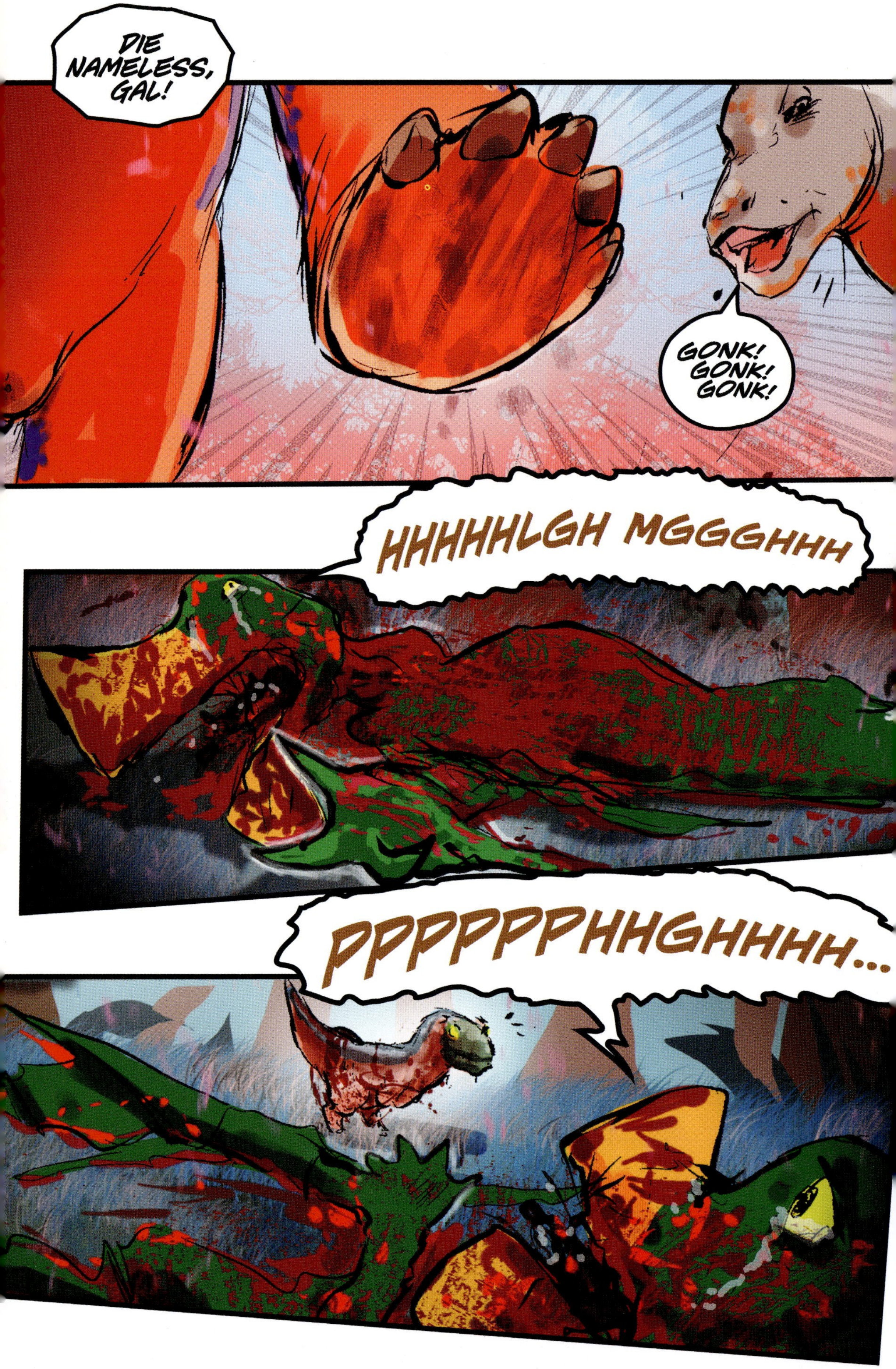
DIE NAMELESS, GAL!
GONK! GONK! GONK!
HHHHHLGH MGGGHHH
PPPPPPHHGHHHH...

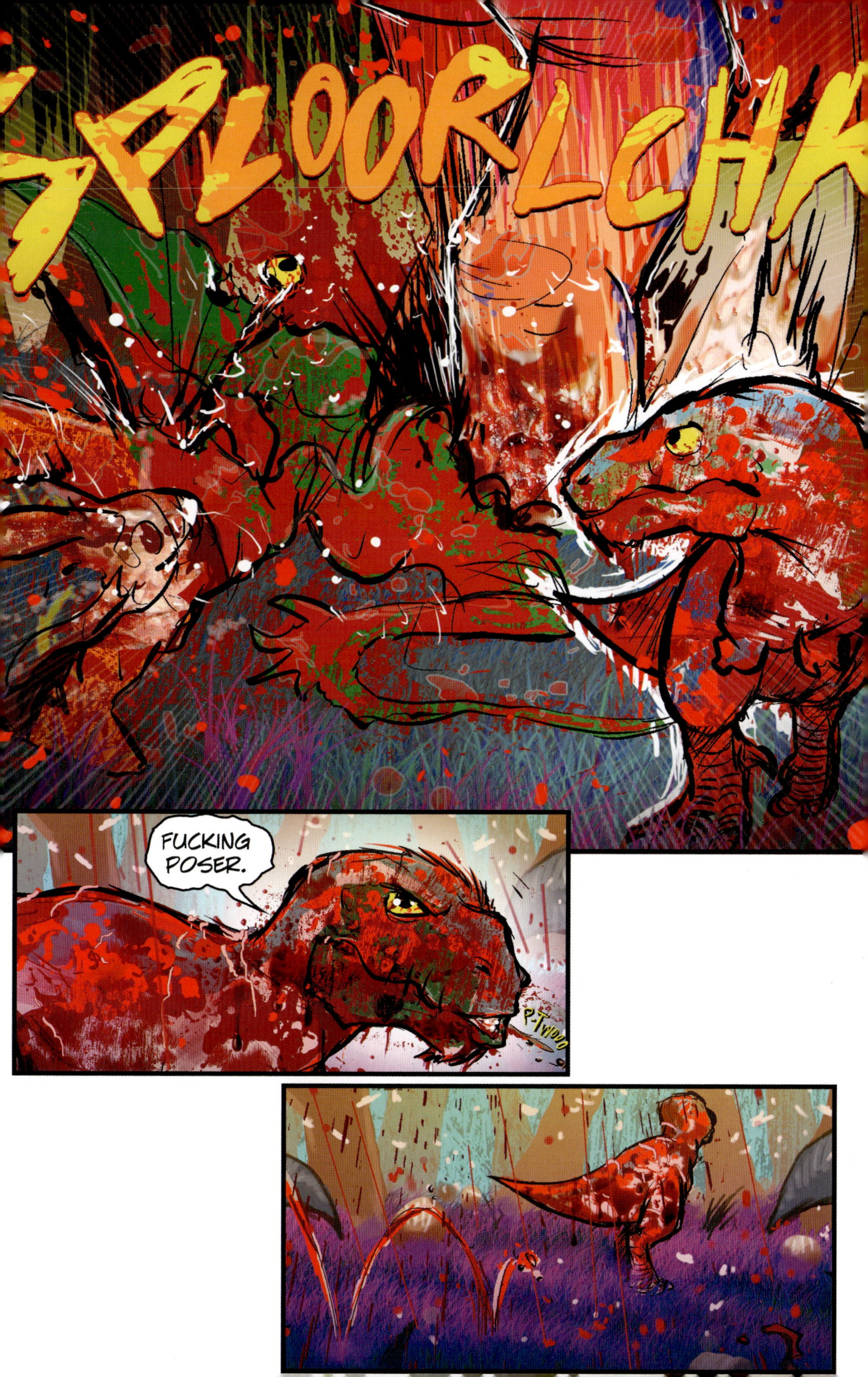
SPLOORLCH
FUCKING POSER.
P-TWOOO

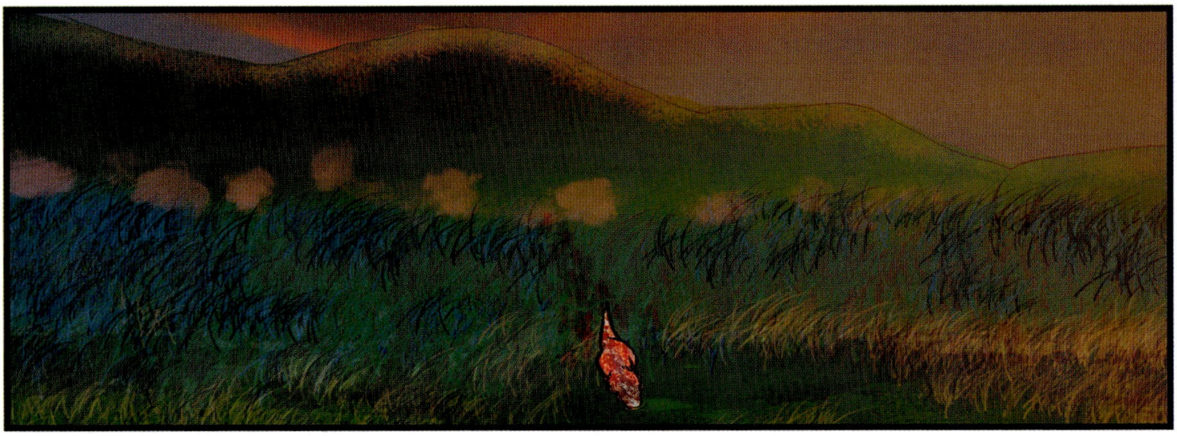
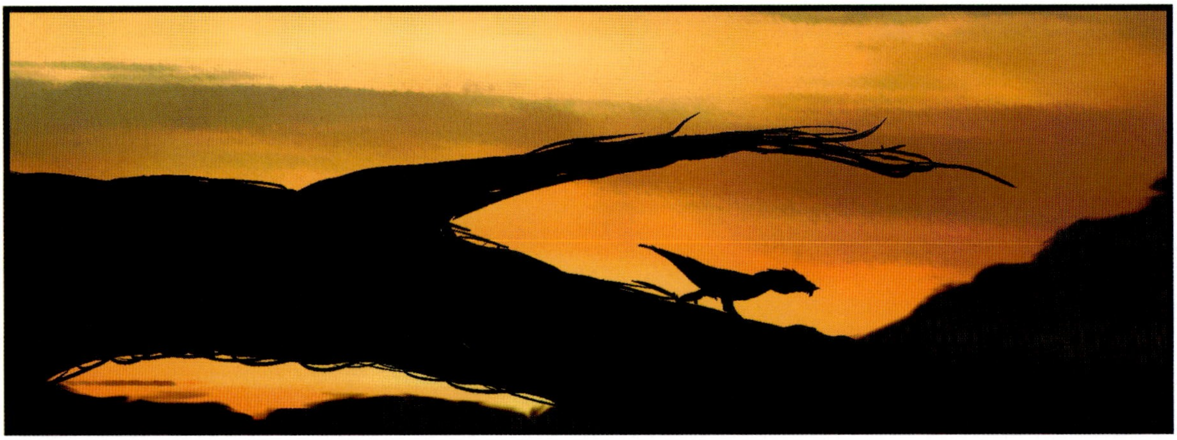
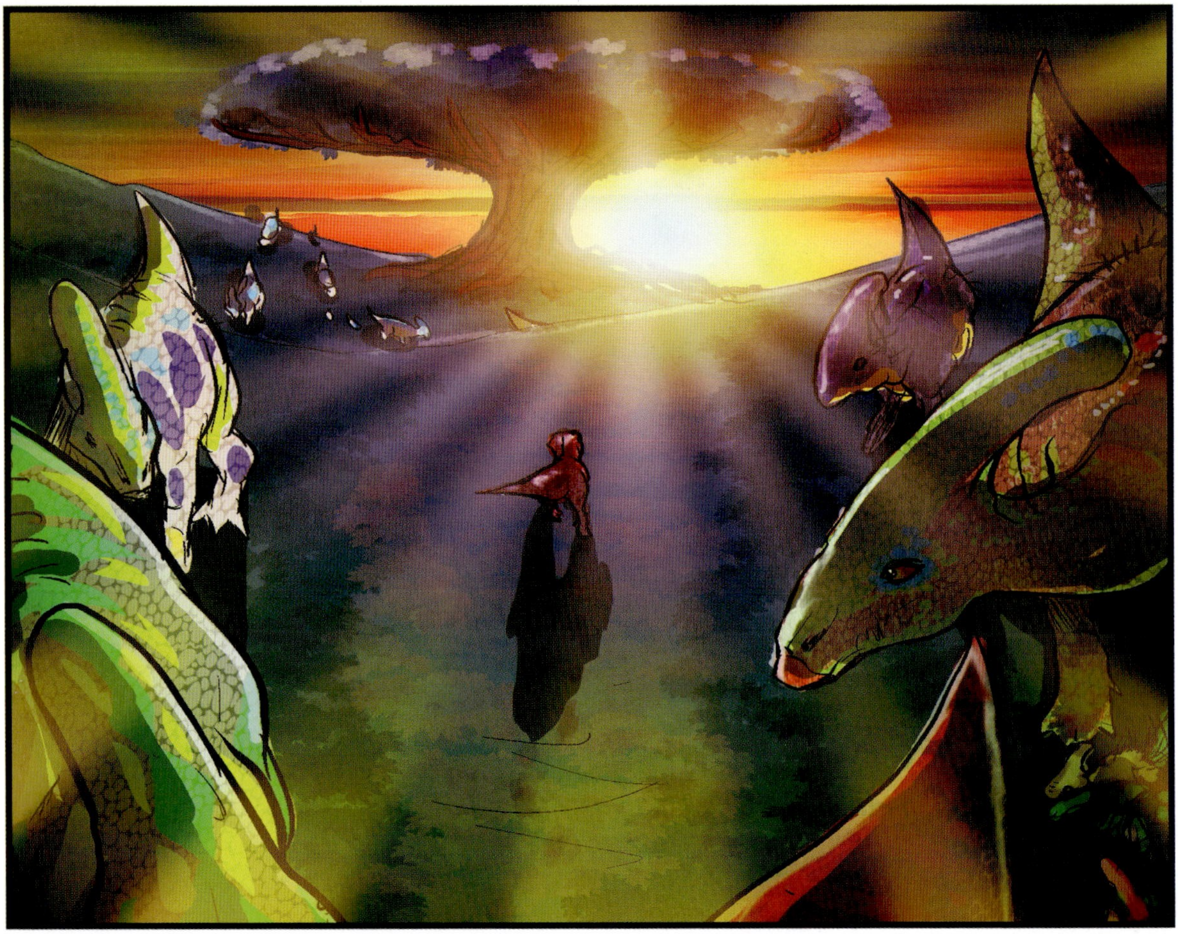

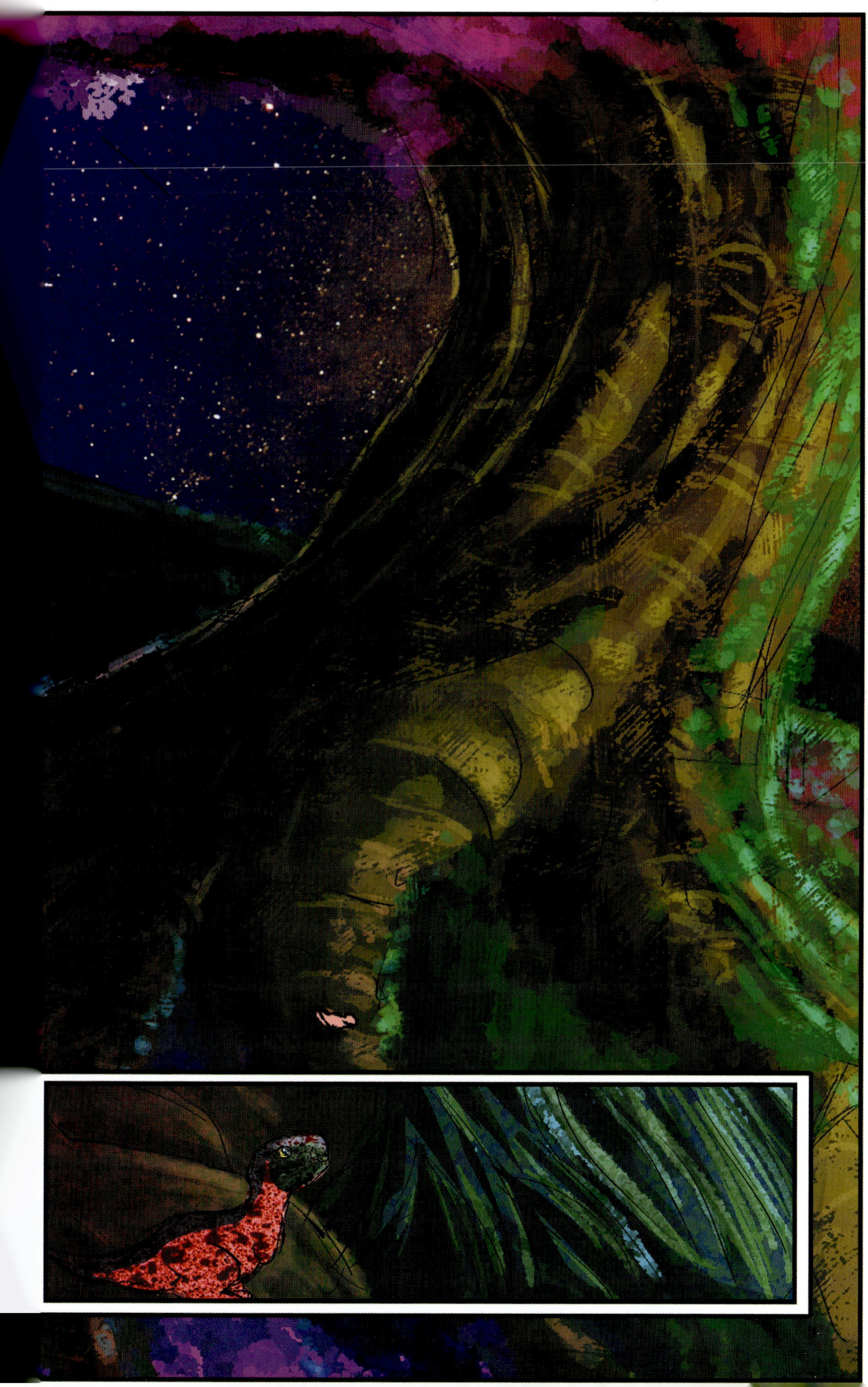

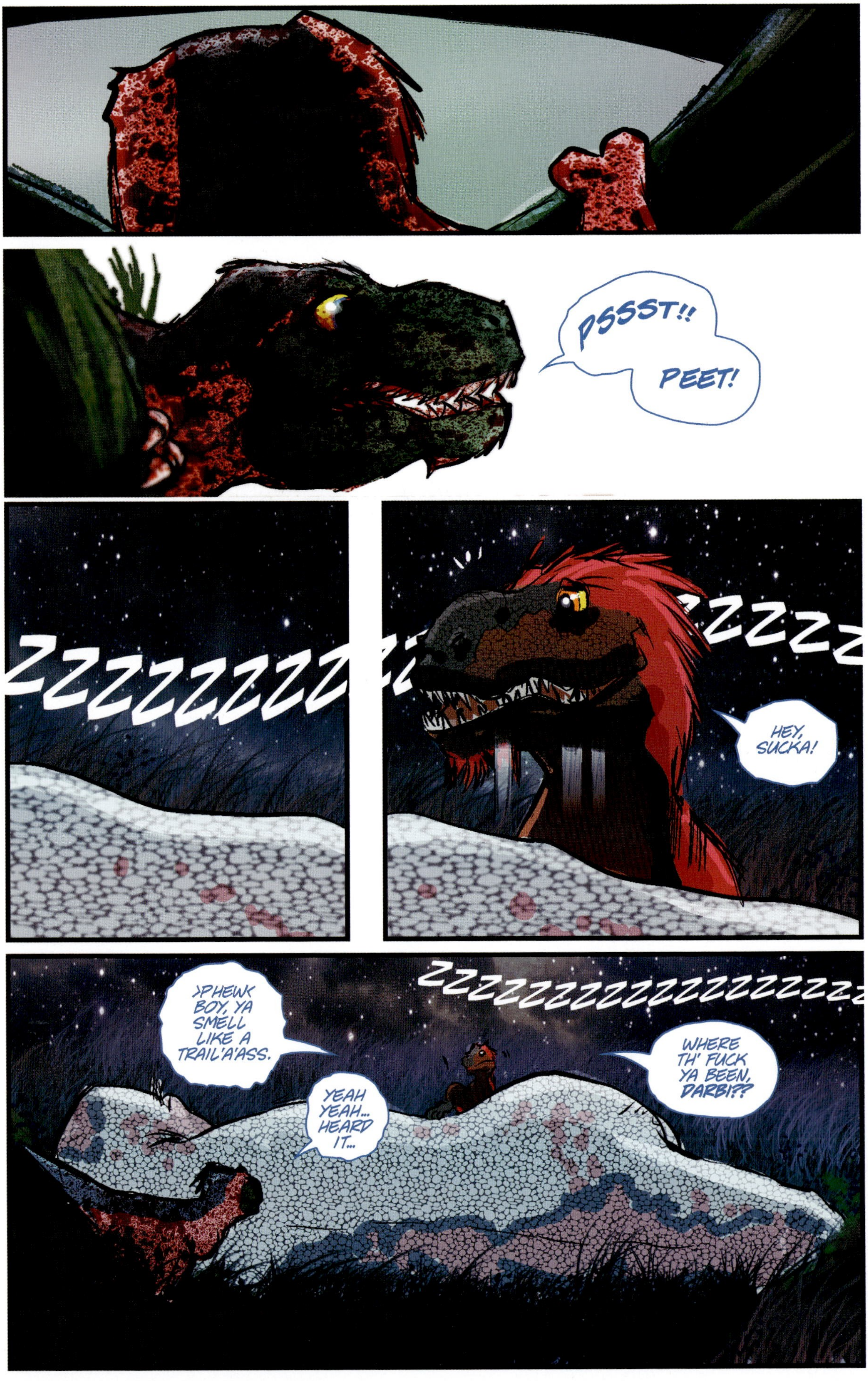
PSSST!!
PEET!
ZZZZZZZZZZZ
ZZZZZ
HEY, SUCKA!
ZZZZZZZZZZZZZZZZZZZZZZ
>PHEW< BOY, YA SMELL LIKE A TRAIL'A'ASS.
YEAH YEAH... HEARD IT...
WHERE TH' FUCK YA BEEN, DARBI??

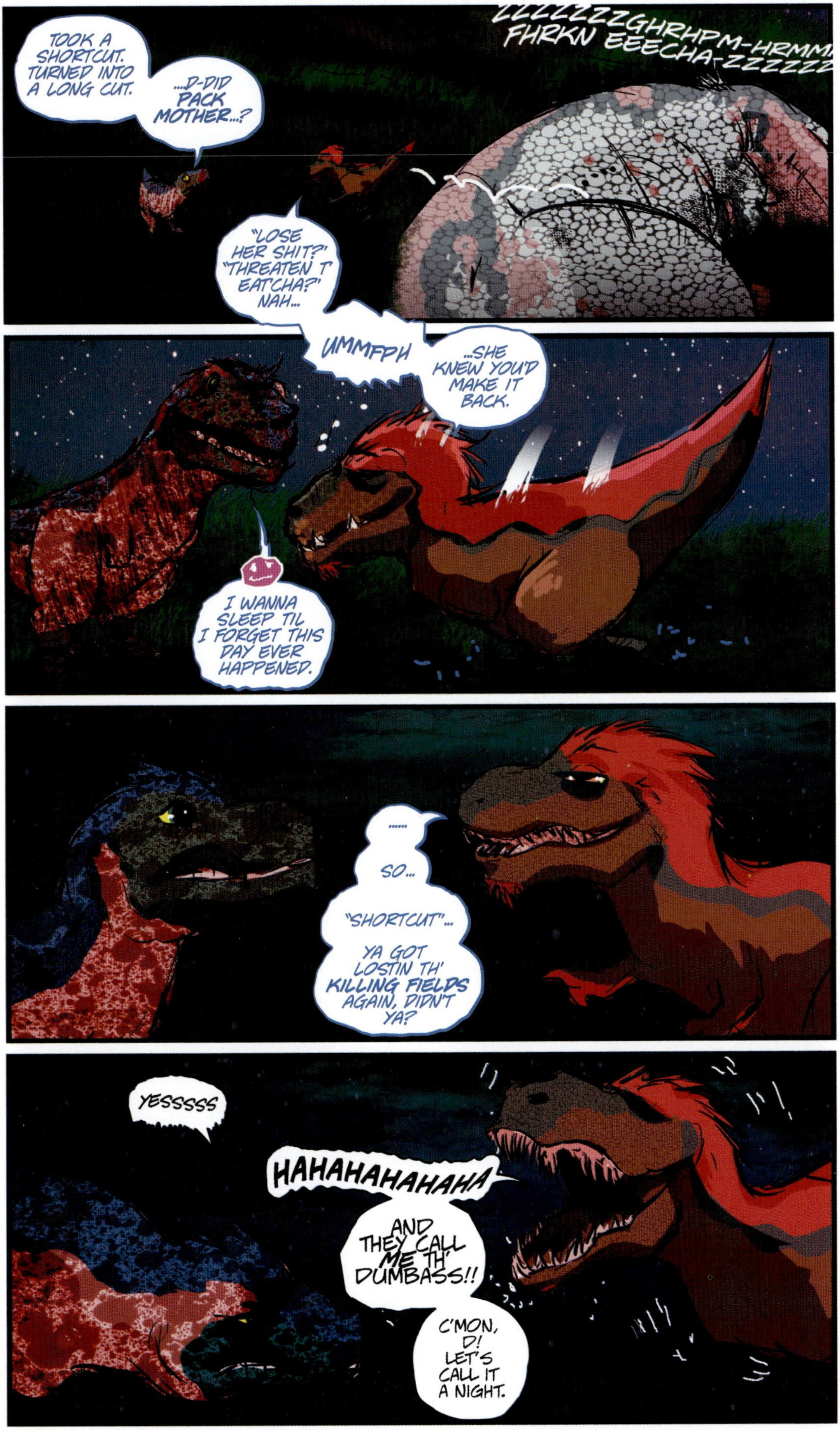
ZZZZZZZZGHRHPM-HRMM FHRKN EEECHA-ZZZZZZ
TOOK A SHORTCUT. TURNED INTO A LONG CUT.
...D-DID PACK MOTHER...?
"LOSE HER SHIT?" "THREATEN T' EAT'CHA?" NAH...
UMMFPH
...SHE KNEW YOU'D MAKE IT BACK.
I WANNA SLEEP TIL I FORGET THIS DAY EVER HAPPENED.
......
SO...
"SHORTCUT"...
YA GOT LOSTIN TH' KILLING FIELDS AGAIN, DIDN'T YA?
YESSSSS
HAHAHAHAHAHA
AND THEY CALL ME TH' DUMBASS!!
C'MON, D! LET'S CALL IT A NIGHT.

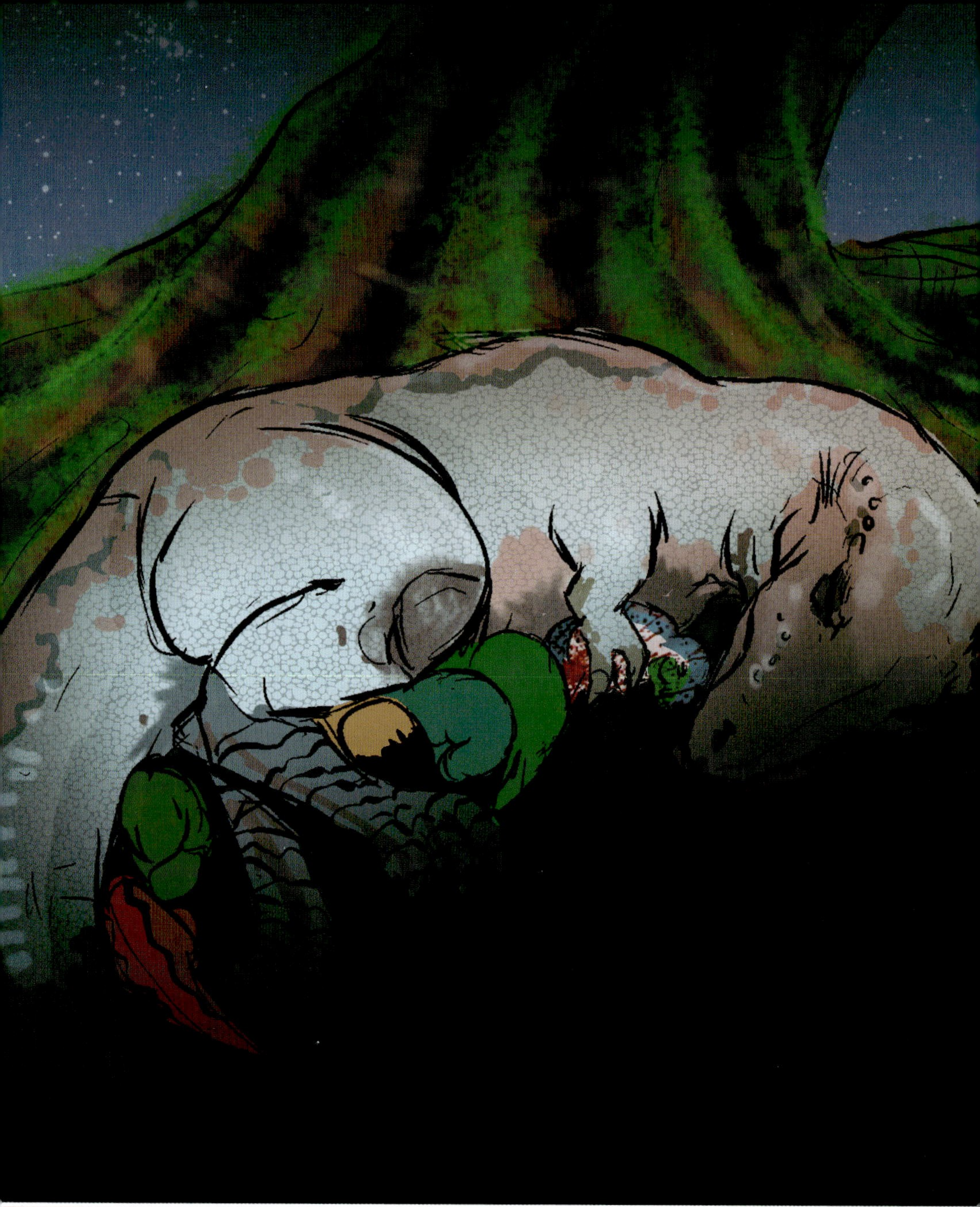
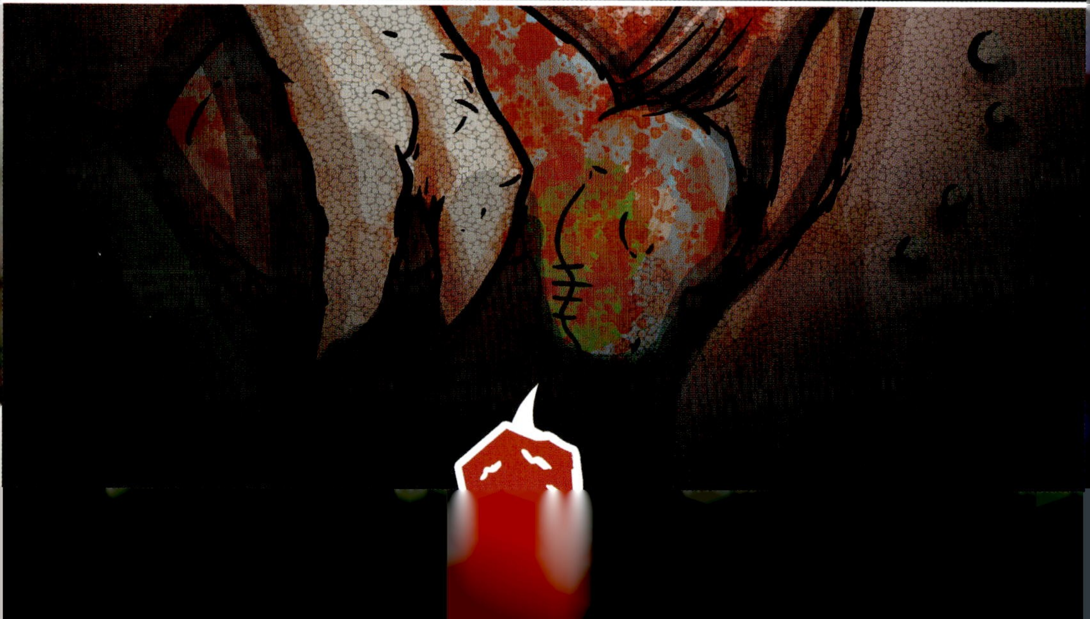

BLOODED

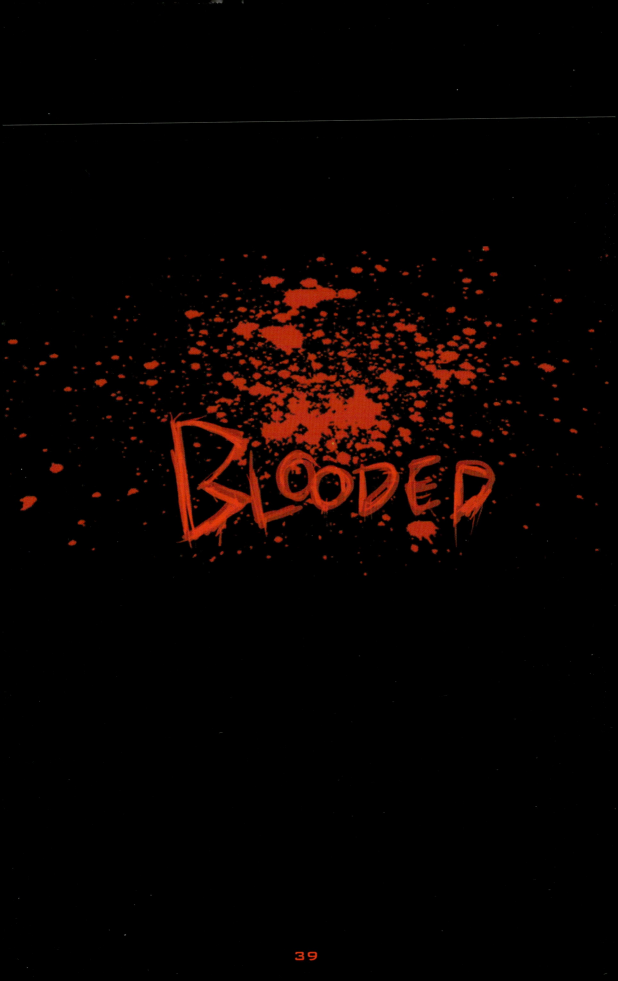

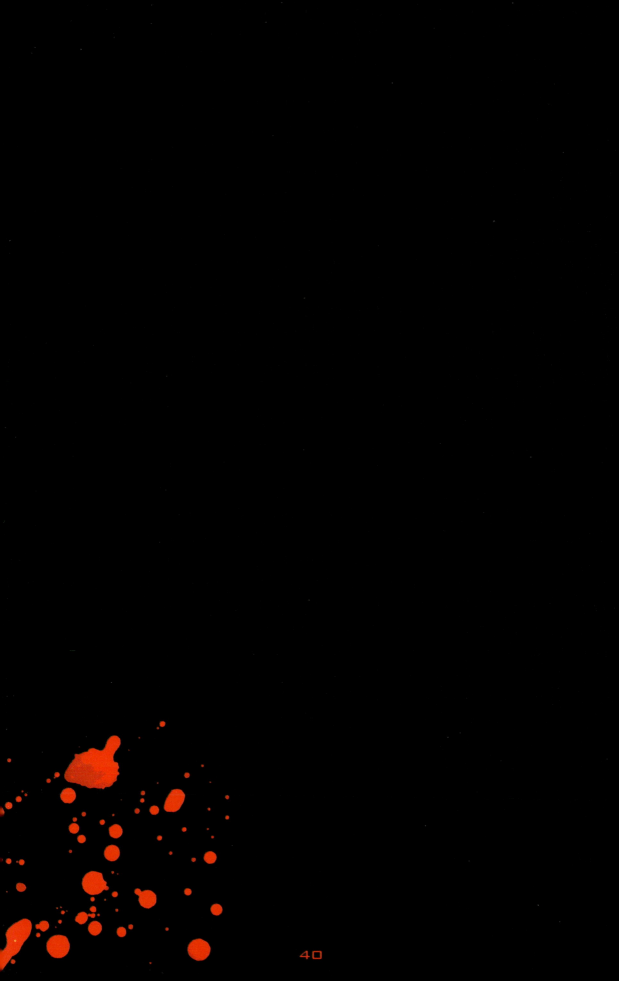

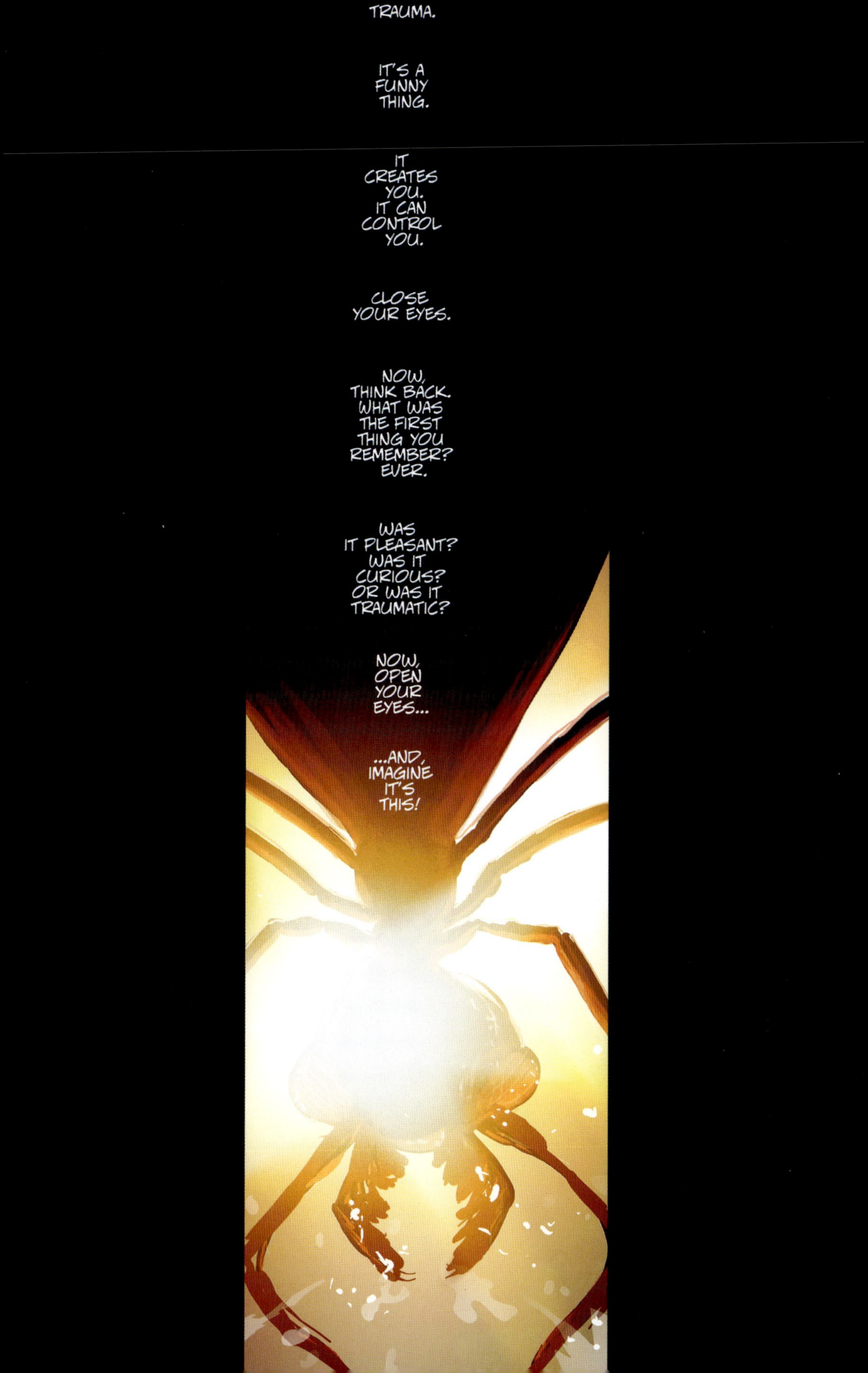
TRAUMA.
IT'S A FUNNY THING.
IT CREATES YOU. IT CAN CONTROL YOU.
CLOSE YOUR EYES.
NOW, THINK BACK. WHAT WAS THE FIRST THING YOU REMEMBER? EVER.
WAS IT PLEASANT? WAS IT CURIOUS? OR WAS IT TRAUMATIC?
NOW, OPEN YOUR EYES...
...AND, IMAGINE IT'S THIS!

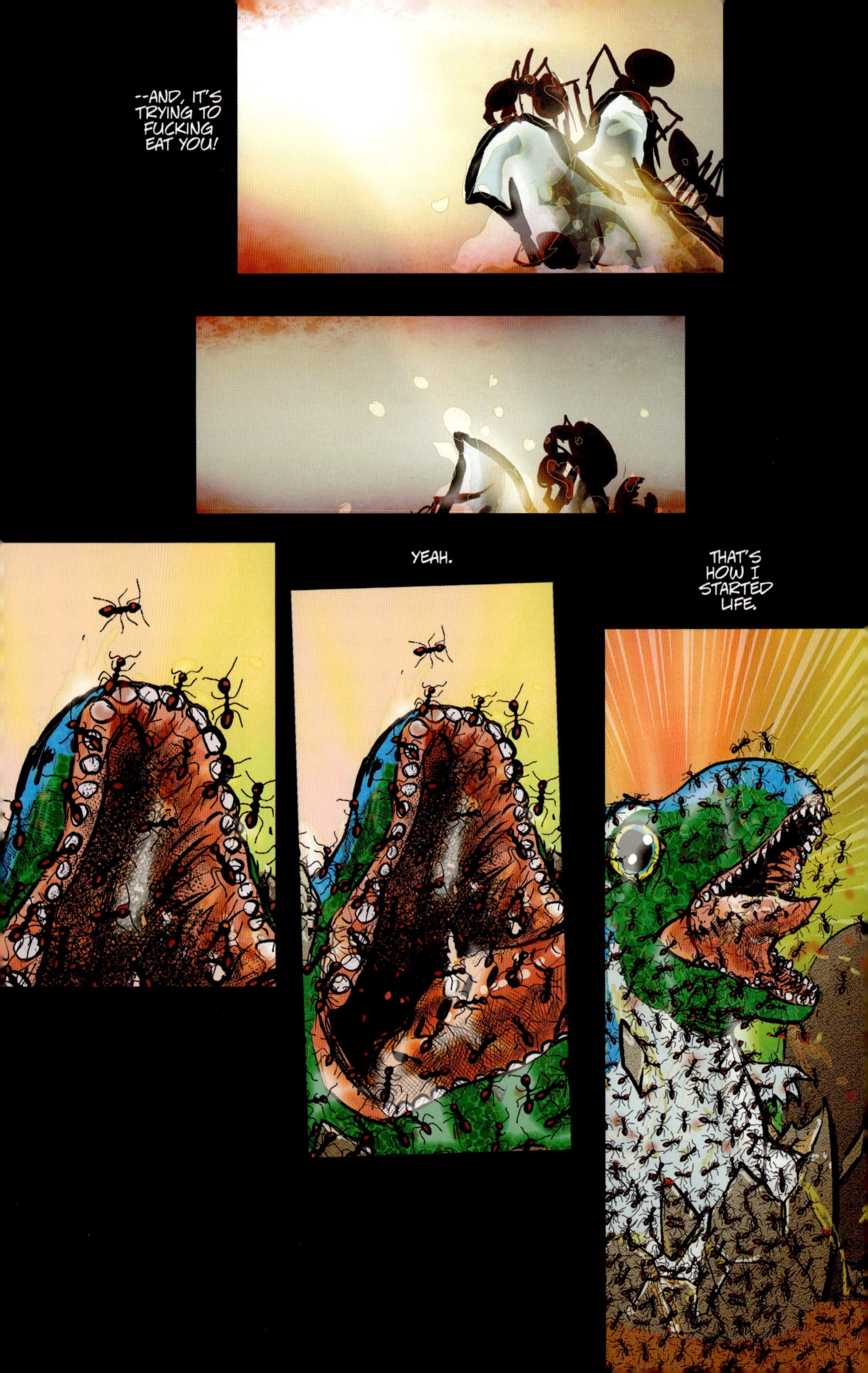
--AND, IT'S TRYING TO FUCKING EAT YOU!
YEAH.
THAT'S HOW I STARTED LIFE.

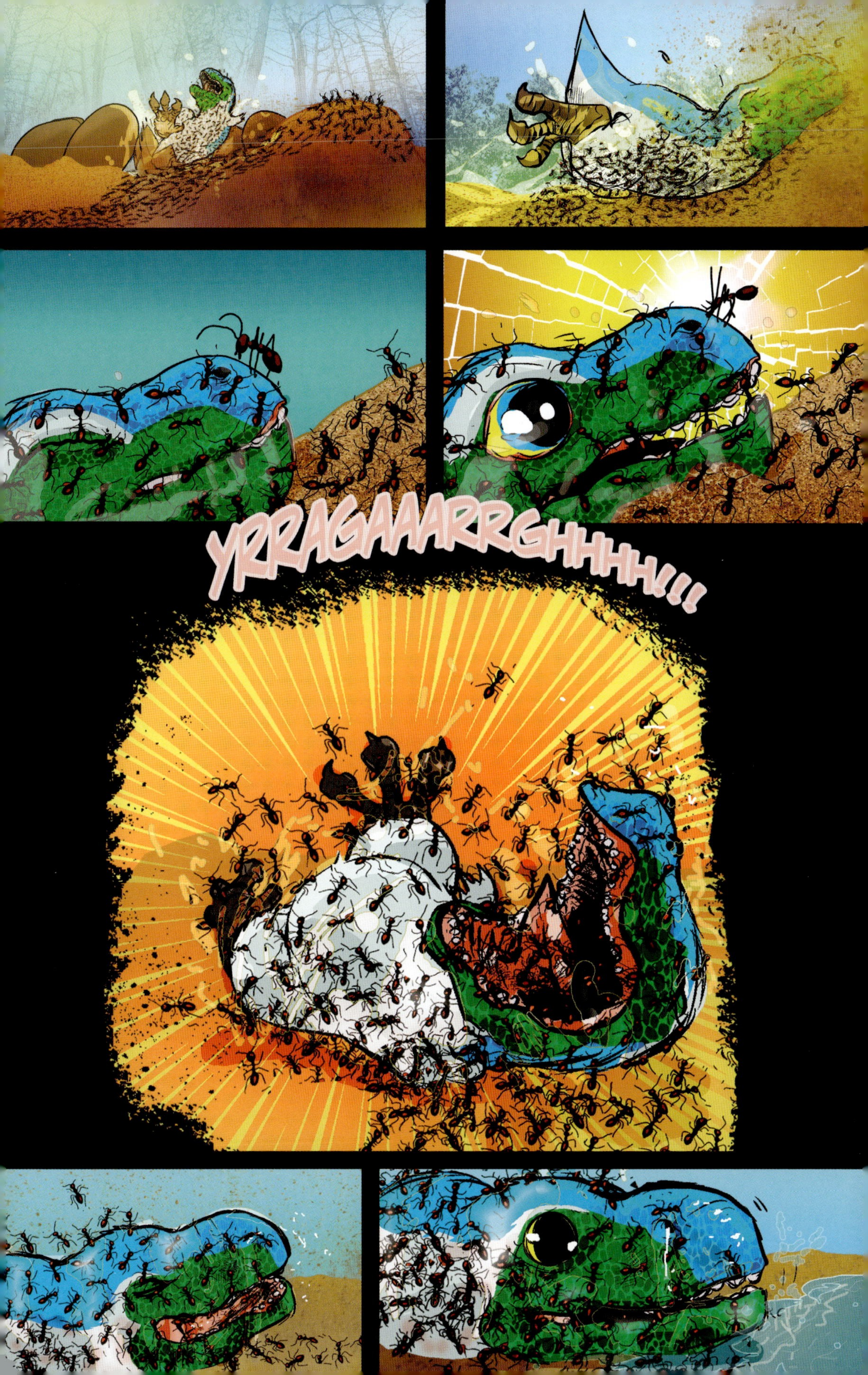
YRRAGAAARRGHHHH!!!

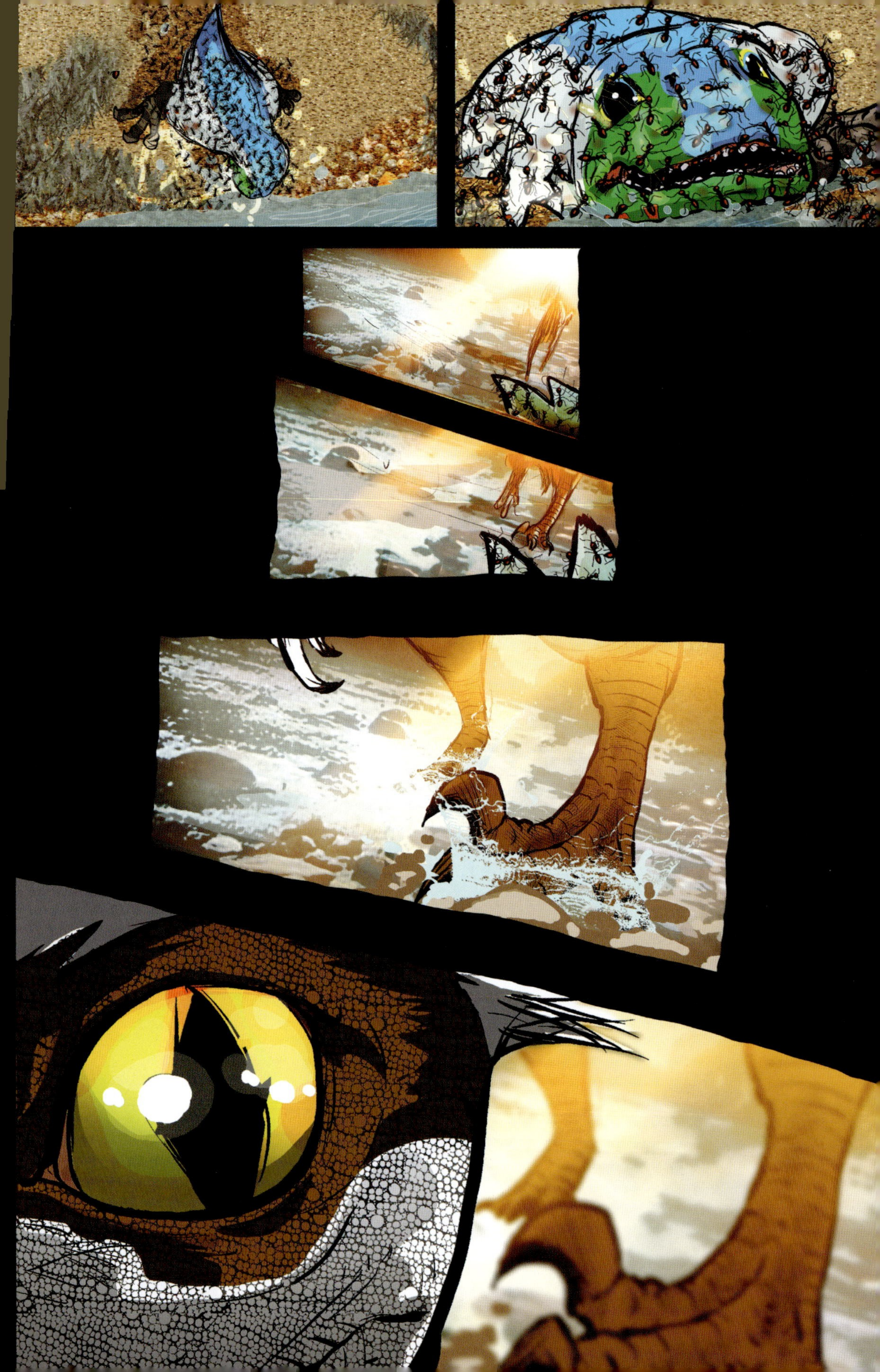

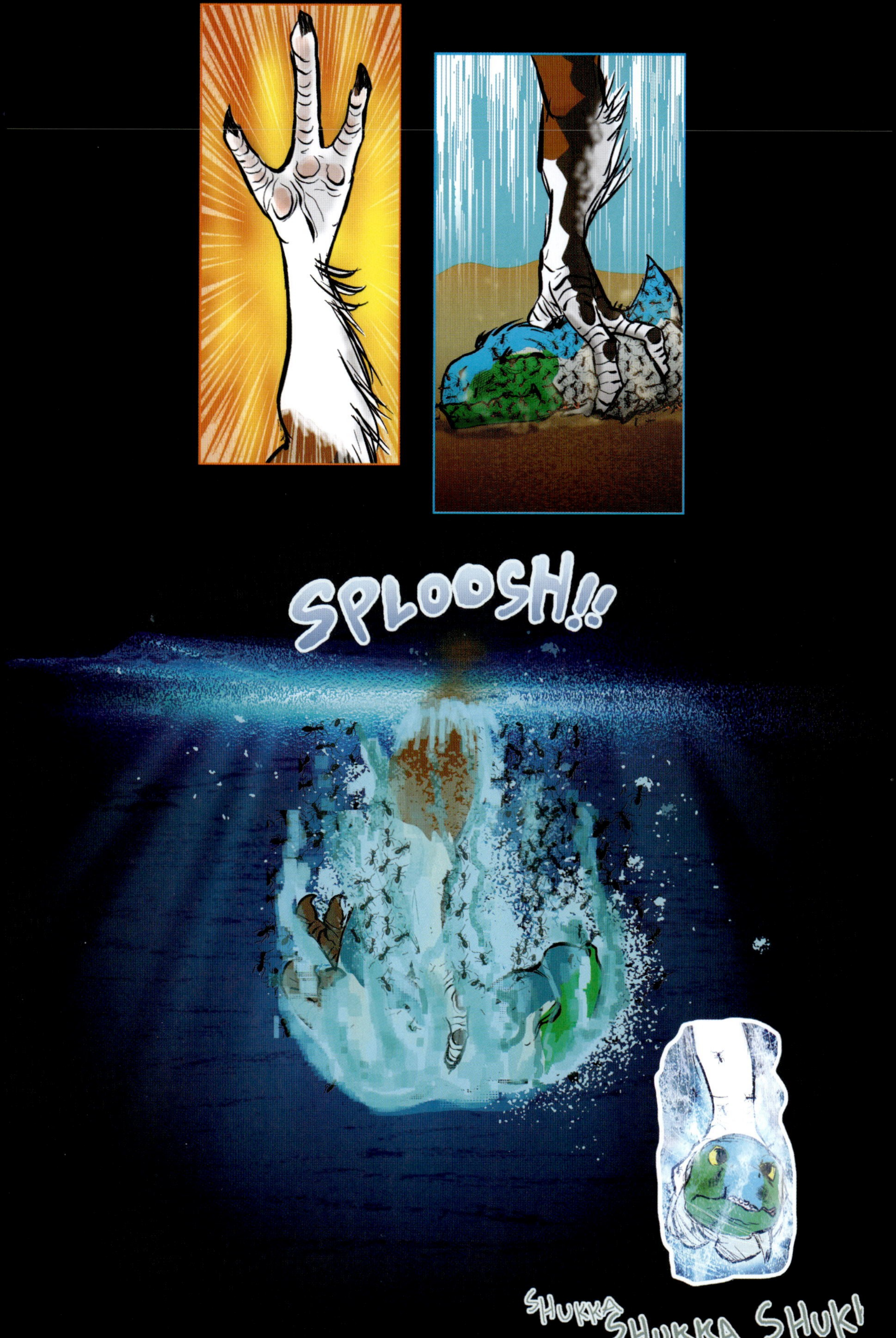
SPLOOSH!!
SHUKKA SHUKKA SHUKI

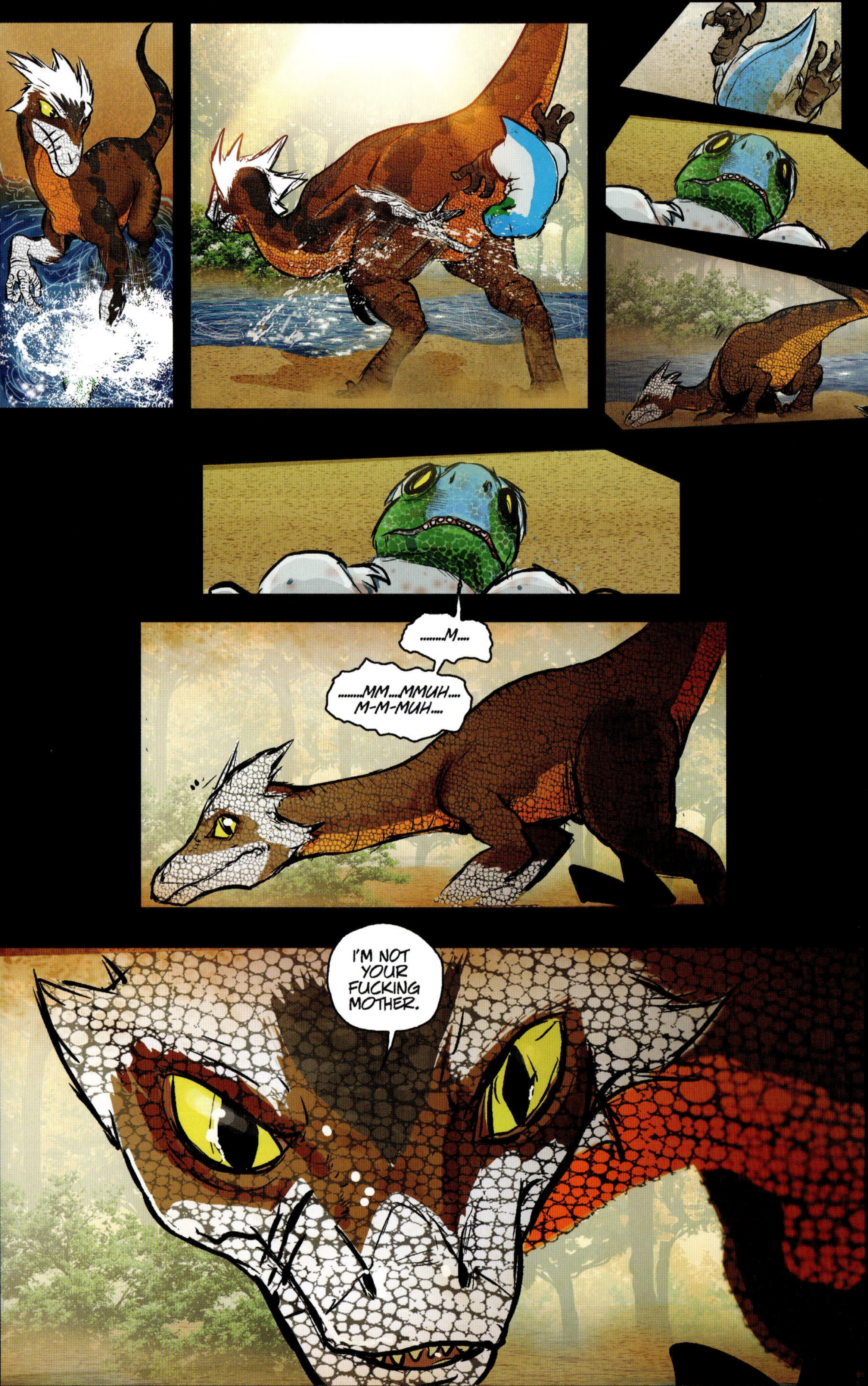
........M....
........MM....MMUH....
M-M-MUH....
I'M NOT YOUR FUCKING MOTHER.

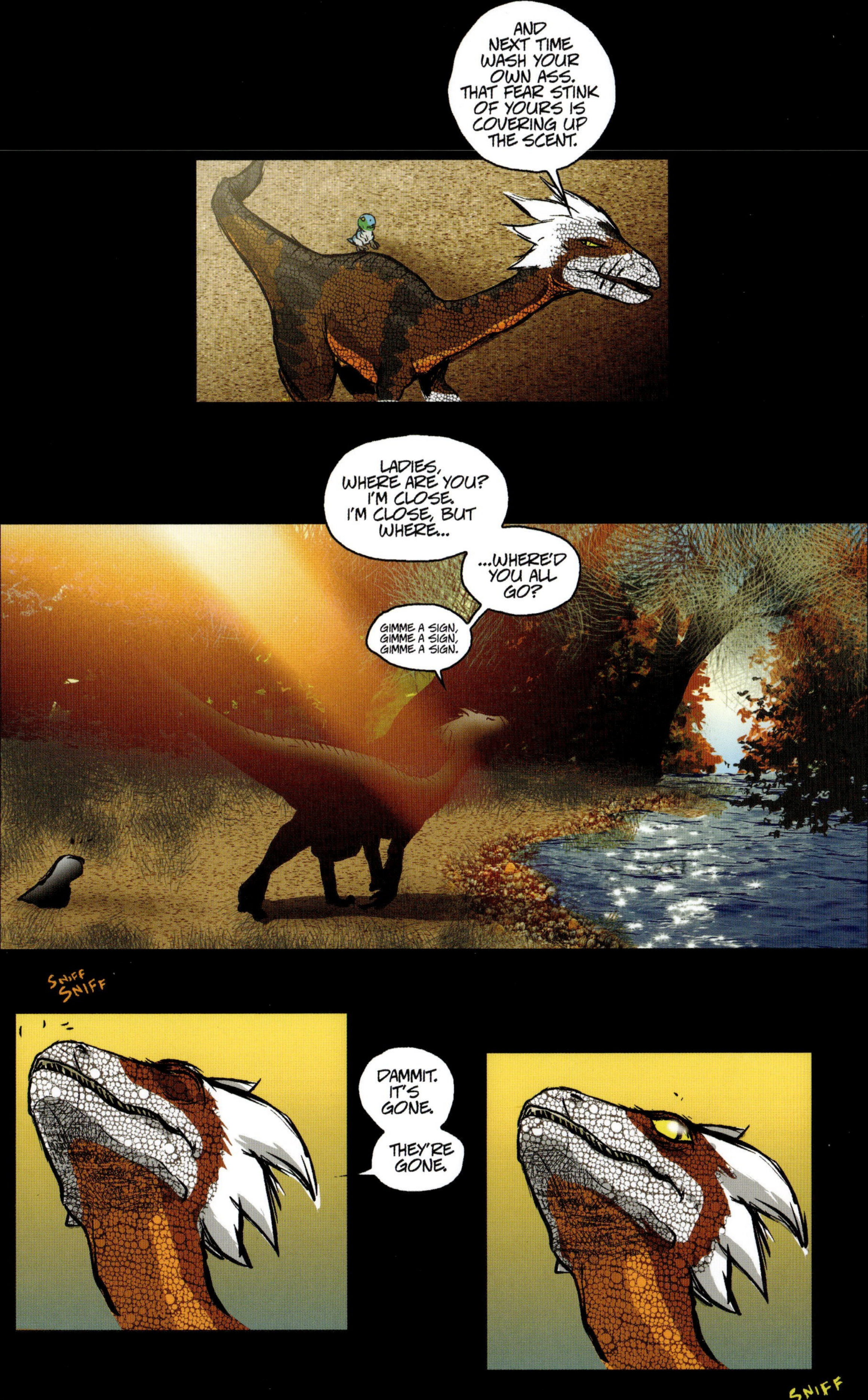
AND NEXT TIME WASH YOUR OWN ASS. THAT FEAR STINK OF YOURS IS COVERING UP THE SCENT.
LADIES, WHERE ARE YOU? I'M CLOSE. I'M CLOSE, BUT WHERE...
...WHERE'D YOU ALL GO?
GIMME A SIGN, GIMME A SIGN, GIMME A SIGN.
SNIFF SNIFF
DAMMIT. IT'S GONE.
THEY'RE GONE.
SNIFF

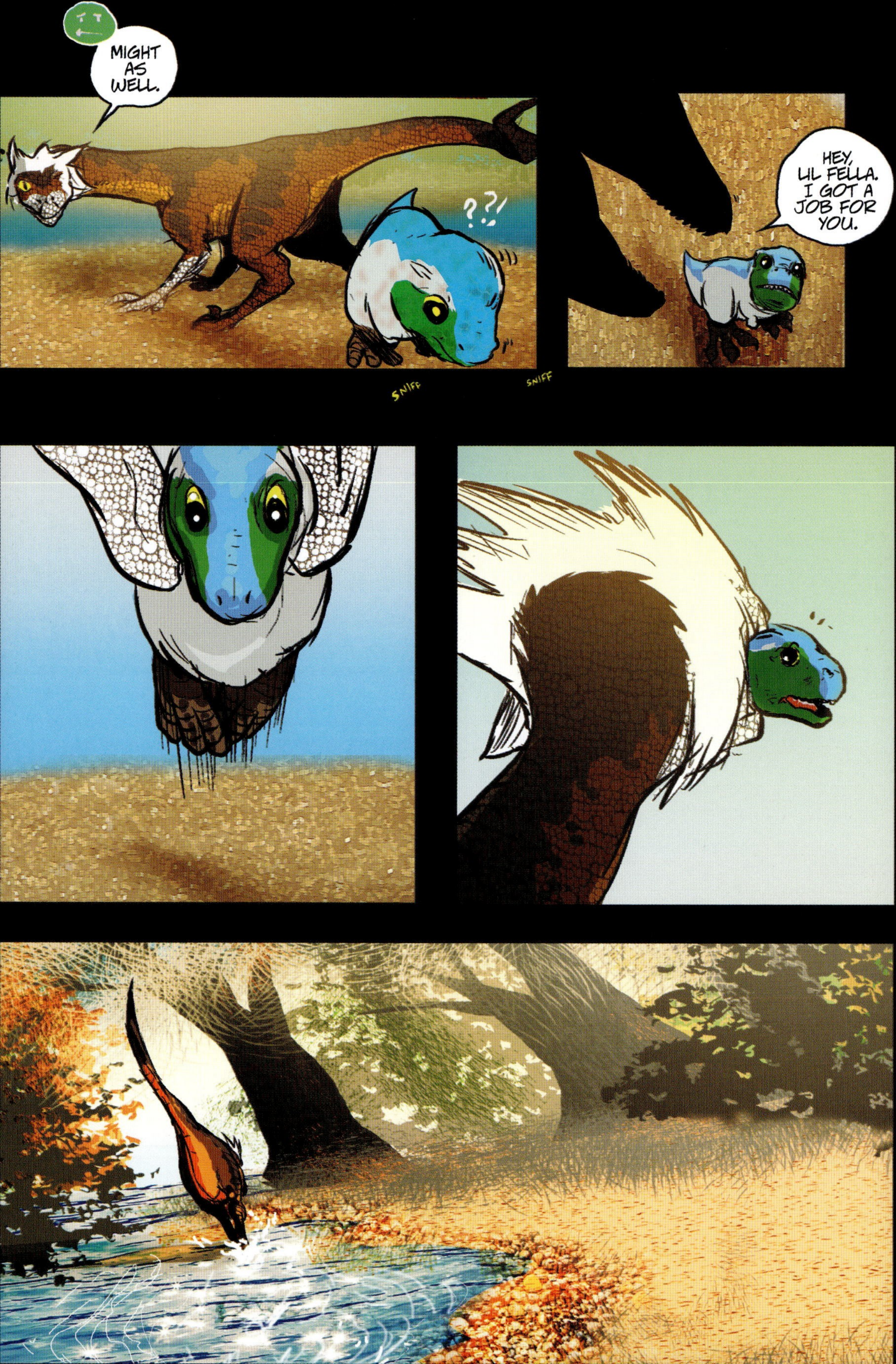
MIGHT AS WELL.
??!
HEY, LIL FELLA. I GOT A JOB FOR YOU.
SNIFF
SNIFF

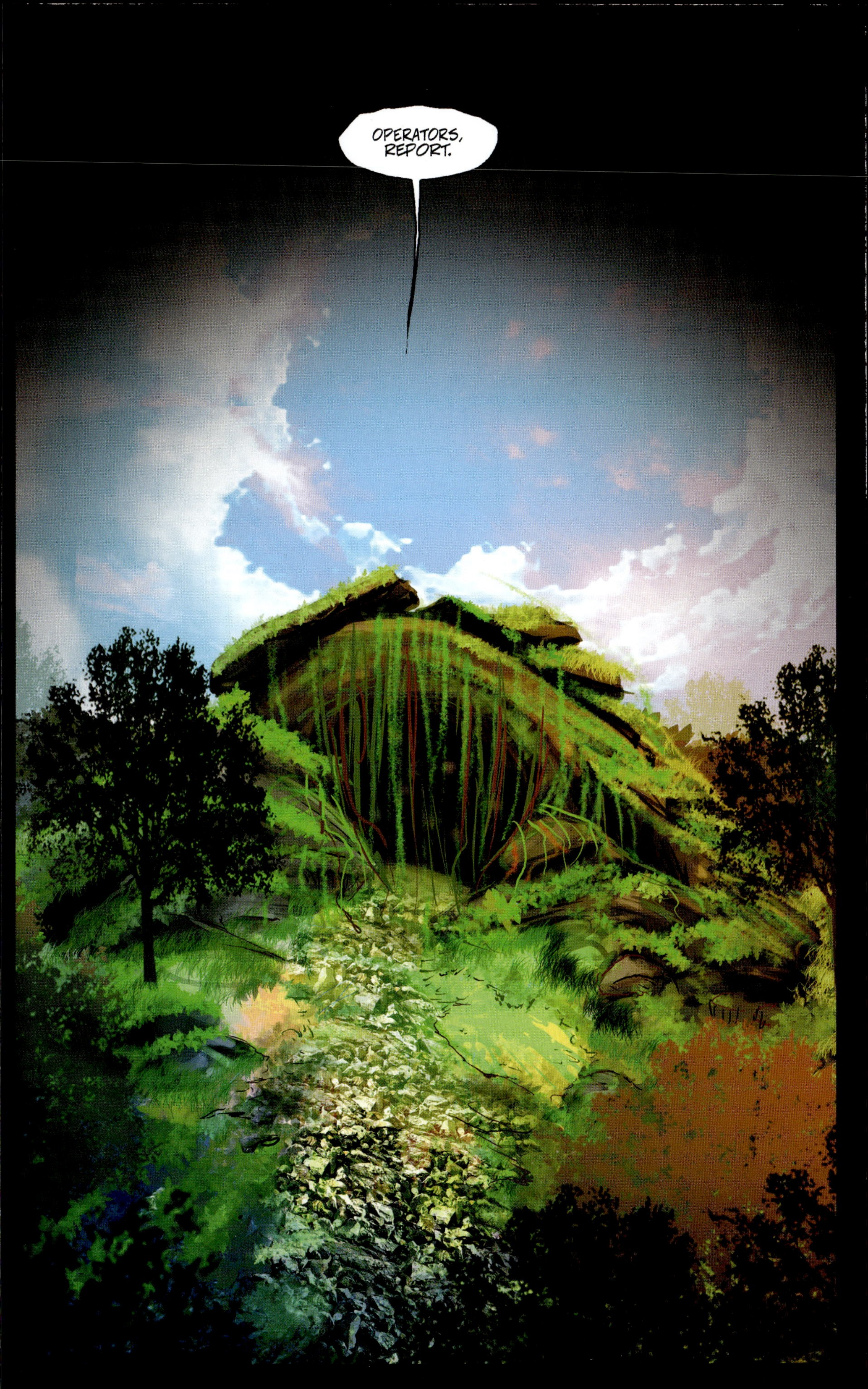
OPERATORS, REPORT.

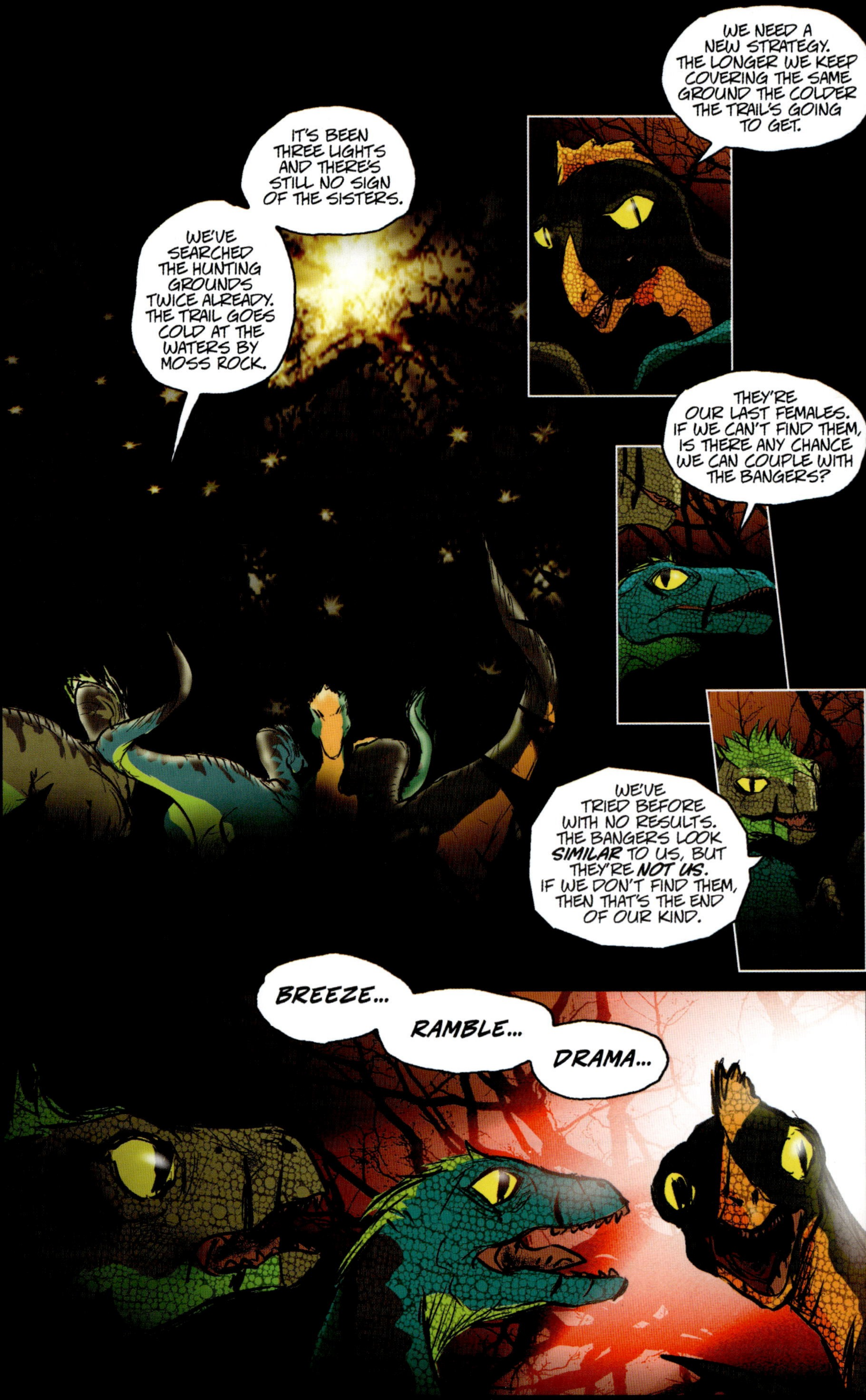

IT'S BEEN THREE LIGHTS AND THERE'S STILL NO SIGN OF THE SISTERS.
WE'VE SEARCHED THE HUNTING GROUNDS TWICE ALREADY. THE TRAIL GOES COLD AT THE WATERS BY MOSS ROCK.
WE NEED A NEW STRATEGY. THE LONGER WE KEEP COVERING THE SAME GROUND THE COLDER THE TRAIL'S GOING TO GET.
THEY'RE OUR LAST FEMALES. IF WE CAN'T FIND THEM, IS THERE ANY CHANCE WE CAN COUPLE WITH THE BANGERS?
WE'VE TRIED BEFORE WITH NO RESULTS. THE BANGERS LOOK SIMILAR TO US, BUT THEY'RE NOT US. IF WE DON'T FIND THEM, THEN THAT'S THE END OF OUR KIND.
BREEZE...
RAMBLE...
DRAMA...

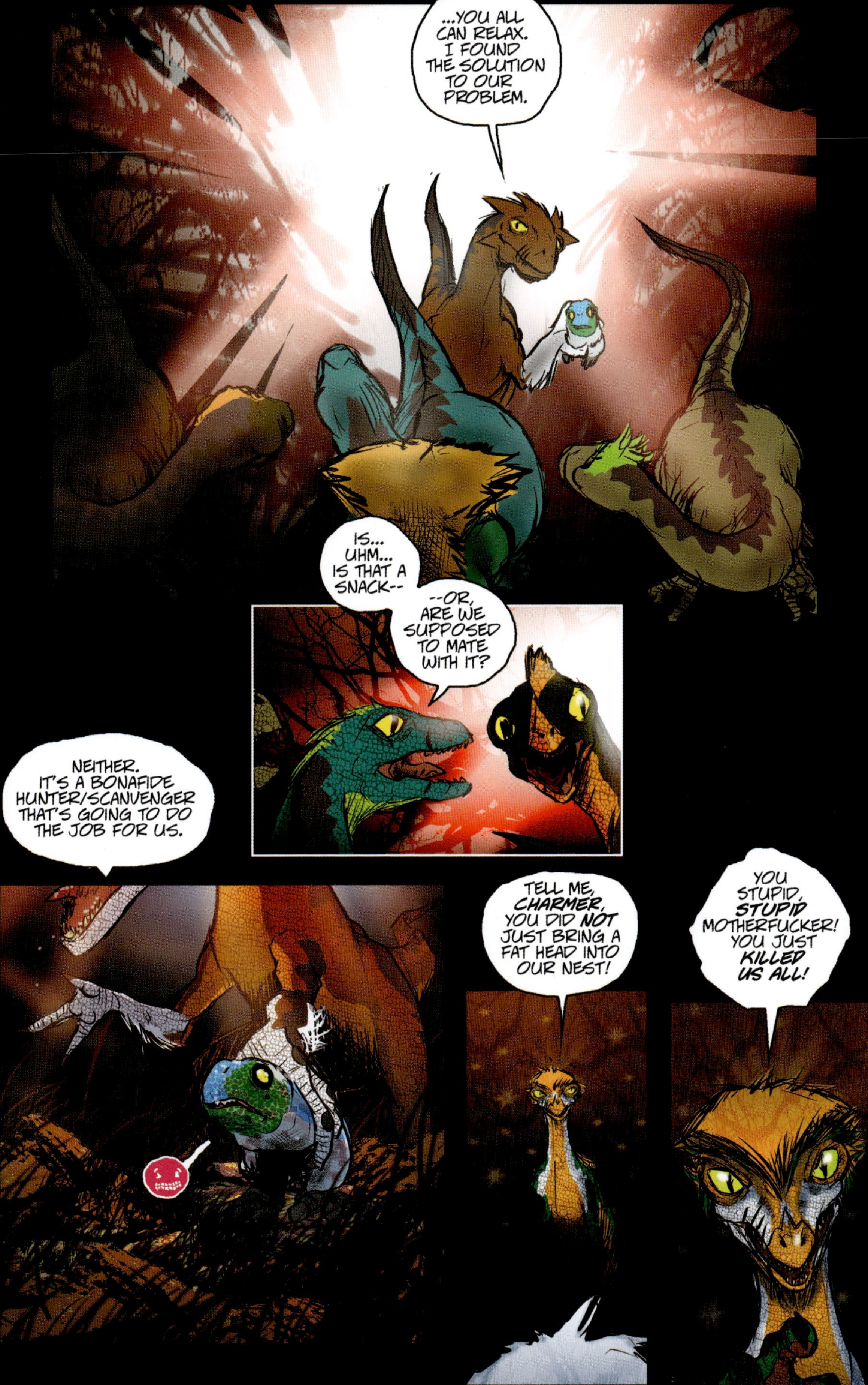
...YOU ALL CAN RELAX. I FOUND THE SOLUTION TO OUR PROBLEM.
IS... UHM... IS THAT A SNACK--
--OR, ARE WE SUPPOSED TO MATE WITH IT?
NEITHER. IT'S A BONAFIDE HUNTER/SCAVENGER THAT'S GOING TO DO THE JOB FOR US.
TELL ME, CHARMER, YOU DID NOT JUST BRING A FAT HEAD INTO OUR NEST!
YOU STUPID, STUPID MOTHERFUCKER! YOU JUST KILLED US ALL!

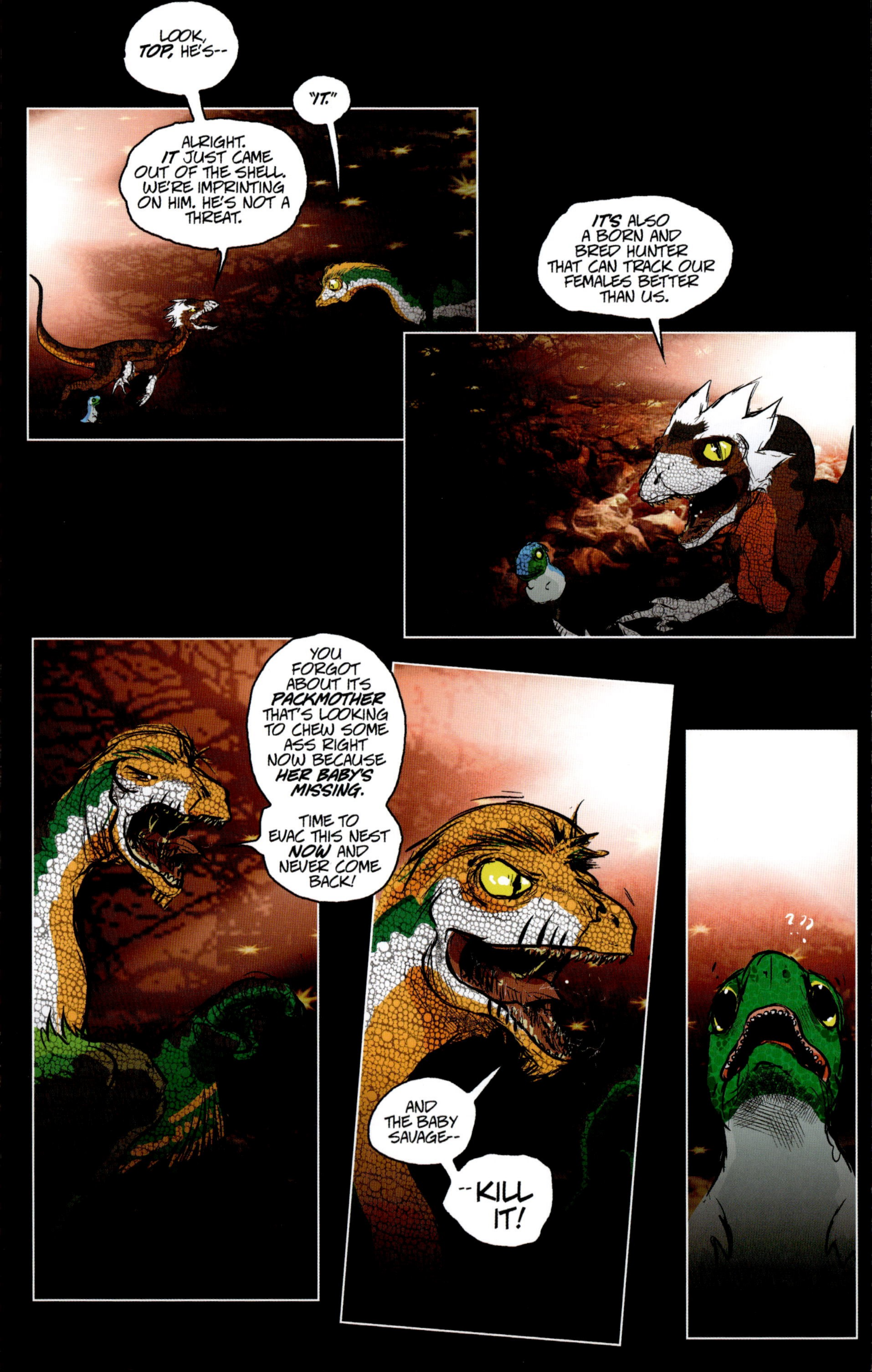
LOOK, *TOP,* HE'S--
ALRIGHT. *IT* JUST CAME OUT OF THE SHELL. WE'RE IMPRINTING ON HIM. HE'S NOT A THREAT.
"IT."
IT'S ALSO A BORN AND BRED HUNTER THAT CAN TRACK OUR FEMALES BETTER THAN US.
YOU FORGOT ABOUT ITS *PACKMOTHER* THAT'S LOOKING TO CHEW SOME ASS RIGHT NOW BECAUSE *HER BABY'S MISSING.*
TIME TO EVAC THIS NEST *NOW* AND NEVER COME BACK!
AND THE BABY SAVAGE--
--KILL IT!
???

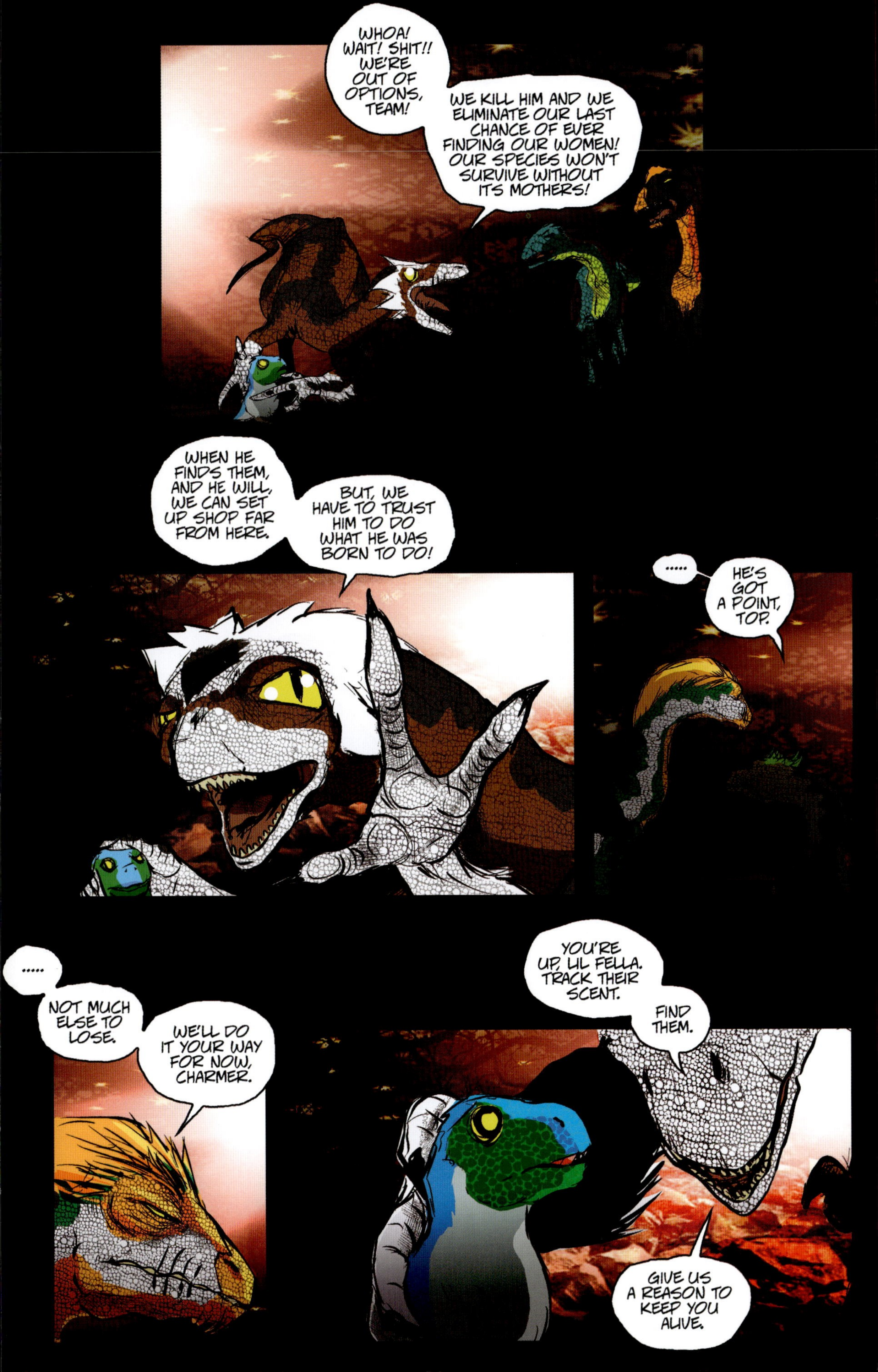
WHOA! WAIT! SHIT!! WE'RE OUT OF OPTIONS, TEAM!
WE KILL HIM AND WE ELIMINATE OUR LAST CHANCE OF EVER FINDING OUR WOMEN! OUR SPECIES WON'T SURVIVE WITHOUT ITS MOTHERS!
WHEN HE FINDS THEM, AND HE WILL, WE CAN SET UP SHOP FAR FROM HERE.
BUT, WE HAVE TO TRUST HIM TO DO WHAT HE WAS BORN TO DO!
.....
HE'S GOT A POINT, TOP.
.....
NOT MUCH ELSE TO LOSE.
WE'LL DO IT YOUR WAY FOR NOW, CHARMER.
YOU'RE UP, LIL FELLA. TRACK THEIR SCENT.
FIND THEM.
GIVE US A REASON TO KEEP YOU ALIVE.

SNIFF

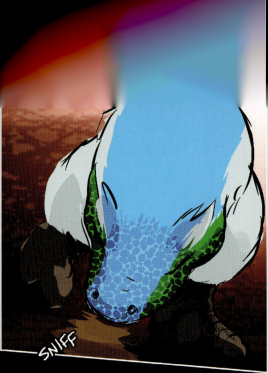

SNIFF

HE'S GOT IT!

FOR THE
FIRST TIME EVER,
THERE WAS NO
TRAUMA.
NO FEAR.

ONLY
PURPOSE.

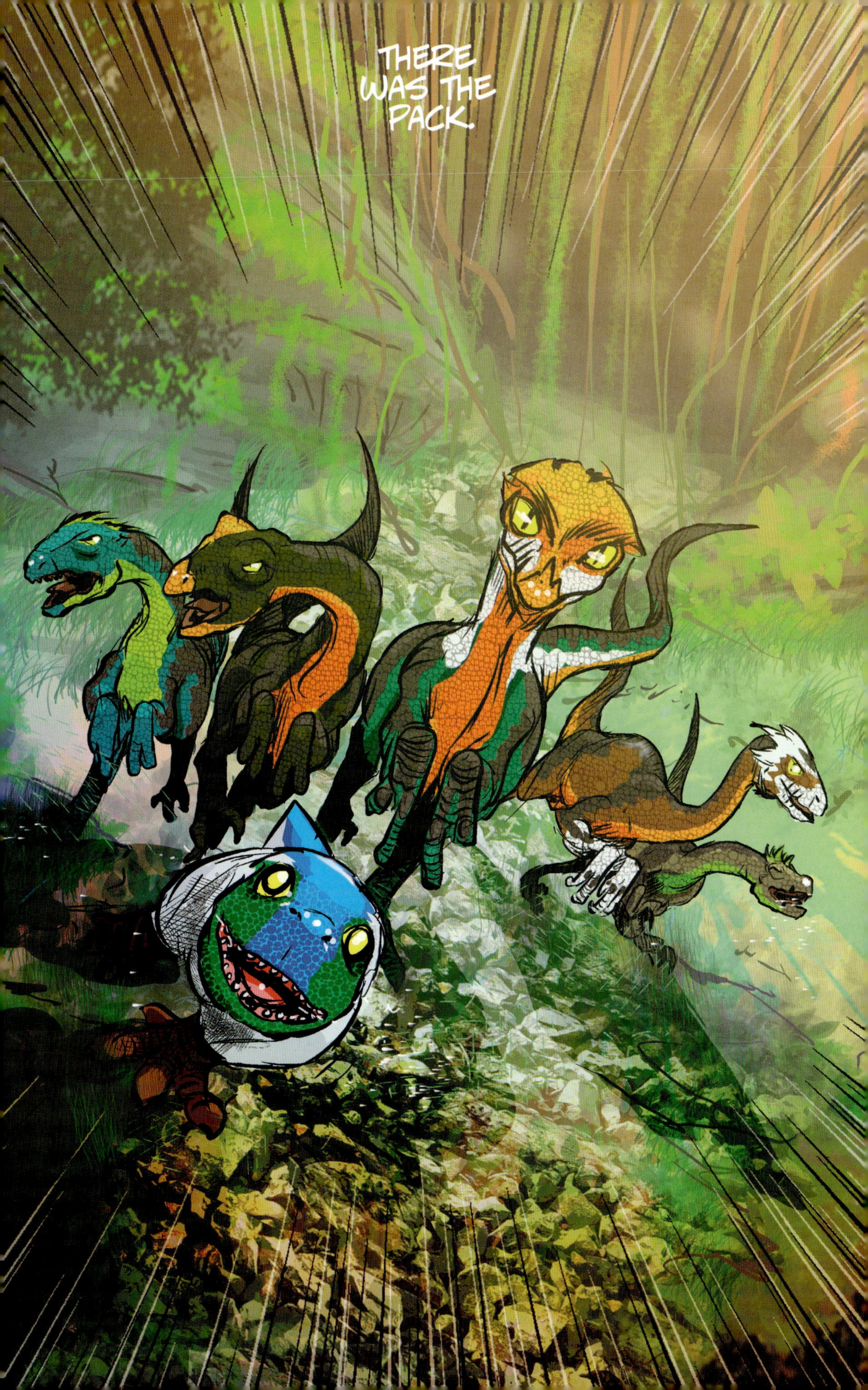
THERE WAS THE PACK.

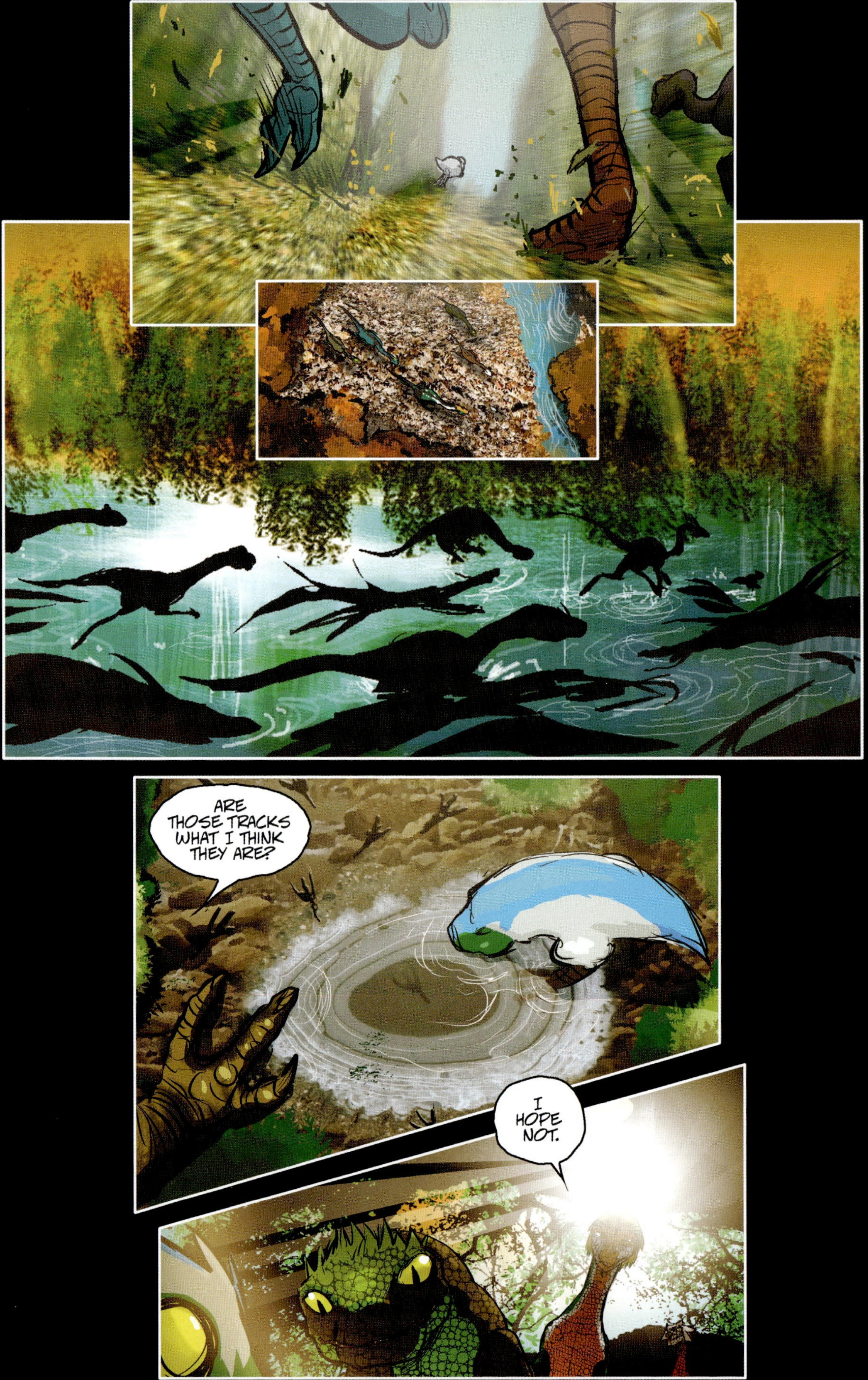
ARE THOSE TRACKS WHAT I THINK THEY ARE?
I HOPE NOT.

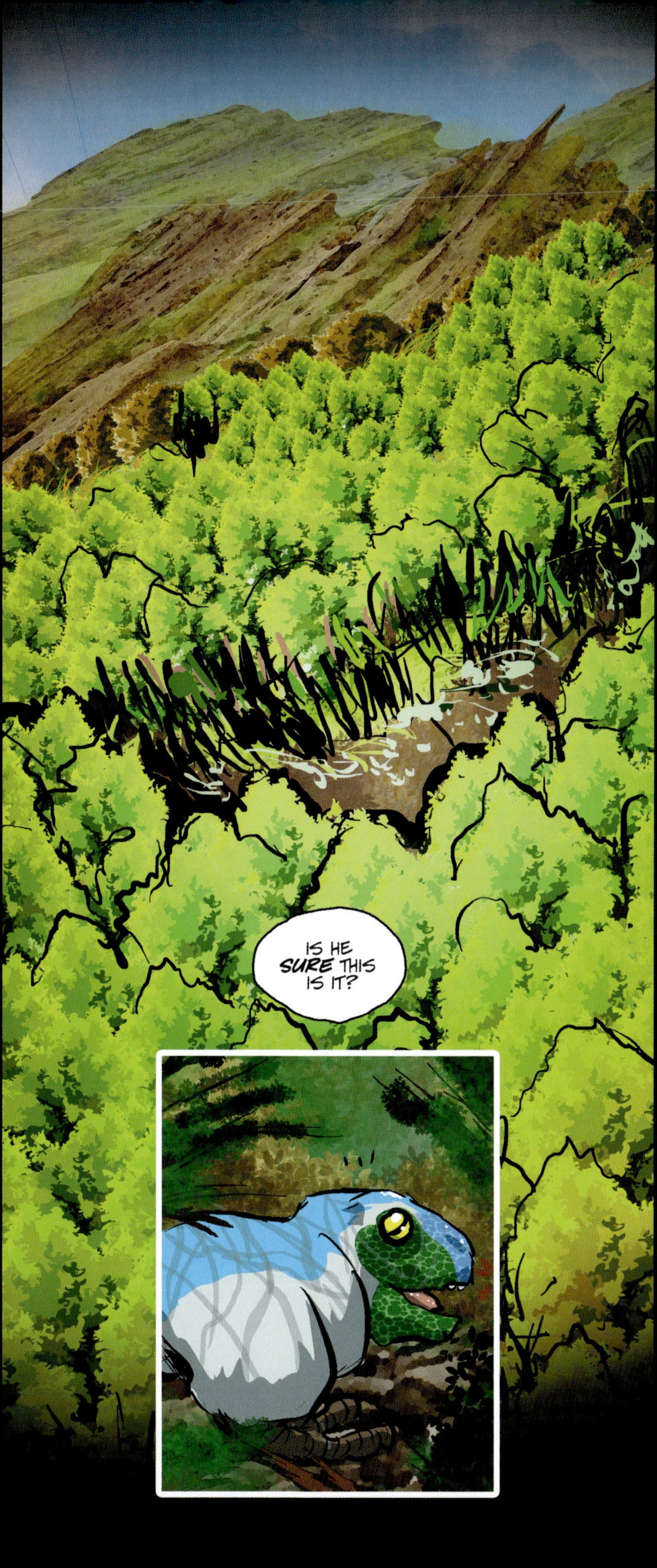
IS HE SURE THIS IS IT?

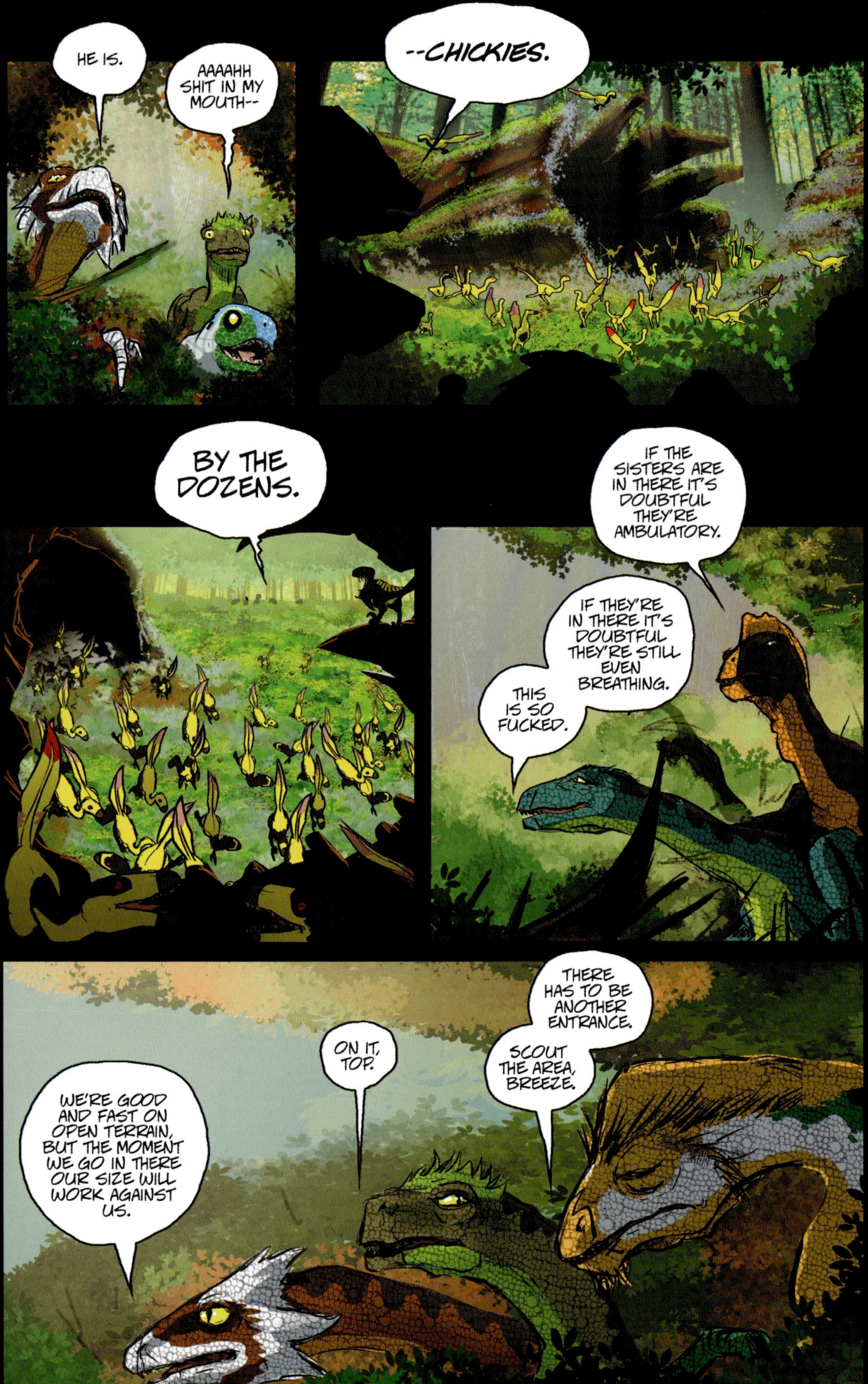
HE IS.
AAAAHH SHIT IN MY MOUTH--
--CHICKIES.
BY THE DOZENS.
IF THE SISTERS ARE IN THERE IT'S DOUBTFUL THEY'RE AMBULATORY.
IF THEY'RE IN THERE IT'S DOUBTFUL THEY'RE STILL EVEN BREATHING.
THIS IS SO FUCKED.
THERE HAS TO BE ANOTHER ENTRANCE.
SCOUT THE AREA, BREEZE.
ON IT, TOP.
WE'RE GOOD AND FAST ON OPEN TERRAIN, BUT THE MOMENT WE GO IN THERE OUR SIZE WILL WORK AGAINST US.

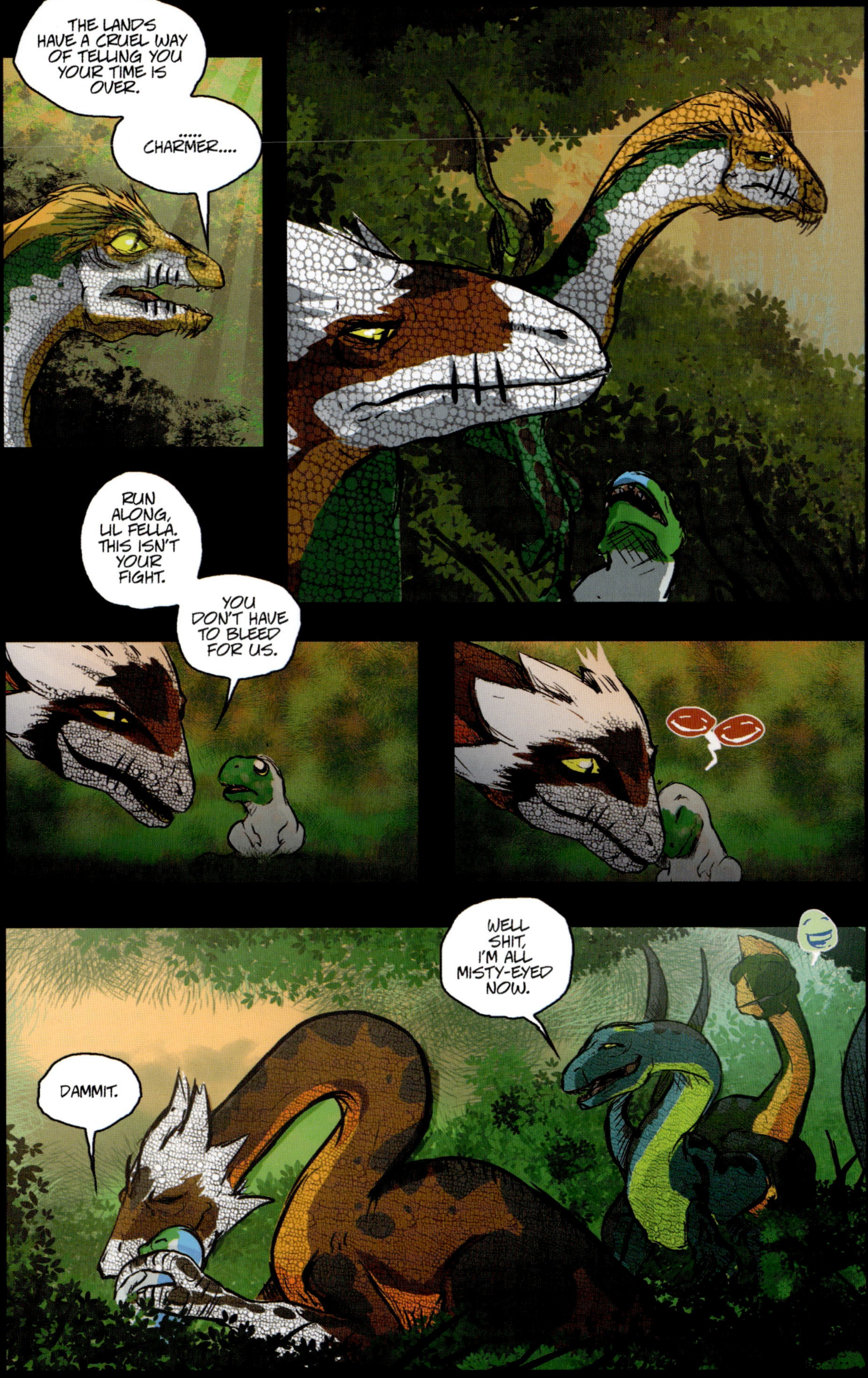
THE LANDS HAVE A CRUEL WAY OF TELLING YOU YOUR TIME IS OVER.
..... CHARMER....
RUN ALONG, LIL FELLA. THIS ISN'T YOUR FIGHT.
YOU DON'T HAVE TO BLEED FOR US.
WELL SHIT, I'M ALL MISTY-EYED NOW.
DAMMIT.

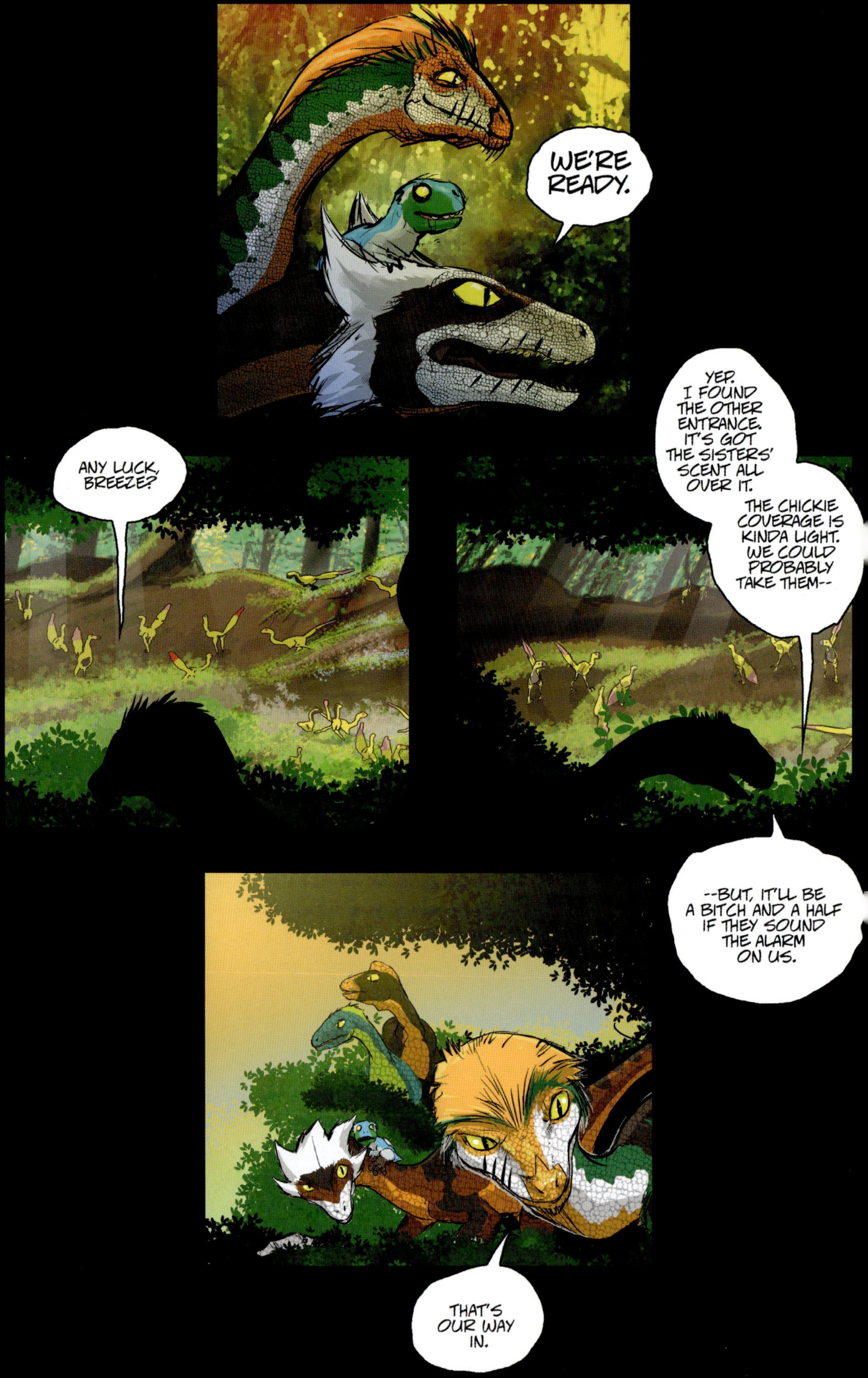
WE'RE READY.
ANY LUCK, BREEZE?
YEP. I FOUND THE OTHER ENTRANCE. IT'S GOT THE SISTERS' SCENT ALL OVER IT.
THE CHICKIE COVERAGE IS KINDA LIGHT. WE COULD PROBABLY TAKE THEM--
--BUT, IT'LL BE A BITCH AND A HALF IF THEY SOUND THE ALARM ON US.
THAT'S OUR WAY IN.

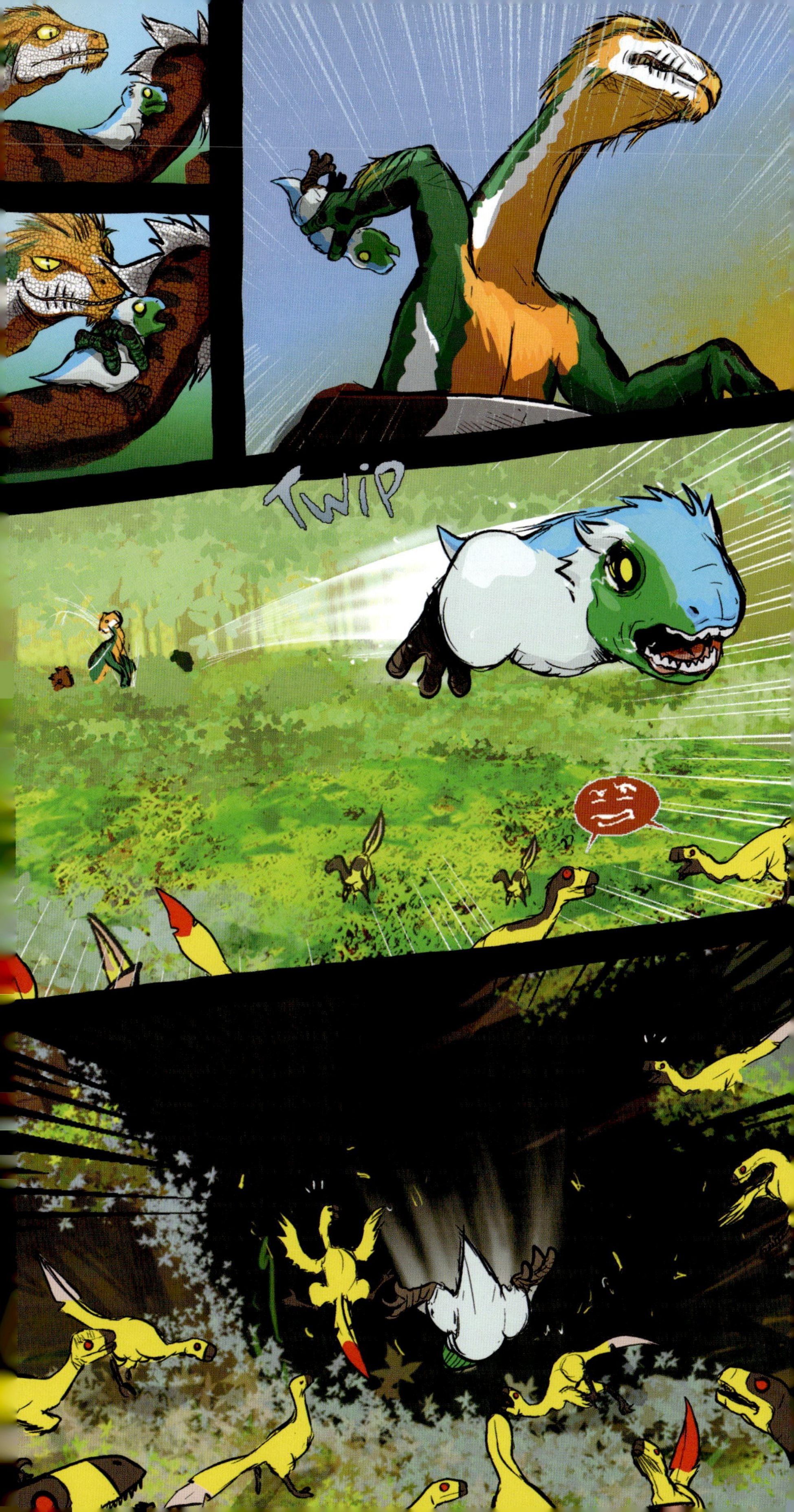
TWIP

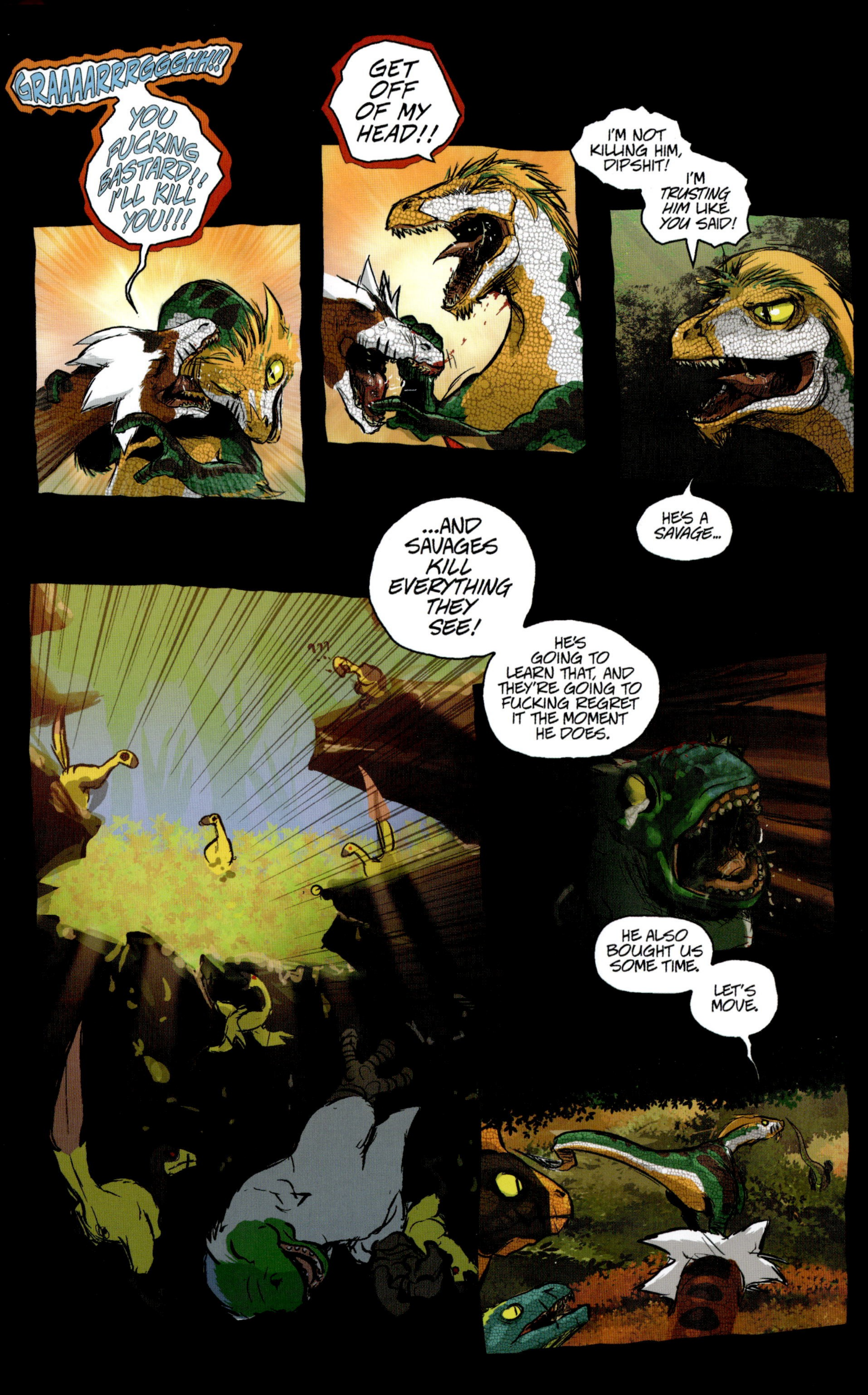
GRAAAARRRGGGHH!!
YOU FUCKING BASTARD!! I'LL KILL YOU!!!
GET OFF OF MY HEAD!!
I'M NOT KILLING HIM, DIPSHIT!
I'M TRUSTING HIM LIKE YOU SAID!
HE'S A SAVAGE...
...AND SAVAGES KILL EVERYTHING THEY SEE!
HE'S GOING TO LEARN THAT, AND THEY'RE GOING TO FUCKING REGRET IT THE MOMENT HE DOES.
HE ALSO BOUGHT US SOME TIME.
LET'S MOVE.

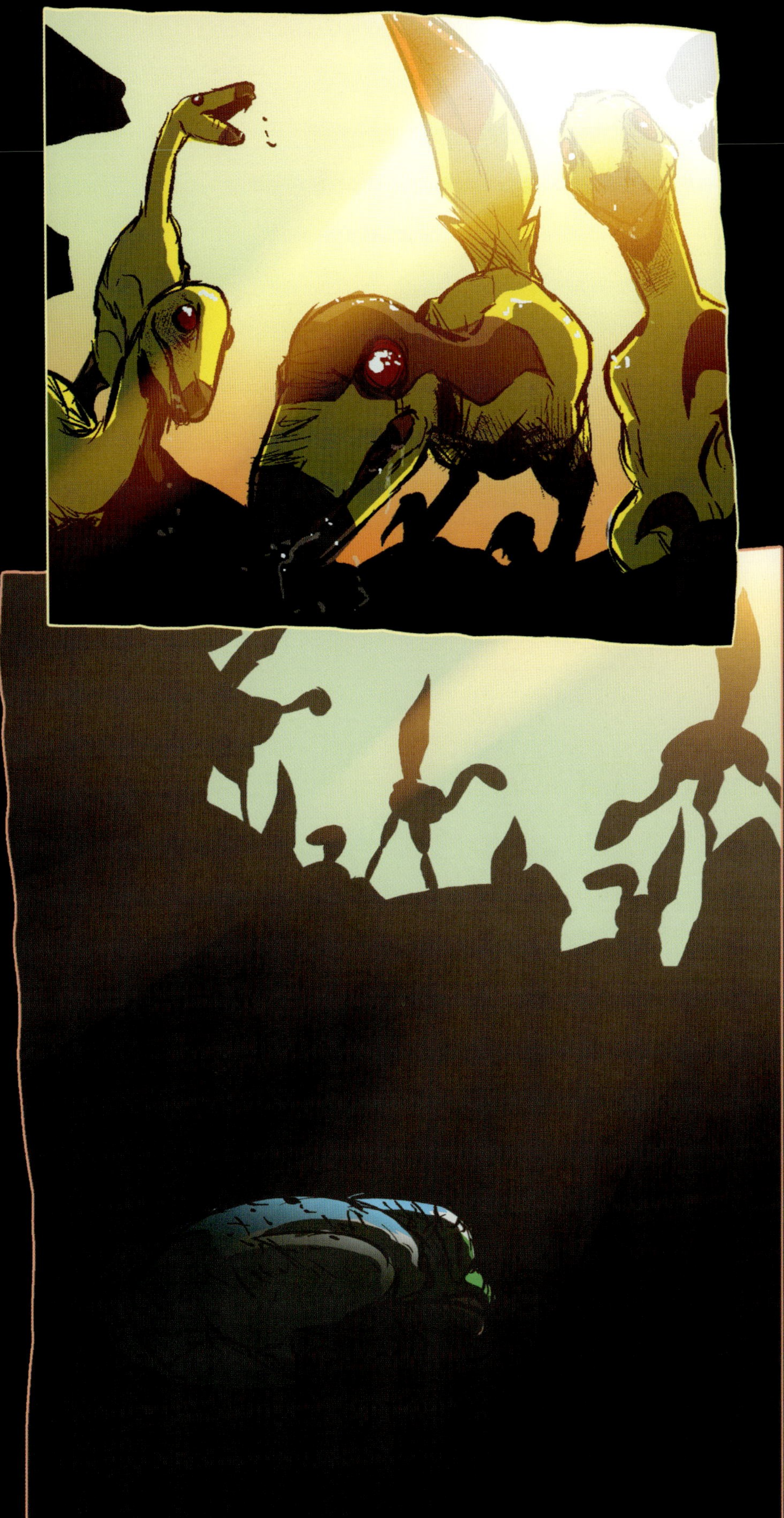

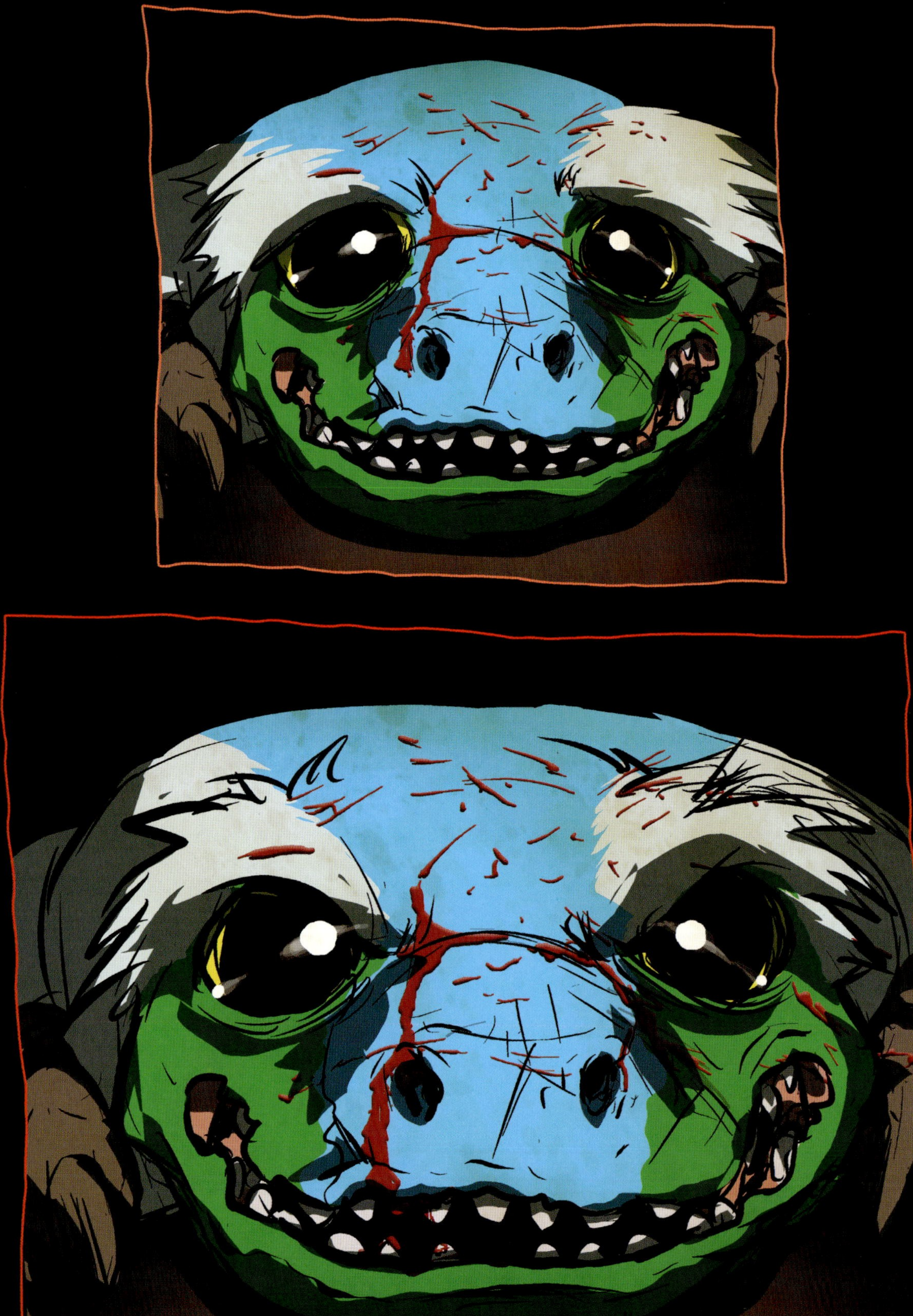

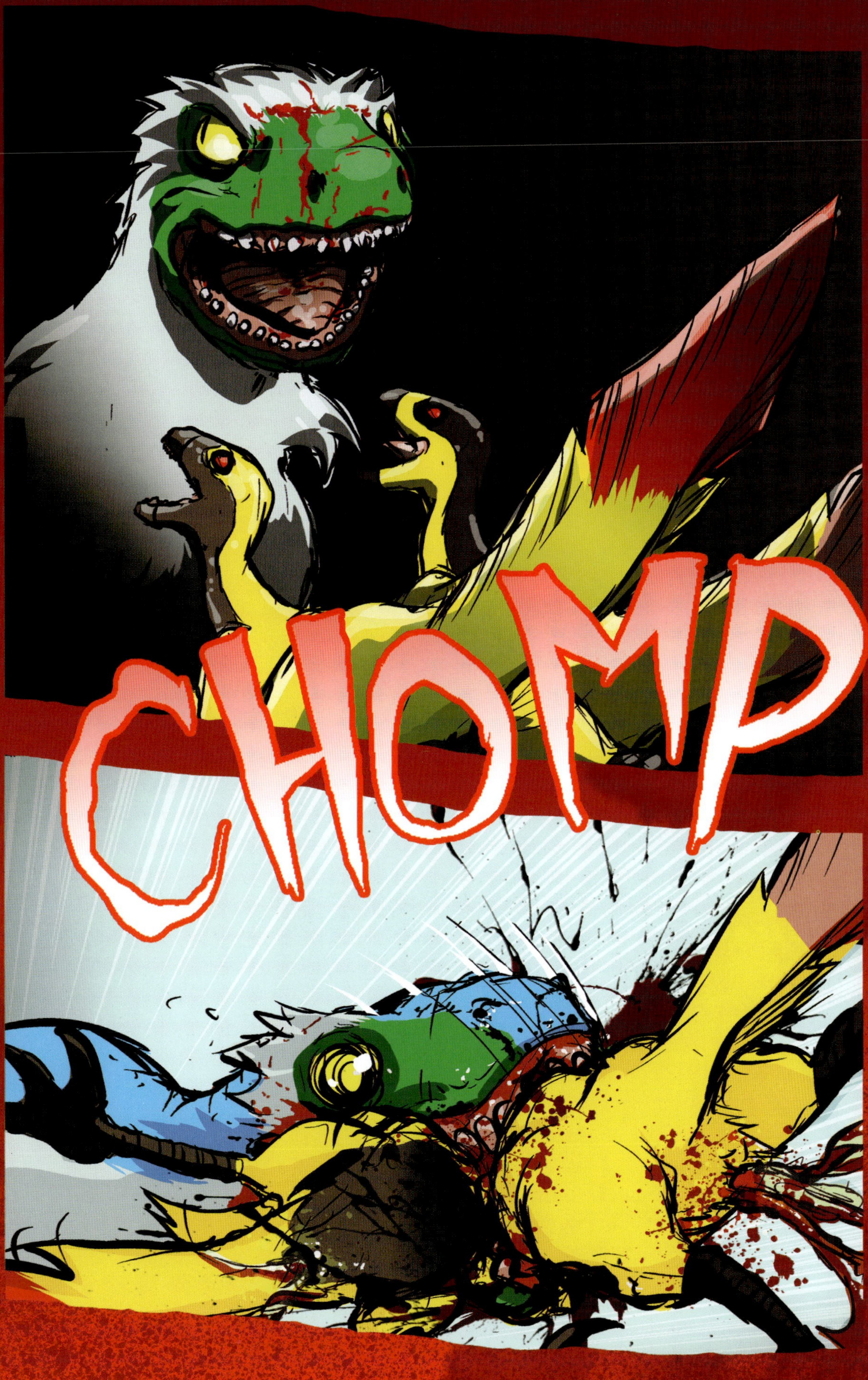
CHOMP

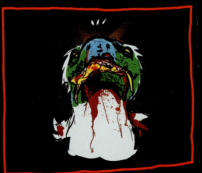

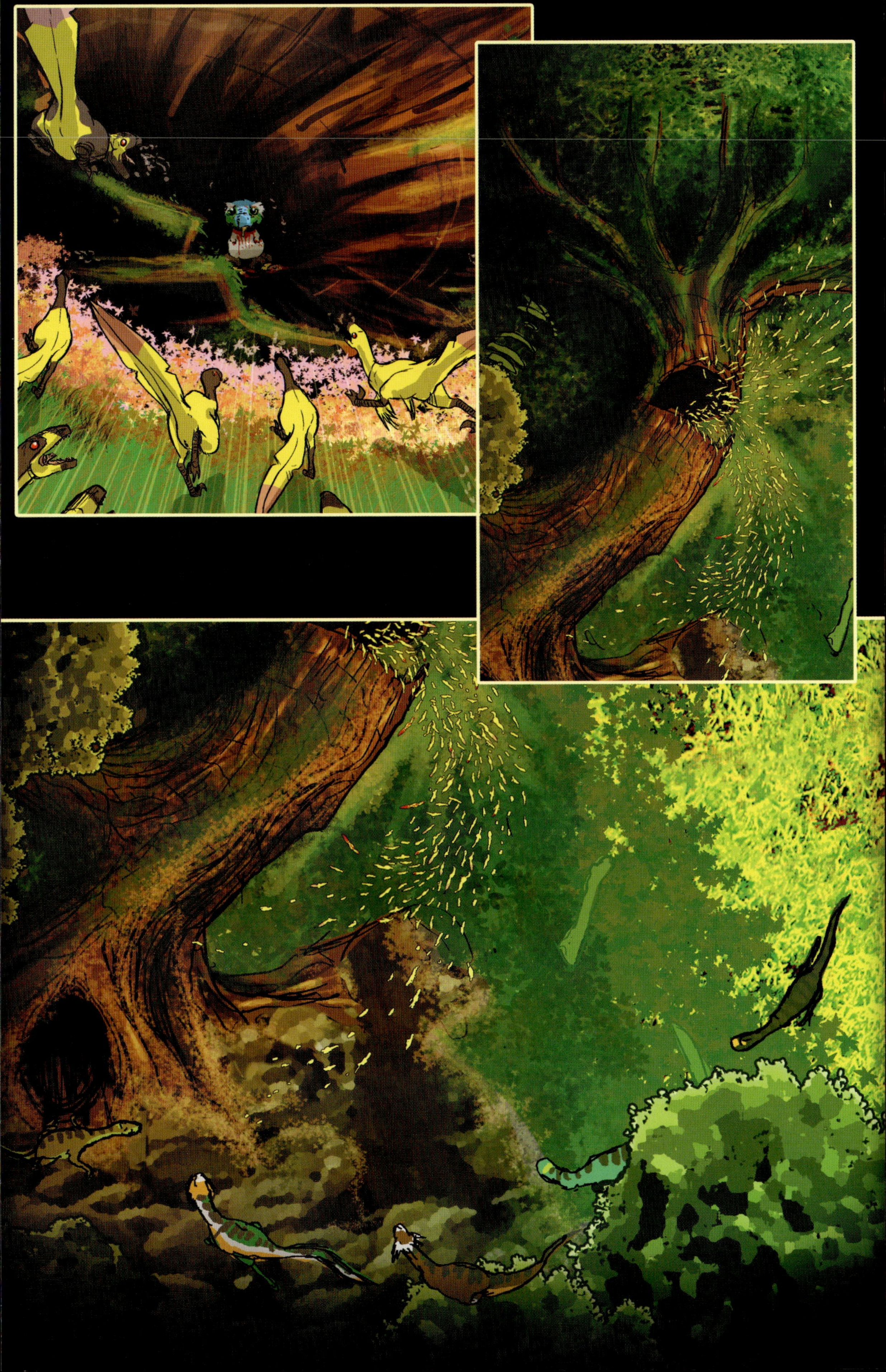

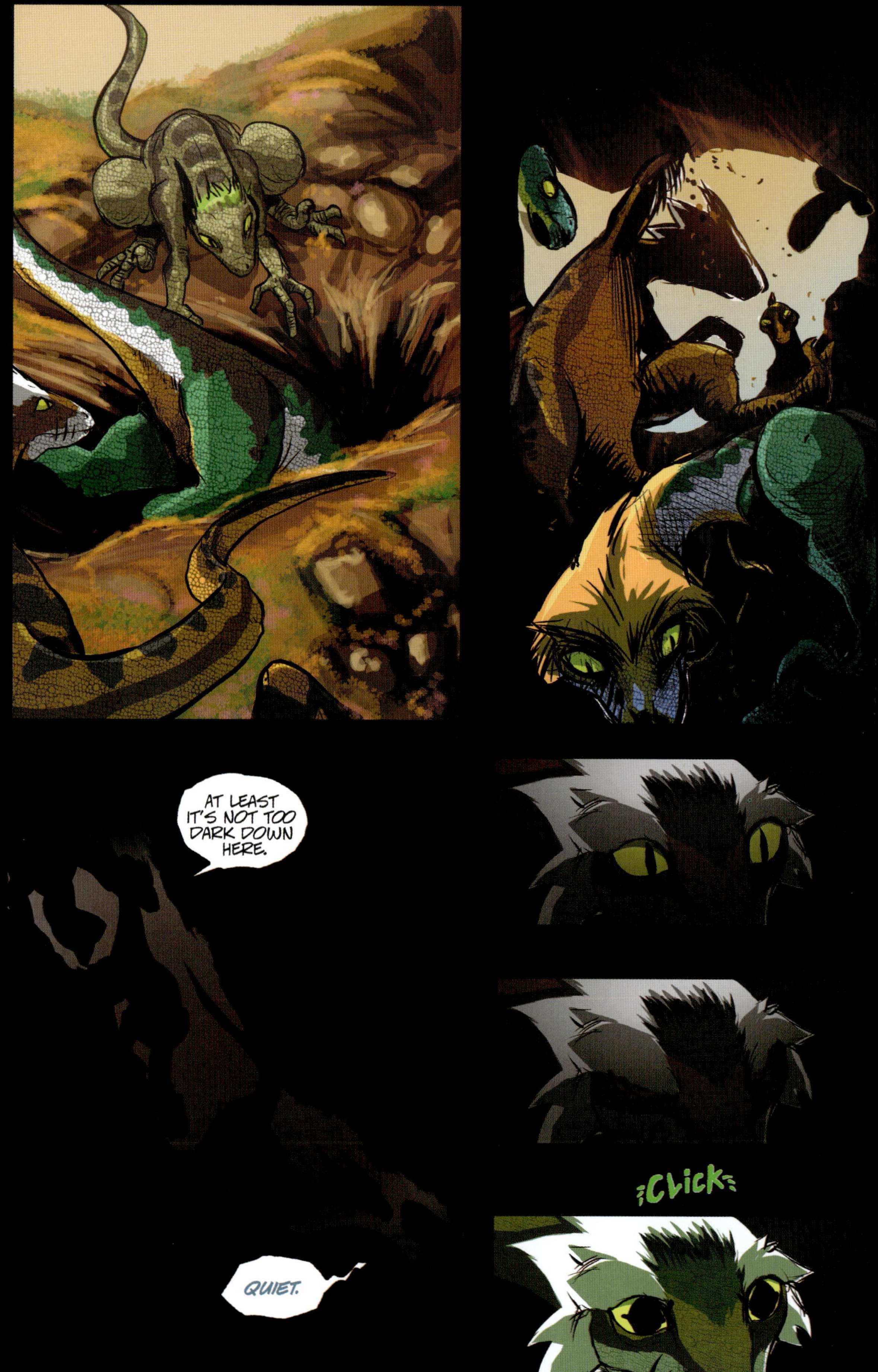
AT LEAST IT'S NOT TOO DARK DOWN HERE.
QUIET.
CLICK

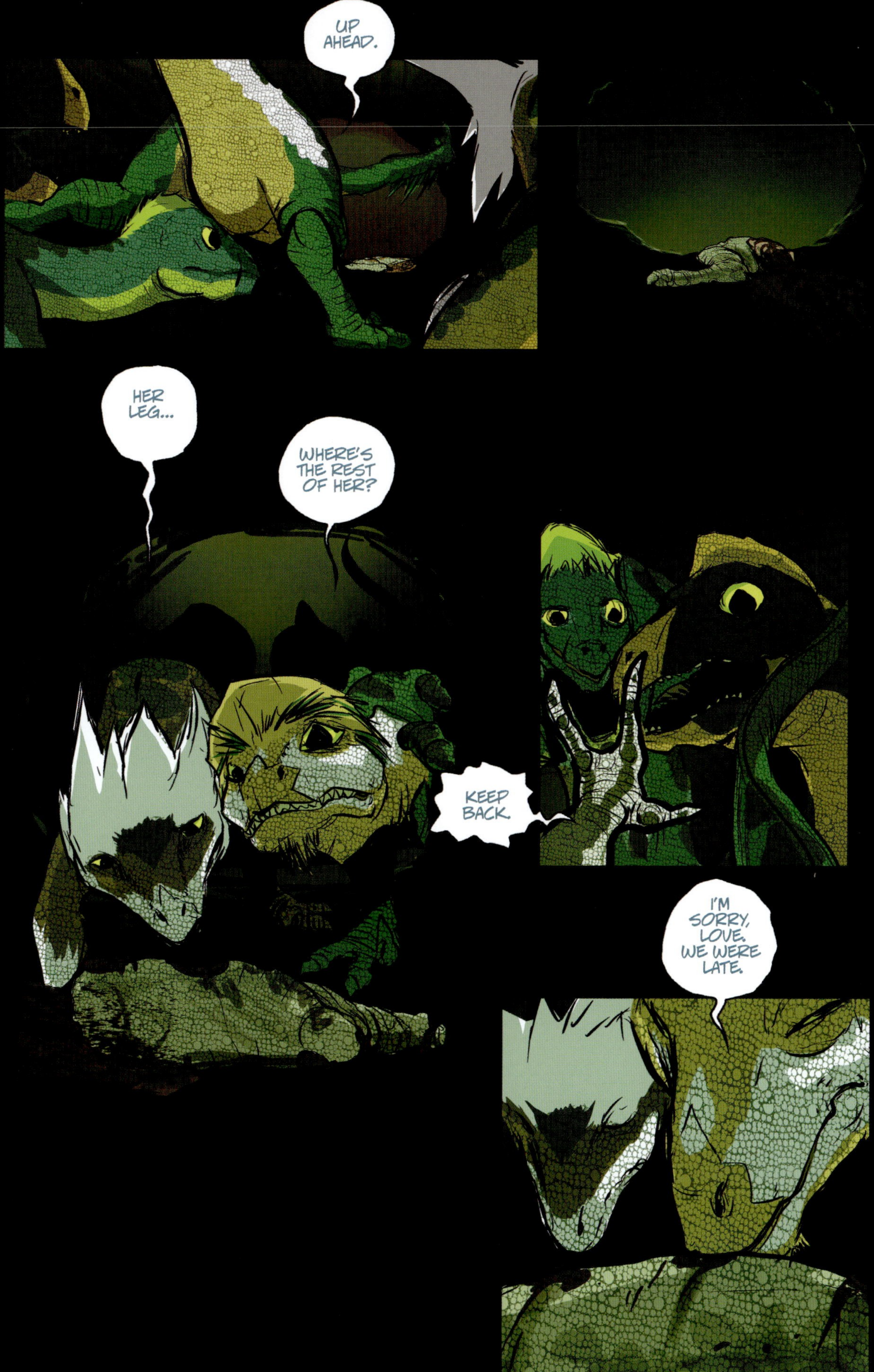
UP AHEAD.
HER LEG...
WHERE'S THE REST OF HER?
KEEP BACK.
I'M SORRY, LOVE. WE WERE LATE.

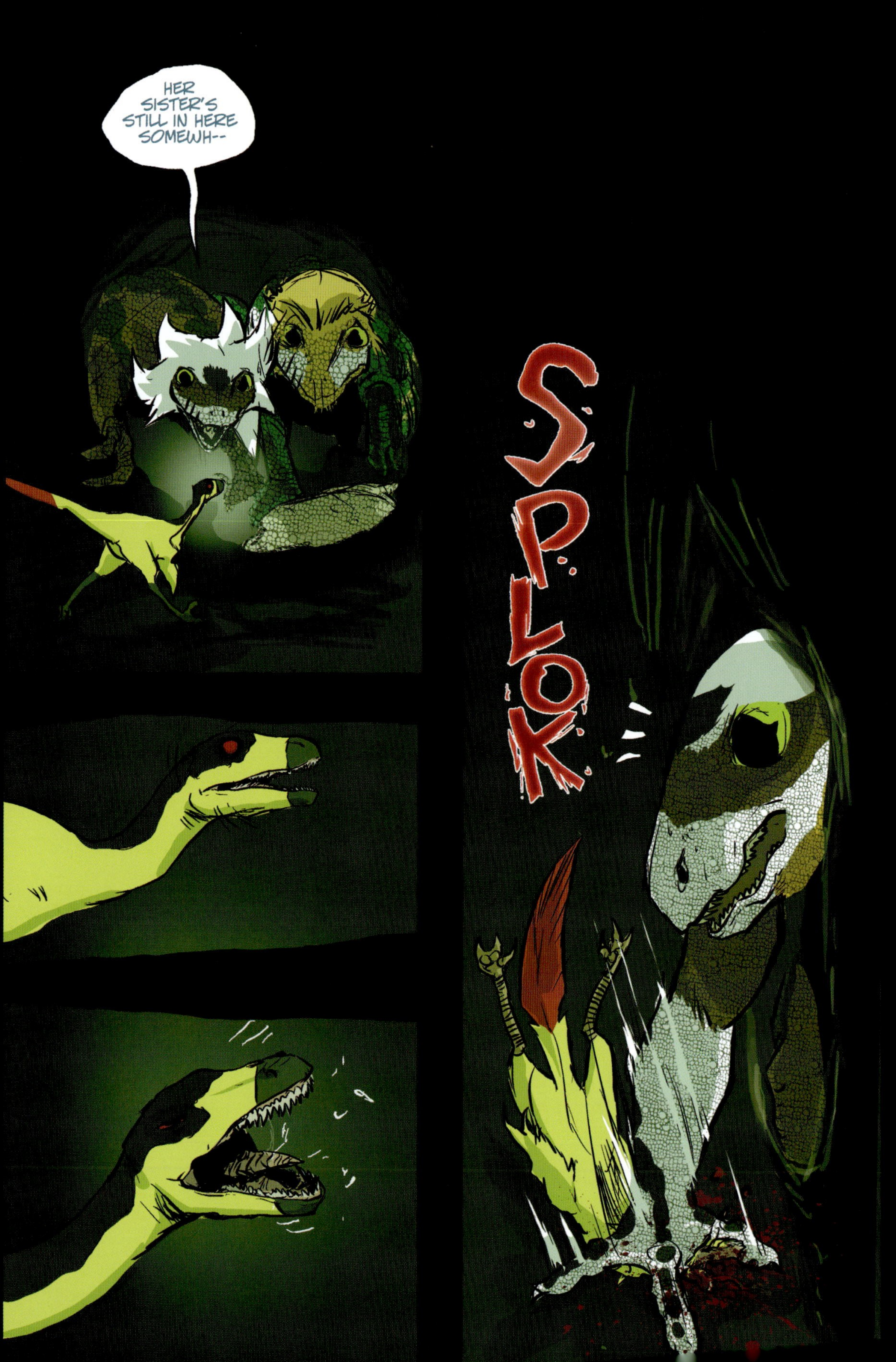
HER SISTER'S STILL IN HERE SOMEWH--
SPLOK

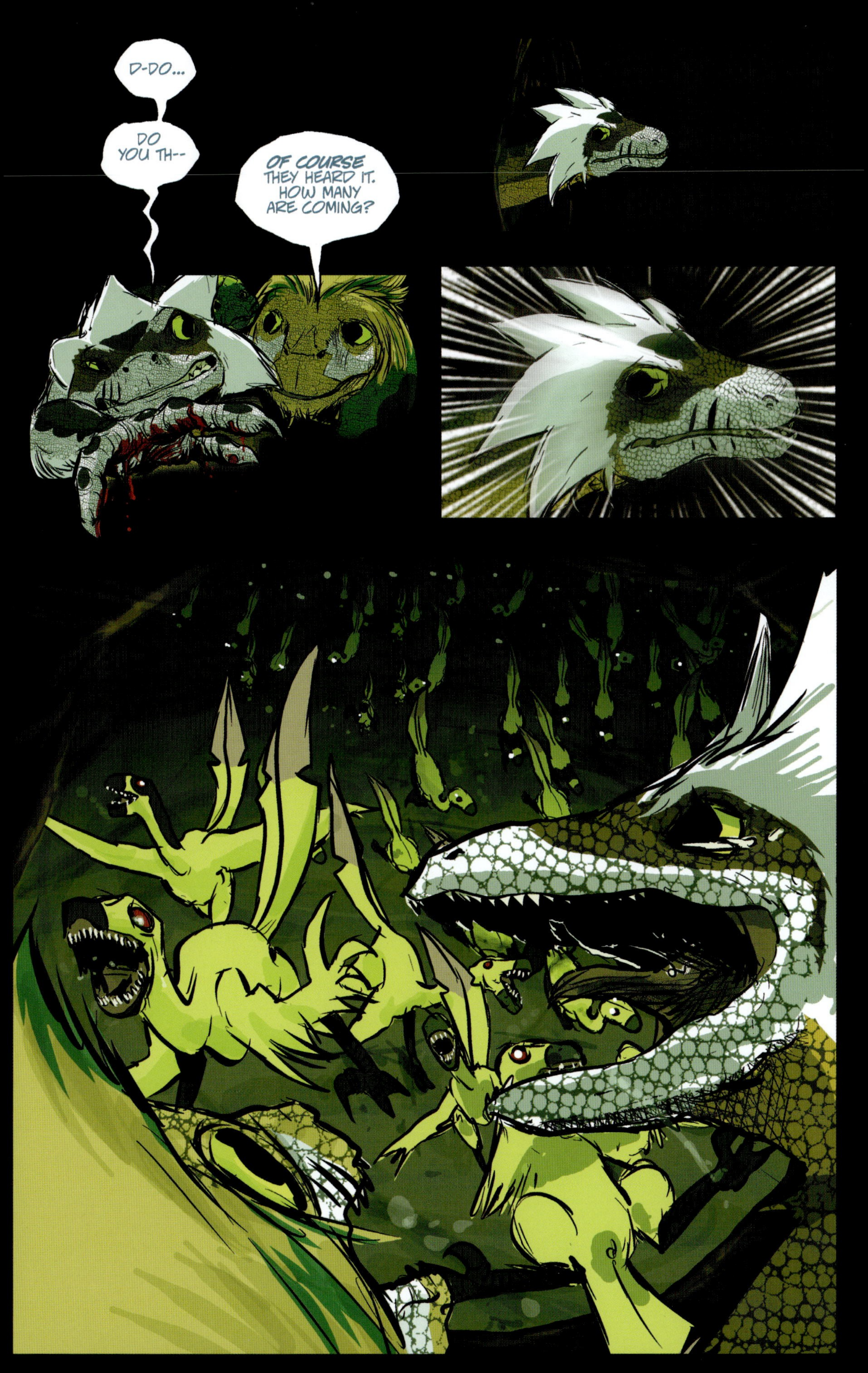
D-DO...
DO YOU TH--
OF COURSE THEY HEARD IT. HOW MANY ARE COMING?

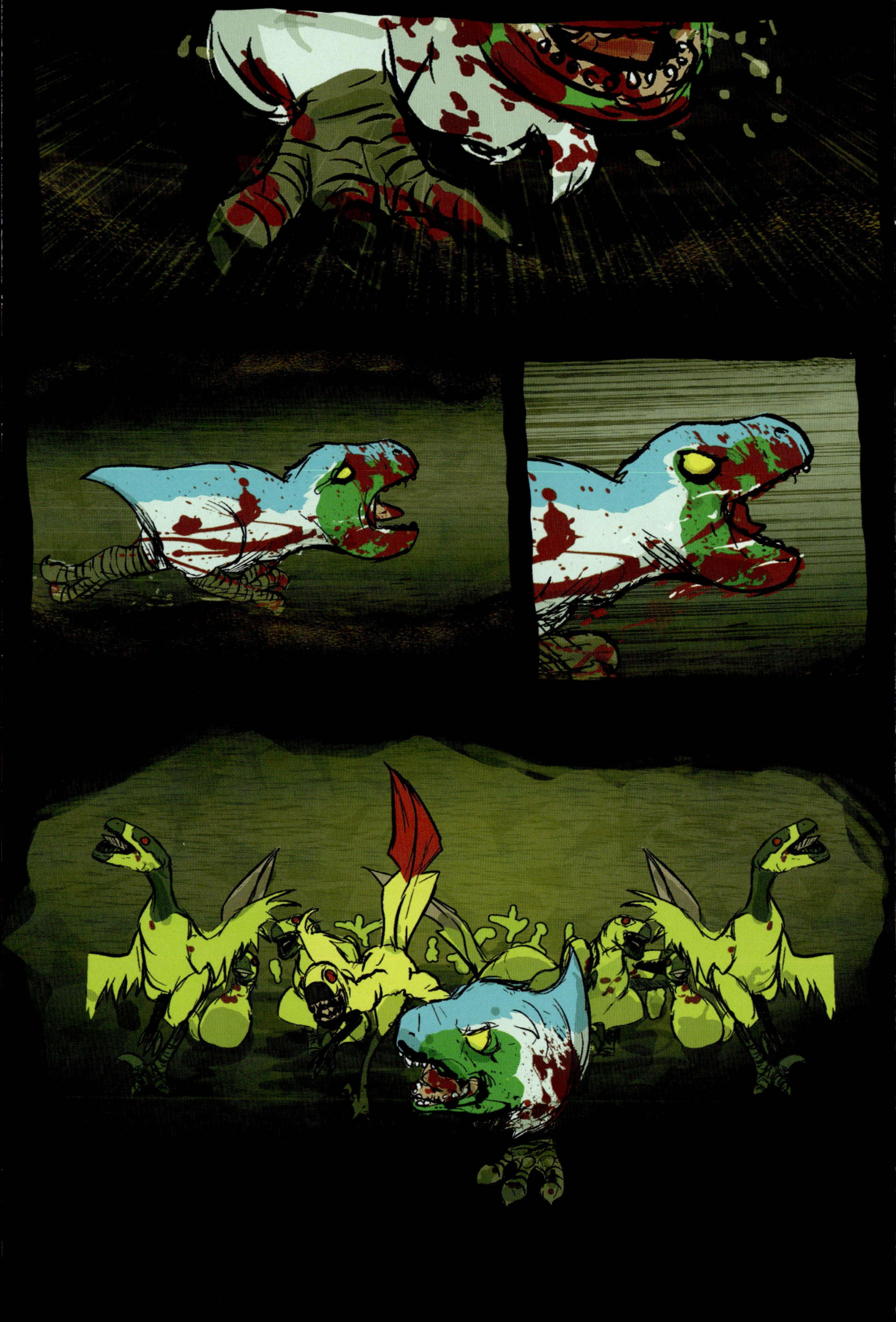

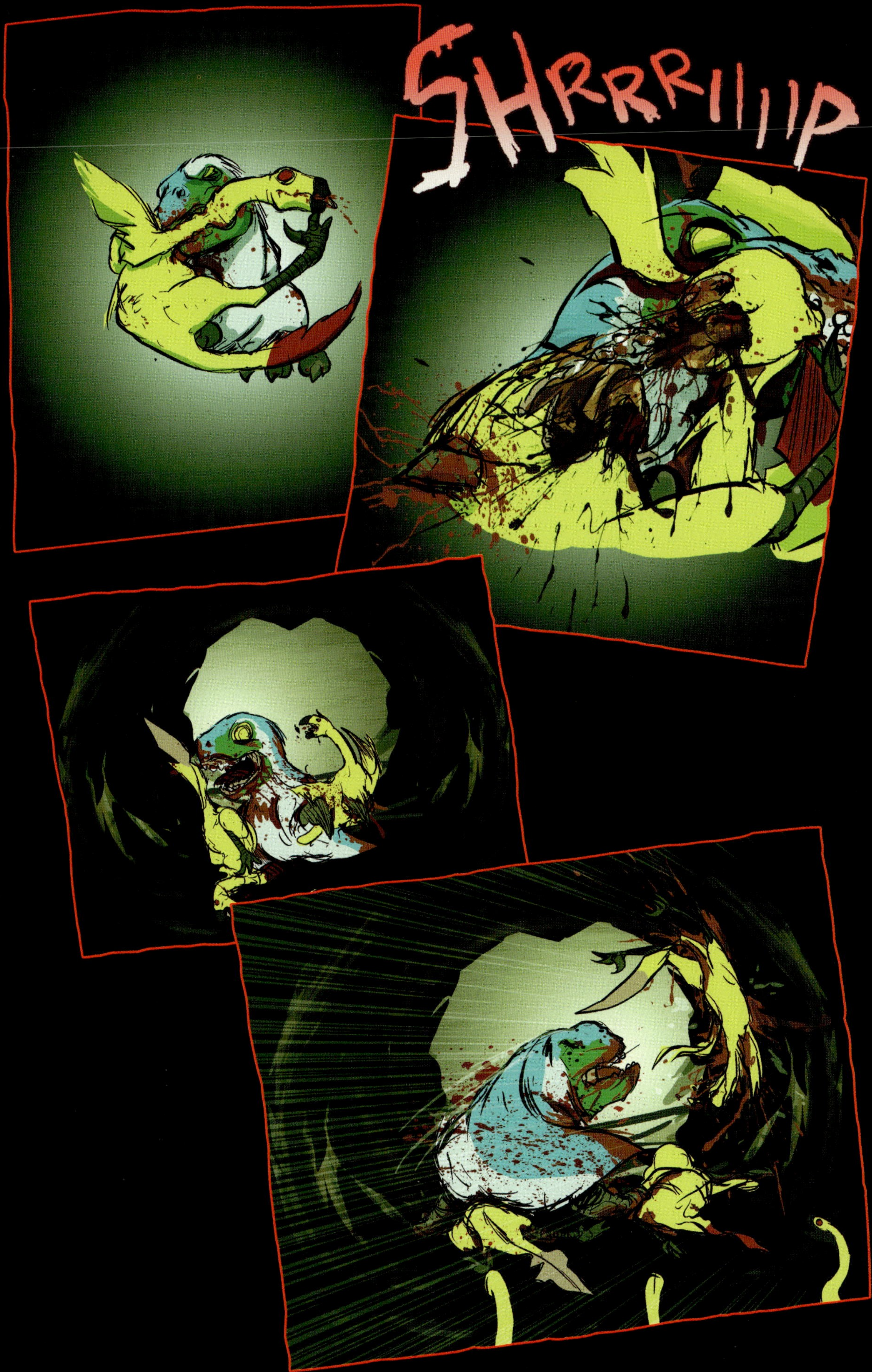
SHRRRIIIIP

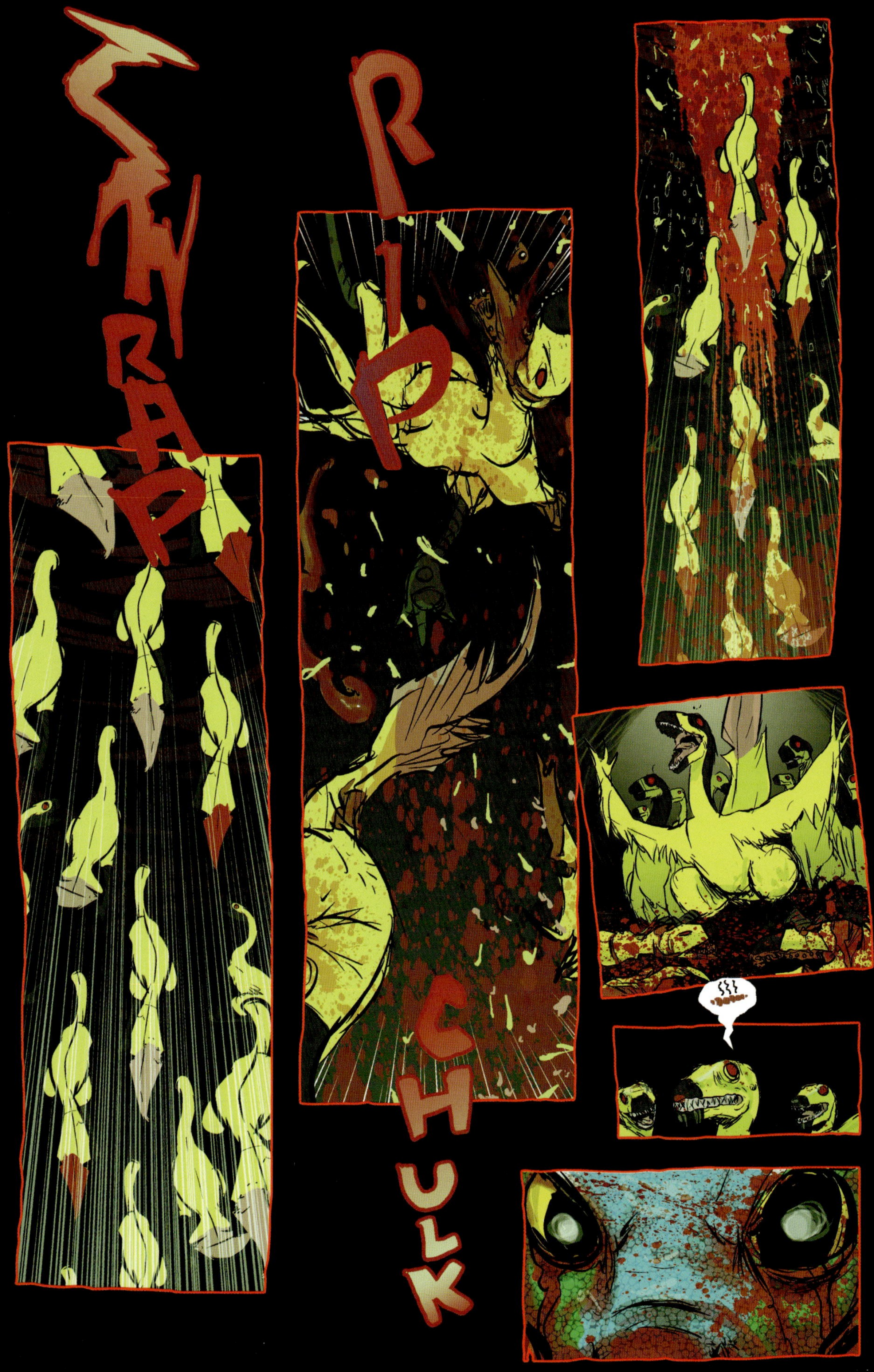

SHRAP
RIP
CHULK

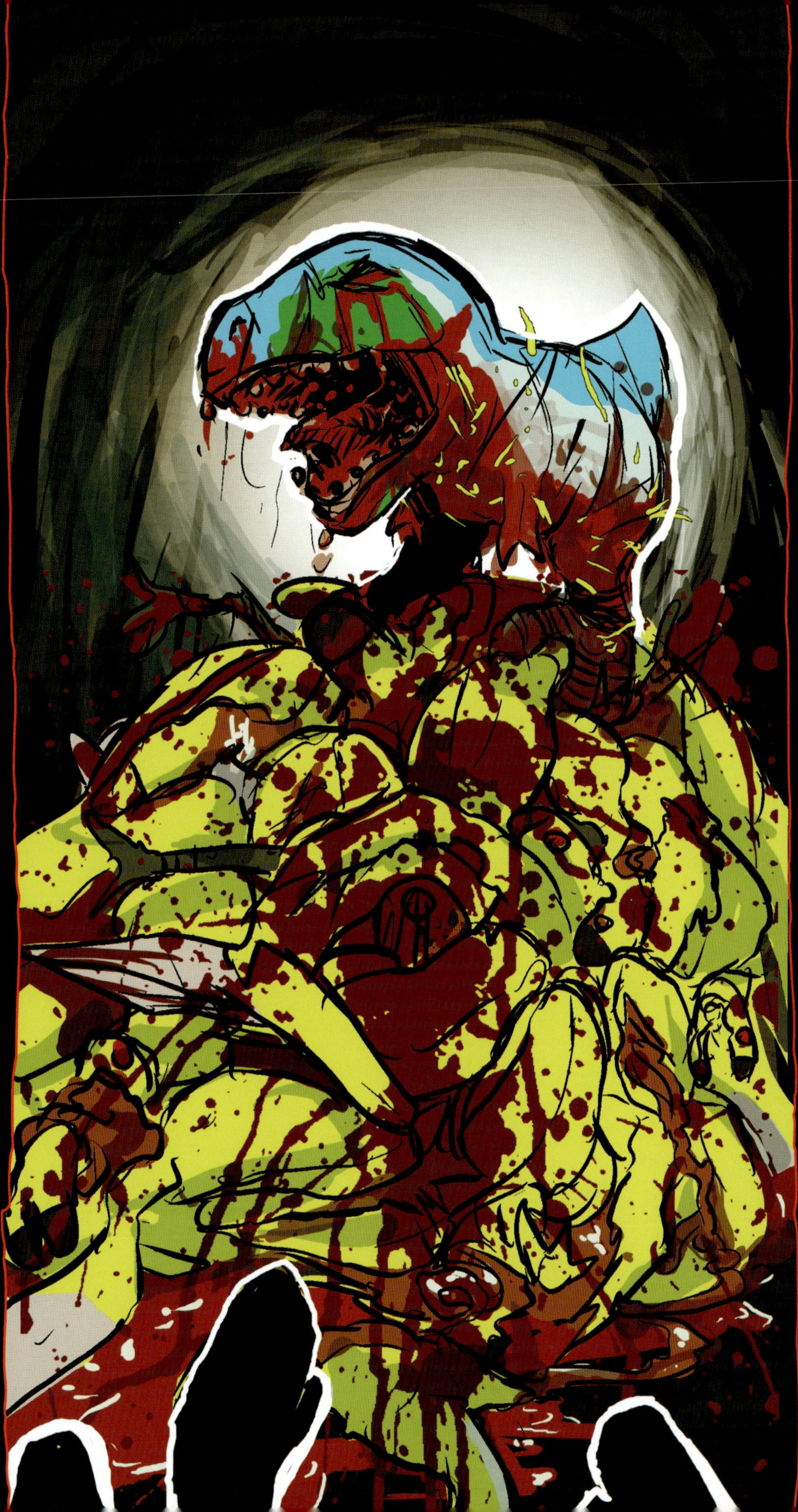

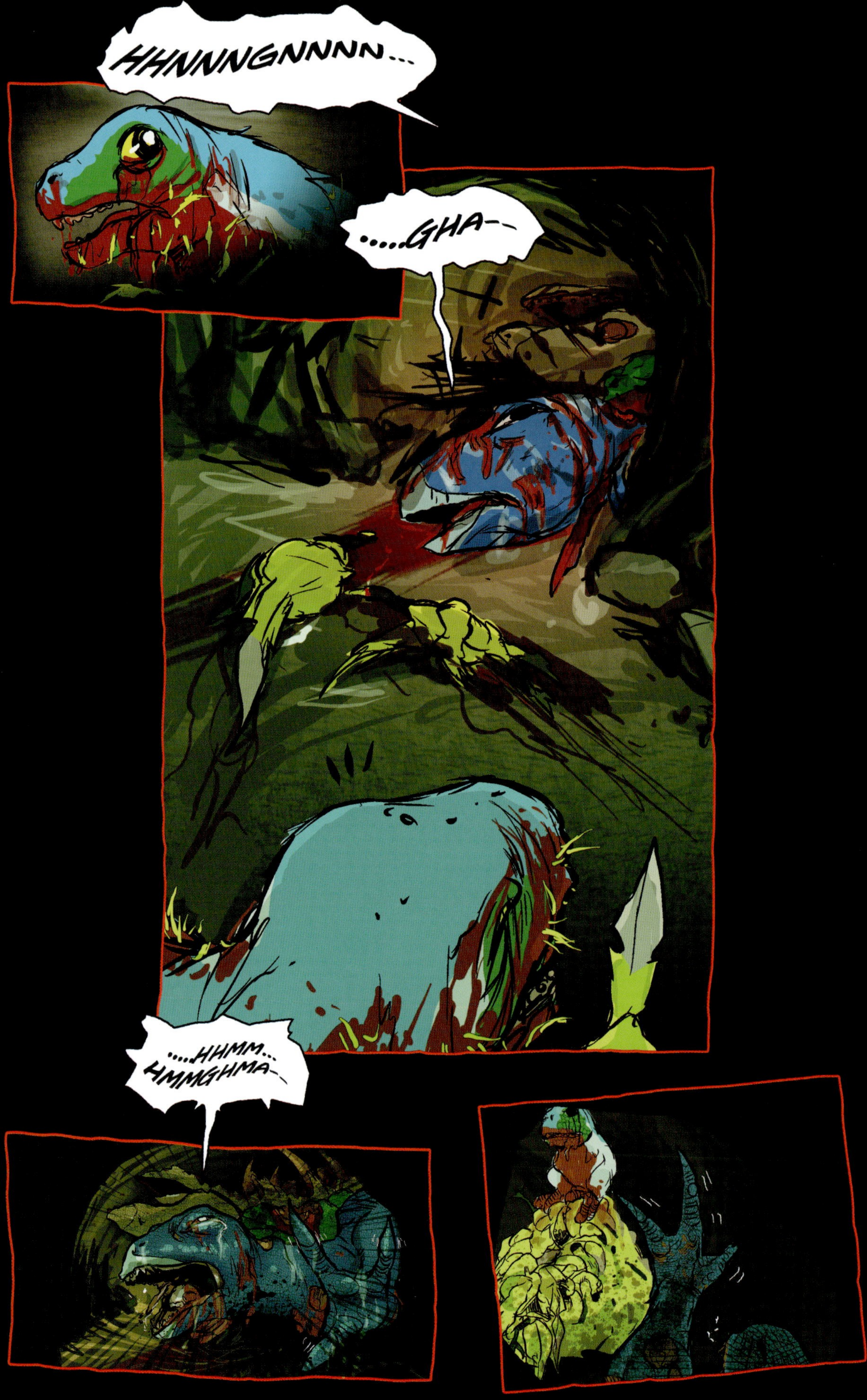
HHNNNGNNNN...
....GHA--
....HHMM...
HMMGHMA--

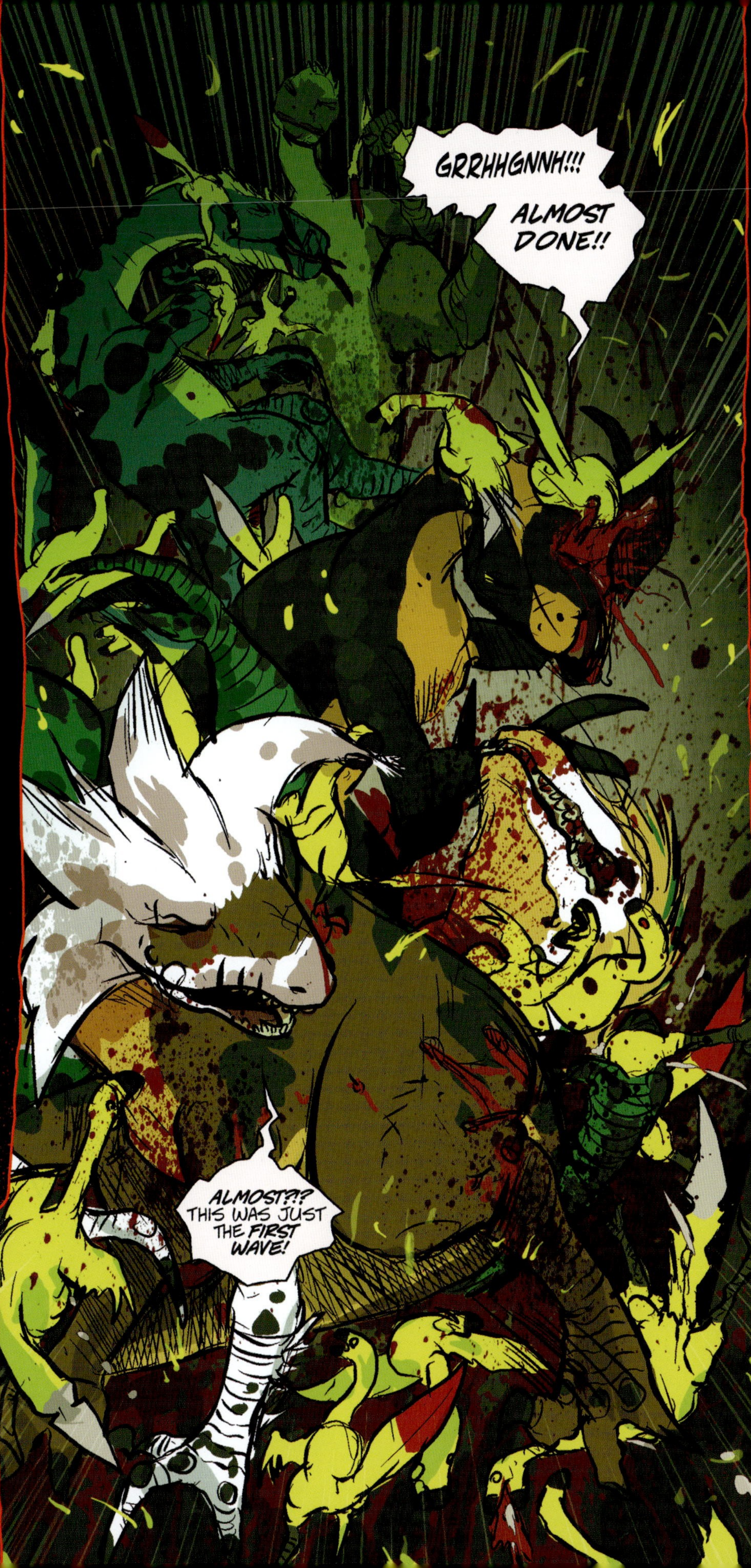
GRRHHGNNH!!!
ALMOST DONE!!
ALMOST?!? THIS WAS JUST THE FIRST WAVE!

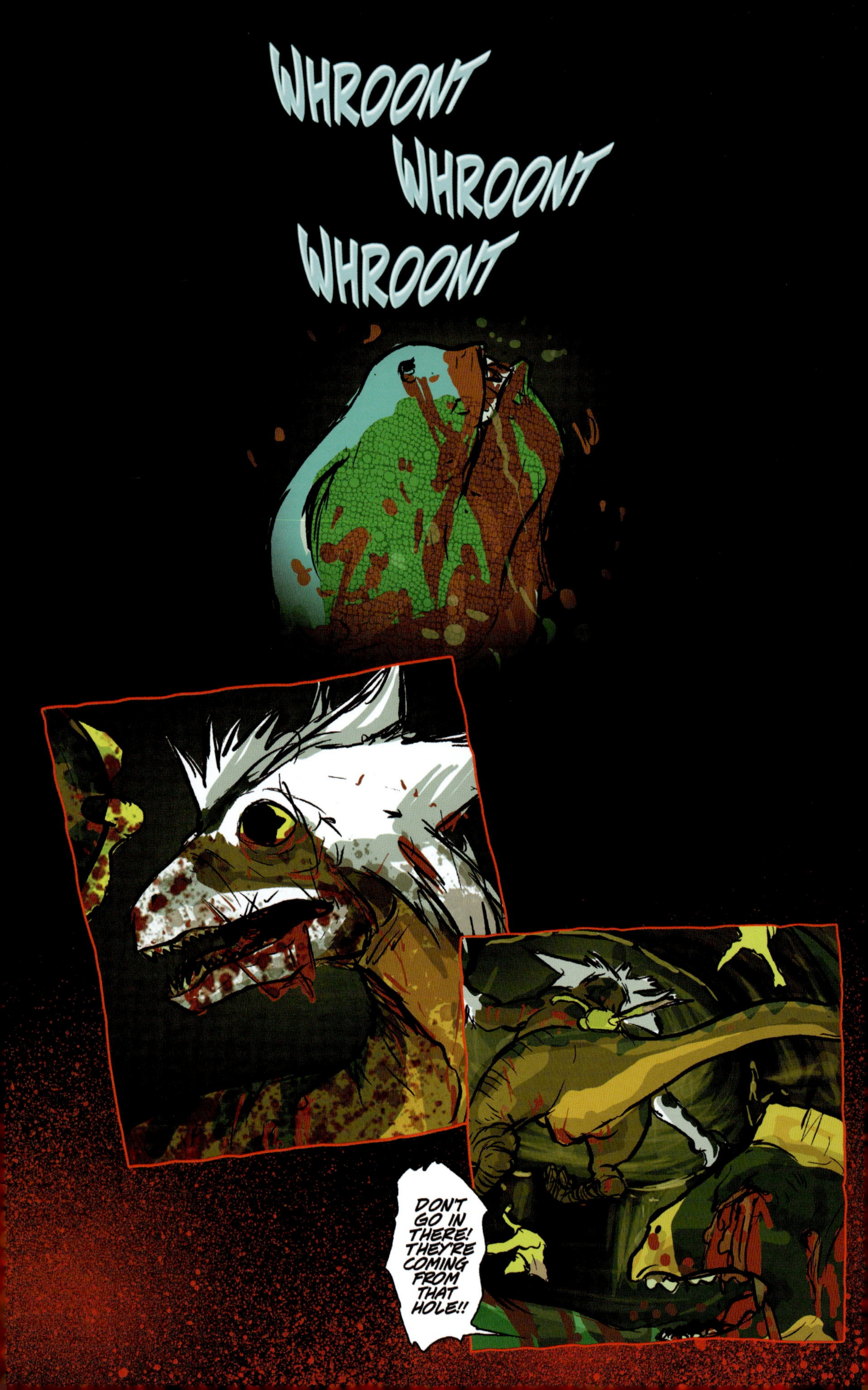
WHROONT
WHROONT
WHROONT
DON'T GO IN THERE! THEY'RE COMING FROM THAT HOLE!!

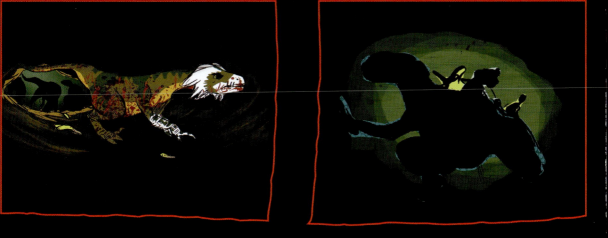

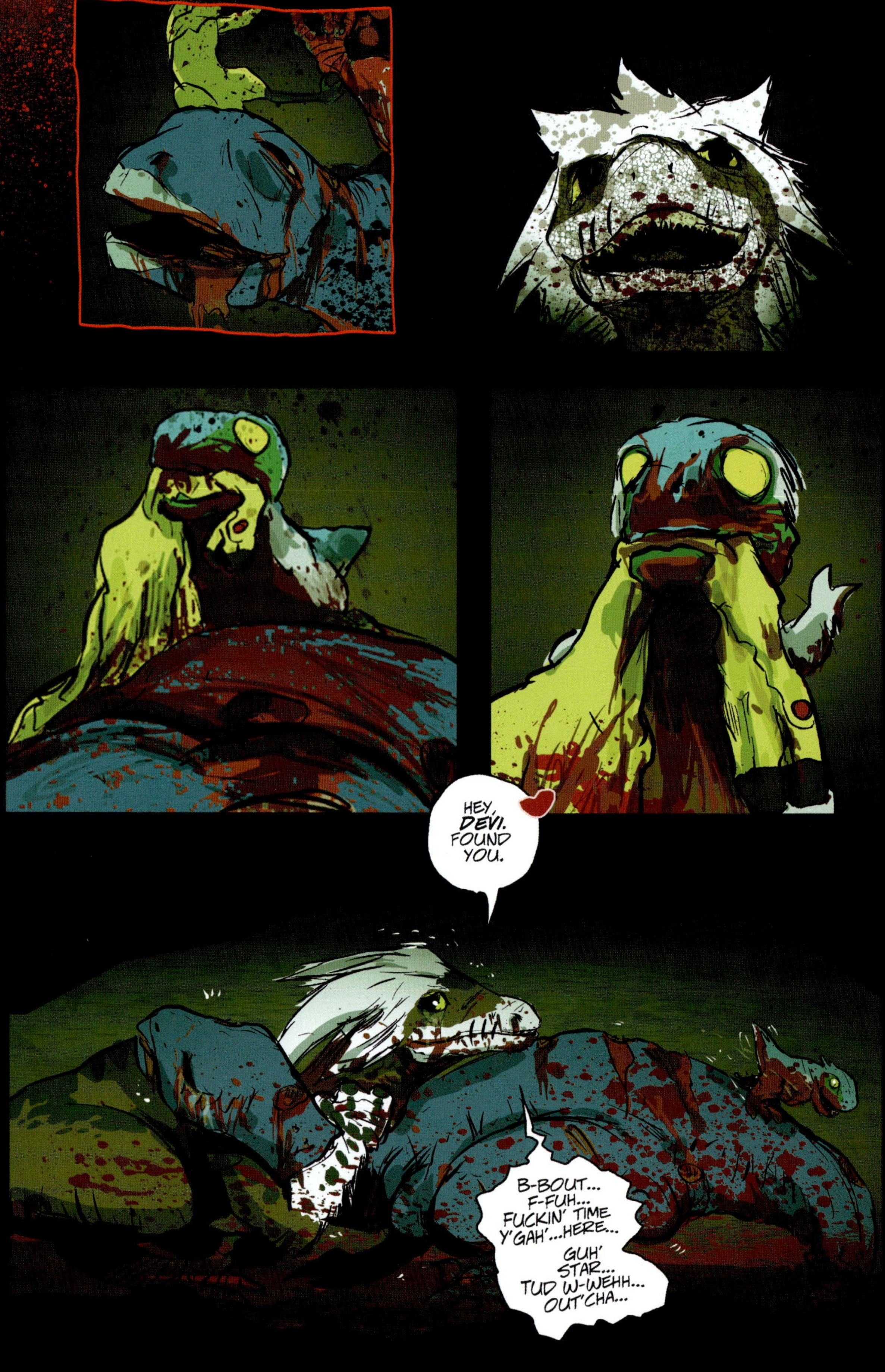
HEY, DEVI. FOUND YOU.
B-BOUT... F-FUH... FUCKIN' TIME Y'GAH'...HERE...
GUH' STAR... TUD W-WEHH... OUT'CHA...

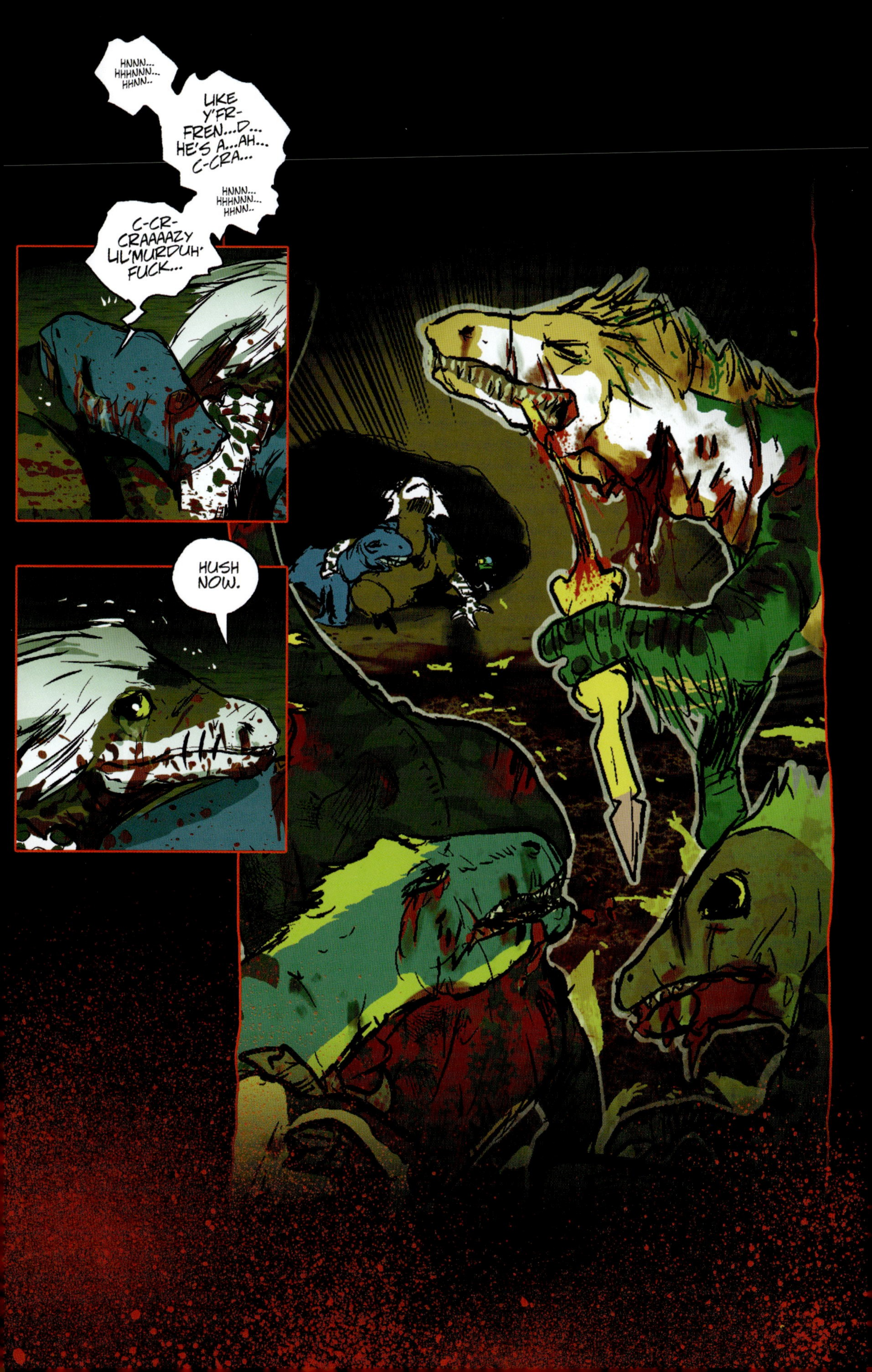
HNNN... HHHNNN... HHNN..
LIKE Y'FR-FREN...D... HE'S A...AH... C-CRA...
HNNN... HHHNNN... HHNN..
C-CR-CRAAAAZY LIL'MURDUH' FUCK...
HUSH NOW.

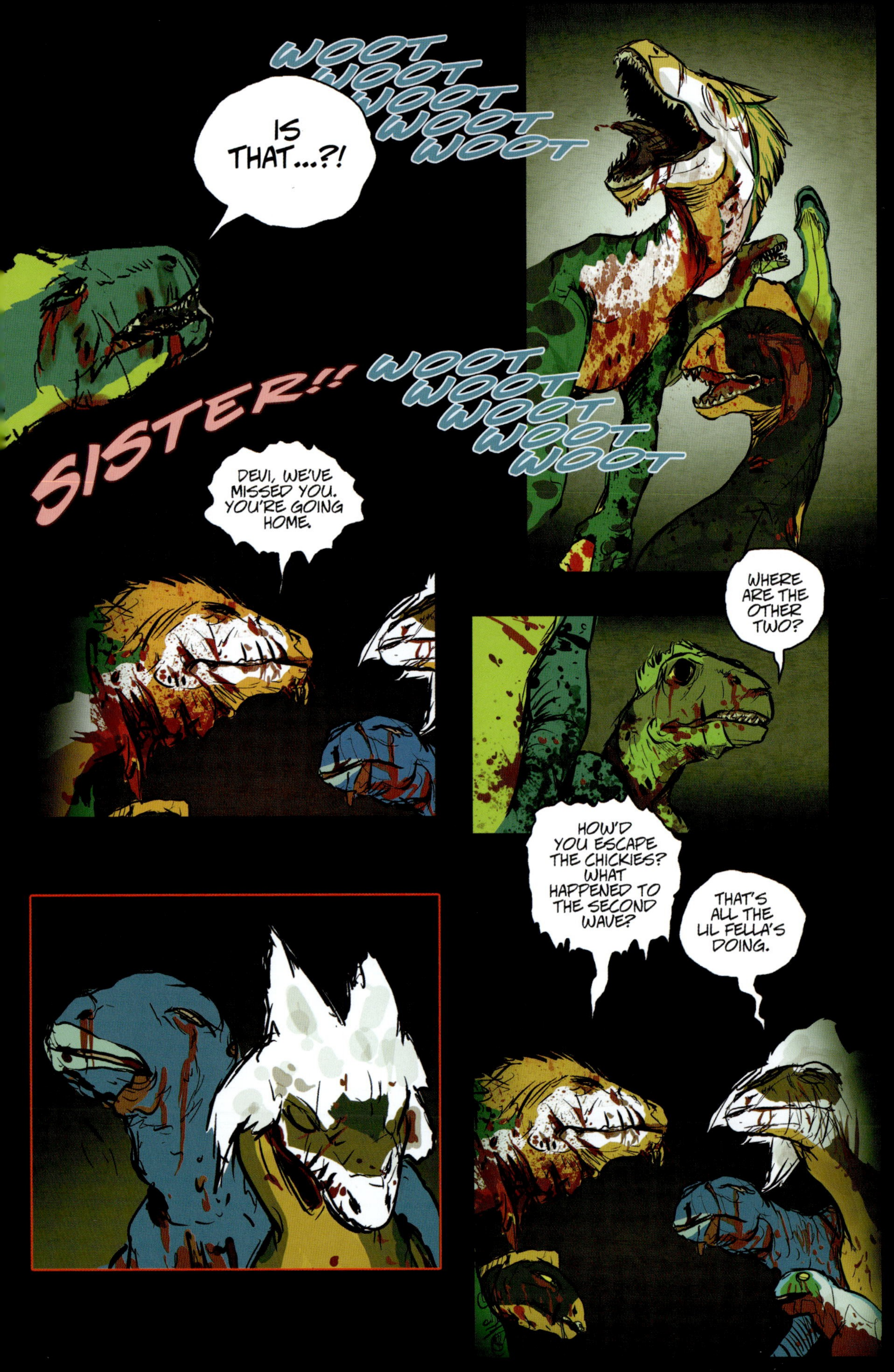
WOOT WOOT WOOT WOOT WOOT
IS THAT...?!
SISTER!!
WOOT WOOT WOOT WOOT WOOT
DEVI, WE'VE MISSED YOU. YOU'RE GOING HOME.
WHERE ARE THE OTHER TWO?
HOW'D YOU ESCAPE THE CHICKIES? WHAT HAPPENED TO THE SECOND WAVE?
THAT'S ALL THE LIL FELLA'S DOING.

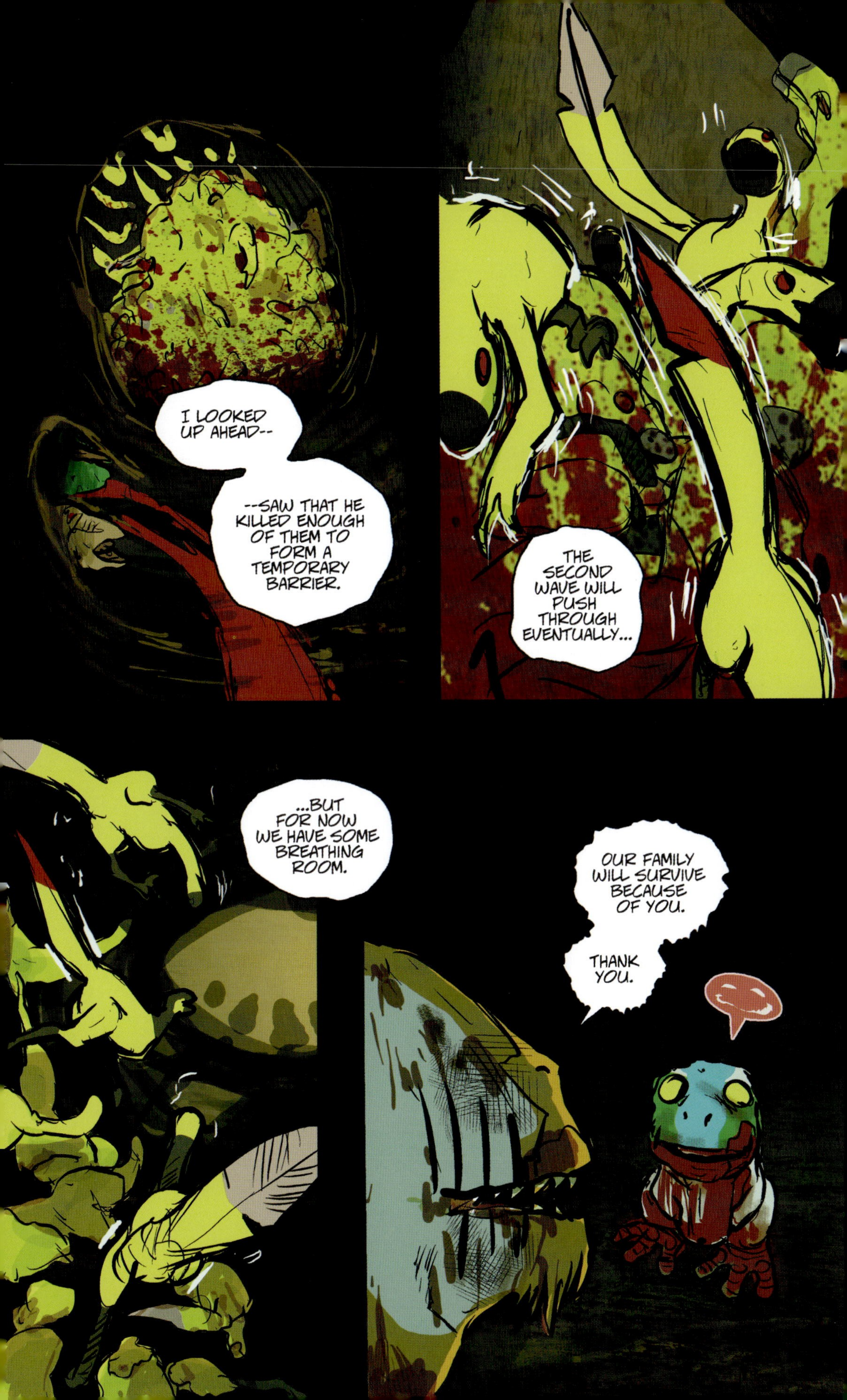
I LOOKED UP AHEAD--
--SAW THAT HE KILLED ENOUGH OF THEM TO FORM A TEMPORARY BARRIER.
THE SECOND WAVE WILL PUSH THROUGH EVENTUALLY...
...BUT FOR NOW WE HAVE SOME BREATHING ROOM.
OUR FAMILY WILL SURVIVE BECAUSE OF YOU.
THANK YOU.

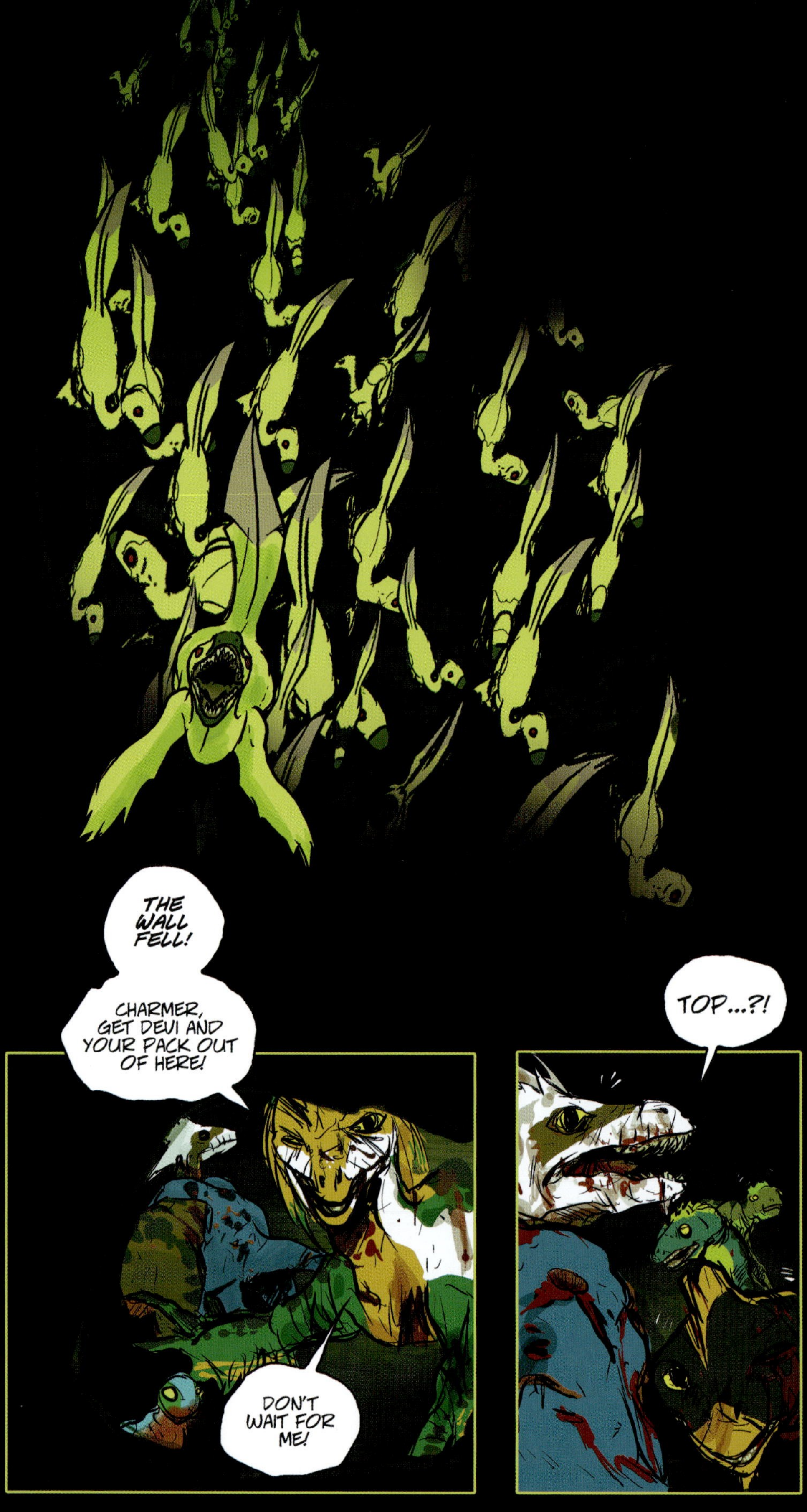
THE WALL FELL!
CHARMER, GET DEVI AND YOUR PACK OUT OF HERE!
DON'T WAIT FOR ME!
TOP...?!

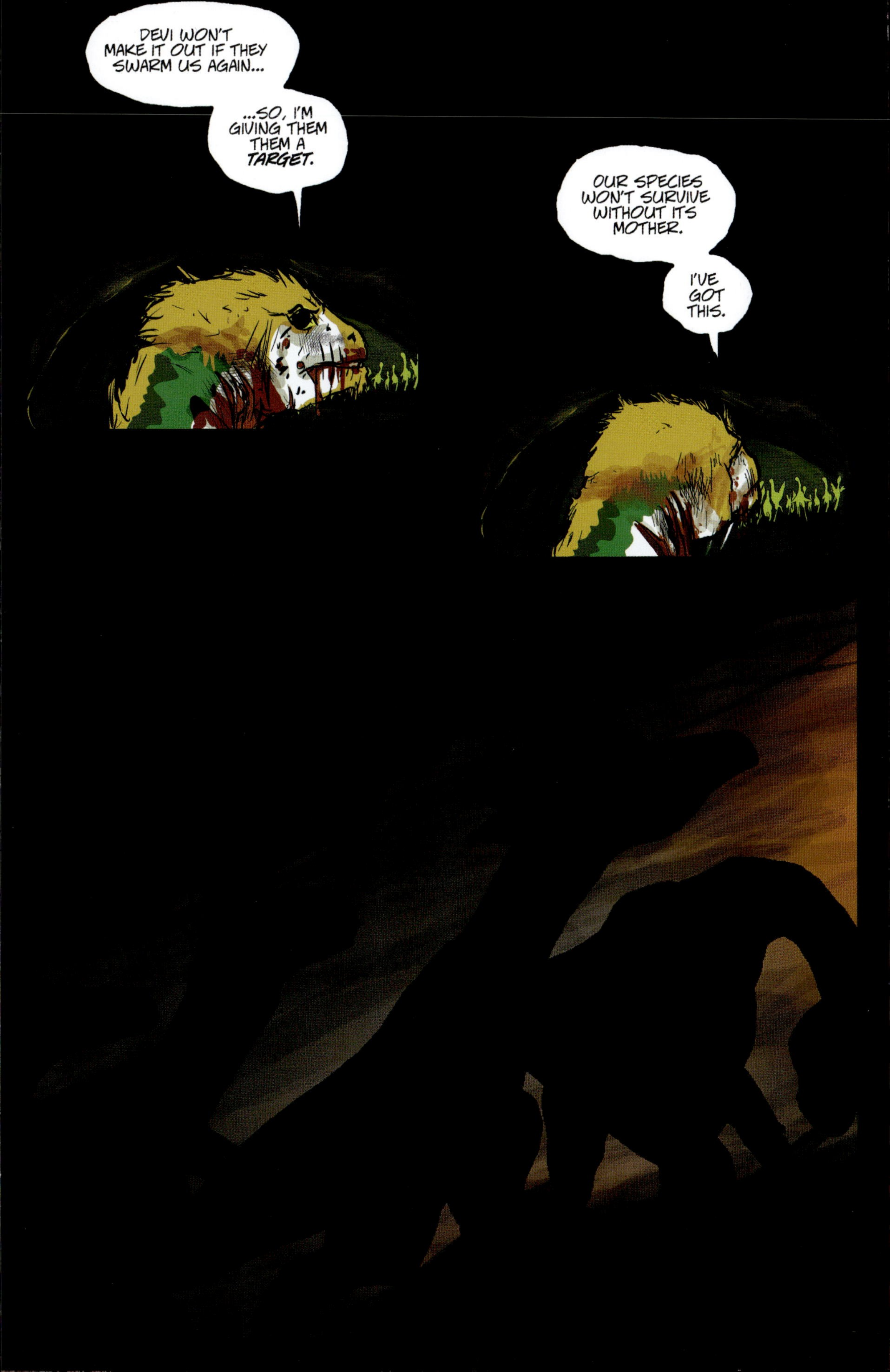
DEVI WON'T MAKE IT OUT IF THEY SWARM US AGAIN...
...SO, I'M GIVING THEM THEM A *TARGET*.
OUR SPECIES WON'T SURVIVE WITHOUT ITS MOTHER.
I'VE GOT THIS.

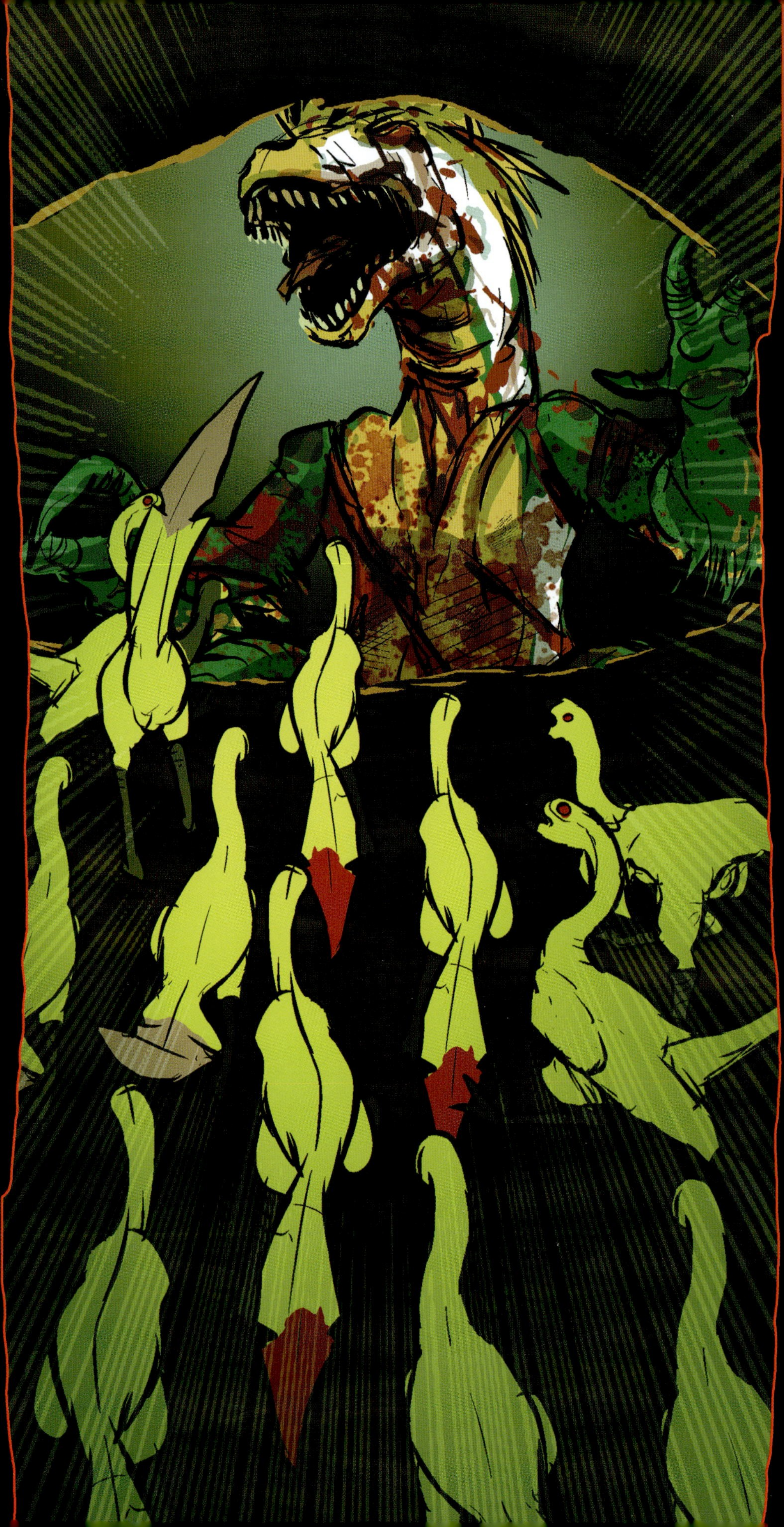

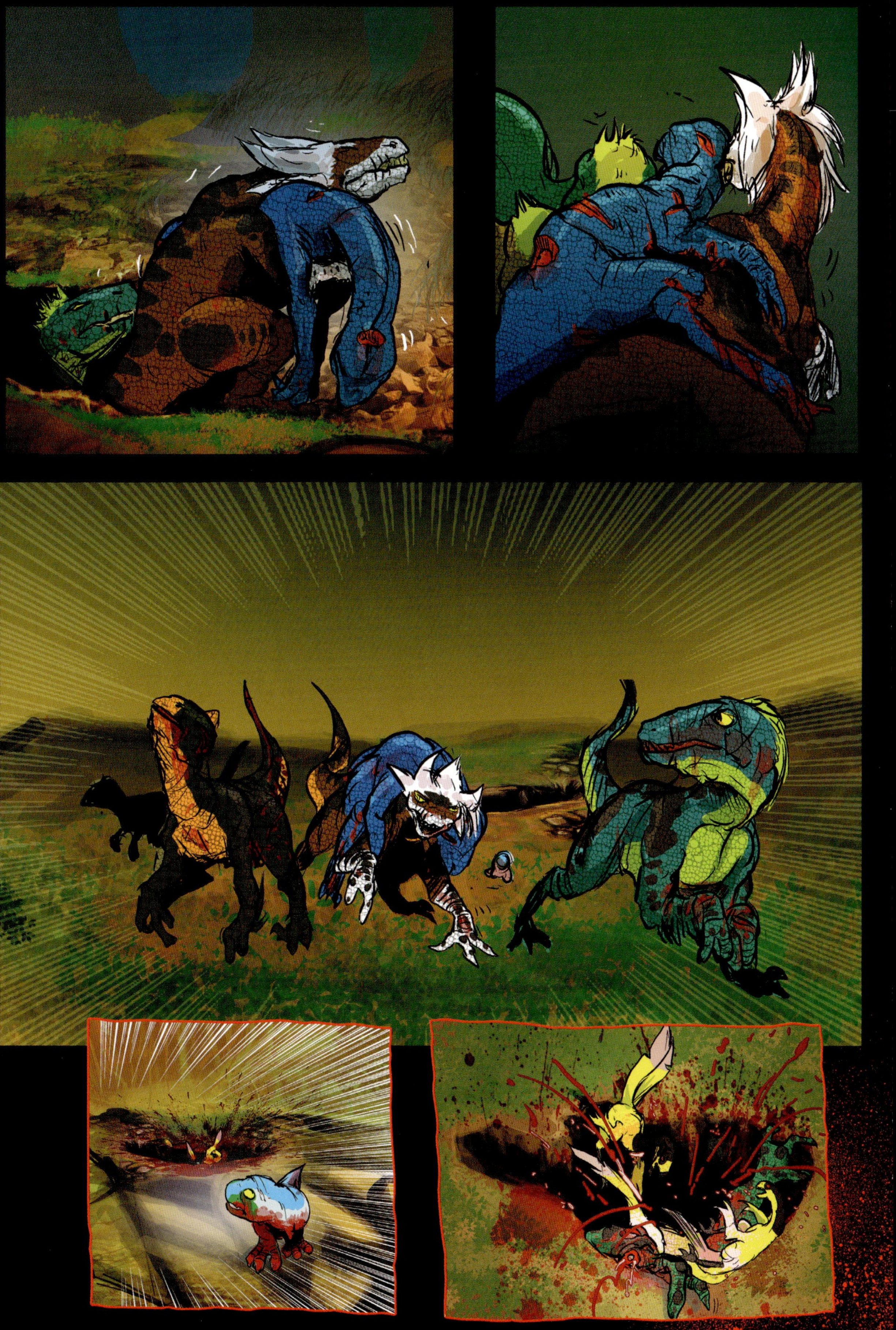

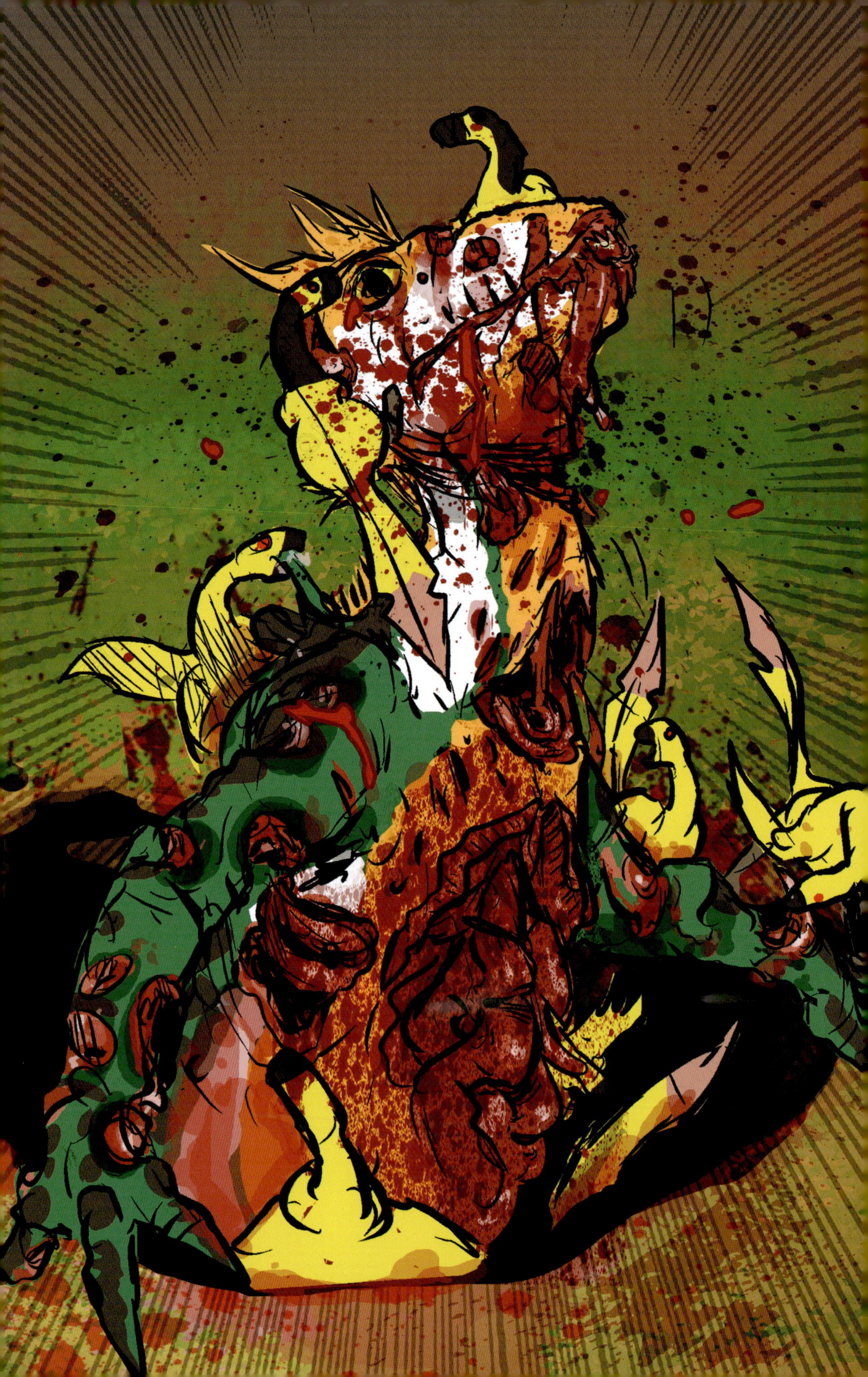

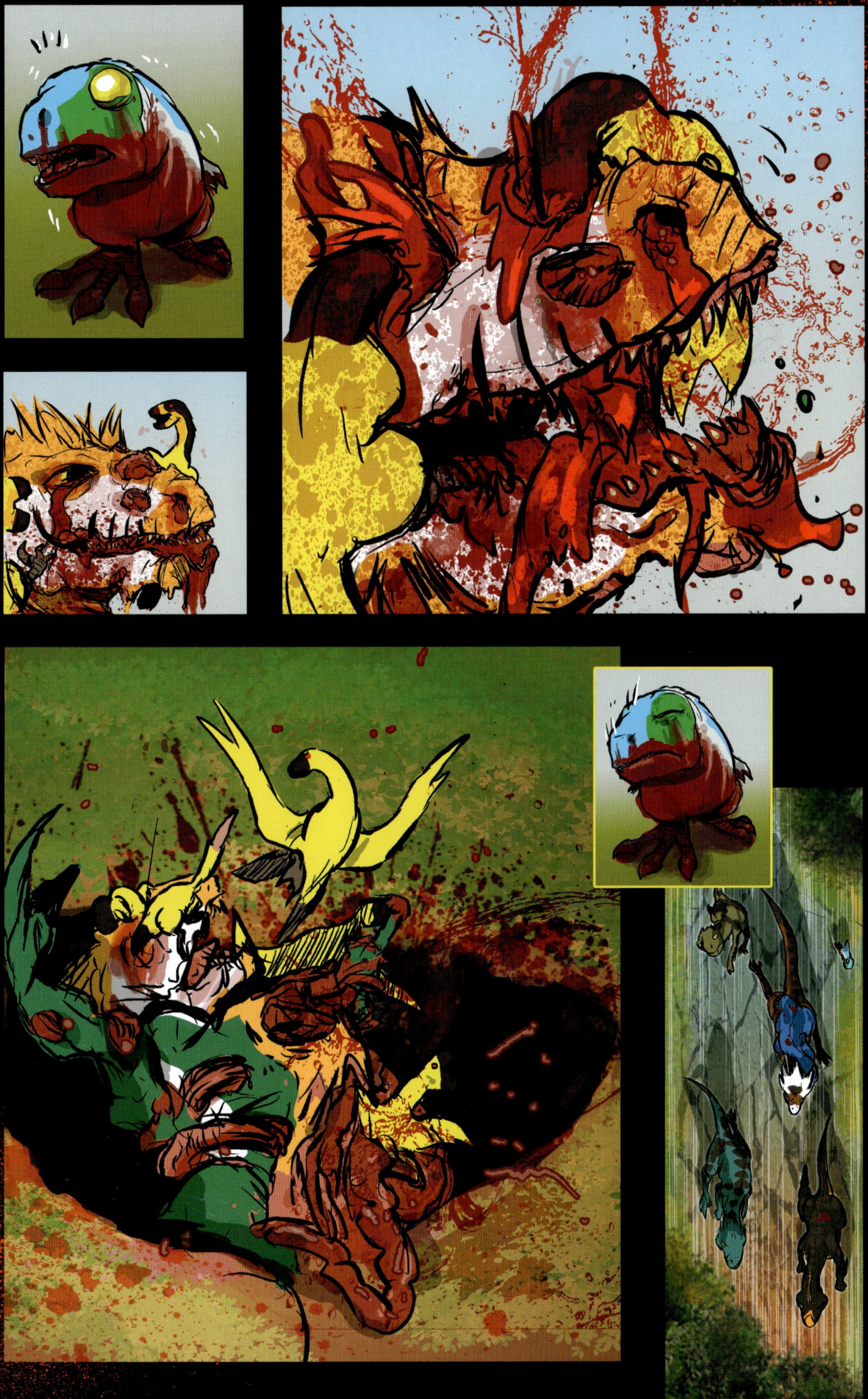

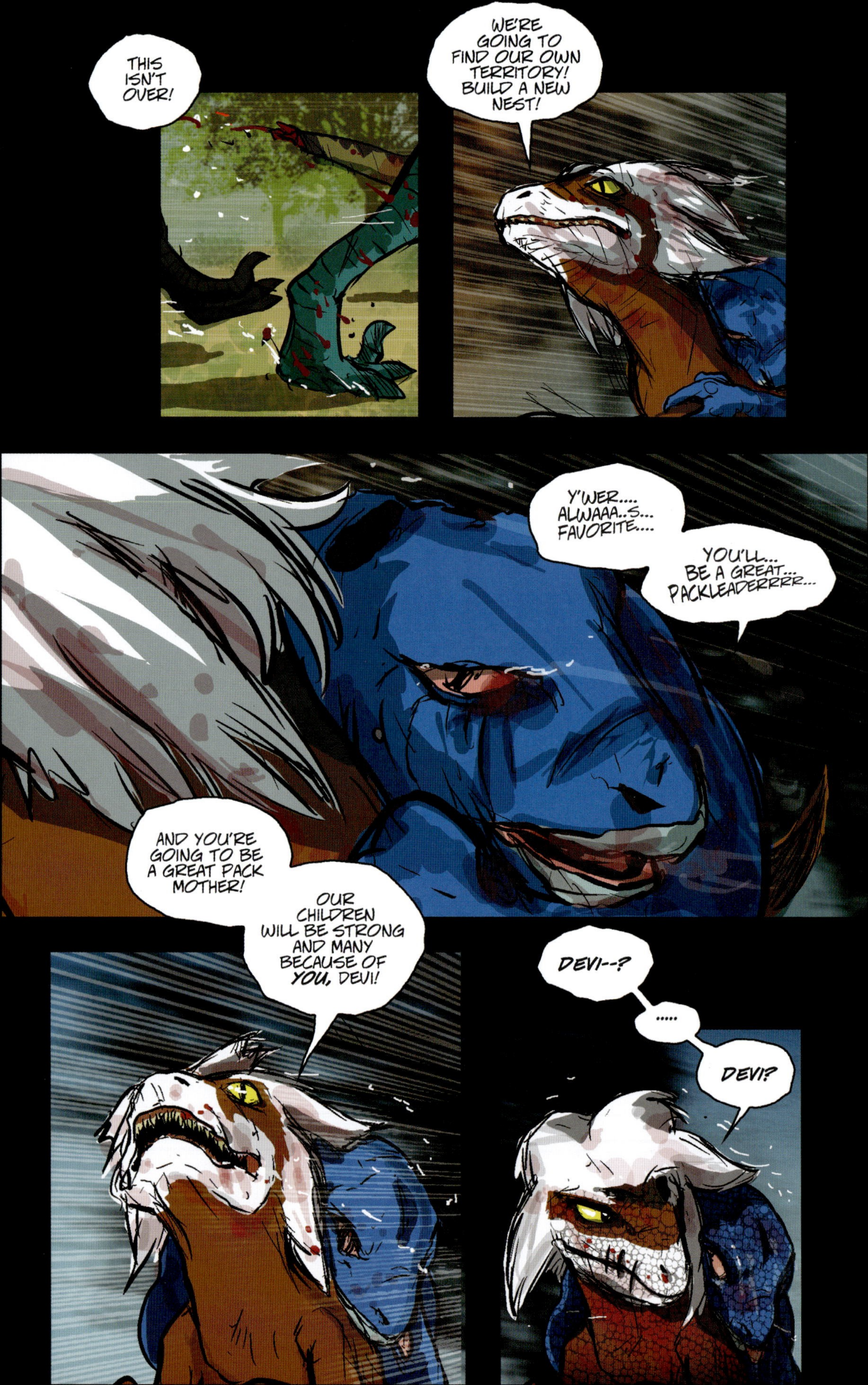
THIS ISN'T OVER!
WE'RE GOING TO FIND OUR OWN TERRITORY! BUILD A NEW NEST!
Y'WER.... ALWAAA..S... FAVORITE....
YOU'LL... BE A GREAT... PACKLEADERRRR...
AND YOU'RE GOING TO BE A GREAT PACK MOTHER!
OUR CHILDREN WILL BE STRONG AND MANY BECAUSE OF YOU, DEVI!
DEVI--?
.....
DEVI?

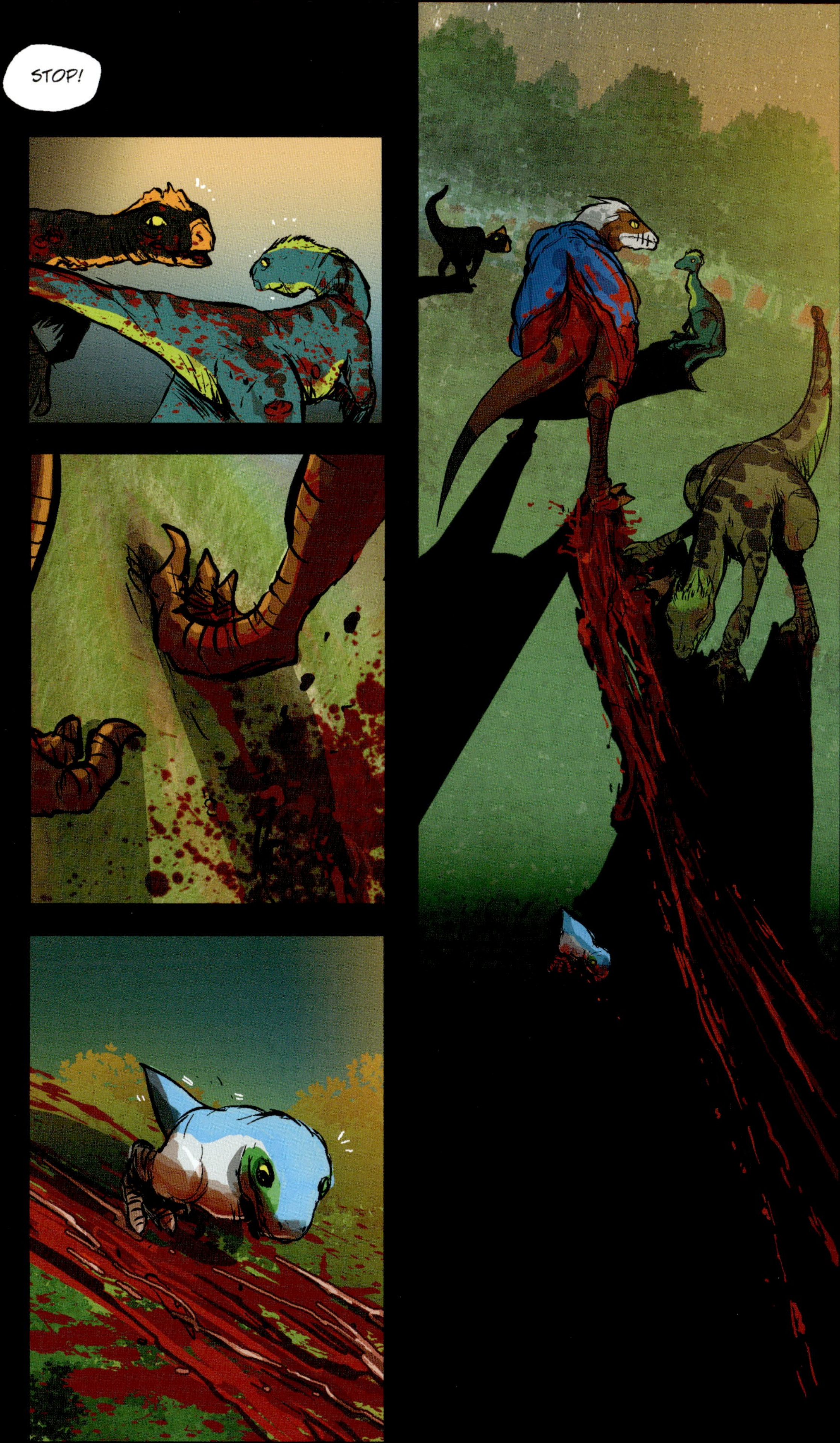
STOP!

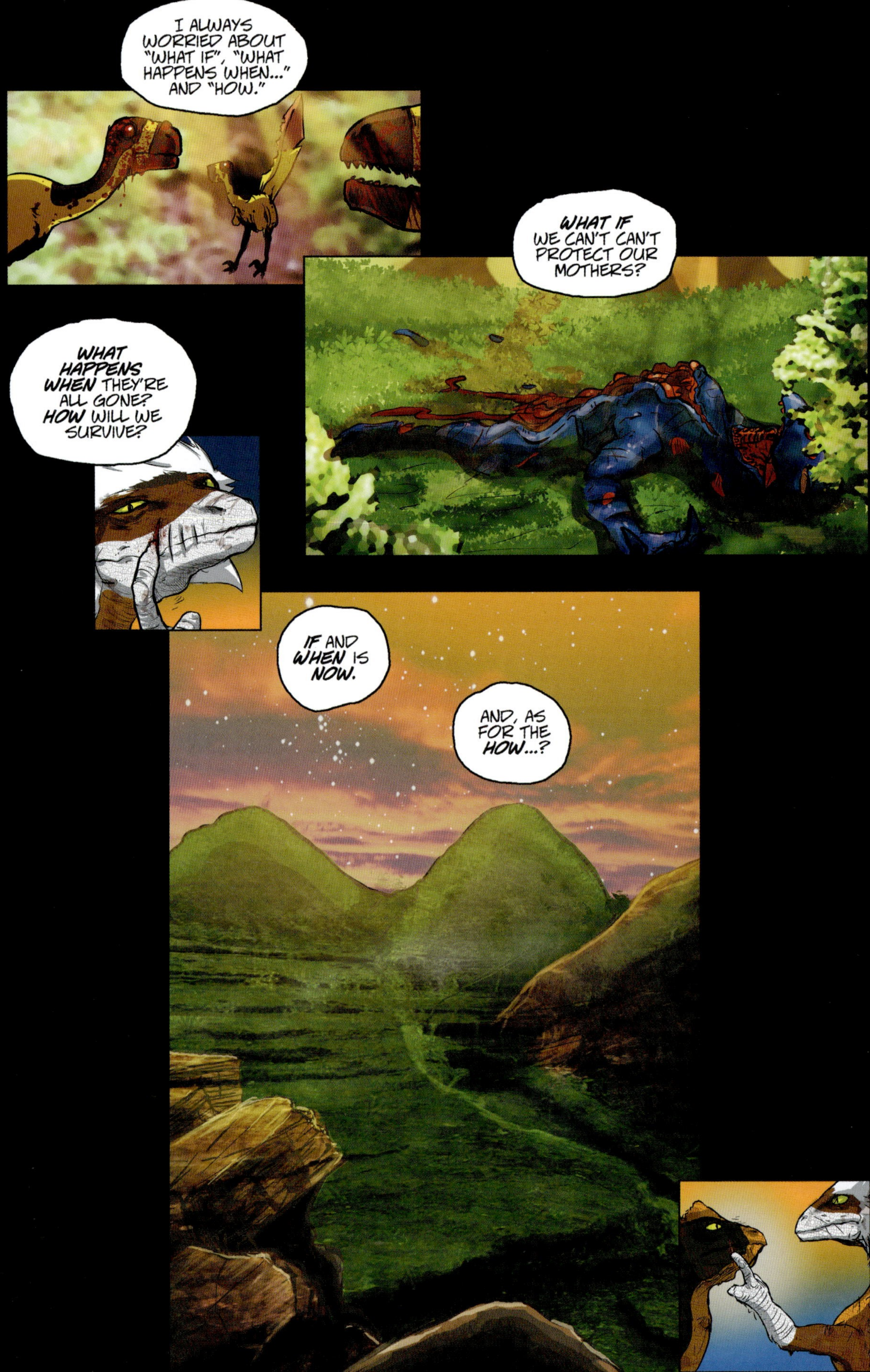
I ALWAYS WORRIED ABOUT "WHAT IF", "WHAT HAPPENS WHEN..." AND "HOW."
WHAT IF WE CAN'T CAN'T PROTECT OUR MOTHERS?
WHAT HAPPENS WHEN THEY'RE ALL GONE? HOW WILL WE SURVIVE?
IF AND WHEN IS NOW.
AND, AS FOR THE HOW...?

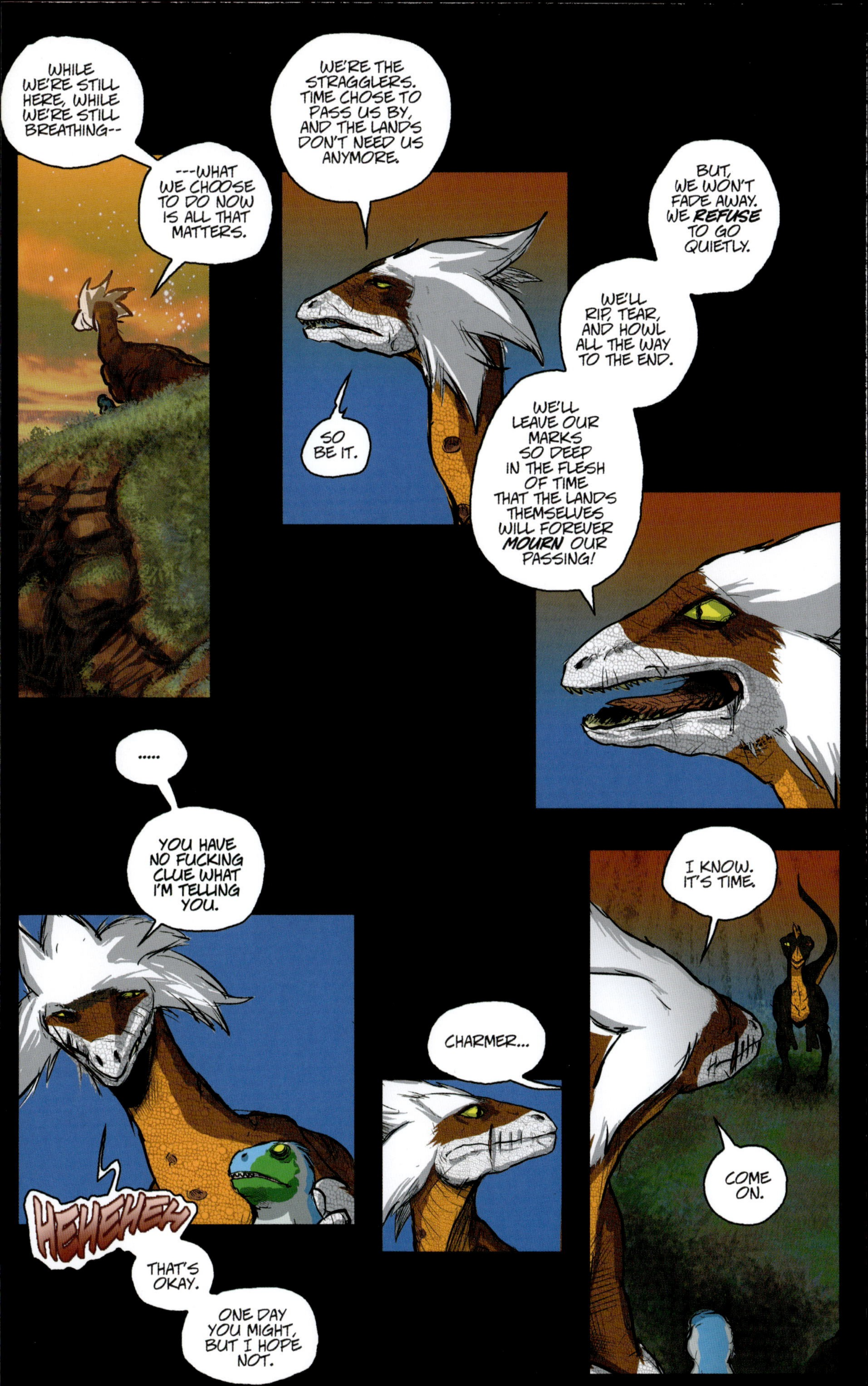
WHILE WE'RE STILL HERE, WHILE WE'RE STILL BREATHING--
---WHAT WE CHOOSE TO DO NOW IS ALL THAT MATTERS.
WE'RE THE STRAGGLERS. TIME CHOSE TO PASS US BY, AND THE LANDS DON'T NEED US ANYMORE.
SO BE IT.
BUT, WE WON'T FADE AWAY. WE REFUSE TO GO QUIETLY.
WE'LL RIP, TEAR, AND HOWL ALL THE WAY TO THE END.
WE'LL LEAVE OUR MARKS SO DEEP IN THE FLESH OF TIME THAT THE LANDS THEMSELVES WILL FOREVER MOURN OUR PASSING!
.....
YOU HAVE NO FUCKING CLUE WHAT I'M TELLING YOU.
HEHEHEH
THAT'S OKAY.
ONE DAY YOU MIGHT, BUT I HOPE NOT.
CHARMER...
I KNOW. IT'S TIME.
COME ON.

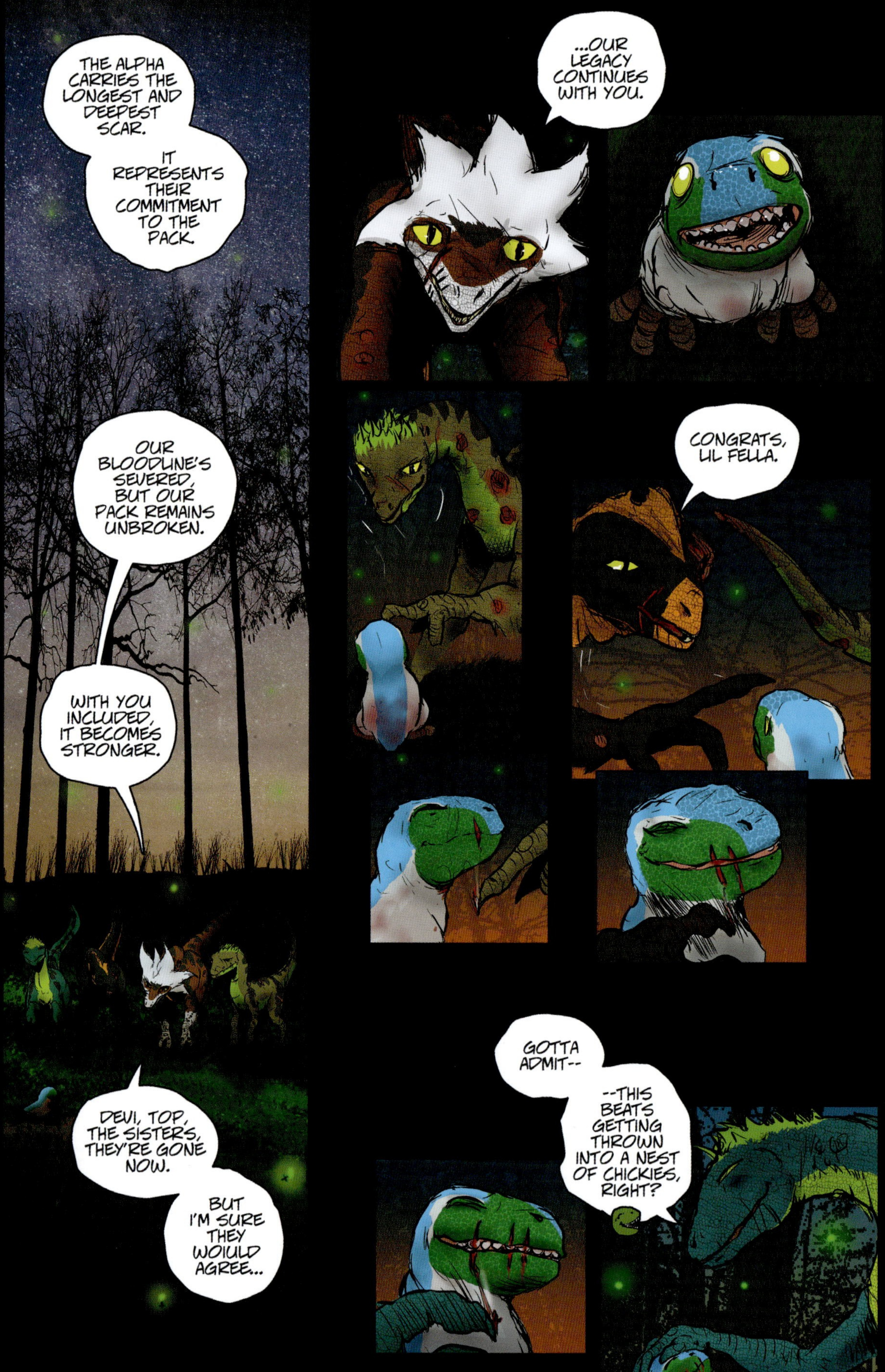
THE ALPHA CARRIES THE LONGEST AND DEEPEST SCAR.
IT REPRESENTS THEIR COMMITMENT TO THE PACK.
...OUR LEGACY CONTINUES WITH YOU.
OUR BLOODLINE'S SEVERED, BUT OUR PACK REMAINS UNBROKEN.
WITH YOU INCLUDED, IT BECOMES STRONGER.
CONGRATS, LIL FELLA.
DEVI, TOP, THE SISTERS, THEY'RE GONE NOW.
BUT I'M SURE THEY WOIULD AGREE...
GOTTA ADMIT--
--THIS BEATS GETTING THROWN INTO A NEST OF CHICKIES, RIGHT?

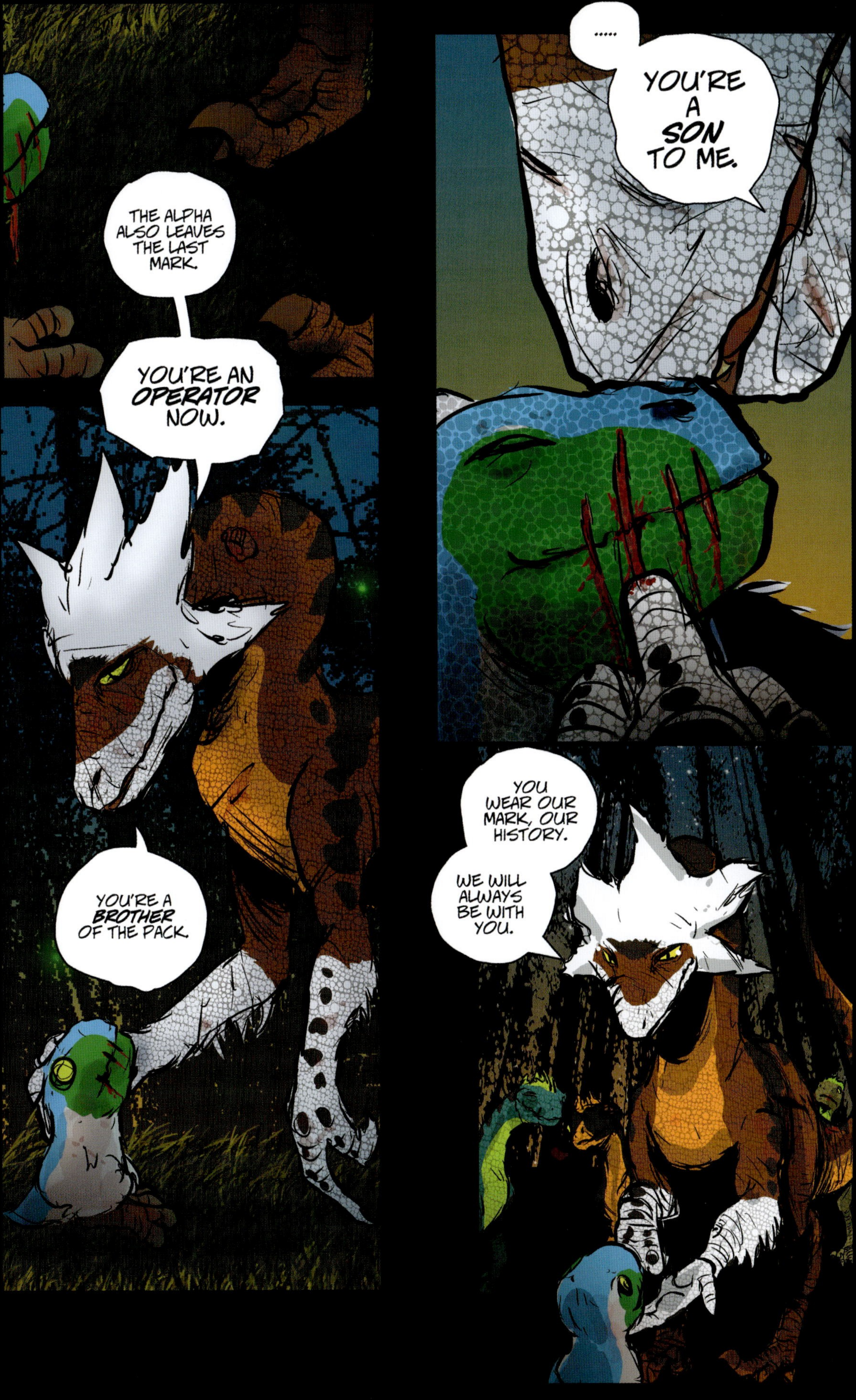
THE ALPHA ALSO LEAVES THE LAST MARK.
YOU'RE AN OPERATOR NOW.
YOU'RE A BROTHER OF THE PACK.
......
YOU'RE A SON TO ME.
YOU WEAR OUR MARK, OUR HISTORY.
WE WILL ALWAYS BE WITH YOU.

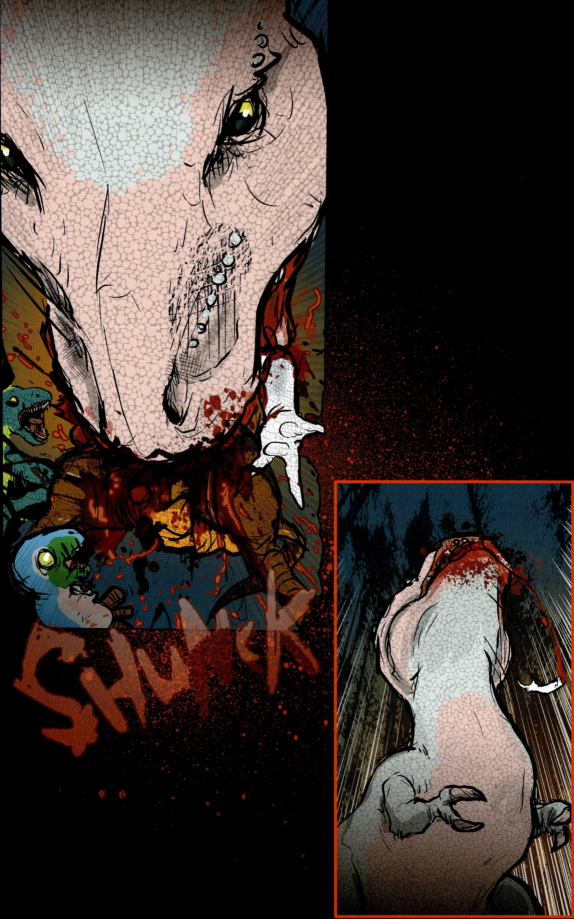

SHUNK

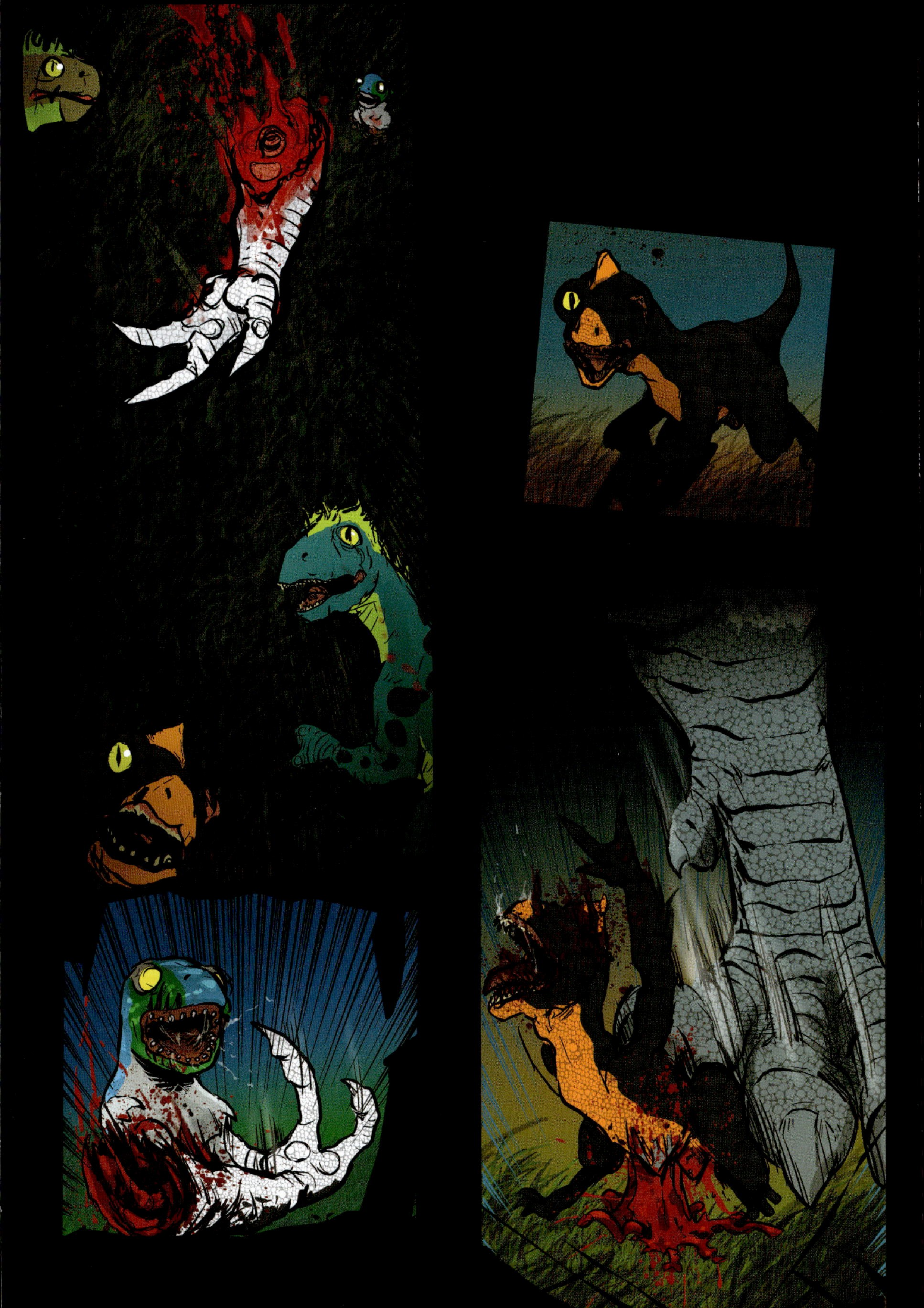

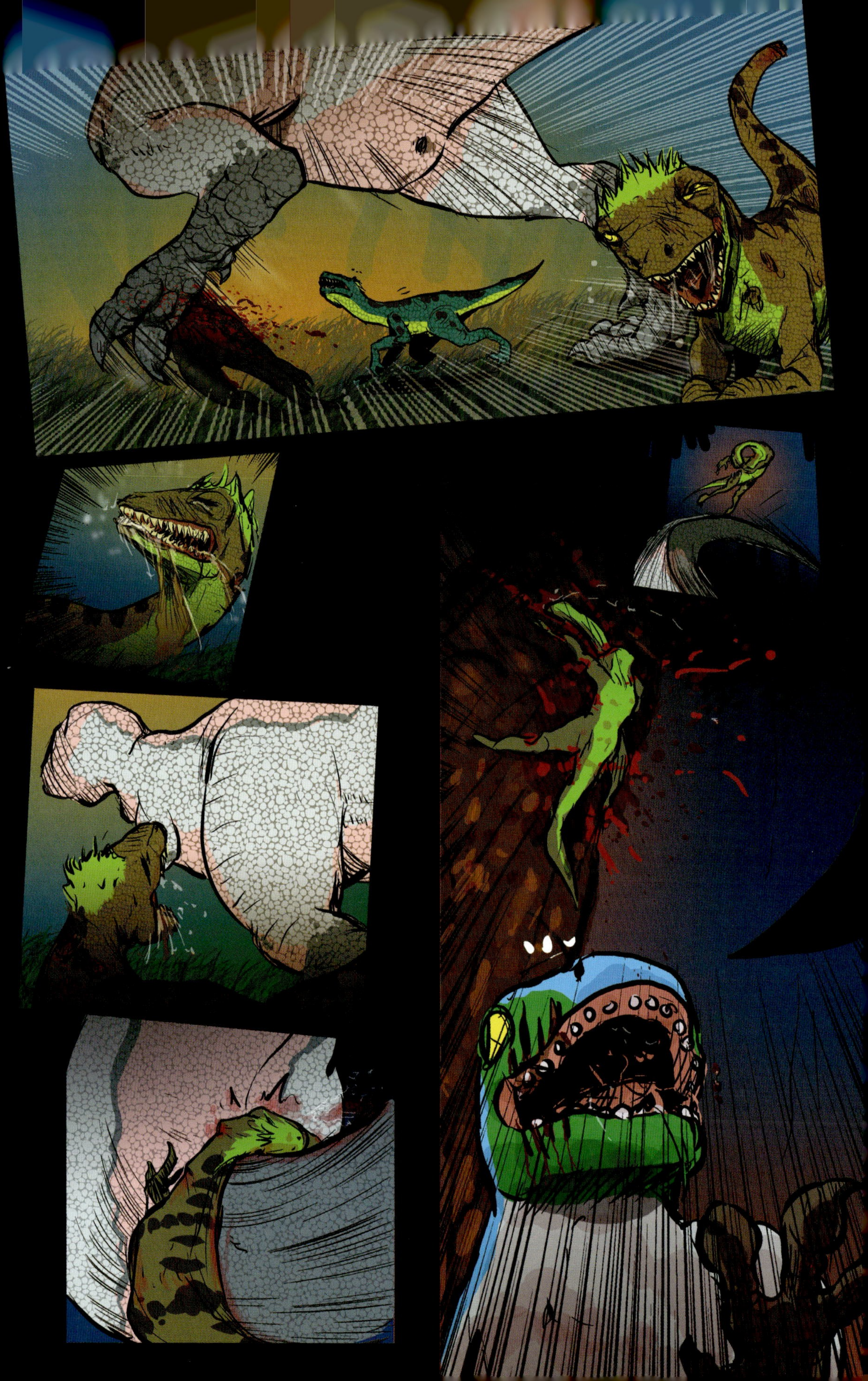

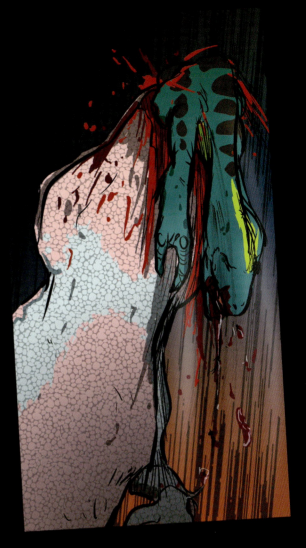

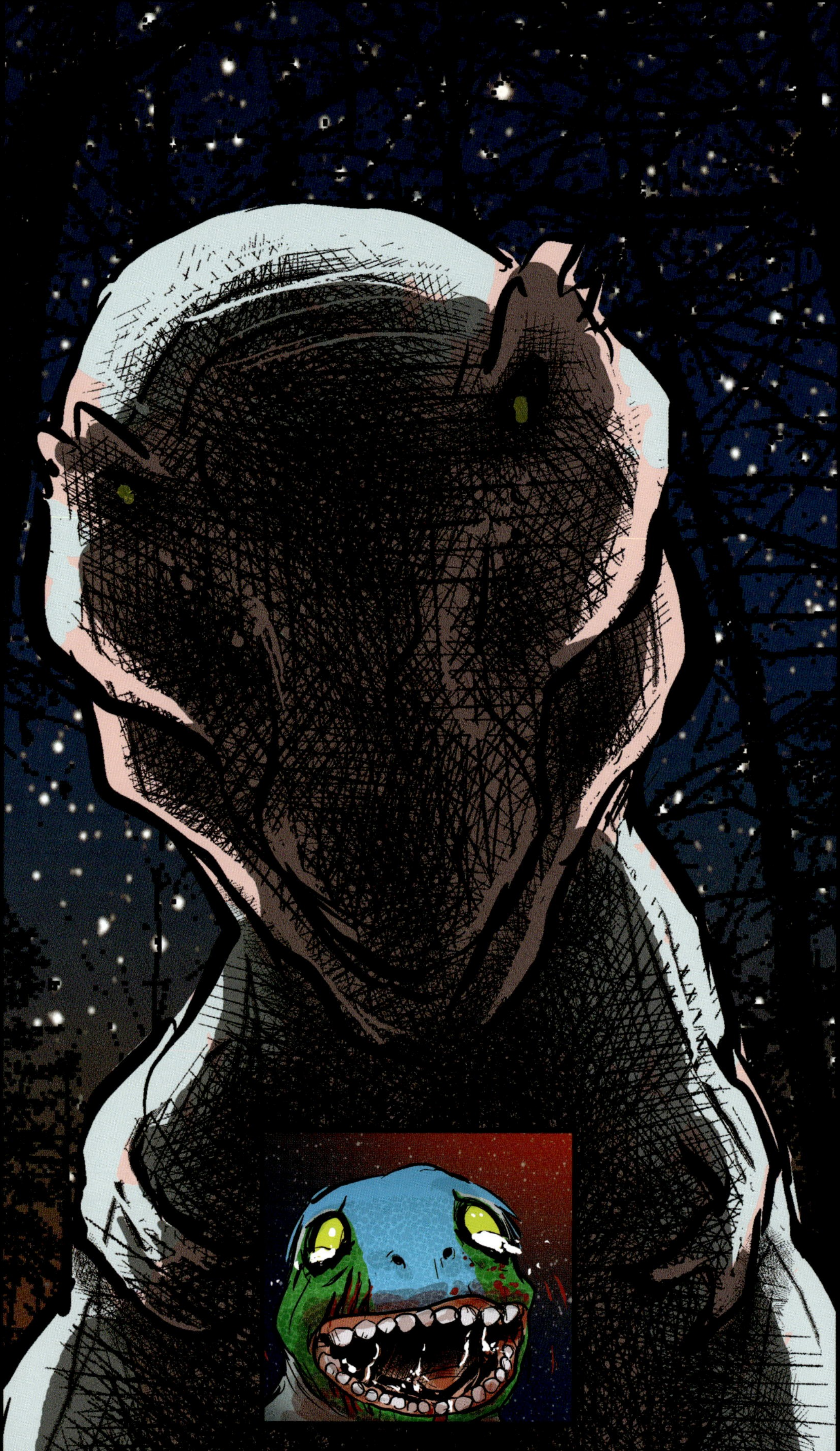

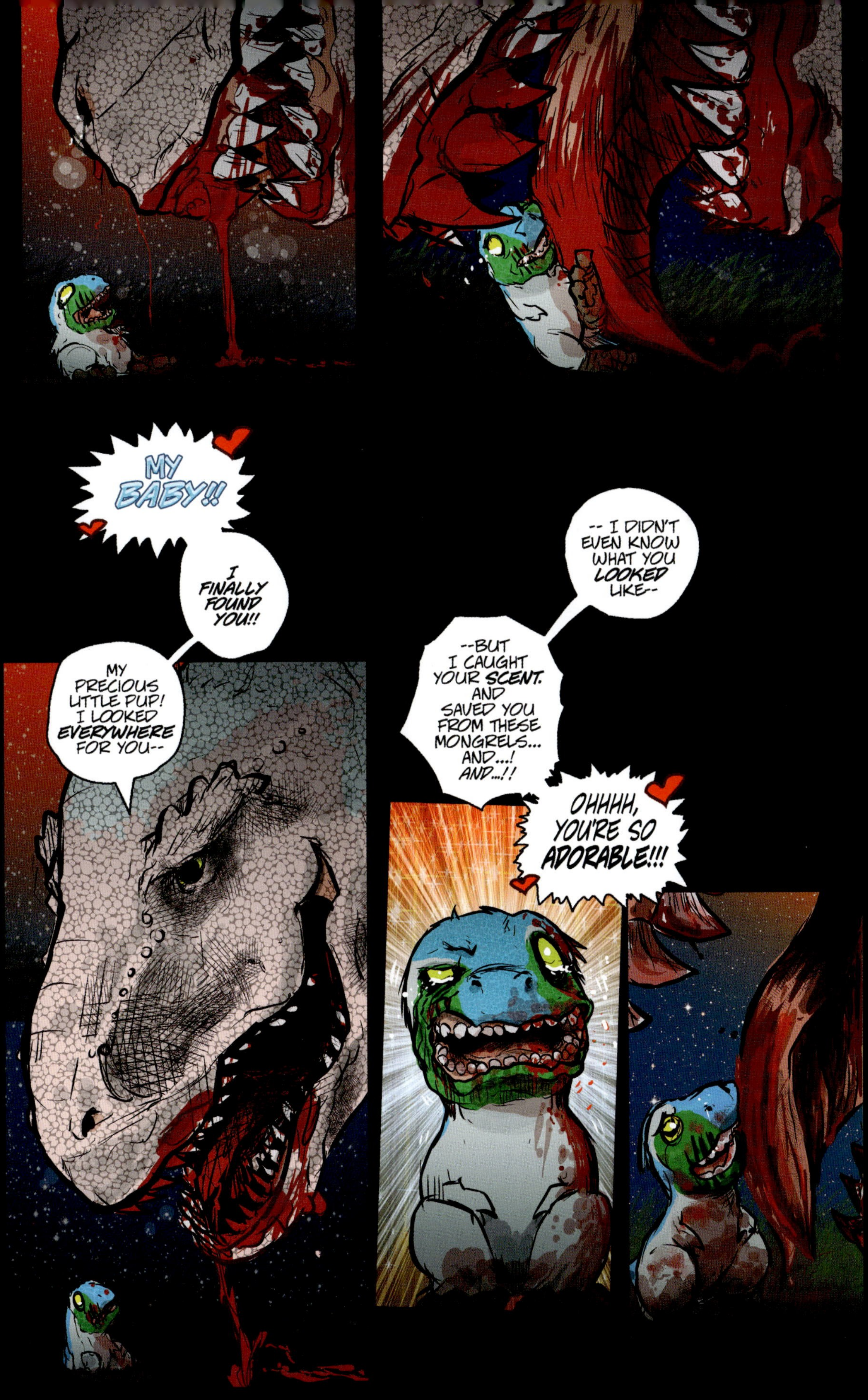

MY BABY!!
I FINALLY FOUND YOU!!
MY PRECIOUS LITTLE PUP! I LOOKED EVERYWHERE FOR YOU--
-- I DIDN'T EVEN KNOW WHAT YOU LOOKED LIKE--
--BUT I CAUGHT YOUR SCENT. AND SAVED YOU FROM THESE MONGRELS... AND...! AND...!!
OHHHH, YOU'RE SO ADORABLE!!!

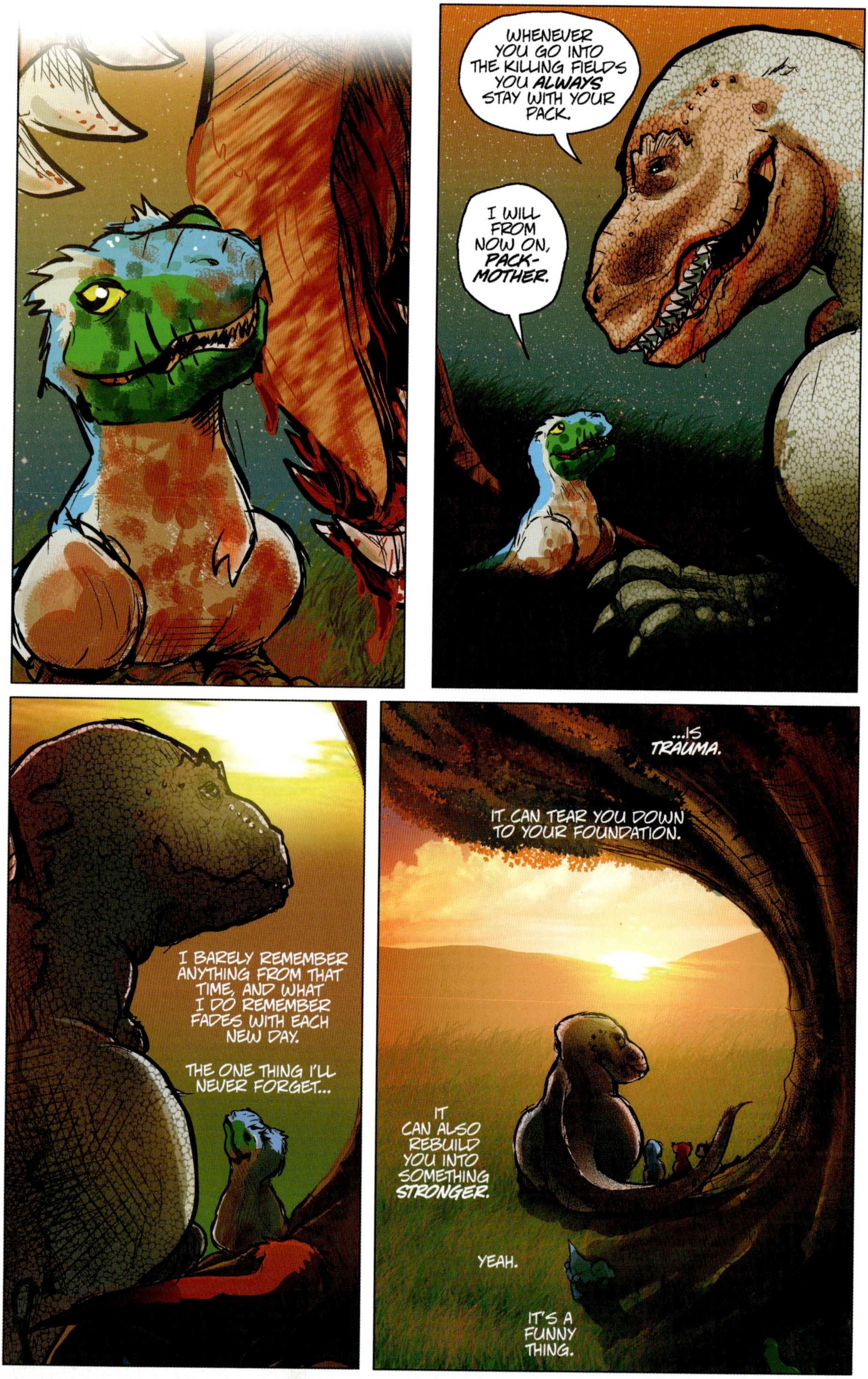
WHENEVER YOU GO INTO THE KILLING FIELDS YOU **ALWAYS** STAY WITH YOUR PACK.
I WILL FROM NOW ON, **PACK-MOTHER.**
I BARELY REMEMBER ANYTHING FROM THAT TIME, AND WHAT I DO REMEMBER FADES WITH EACH NEW DAY.
THE ONE THING I'LL NEVER FORGET...
...IS **TRAUMA.**
IT CAN TEAR YOU DOWN TO YOUR FOUNDATION.
IT CAN ALSO REBUILD YOU INTO SOMETHING **STRONGER.**
YEAH.
IT'S A FUNNY THING.

CRETACEOUS BOOGALOO

WOOOOO!!!

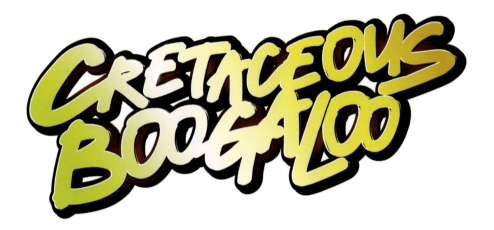

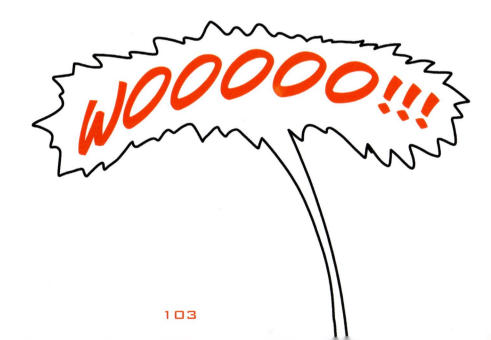

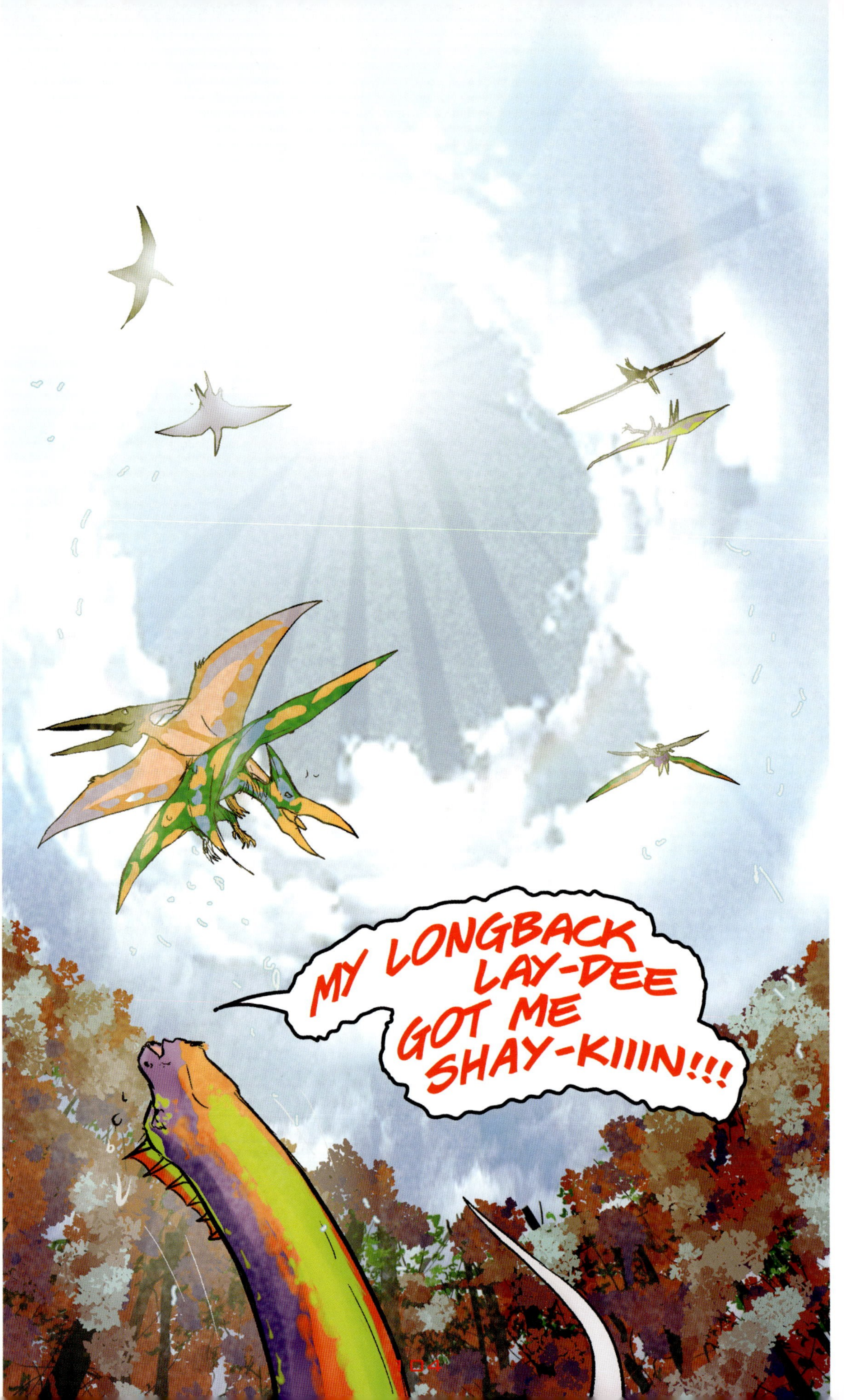
MY LONGBACK LAY-DEE GOT ME SHAY-KIIIN!!!

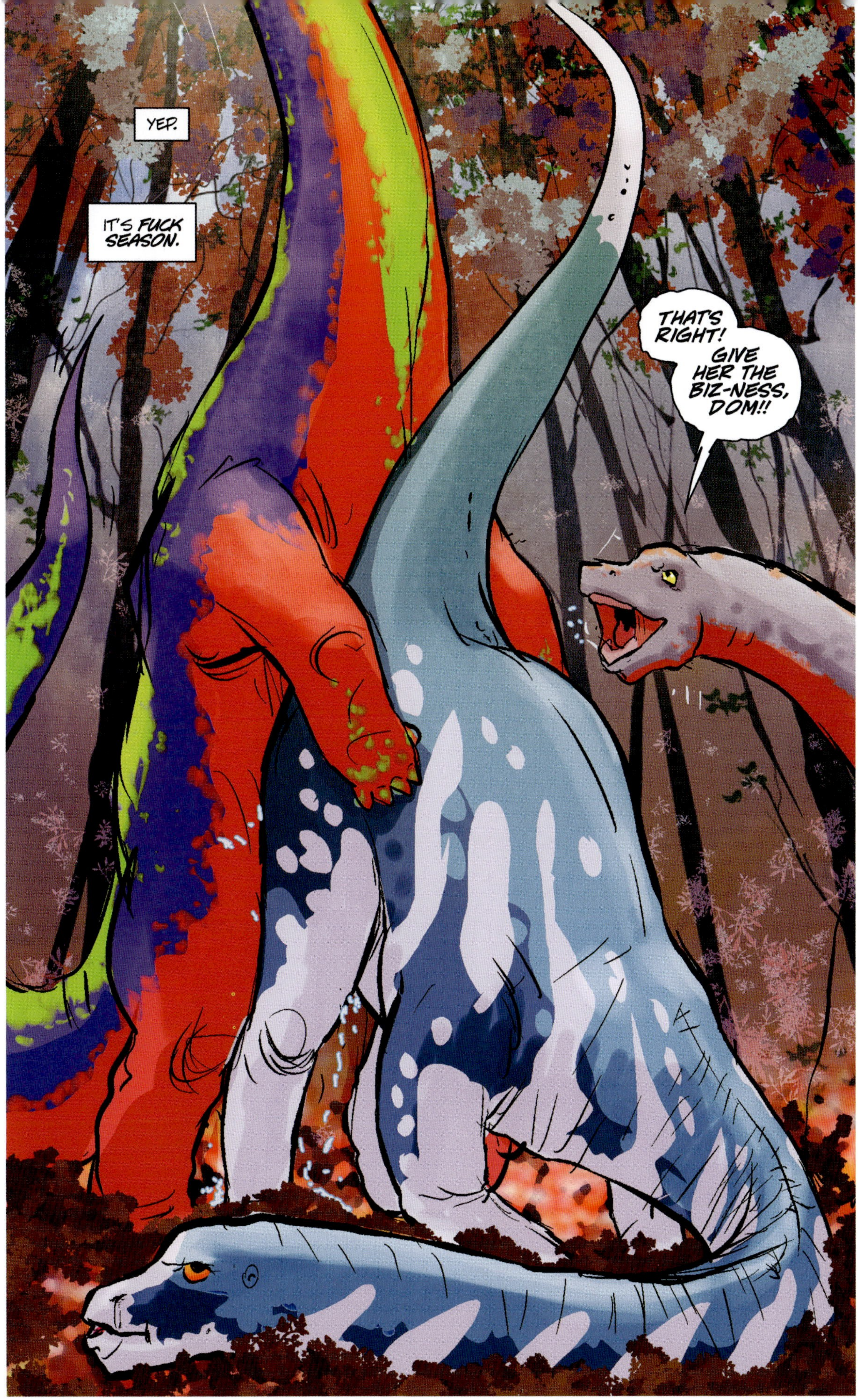
YEP.
IT'S FUCK SEASON.
THAT'S RIGHT! GIVE HER THE BIZ-NESS, DOM!!

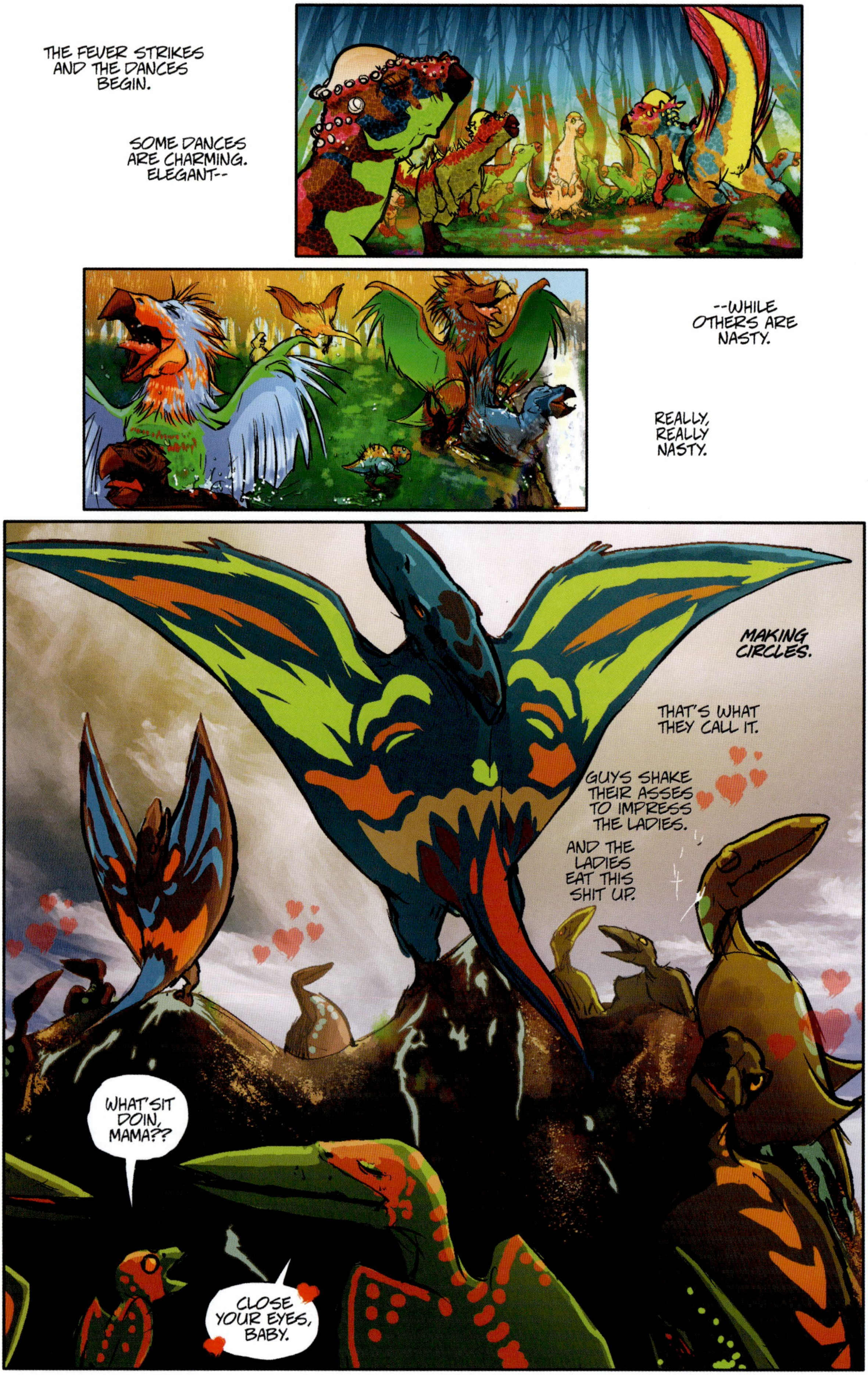
THE FEVER STRIKES AND THE DANCES BEGIN.
SOME DANCES ARE CHARMING. ELEGANT--
--WHILE OTHERS ARE NASTY.
REALLY, REALLY NASTY.
MAKING CIRCLES.
THAT'S WHAT THEY CALL IT.
GUYS SHAKE THEIR ASSES TO IMPRESS THE LADIES.
AND THE LADIES EAT THIS SHIT UP.
WHAT'SIT DOIN, MAMA??
CLOSE YOUR EYES, BABY.

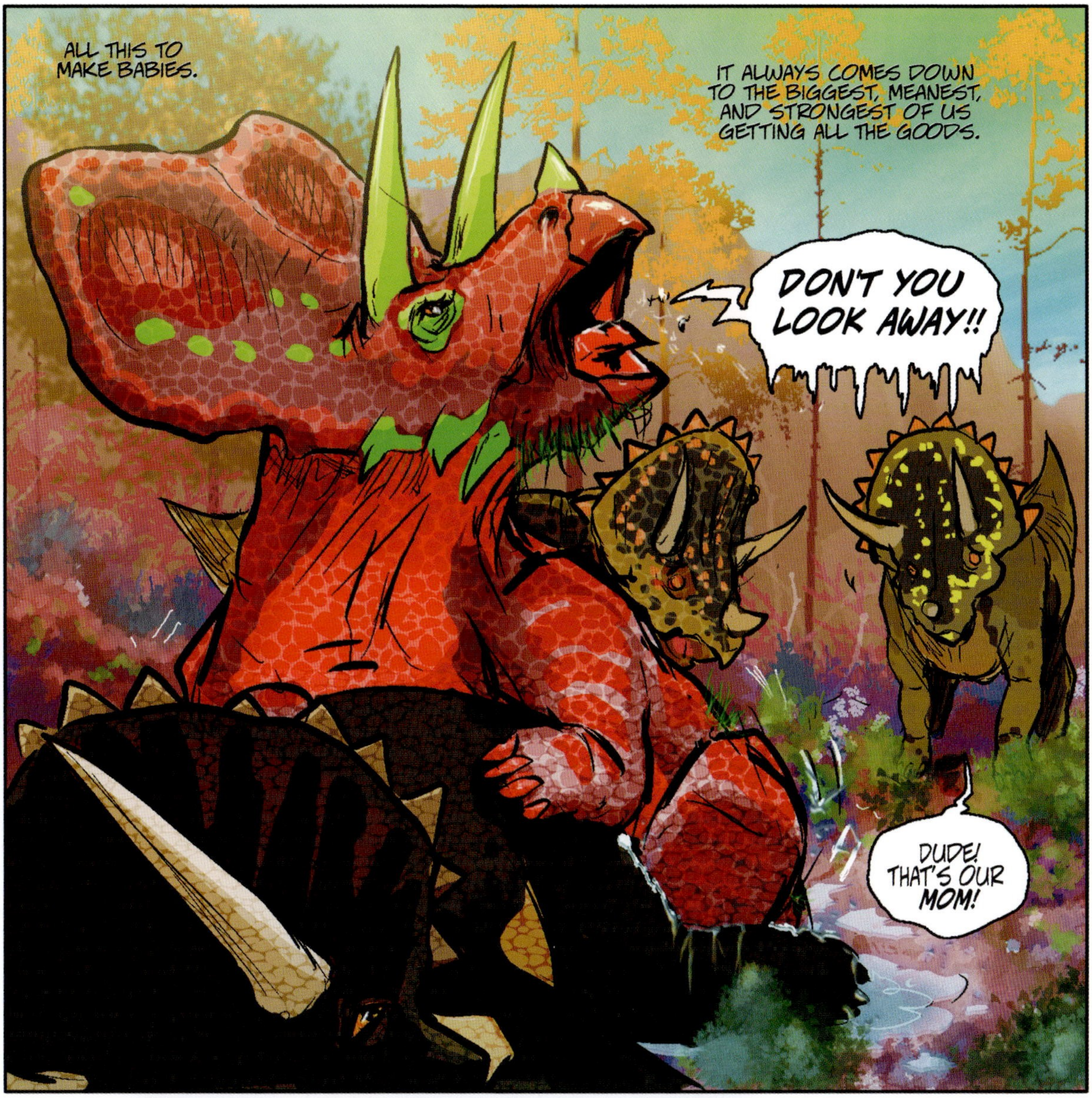
ALL THIS TO MAKE BABIES.
IT ALWAYS COMES DOWN TO THE BIGGEST, MEANEST, AND STRONGEST OF US GETTING ALL THE GOODS.
DON'T YOU LOOK AWAY!!
DUDE! THAT'S OUR *MOM!*

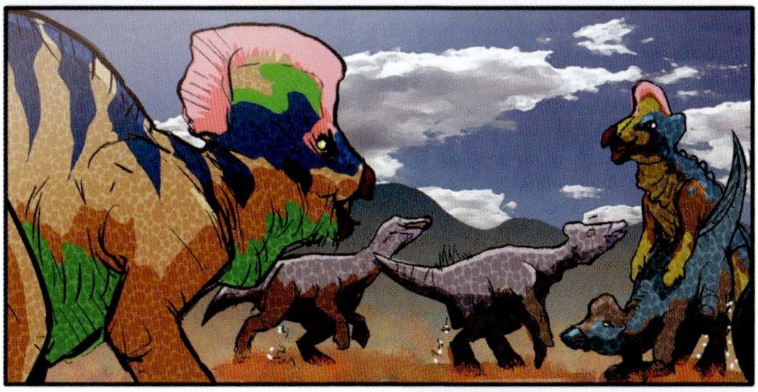

BUT WHY?

THE GIRLS OUTNUMBER THE BOYS ***FOUR*** TO ***ONE.*** MORE THAN ENOUGH TO GO AROUND.

YOU'D FIGURE THESE DUMBASS DUDES WOULD LEARN TO WORK TOGETHER--

--SO THAT EVERYBODY COULD GET A PIECE.

AND, NOT BUTT HEADS--

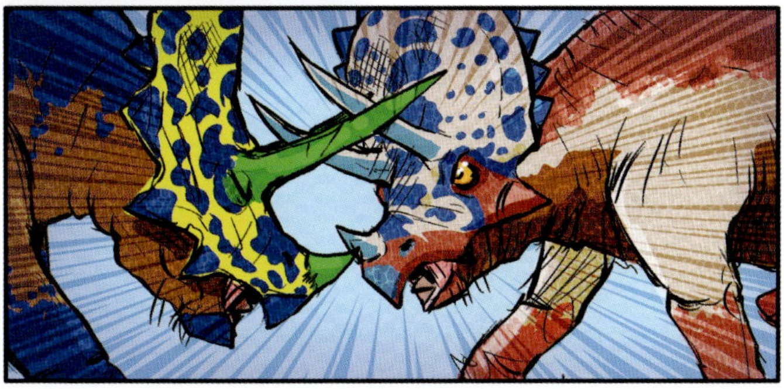

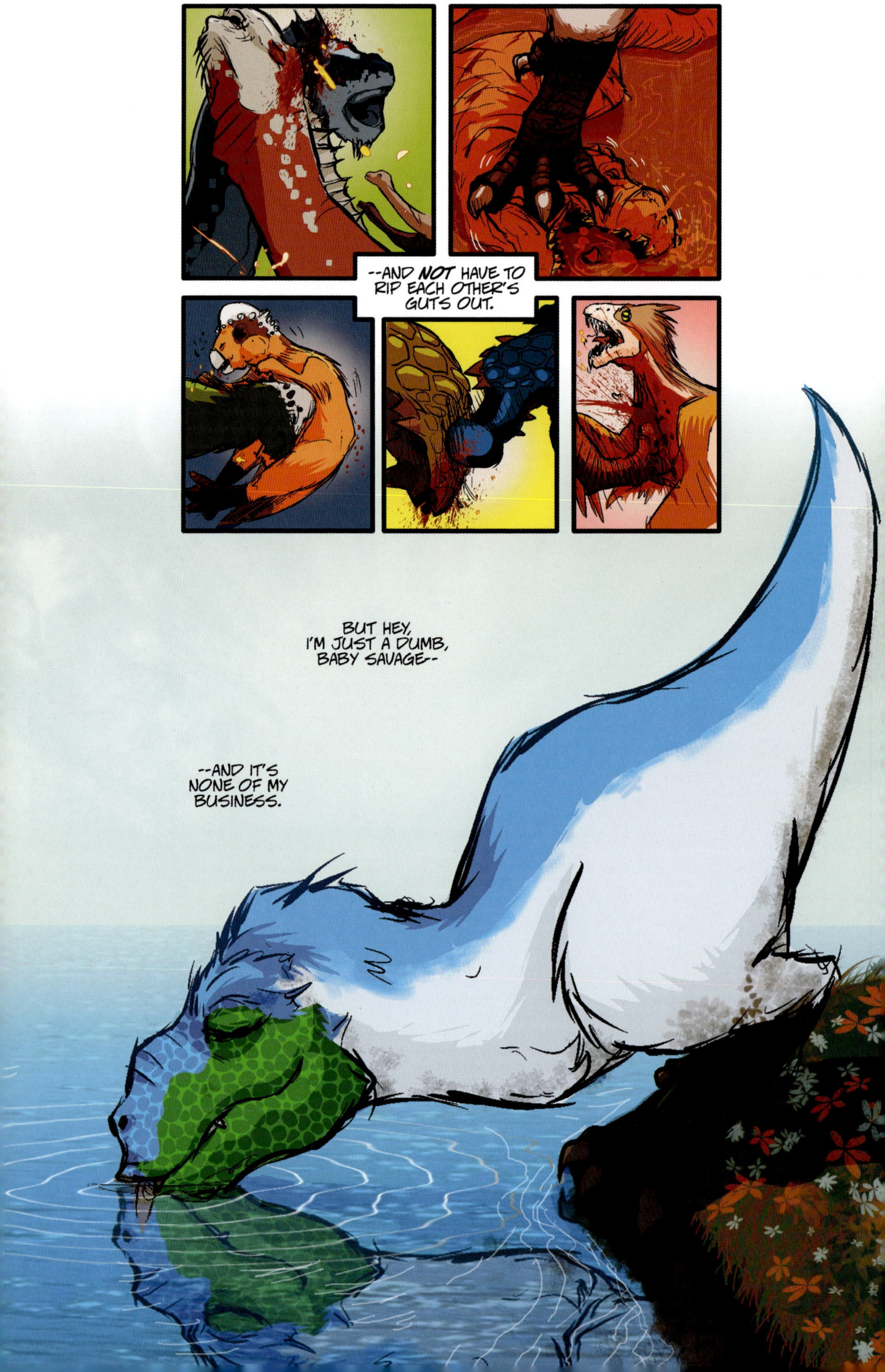
--AND NOT HAVE TO RIP EACH OTHER'S GUTS OUT.
BUT HEY, I'M JUST A DUMB, BABY SAVAGE--
--AND IT'S NONE OF MY BUSINESS.

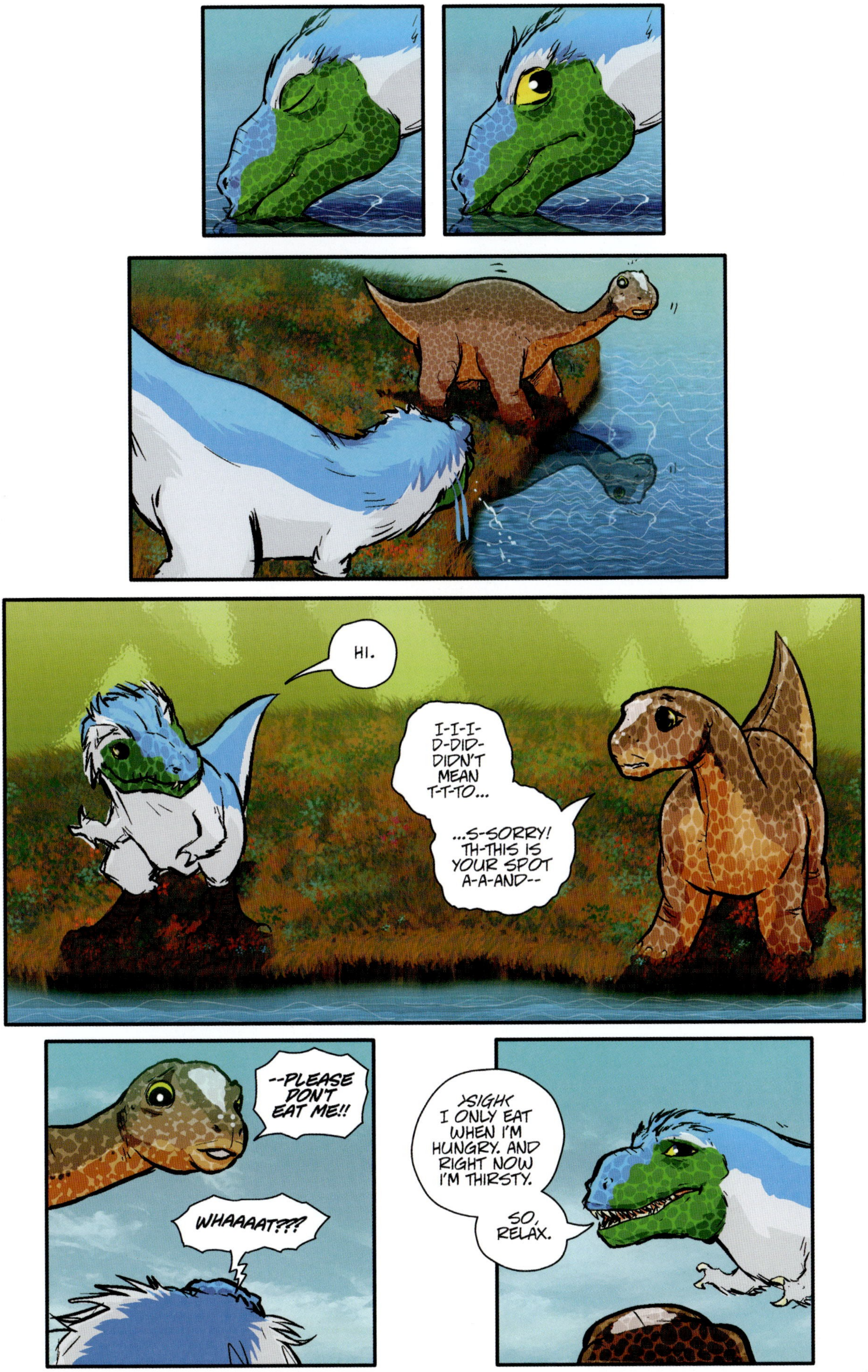
HI.
I-I-I-
D-DID-
DIDN'T
MEAN
T-T-TO...
...S-SORRY!
TH-THIS IS
YOUR SPOT
A-A-AND--
--PLEASE
DON'T
EAT ME!!
WHAAAAT???
>SIGH<
I ONLY EAT
WHEN I'M
HUNGRY. AND
RIGHT NOW
I'M THIRSTY.
SO,
RELAX.

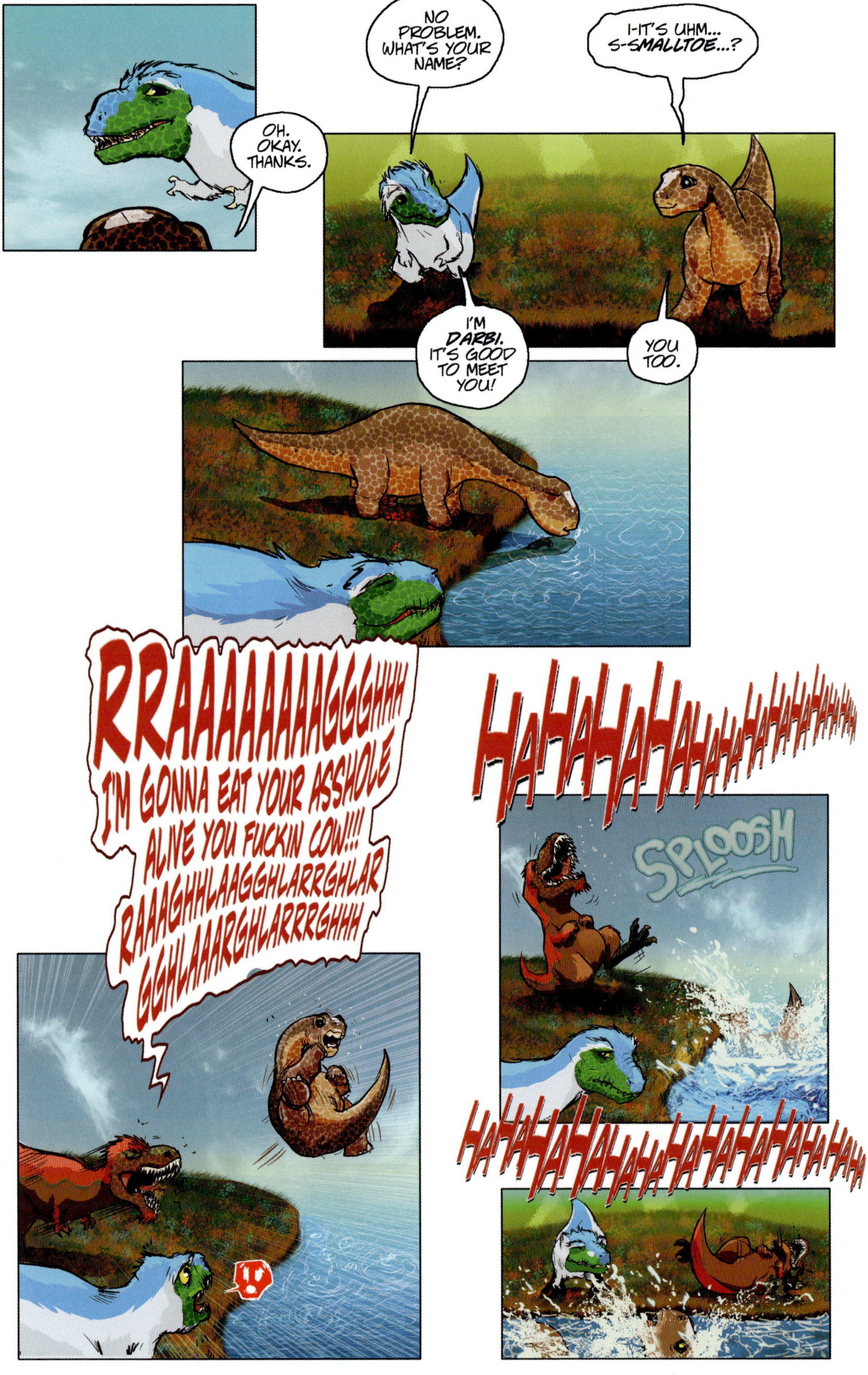
OH. OKAY. THANKS.
NO PROBLEM. WHAT'S YOUR NAME?
I'M DARBI. IT'S GOOD TO MEET YOU!
I-IT'S UHM... S-SMALLTOE...?
YOU TOO.
RRAAAAAAAGGGHHH I'M GONNA EAT YOUR ASSHOLE ALIVE YOU FUCKIN COW!!! RAAAGHHLAAGGHLARRGHLAR GGHLAAARGHLARRRGHHH
HAHAHAHAHAHAHAHAHAHAHAHAHAHAHAHA
SPLOOSH
HAHAHAHAHAHAHAHAHAHAHAHAHAHAHAHA

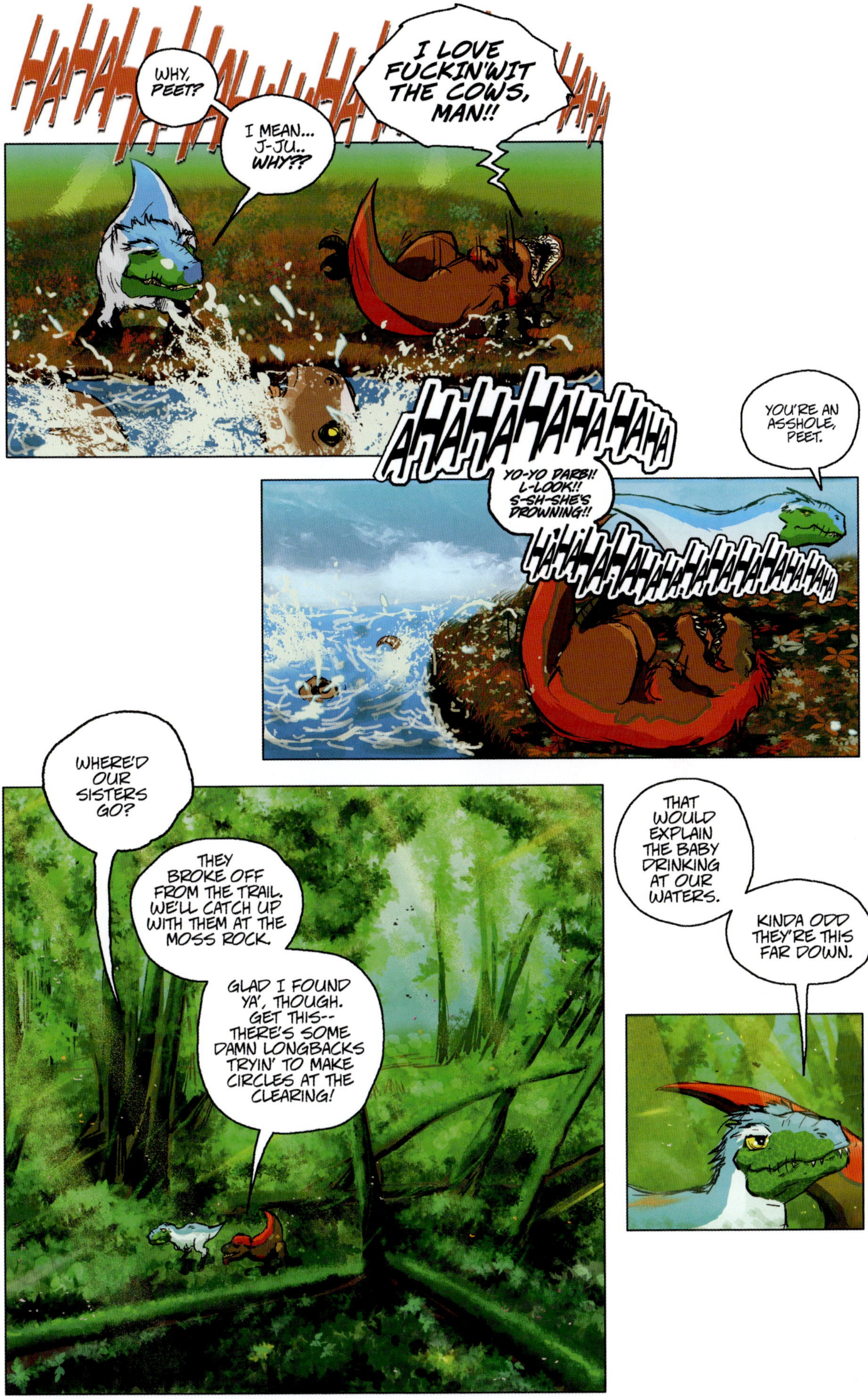
HAHAHAHAHAHAHAHAHA
WHY, PEET?
I MEAN... J-JU.. WHY??
I LOVE FUCKIN'WIT THE COWS, MAN!!
AHAHAHAHAHAHAHA
YO-YO DARBI! L-LOOK!! S-SH-SHE'S DROWNING!!
HAHAHAHAHAHAHAHAHAHAHAHAHA
YOU'RE AN ASSHOLE, PEET.
WHERE'D OUR SISTERS GO?
THEY BROKE OFF FROM THE TRAIL. WE'LL CATCH UP WITH THEM AT THE MOSS ROCK.
GLAD I FOUND YA', THOUGH. GET THIS-- THERE'S SOME DAMN LONGBACKS TRYIN' TO MAKE CIRCLES AT THE CLEARING!
THAT WOULD EXPLAIN THE BABY DRINKING AT OUR WATERS.
KINDA ODD THEY'RE THIS FAR DOWN.

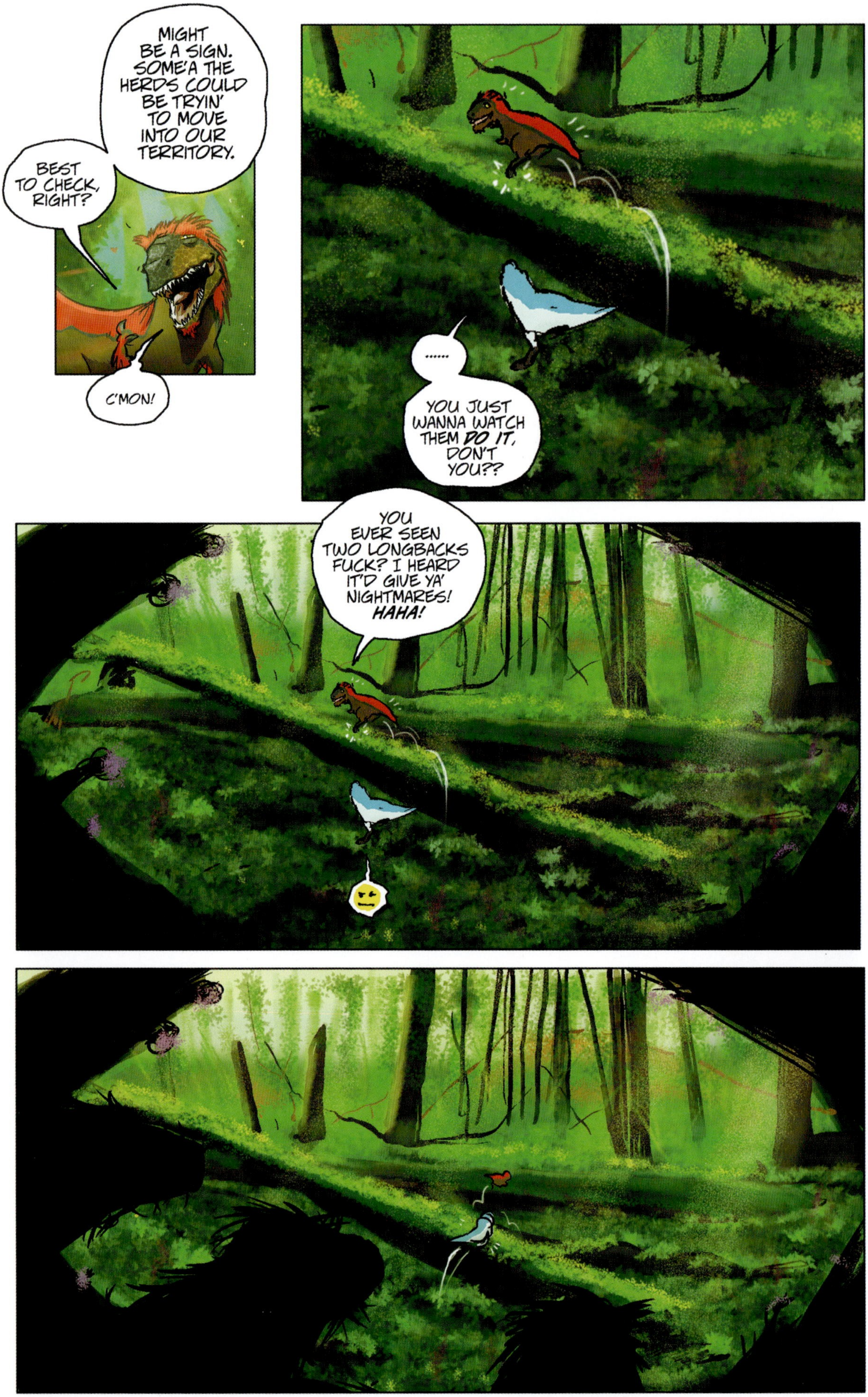

MIGHT BE A SIGN. SOME'A THE HERDS COULD BE TRYIN' TO MOVE INTO OUR TERRITORY.
BEST TO CHECK, RIGHT?
C'MON!
......
YOU JUST WANNA WATCH THEM *DO IT*, DON'T YOU??
YOU EVER SEEN TWO LONGBACKS FUCK? I HEARD IT'D GIVE YA' NIGHTMARES! ***HAHA!***

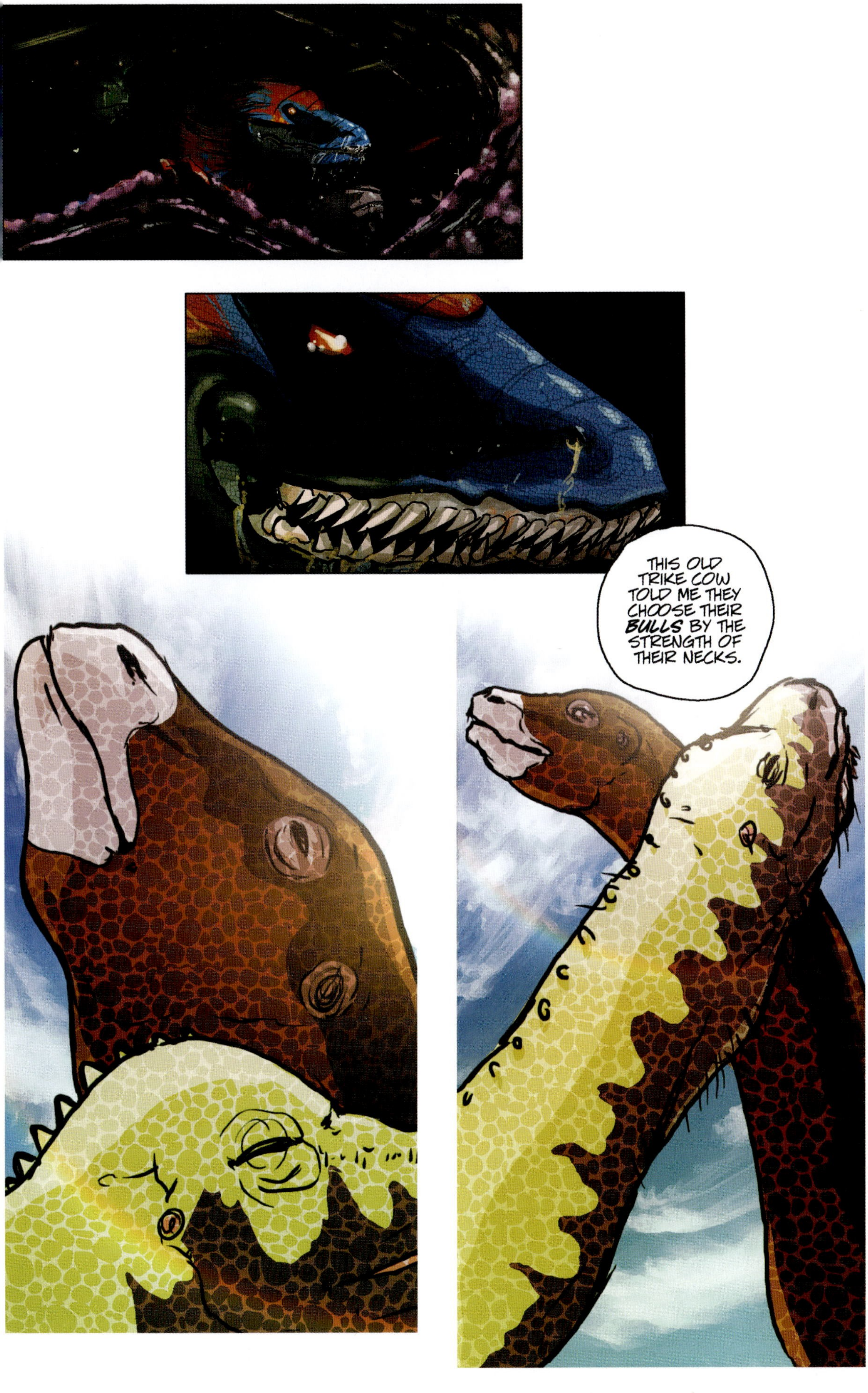
THIS OLD TRIKE COW TOLD ME THEY CHOOSE THEIR **BULLS** BY THE STRENGTH OF THEIR NECKS.

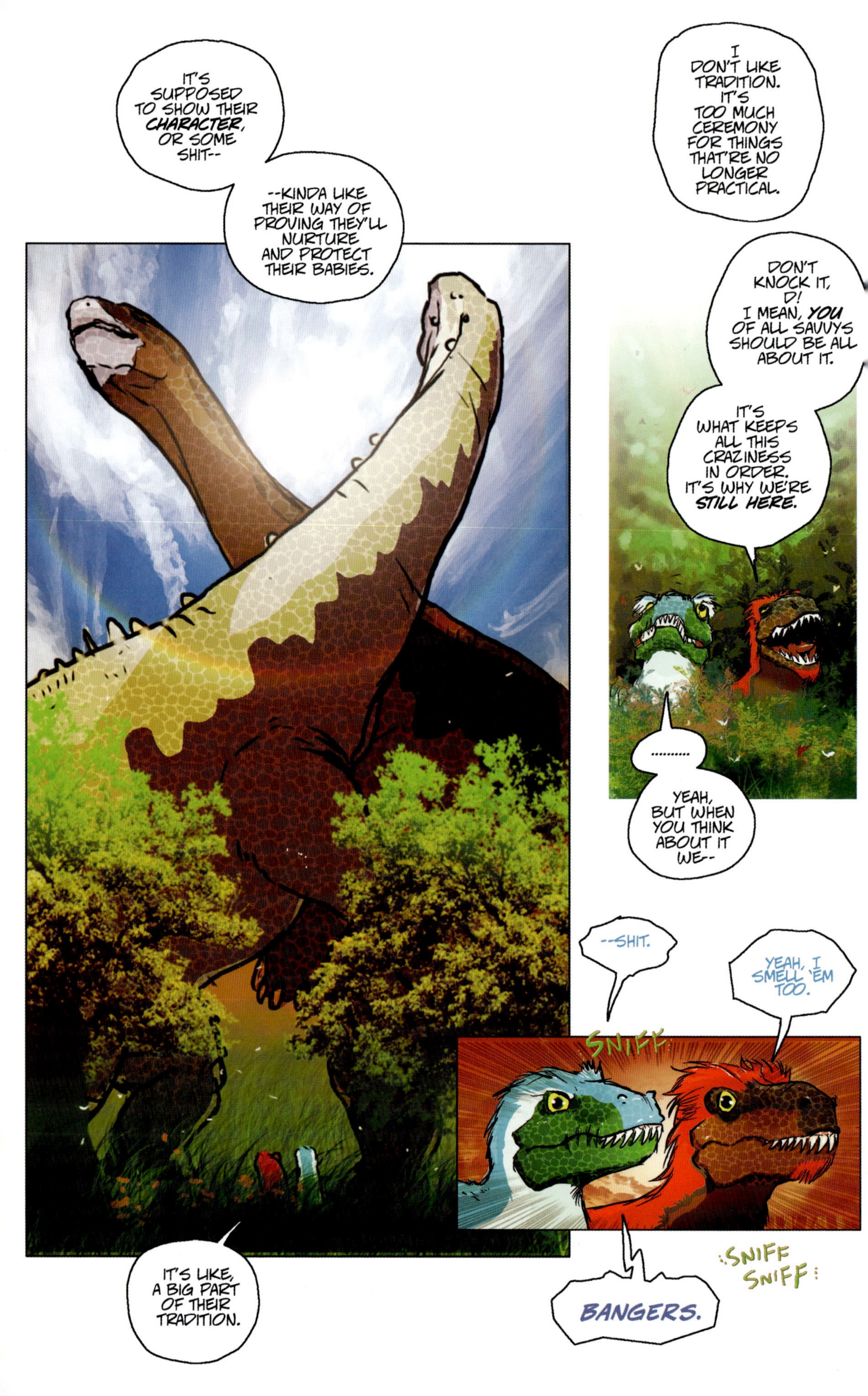
IT'S SUPPOSED TO SHOW THEIR CHARACTER, OR SOME SHIT--
--KINDA LIKE THEIR WAY OF PROVING THEY'LL NURTURE AND PROTECT THEIR BABIES.
IT'S LIKE, A BIG PART OF THEIR TRADITION.
I DON'T LIKE TRADITION. IT'S TOO MUCH CEREMONY FOR THINGS THAT'RE NO LONGER PRACTICAL.
DON'T KNOCK IT, D! I MEAN, YOU OF ALL SAVVYS SHOULD BE ALL ABOUT IT.
IT'S WHAT KEEPS ALL THIS CRAZINESS IN ORDER. IT'S WHY WE'RE STILL HERE.
....
YEAH, BUT WHEN YOU THINK ABOUT IT WE--
--SHIT.
YEAH, I SMELL 'EM TOO.
SNIFF
SNIFF SNIFF
BANGERS.

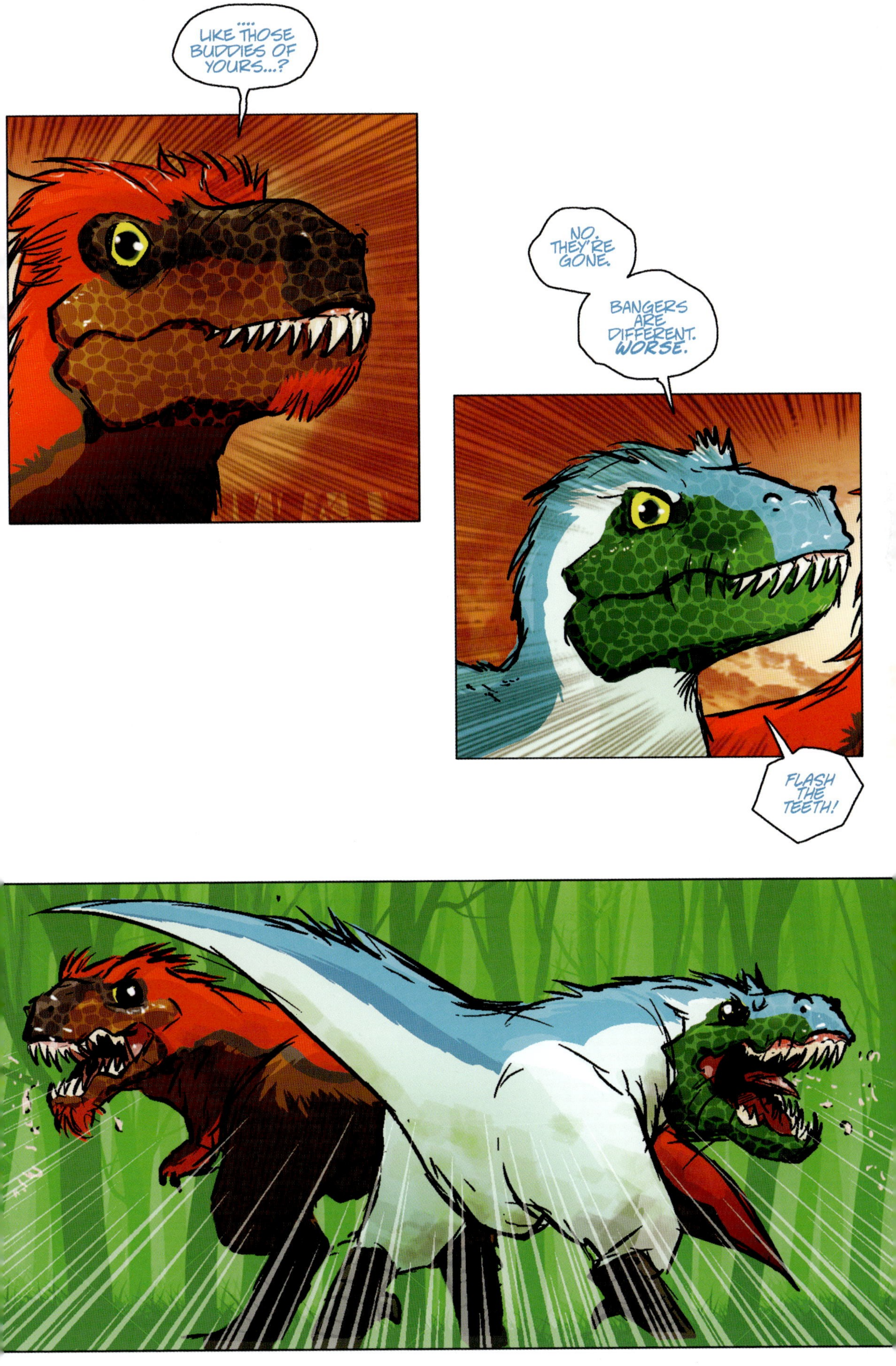
....
LIKE THOSE BUDDIES OF YOURS...?
NO. THEY'RE GONE.
BANGERS ARE DIFFERENT. *WORSE.*
FLASH THE TEETH!

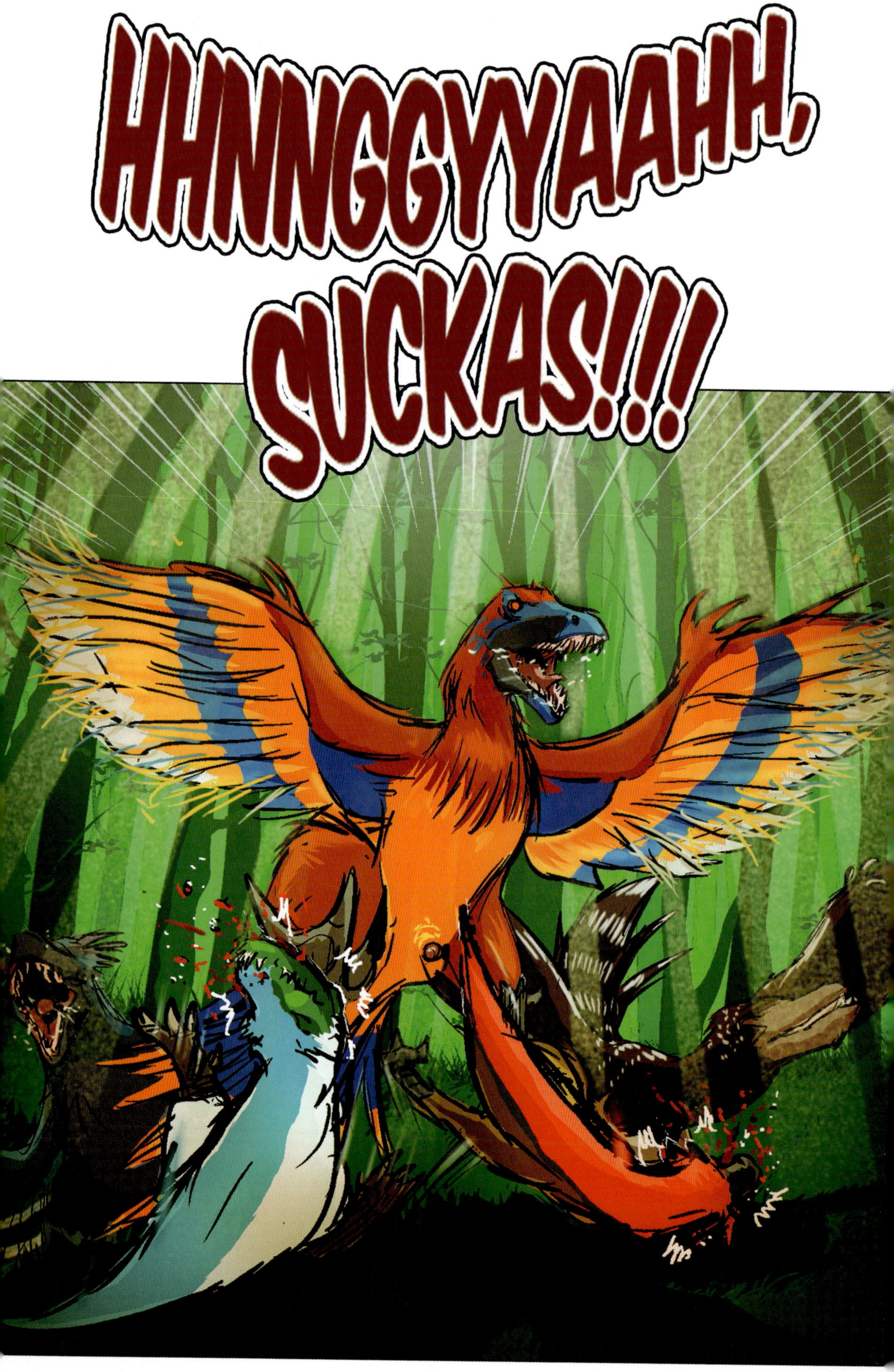
HHNNGGYYAAHH,
SUCKAS!!!

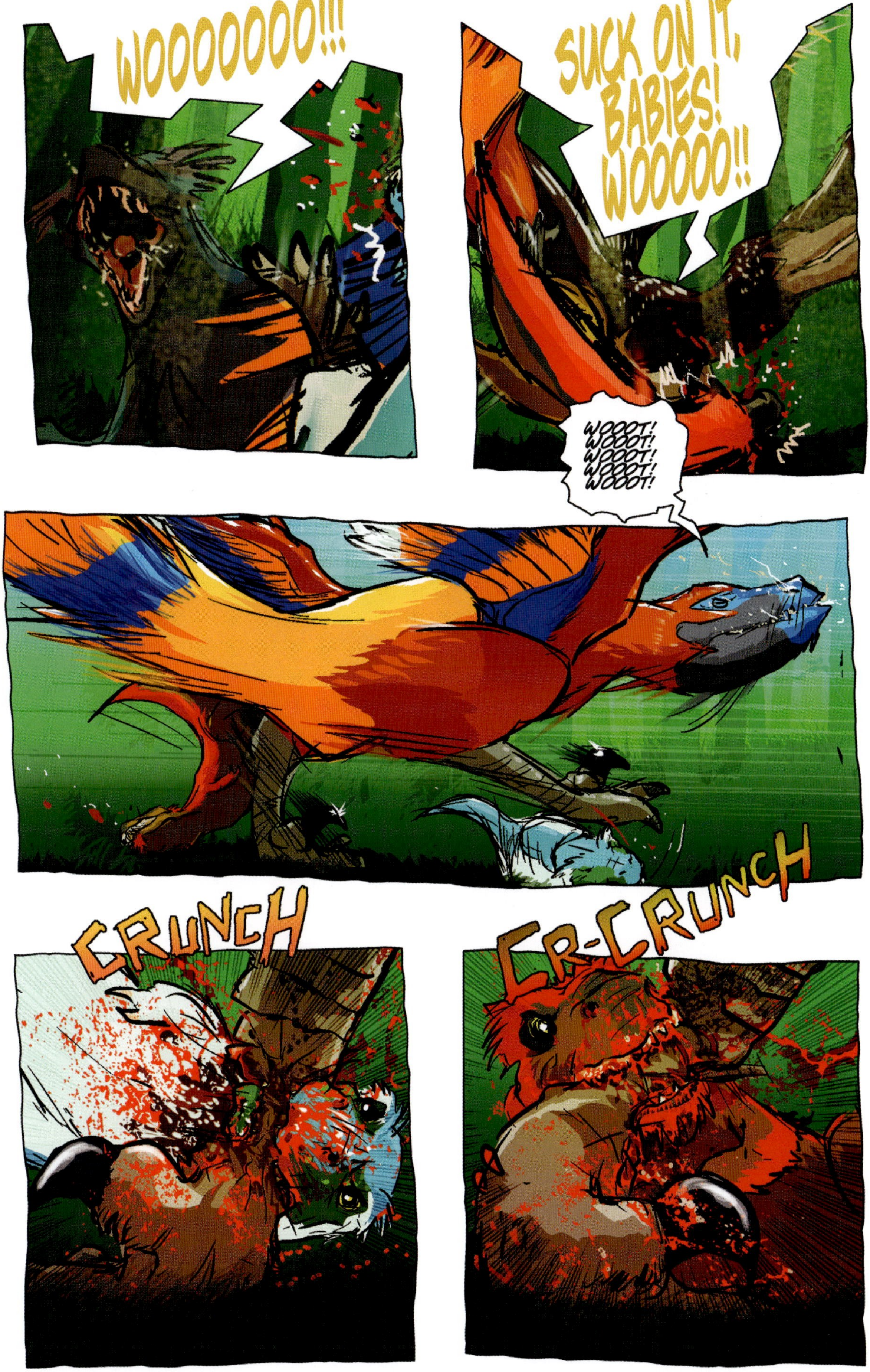
WOOOOOOO!!!
SUCK ON IT, BABIES! WOOOOO!!
WOOOT! WOOOT! WOOOT! WOOOT! WOOOT!
CRUNCH
CR-CRUNCH

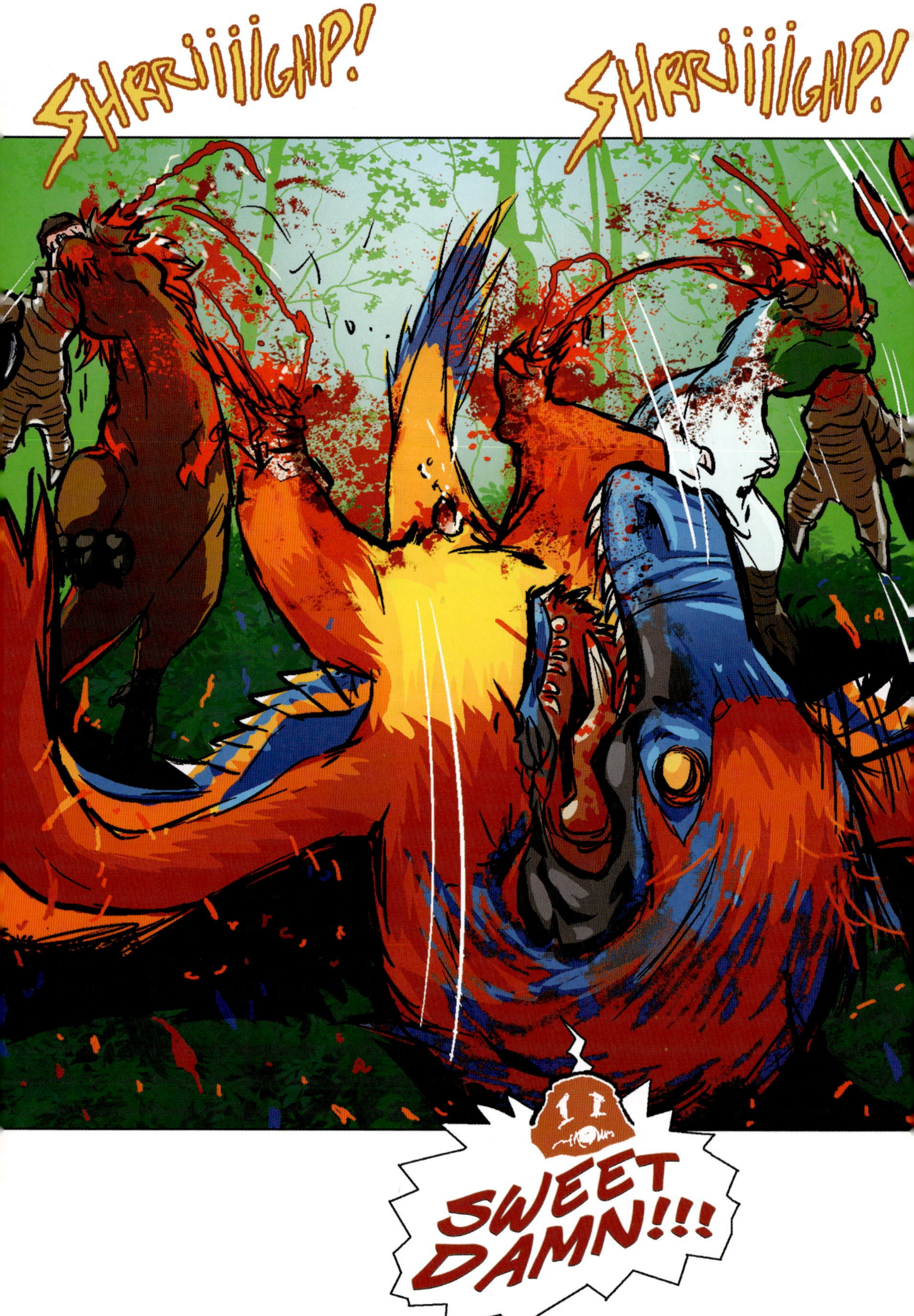
SHRRIIIIGHP!
SHRRIIIIGHP!
SWEET DAMN!!!

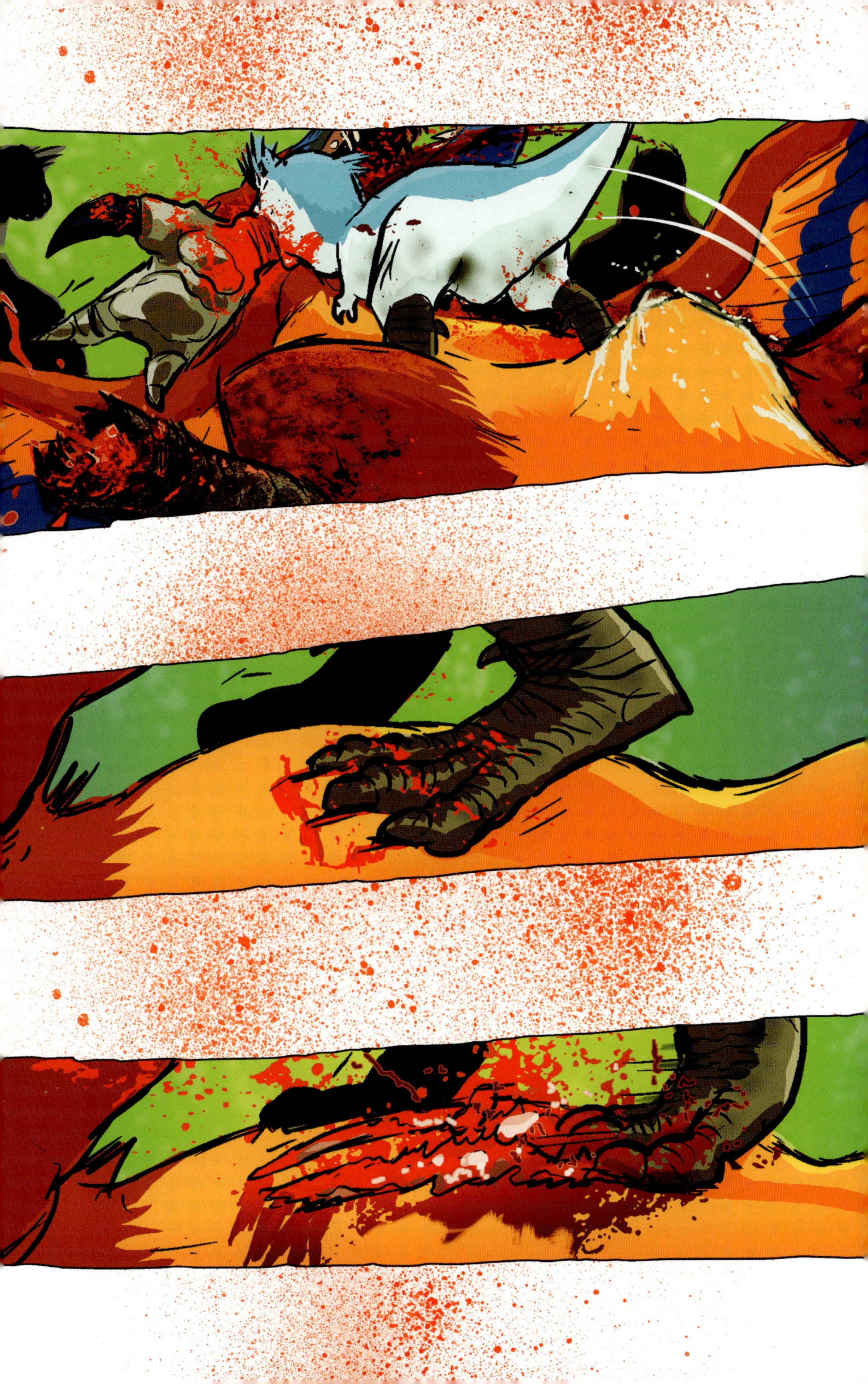

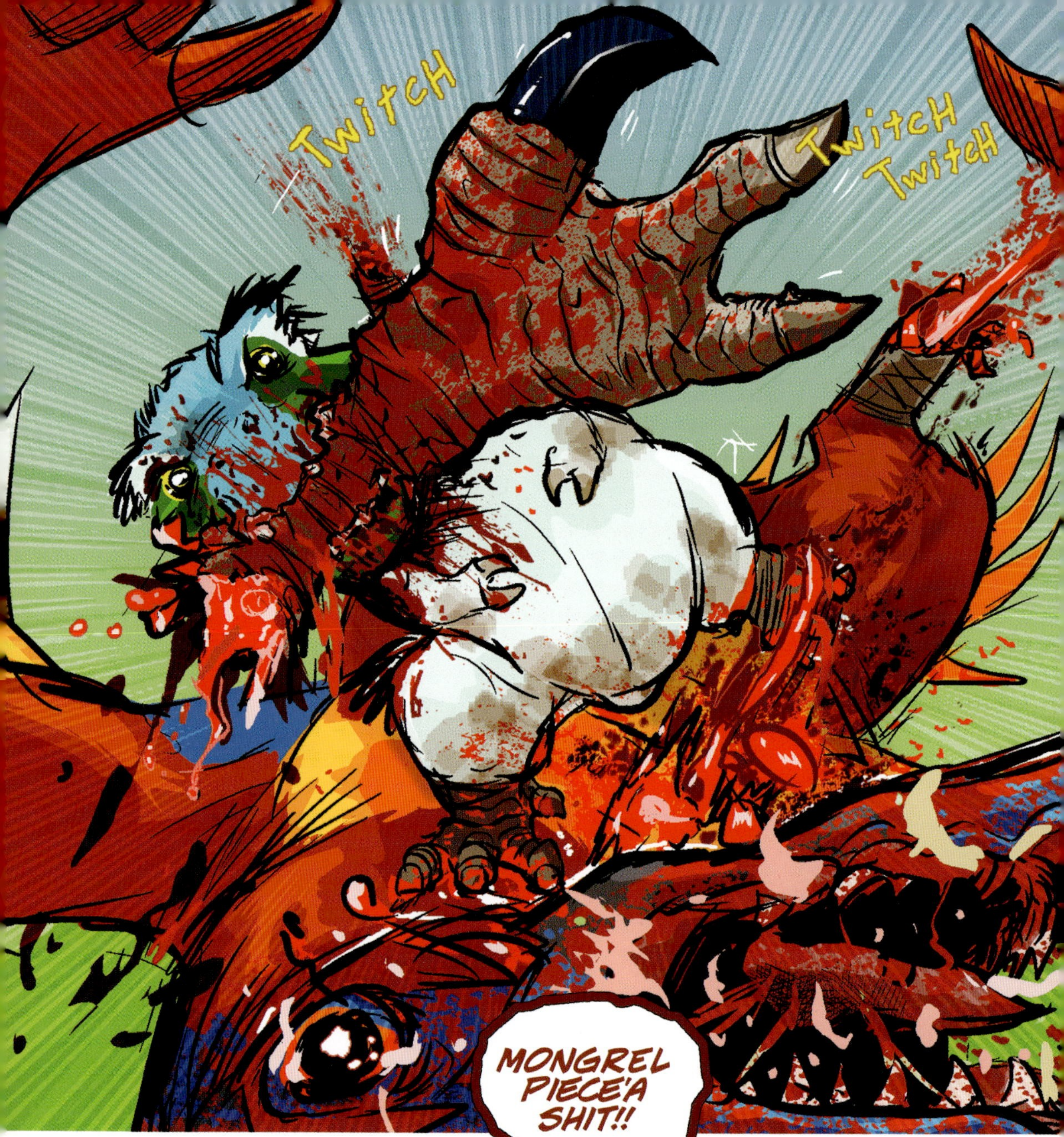
TWITCH
TWITCH
TWITCH
MONGREL PIECE'A SHIT!!
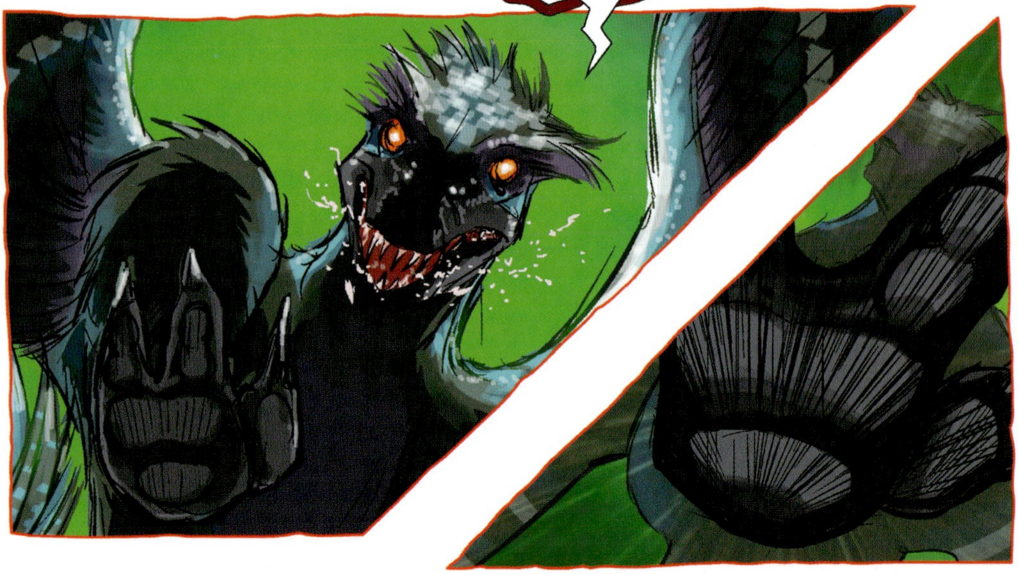

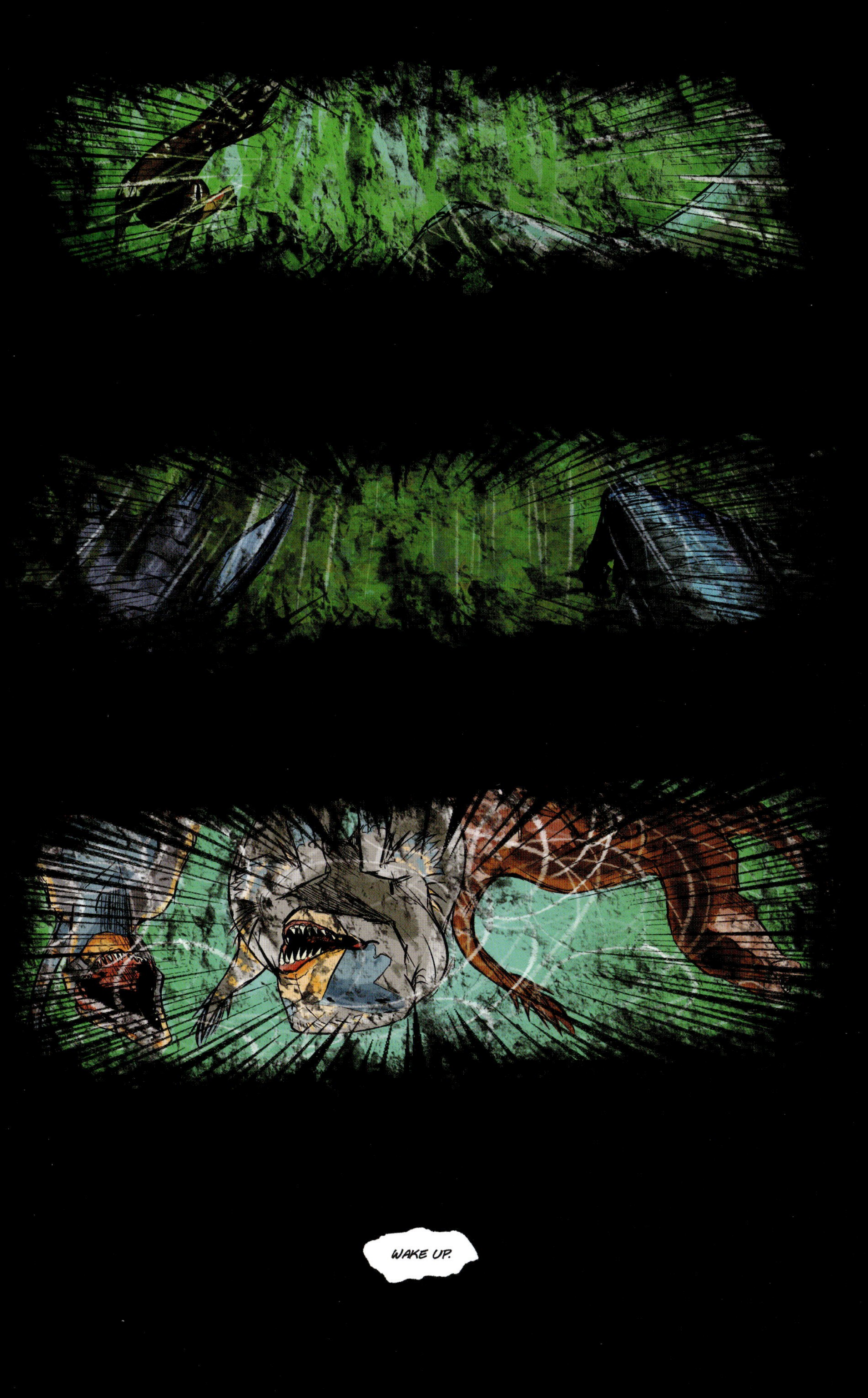
WAKE UP.

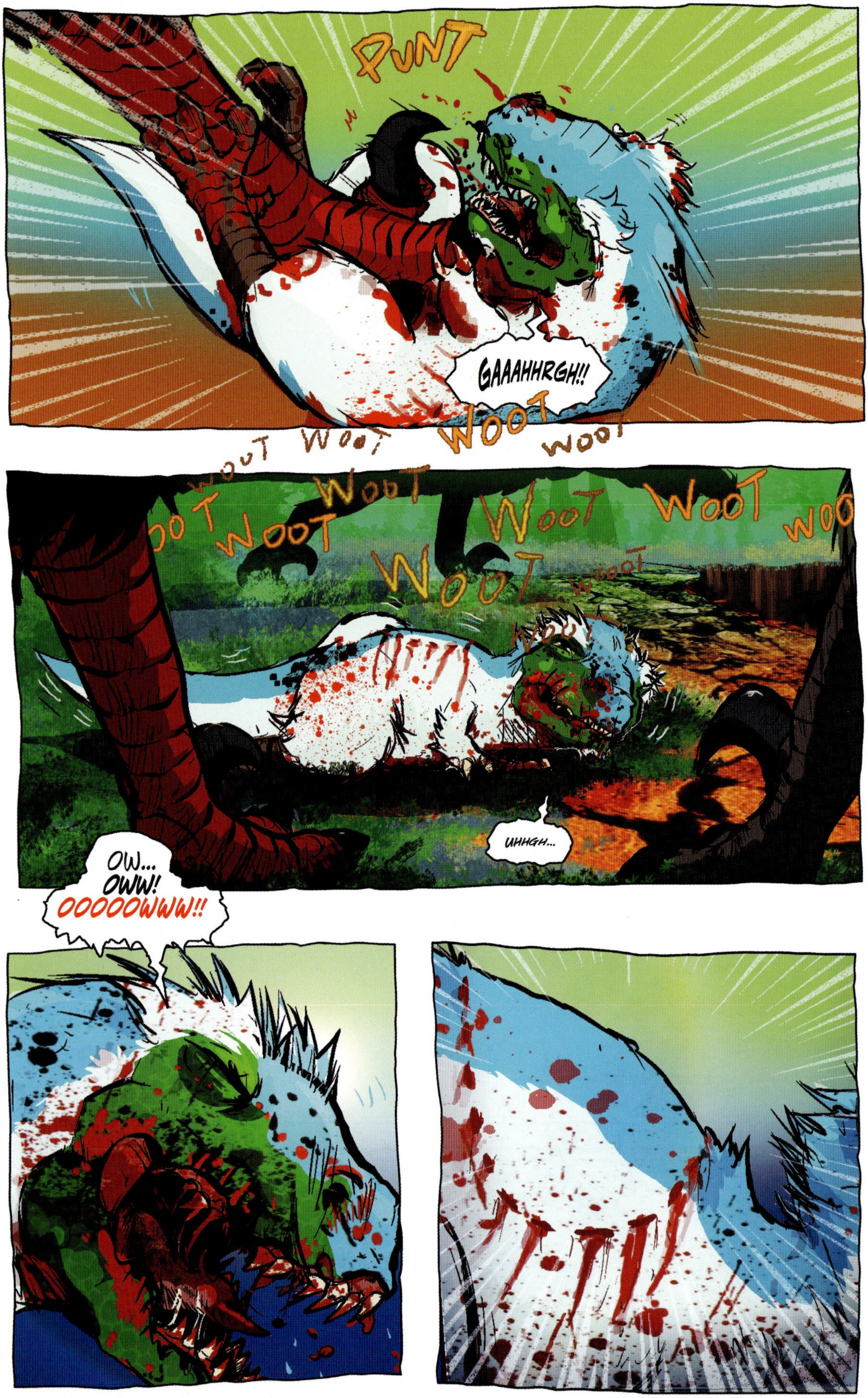
PUNT
GAAAHHRGH!!
WOOT WOOT WOOT WOOT
WOOT WOOT WOOT WOOT WOOT WOOT WOO WOOT
UHHGH...
OW... OWW! OOOOOWWW!!

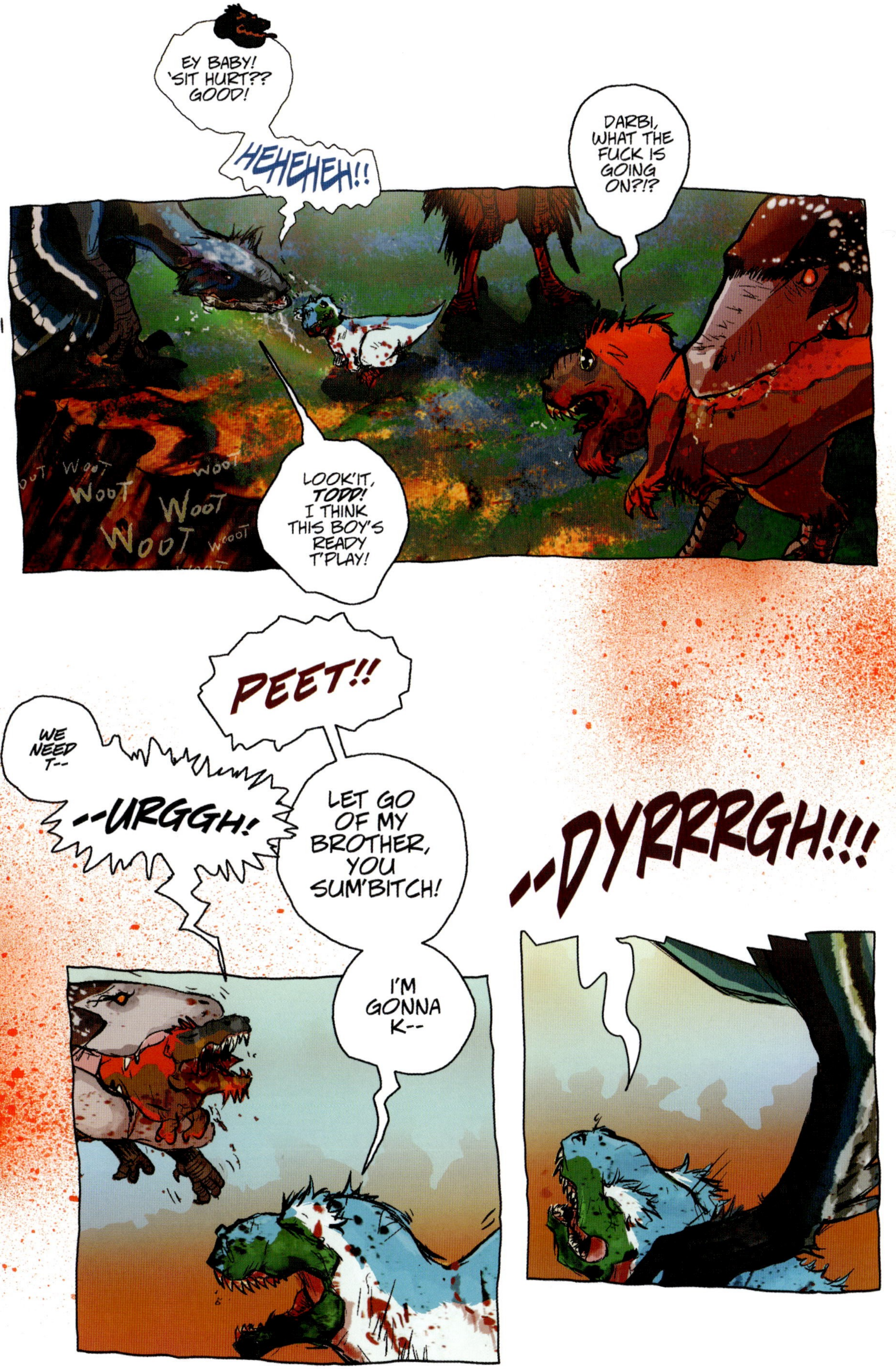
EY BABY! 'SIT HURT?? GOOD!
HEHEHEH!!
DARBI, WHAT THE FUCK IS GOING ON?!?
WOOT WOOT WOOT WOOT WOOT WOOT
LOOK'IT, TODD! I THINK THIS BOY'S READY T'PLAY!
WE NEED T--
--URGGH!
PEET!!
LET GO OF MY BROTHER, YOU SUM'BITCH!
I'M GONNA K--
--DYRRRGH!!!

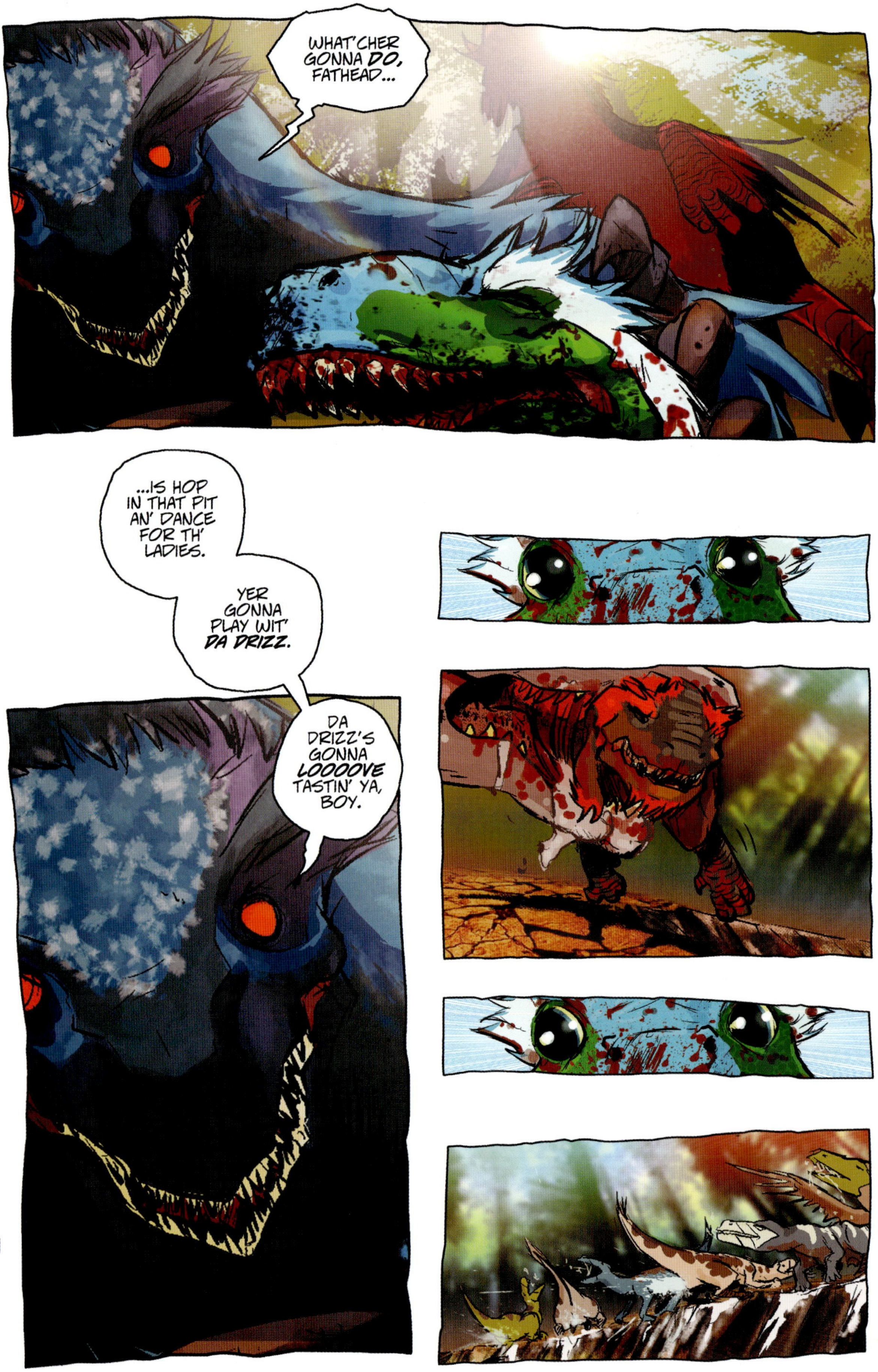
WHAT'CHER GONNA DO, FATHEAD...
...IS HOP IN THAT PIT AN' DANCE FOR TH' LADIES.
YER GONNA PLAY WIT' DA DRIZZ.
DA DRIZZ'S GONNA LOOOOVE TASTIN' YA, BOY.

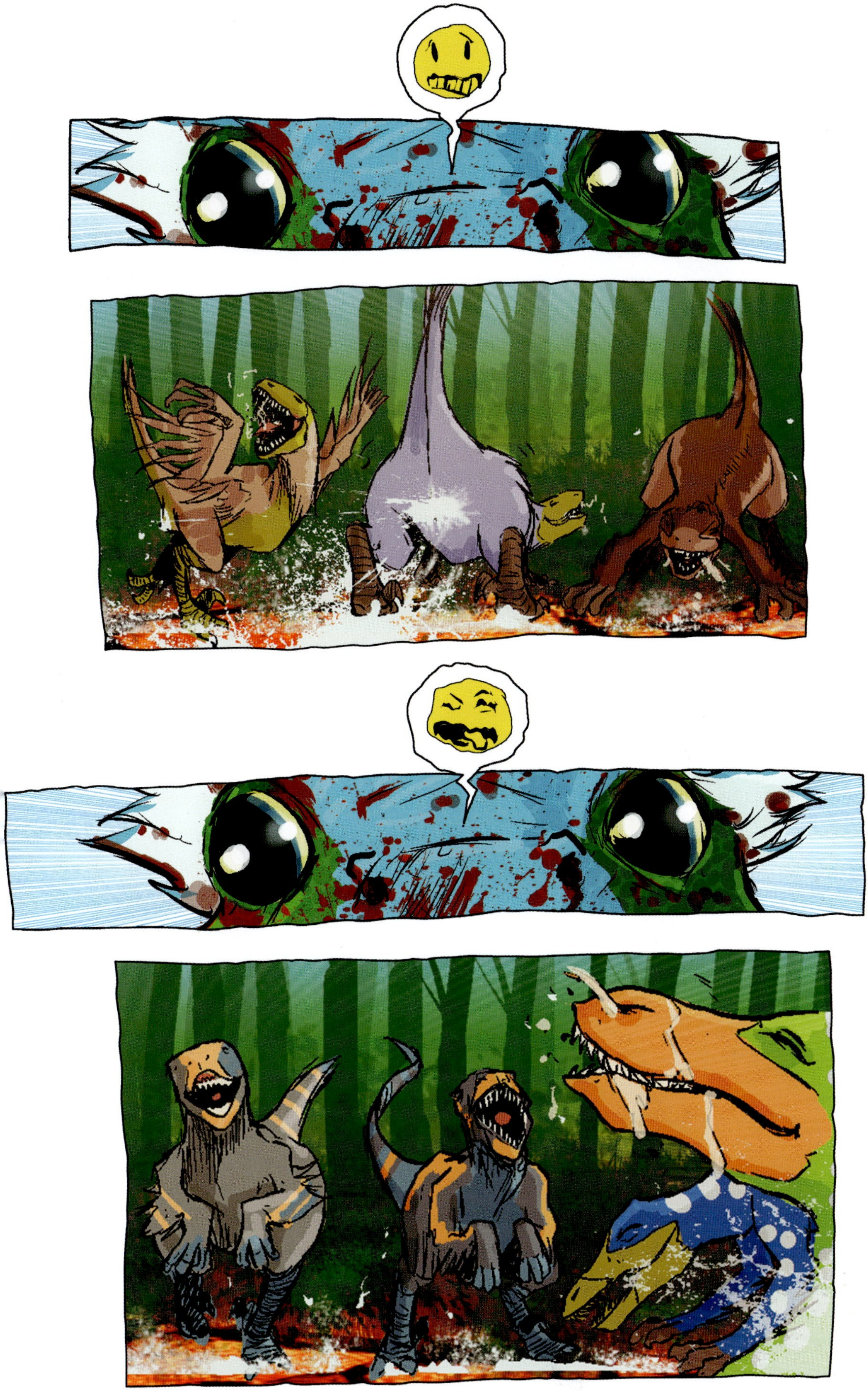

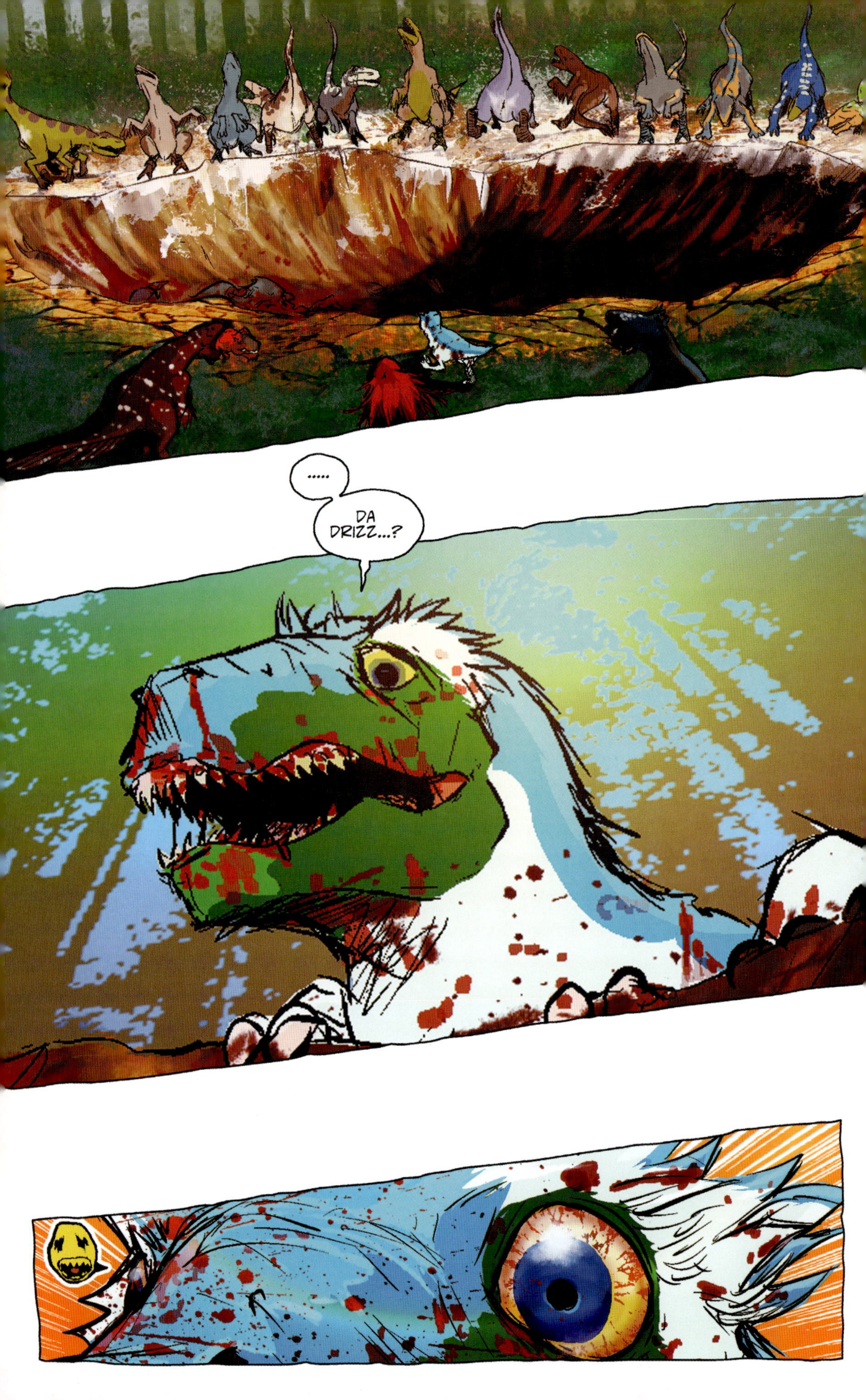
.....
DA DRIZZ...?

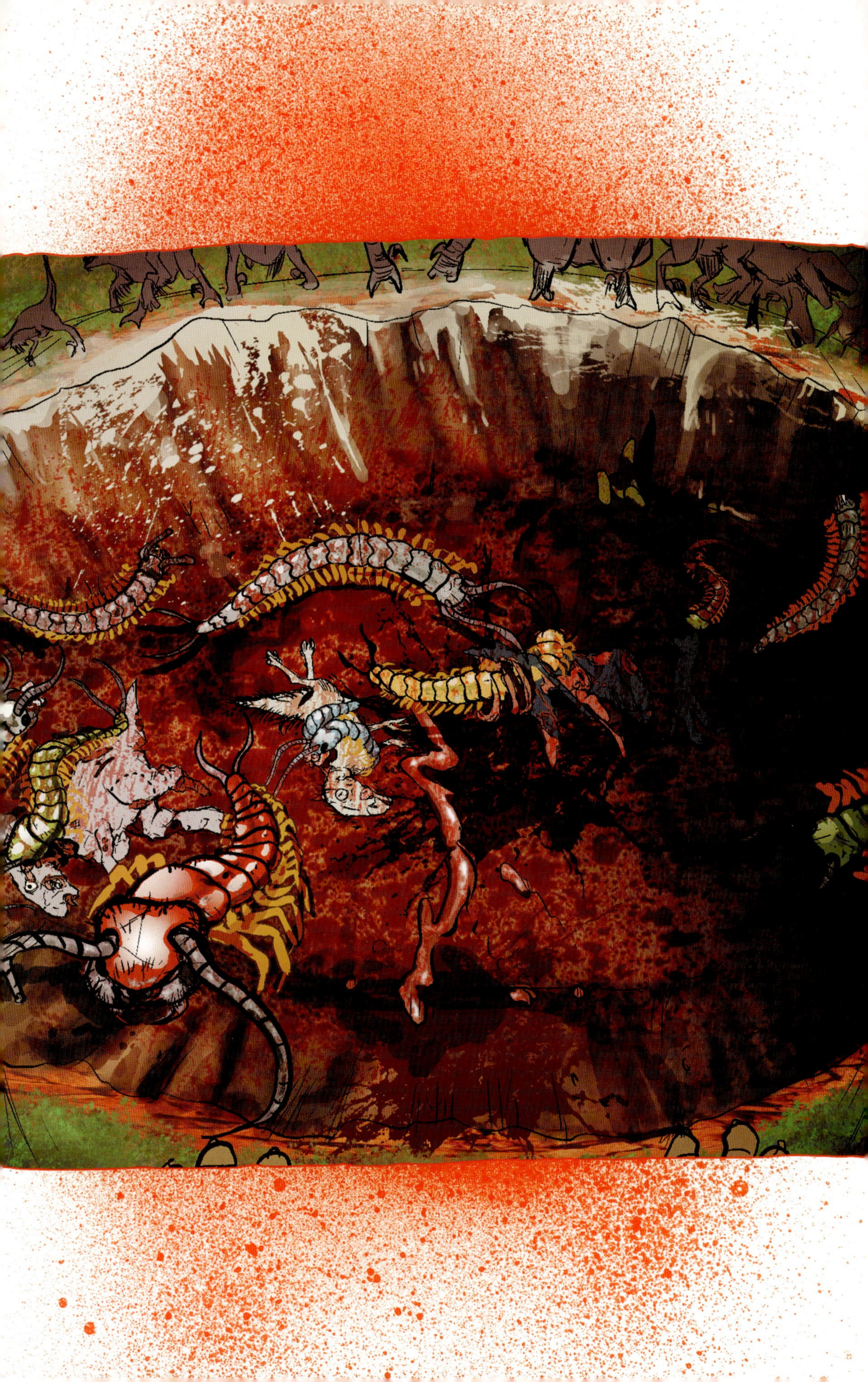

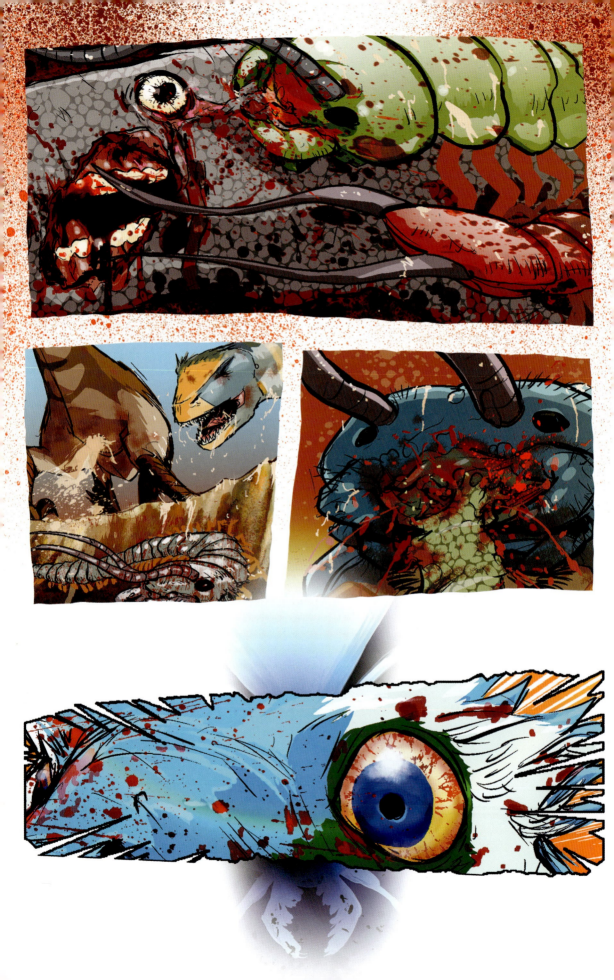

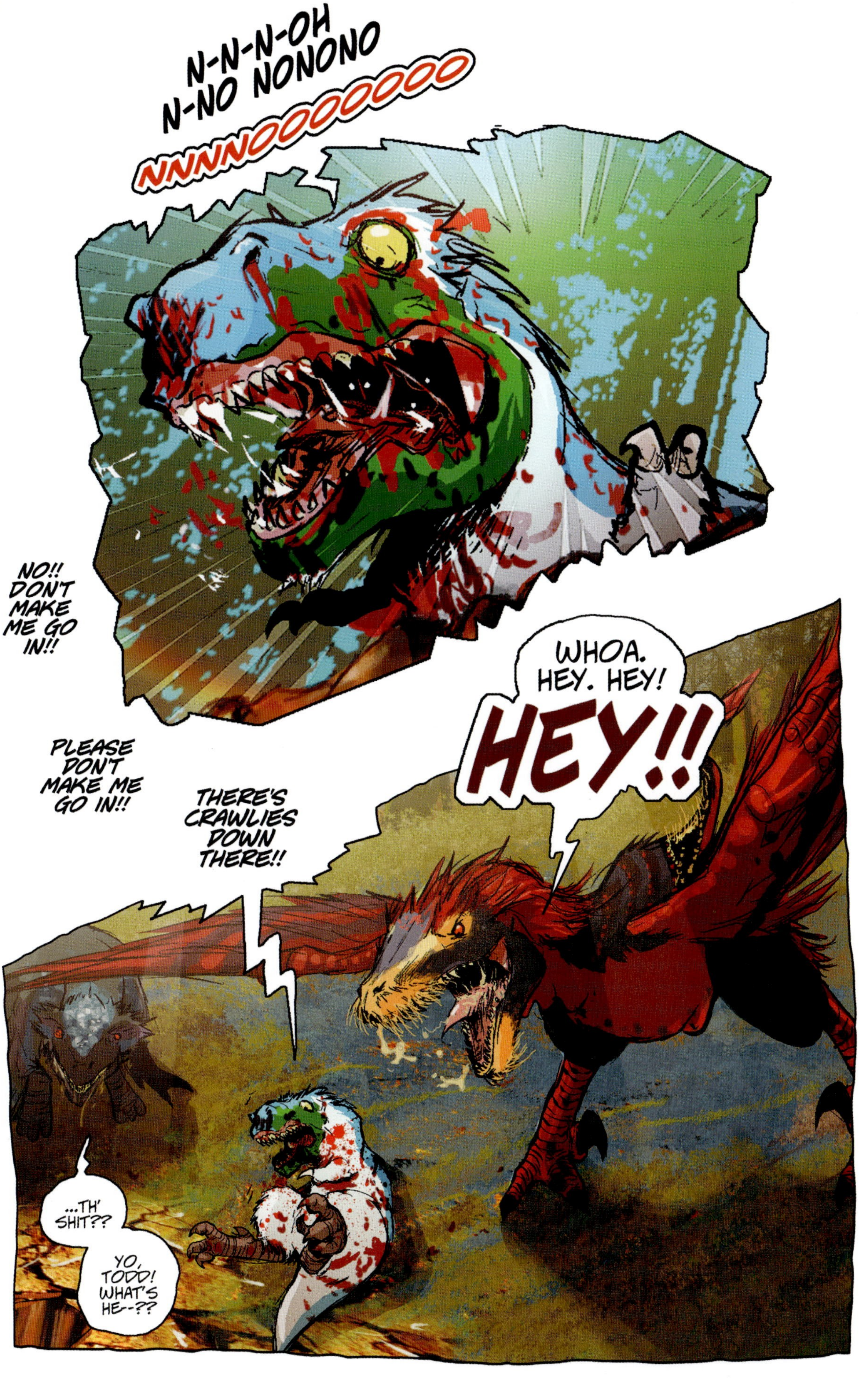
N-N-N-OH
N-NO NONONO
NNNNOOOOOOOO
NO!! DON'T MAKE ME GO IN!!
PLEASE DON'T MAKE ME GO IN!!
THERE'S CRAWLIES DOWN THERE!!
WHOA. HEY. HEY!
HEY!!
...TH' SHIT??
YO, TODD! WHAT'S HE--??

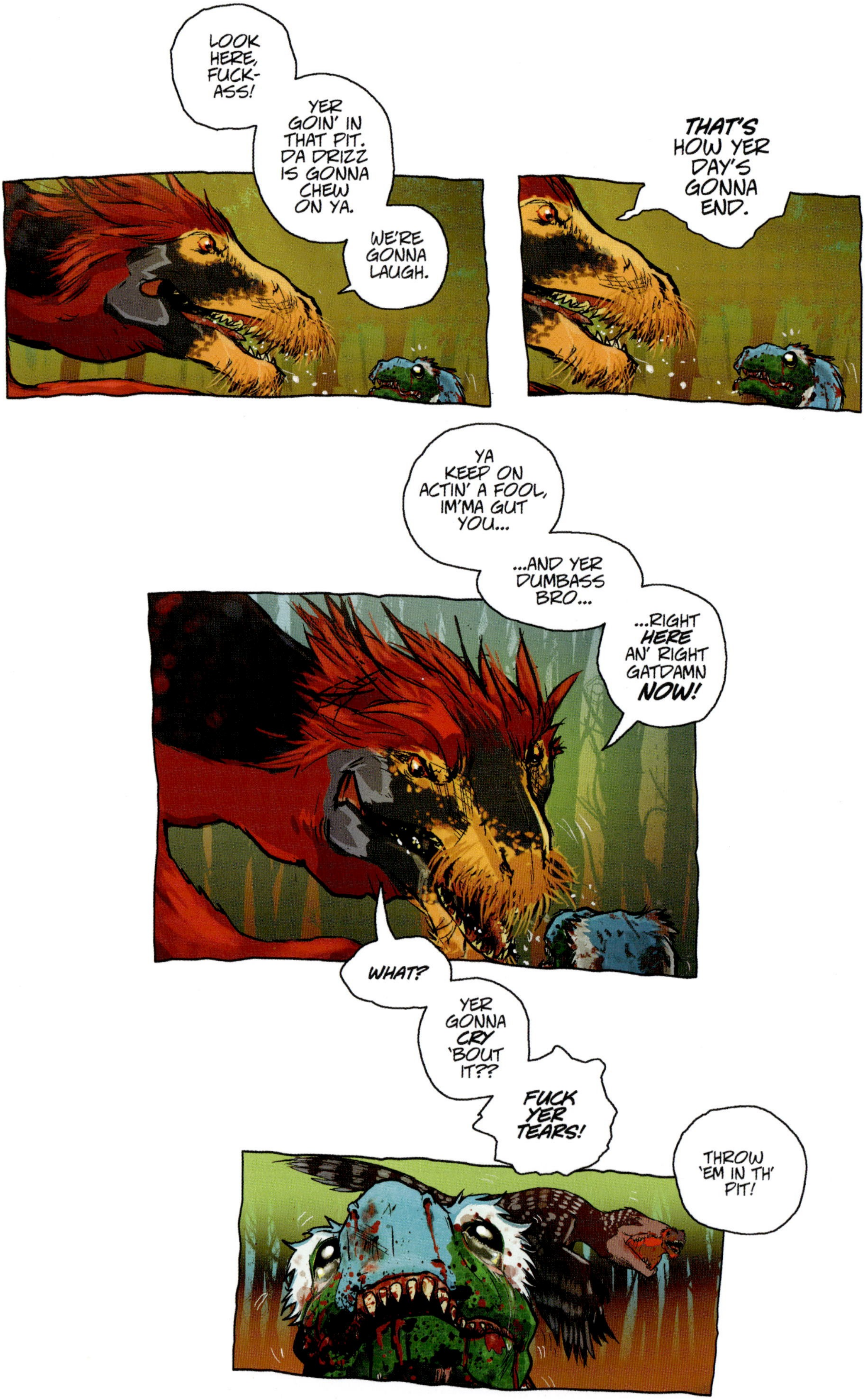
LOOK HERE, FUCK-ASS!
YER GOIN' IN THAT PIT. DA DRIZZ IS GONNA CHEW ON YA.
WE'RE GONNA LAUGH.
THAT'S HOW YER DAY'S GONNA END.
YA KEEP ON ACTIN' A FOOL, IM'MA GUT YOU...
...AND YER DUMBASS BRO...
...RIGHT HERE AN' RIGHT GATDAMN NOW!
WHAT?
YER GONNA CRY 'BOUT IT??
FUCK YER TEARS!
THROW 'EM IN TH' PIT!

GO FETCH.

G'ON NOW!

BOOT!

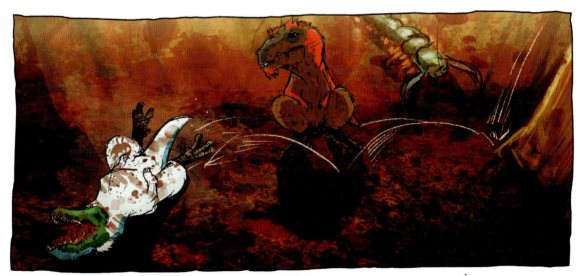

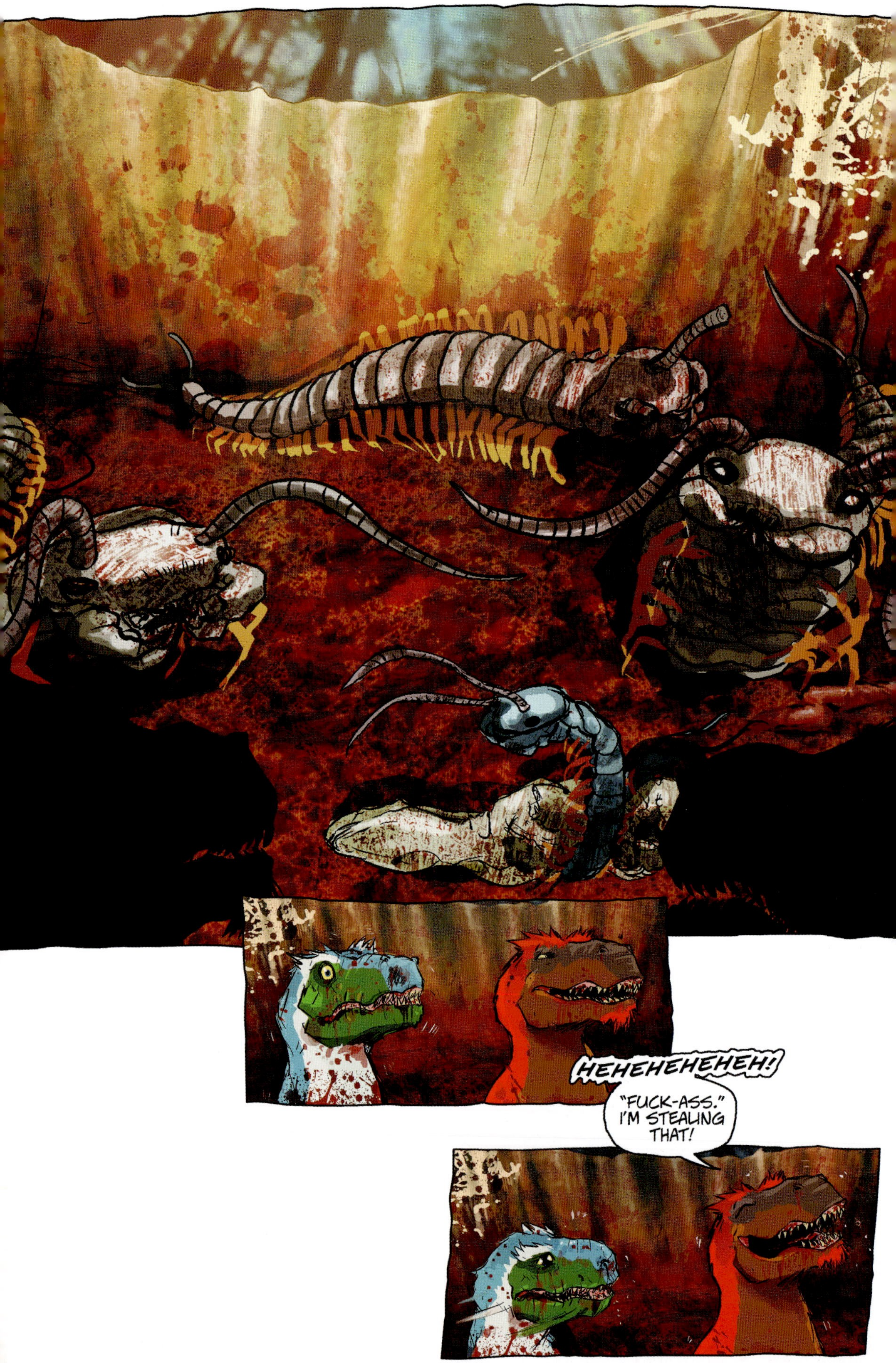
HEHEHEHEHEHEH!
"FUCK-ASS." I'M STEALING THAT!

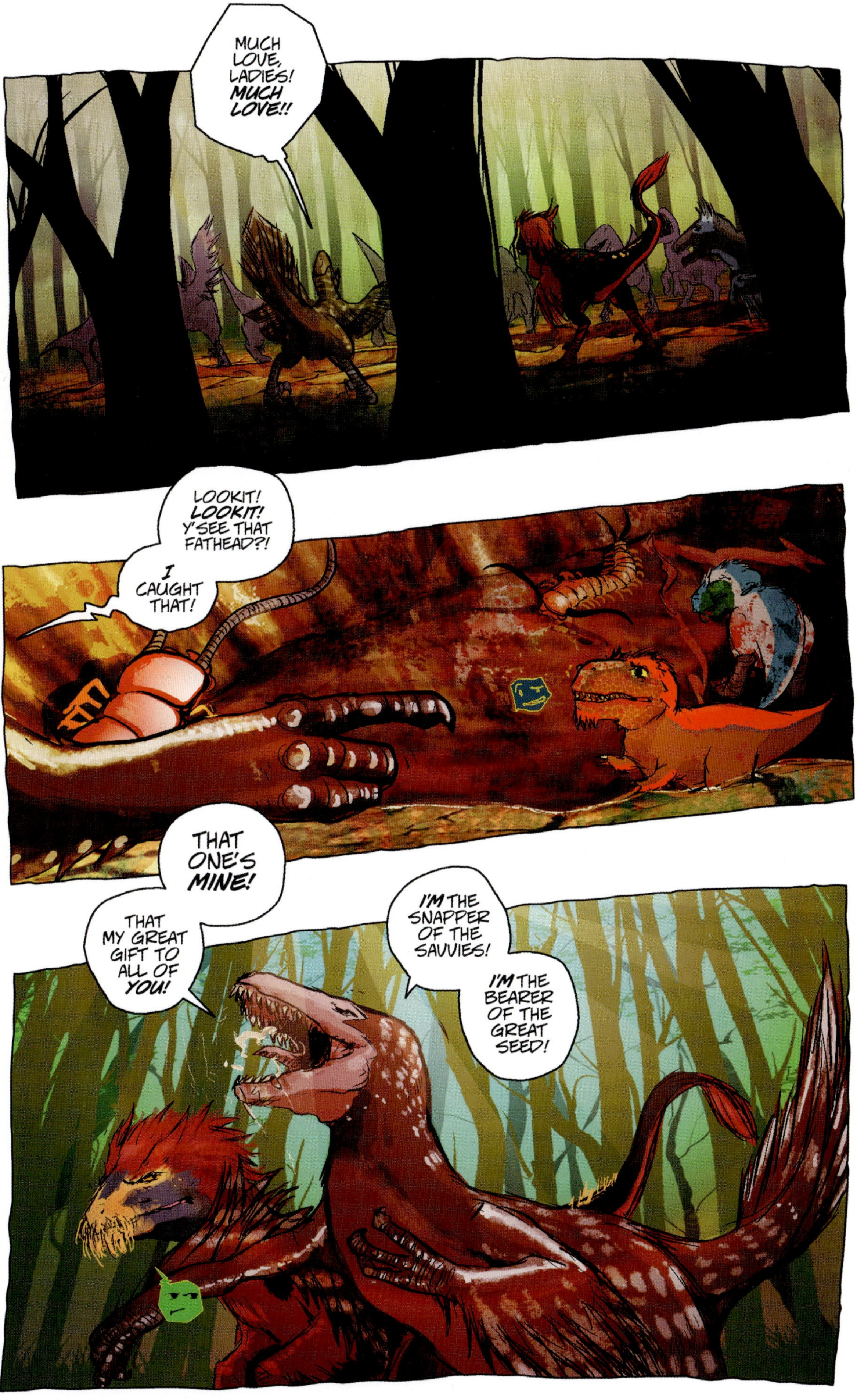
MUCH LOVE, LADIES! MUCH LOVE!!
LOOKIT! LOOKIT! Y'SEE THAT FATHEAD?!
I CAUGHT THAT!
THAT ONE'S MINE!
THAT MY GREAT GIFT TO ALL OF YOU!
I'M THE SNAPPER OF THE SAUVIES!
I'M THE BEARER OF THE GREAT SEED!

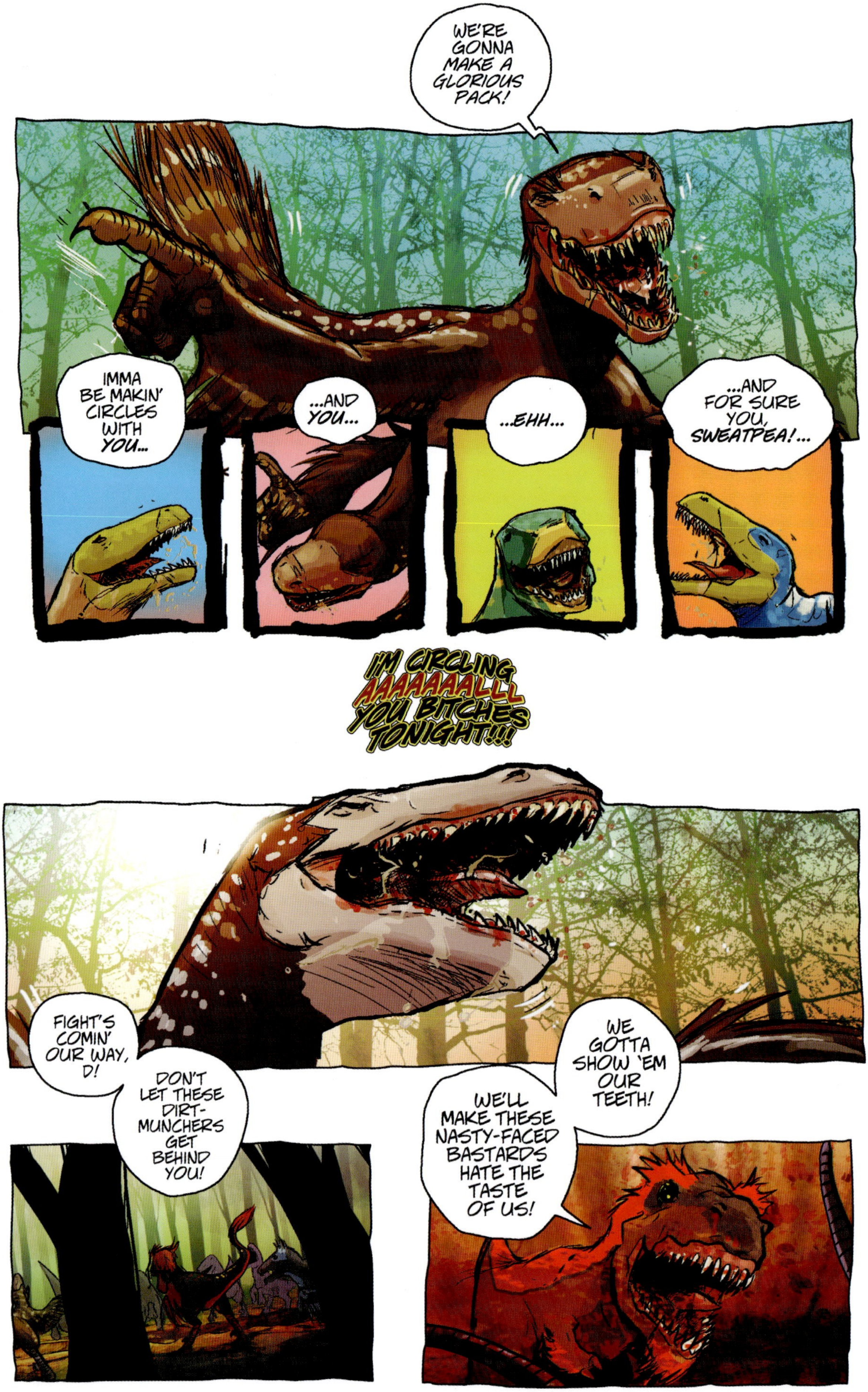
WE'RE GONNA MAKE A GLORIOUS PACK!
IMMA BE MAKIN' CIRCLES WITH YOU...
...AND YOU...
...EHH...
...AND FOR SURE YOU, SWEATPEA!...
I'M CIRCLING AAAAAAALLL YOU BITCHES TONIGHT!!!
FIGHT'S COMIN' OUR WAY, D!
DON'T LET THESE DIRT-MUNCHERS GET BEHIND YOU!
WE GOTTA SHOW 'EM OUR TEETH!
WE'LL MAKE THESE NASTY-FACED BASTARDS HATE THE TASTE OF US!

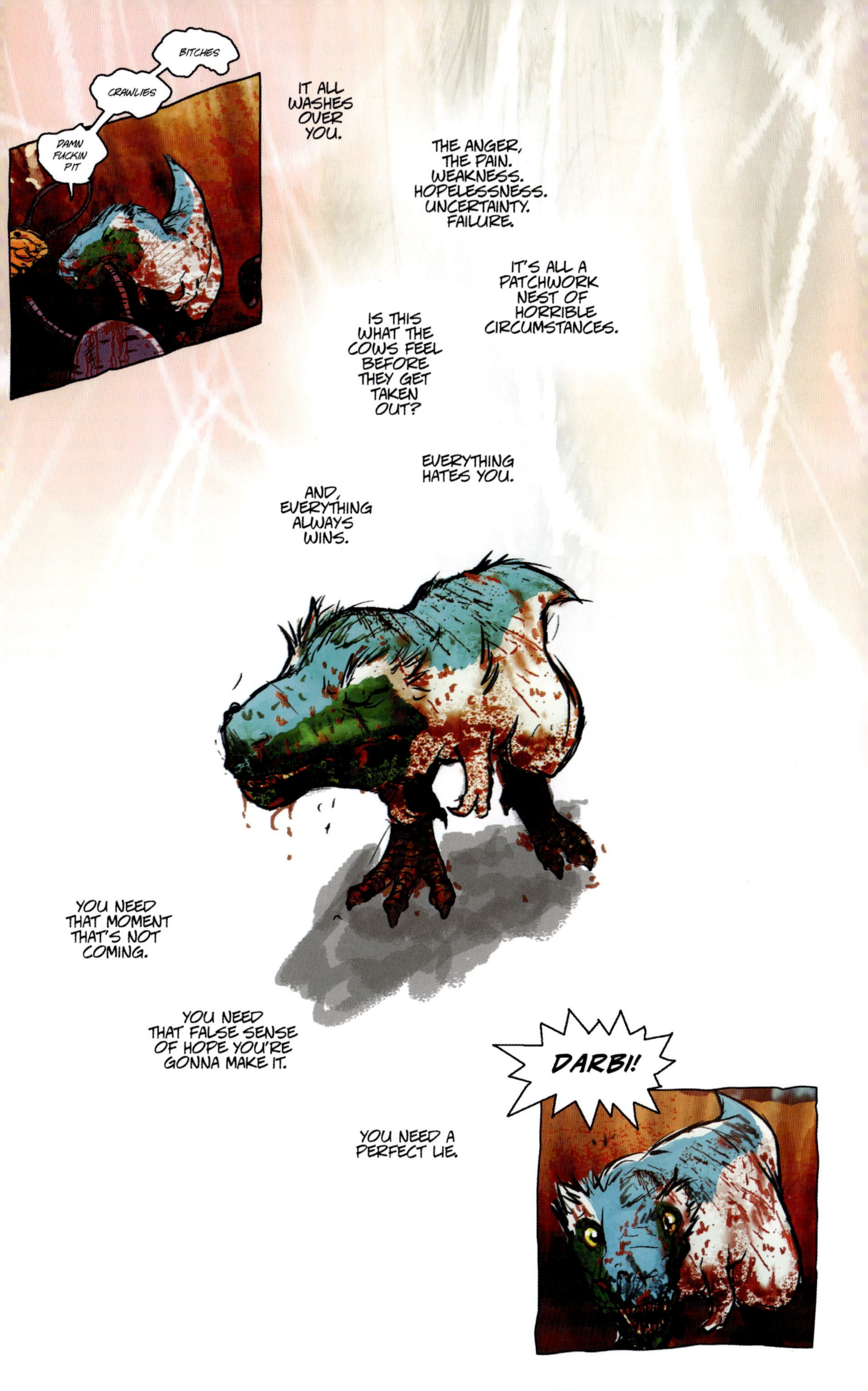
DAMN FUCKIN PIT
CRAWLIES
BITCHES
IT ALL WASHES OVER YOU.
THE ANGER, THE PAIN. WEAKNESS. HOPELESSNESS. UNCERTAINTY. FAILURE.
IT'S ALL A PATCHWORK NEST OF HORRIBLE CIRCUMSTANCES.
IS THIS WHAT THE COWS FEEL BEFORE THEY GET TAKEN OUT?
EVERYTHING HATES YOU.
AND, EVERYTHING ALWAYS WINS.
YOU NEED THAT MOMENT THAT'S NOT COMING.
YOU NEED THAT FALSE SENSE OF HOPE YOU'RE GONNA MAKE IT.
DARBI!
YOU NEED A PERFECT LIE.

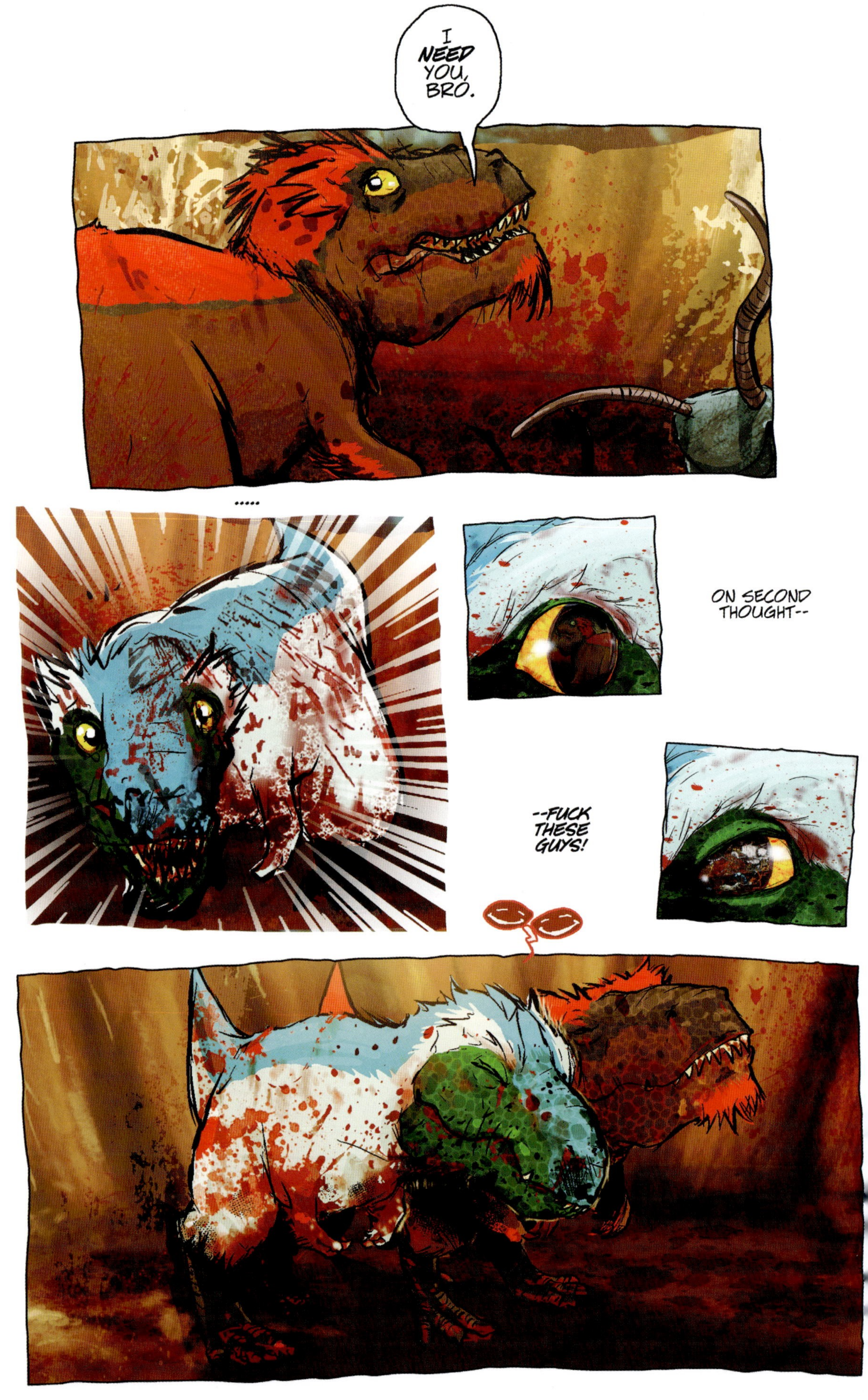
I NEED YOU, BRO.
.....
ON SECOND THOUGHT--
--FUCK THESE GUYS!

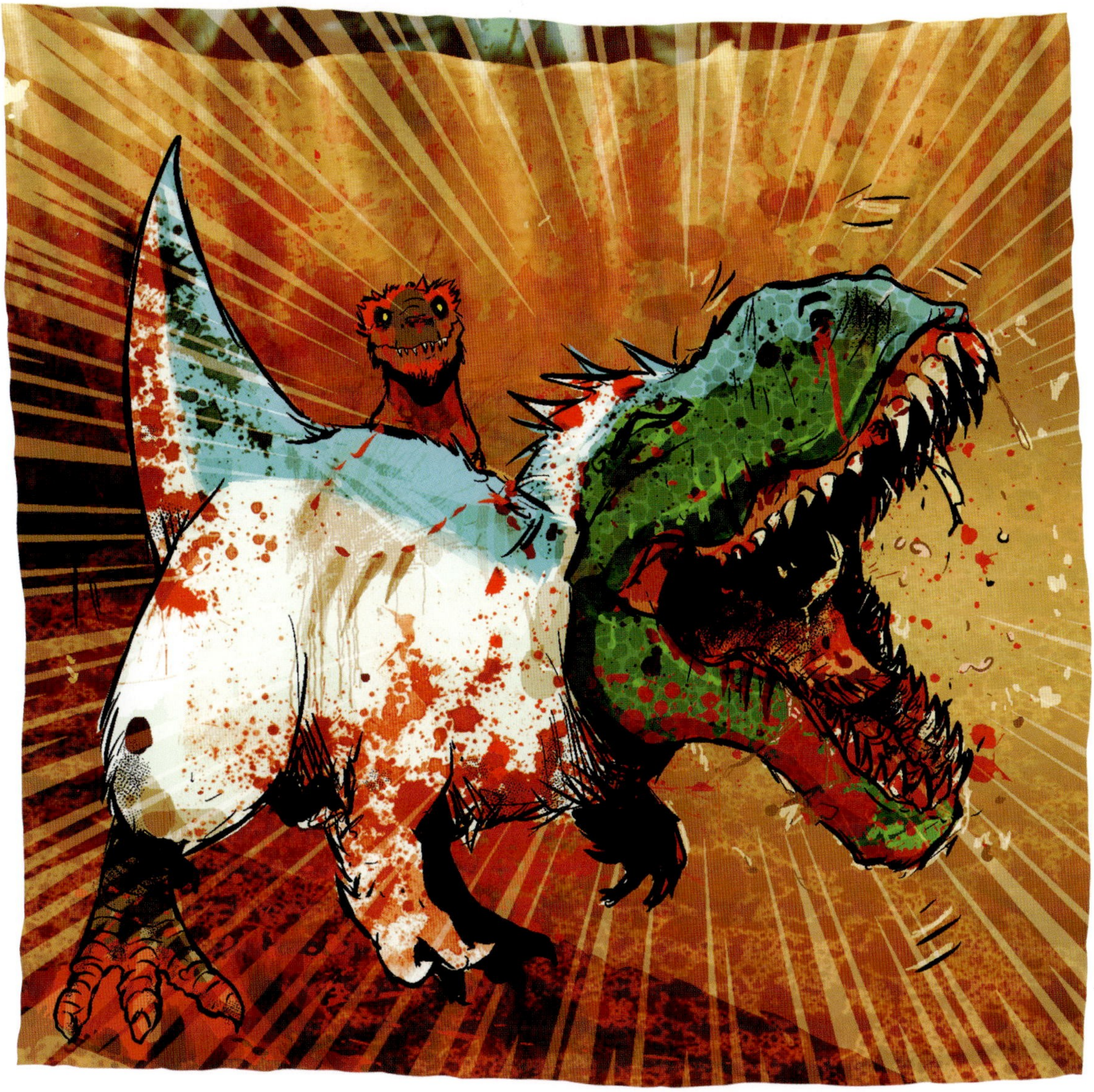

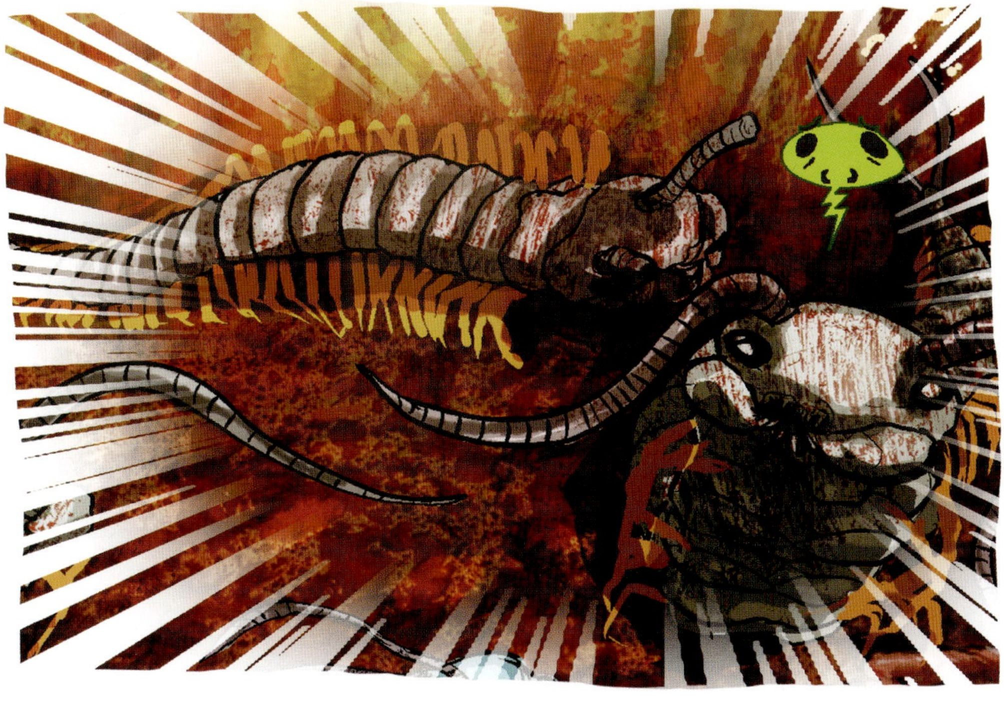

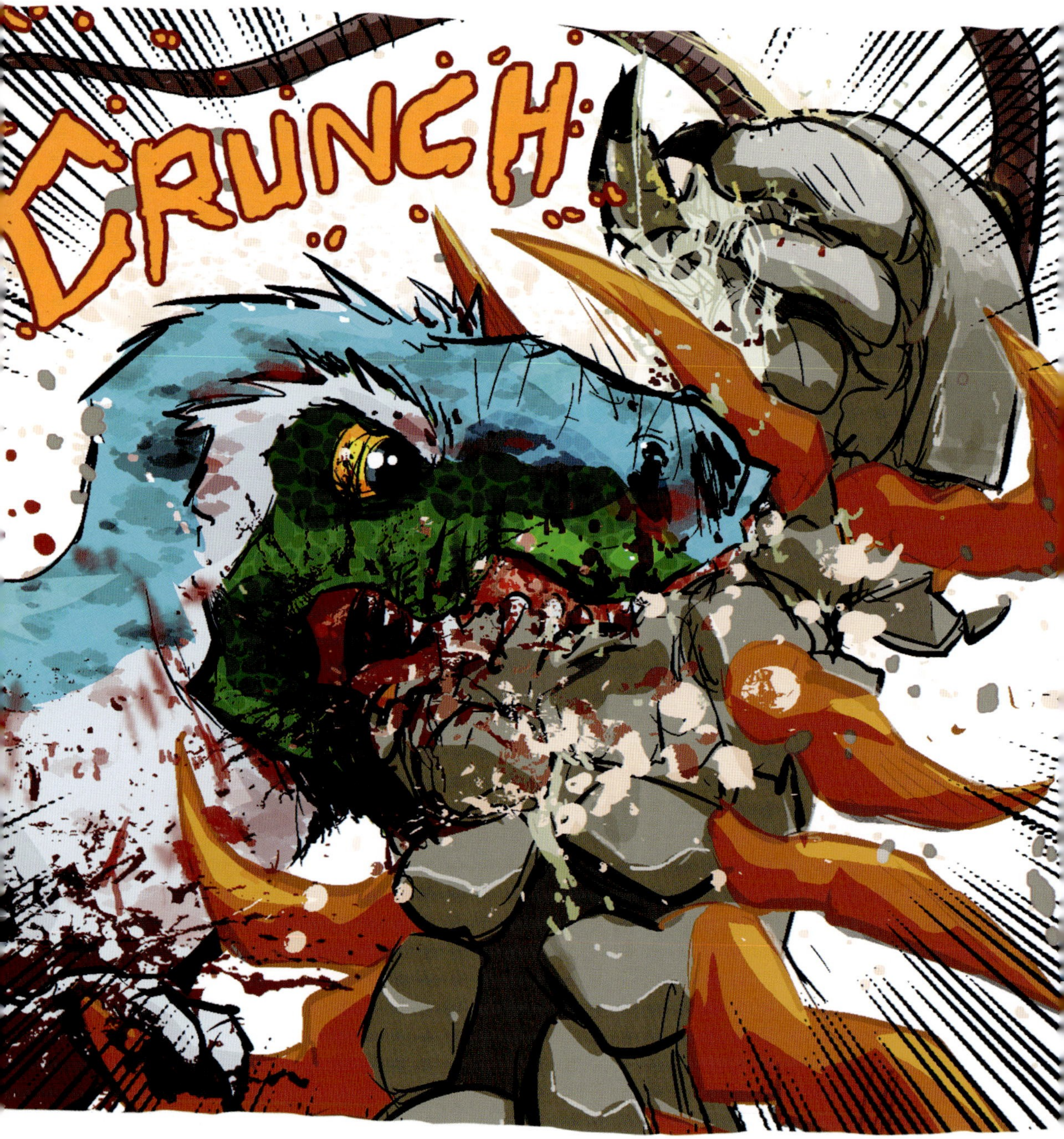
CRUNCH

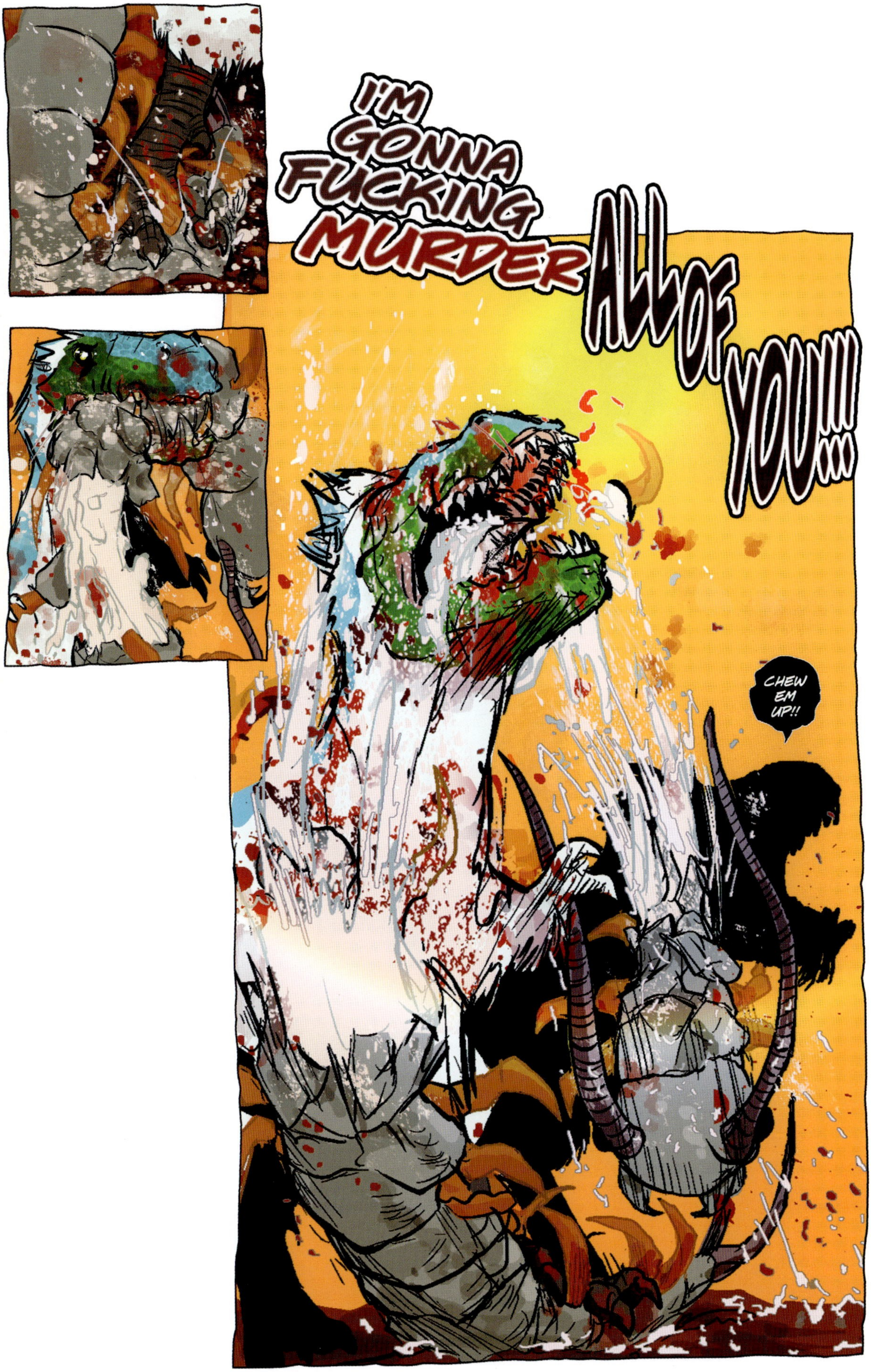
I'M GONNA FUCKING MURDER ALL OF YOU!!!
CHEW EM UP!!

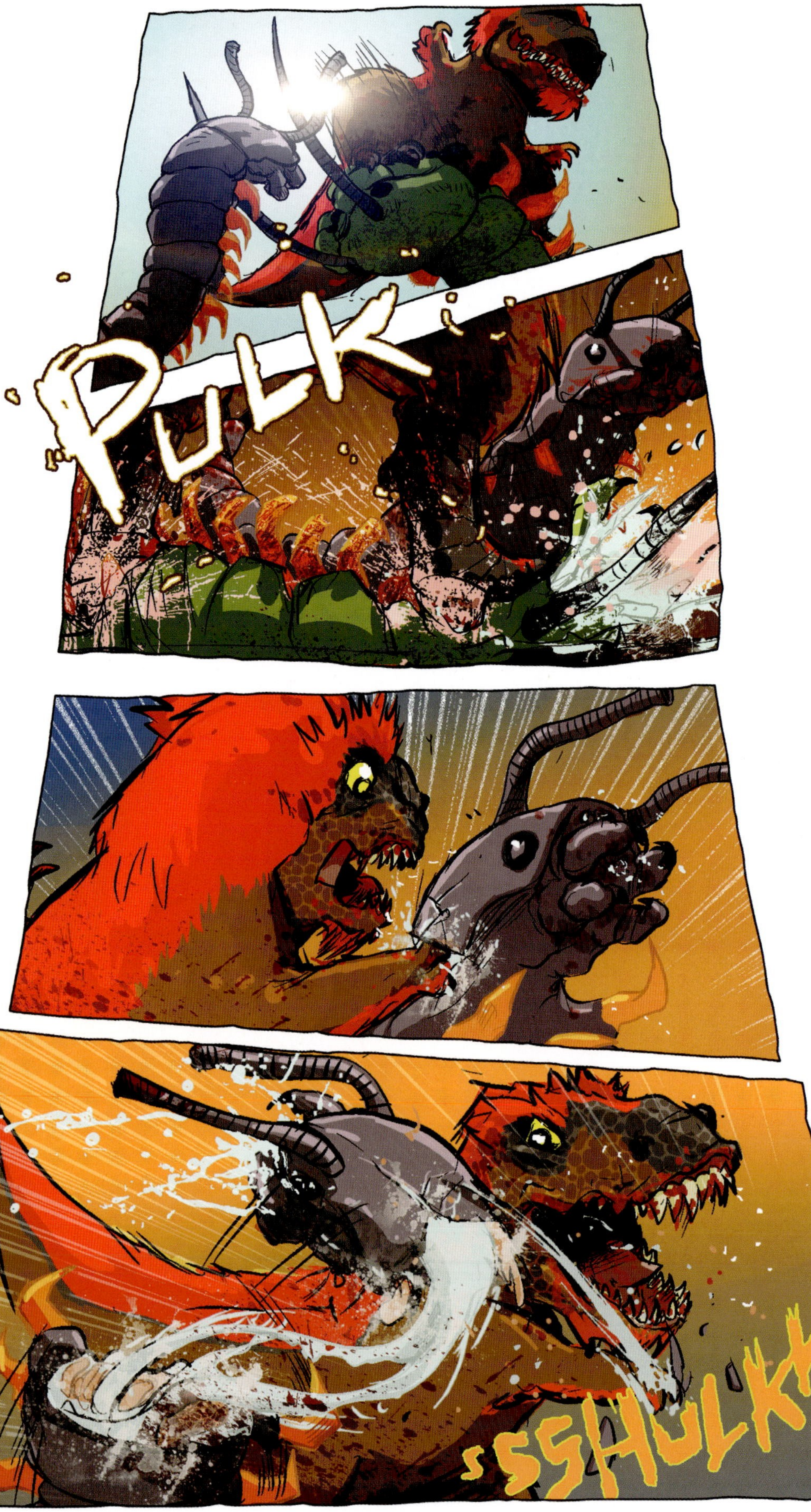
PULK
sSSHULKK

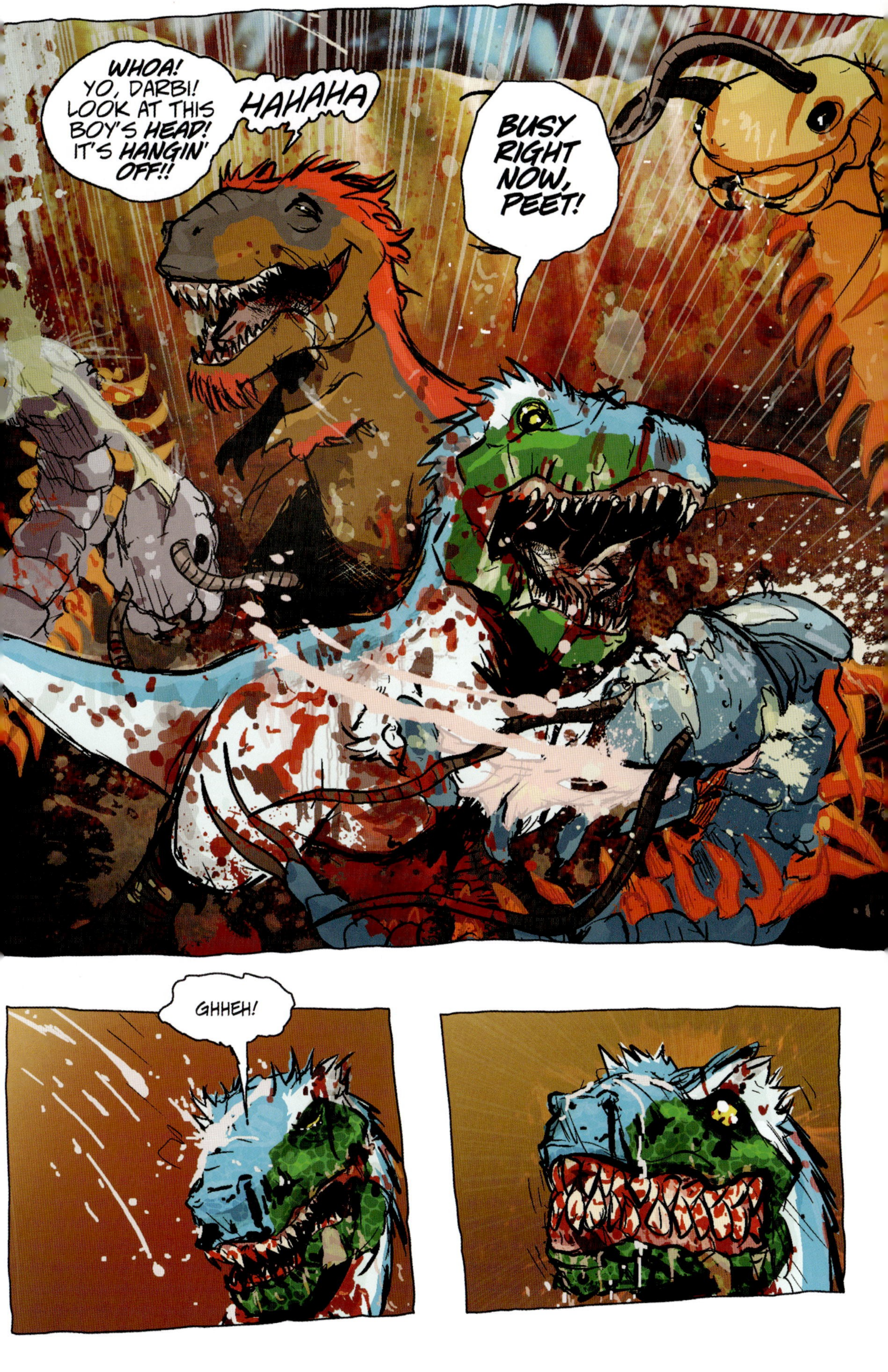
WHOA! YO, DARBI! LOOK AT THIS BOY'S HEAD! IT'S HANGIN' OFF!!
HAHAHA
BUSY RIGHT NOW, PEET!
GHHEH!

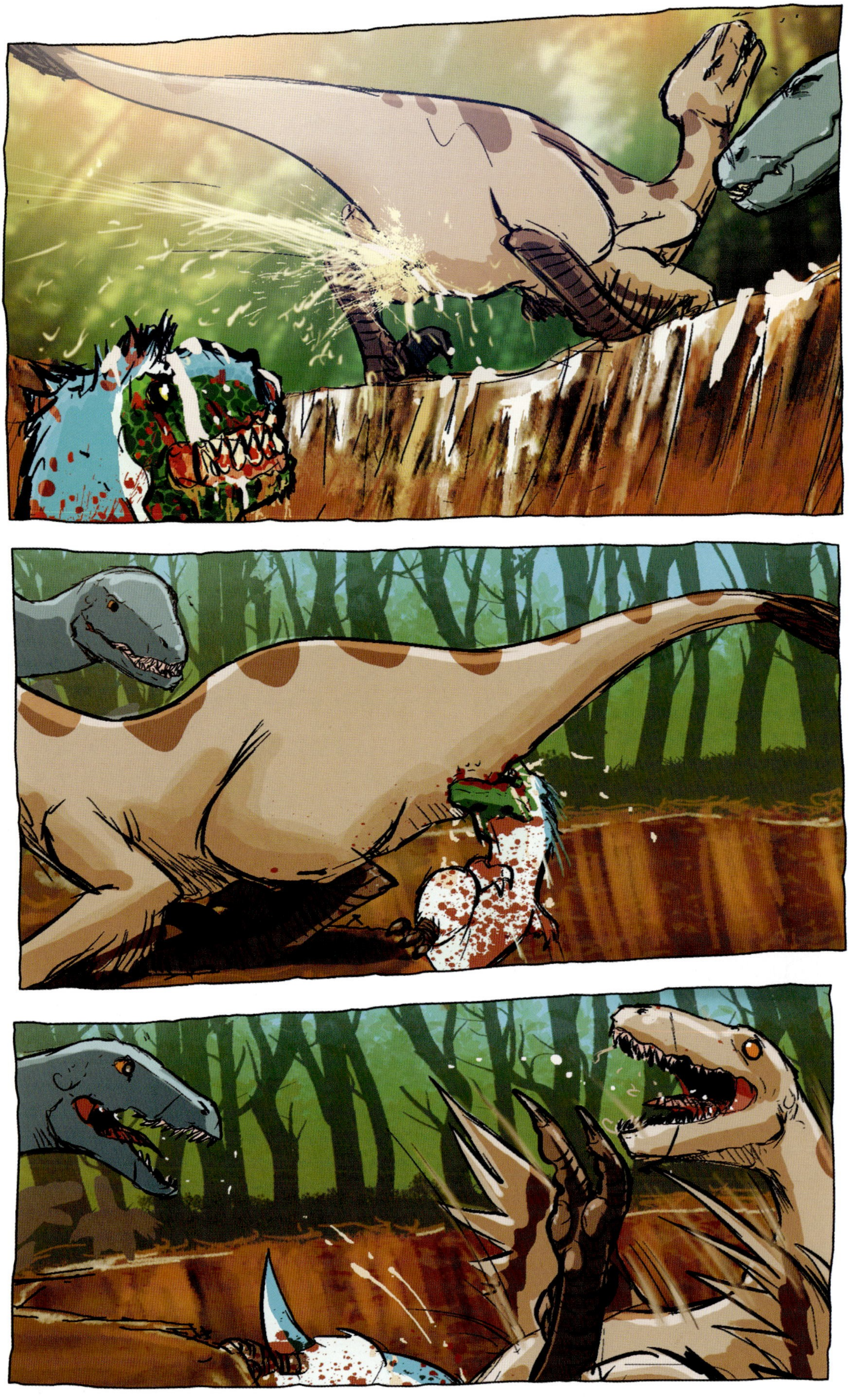

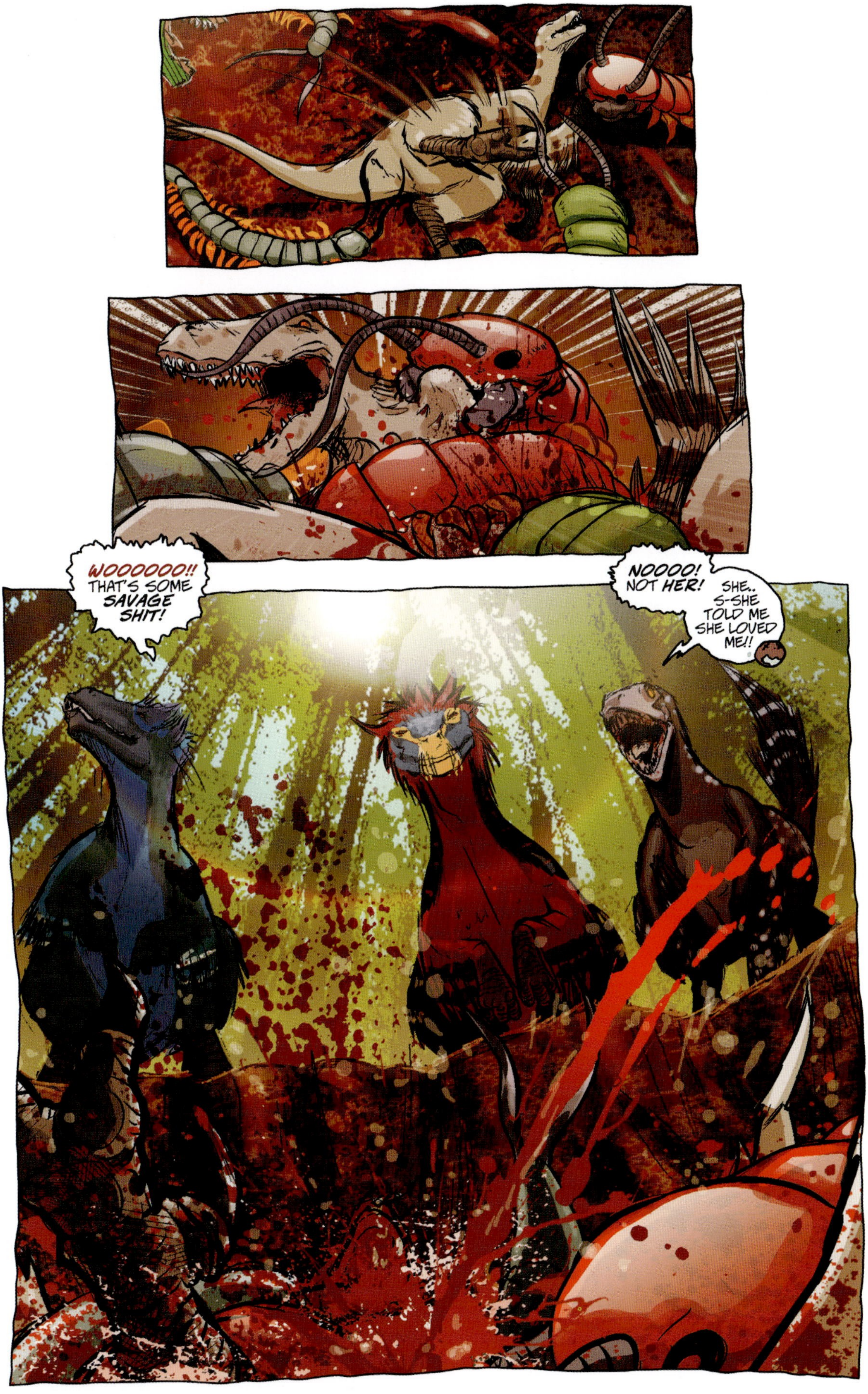
WOOOOOO!! THAT'S SOME SAVAGE SHIT!
NOOOO! NOT HER!
SHE.. S-SHE TOLD ME SHE LOVED ME!!

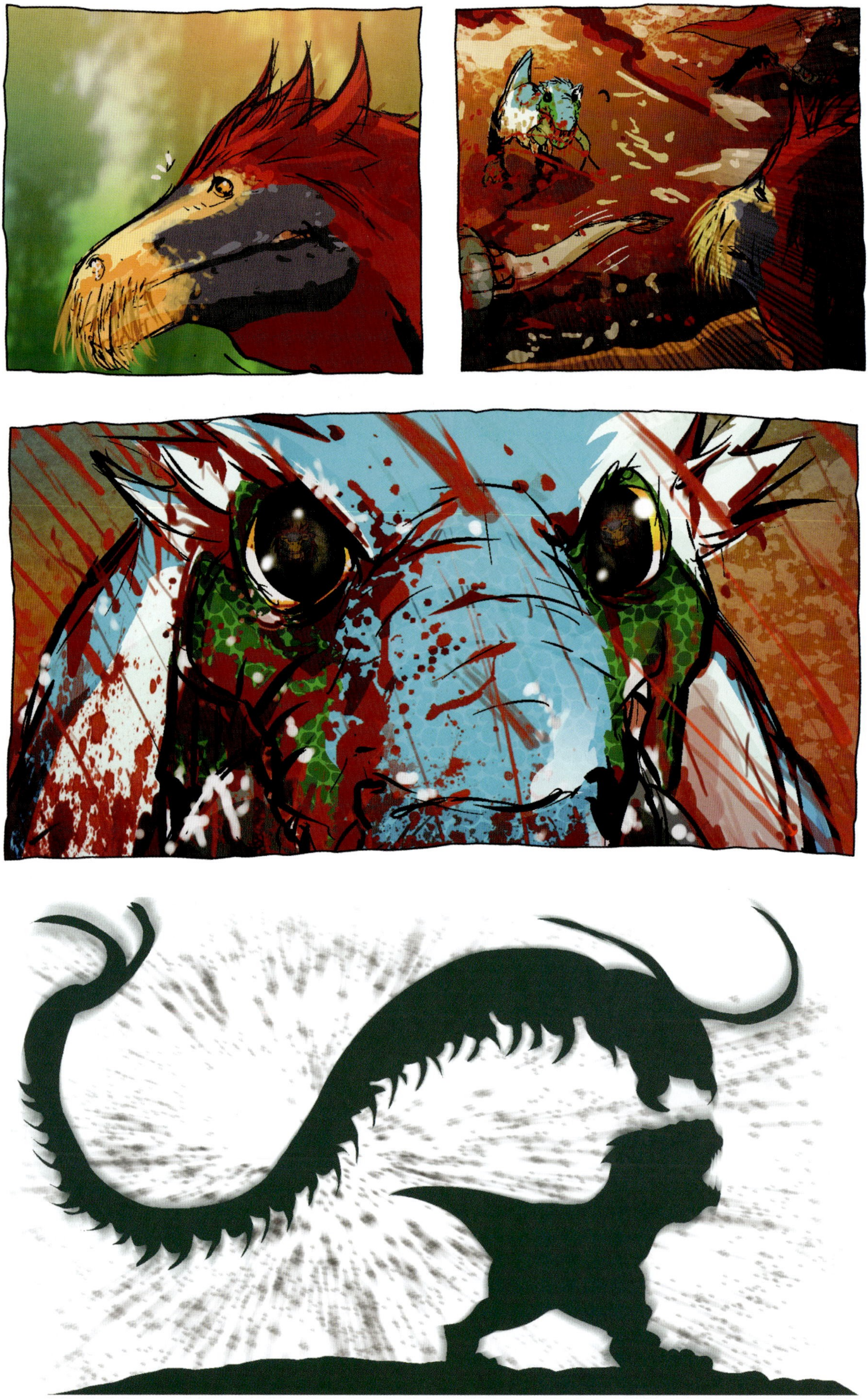

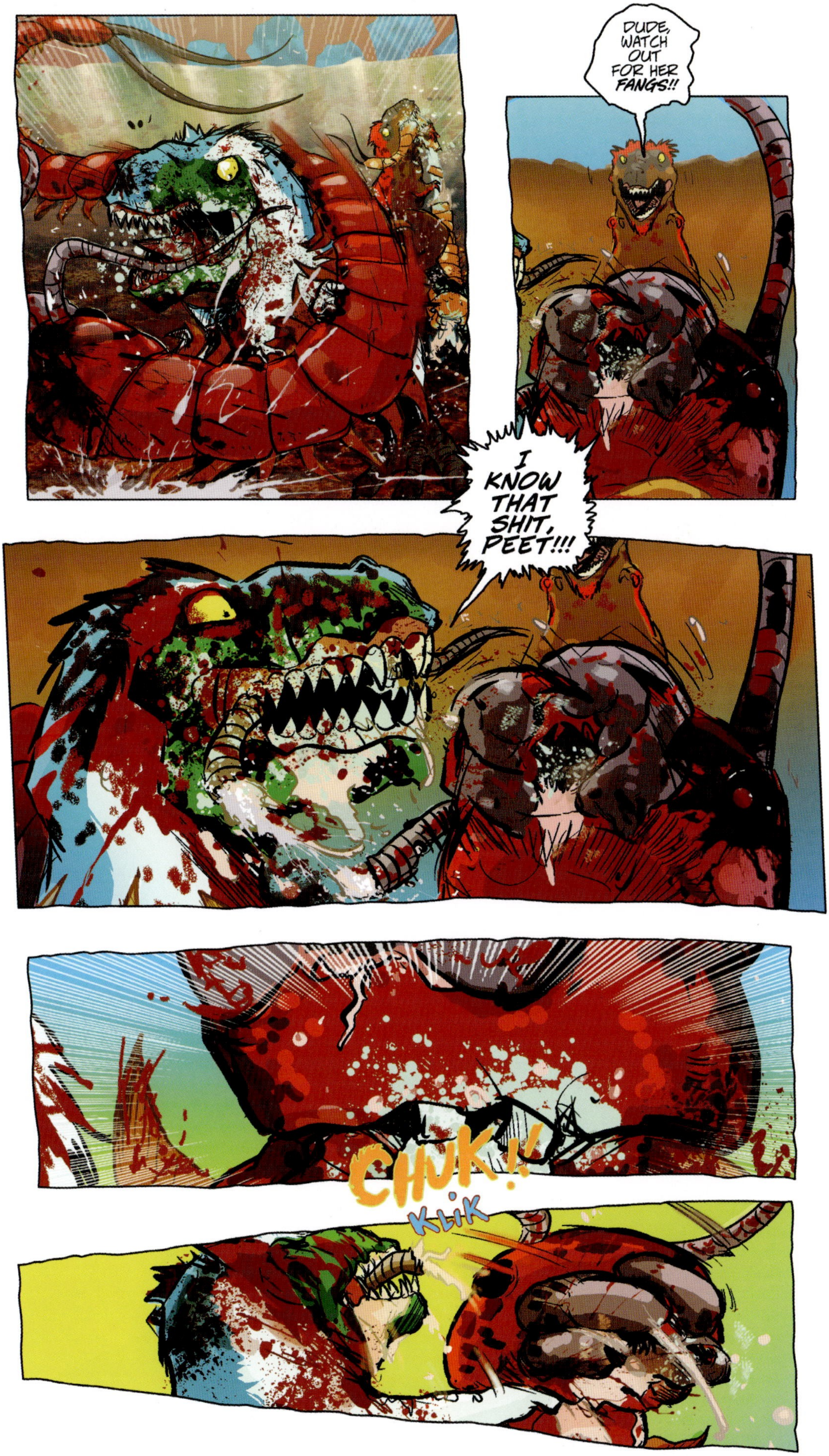
DUDE, WATCH OUT FOR HER FANGS!!
I KNOW THAT SHIT, PEET!!!
CHUK!!
KLIK

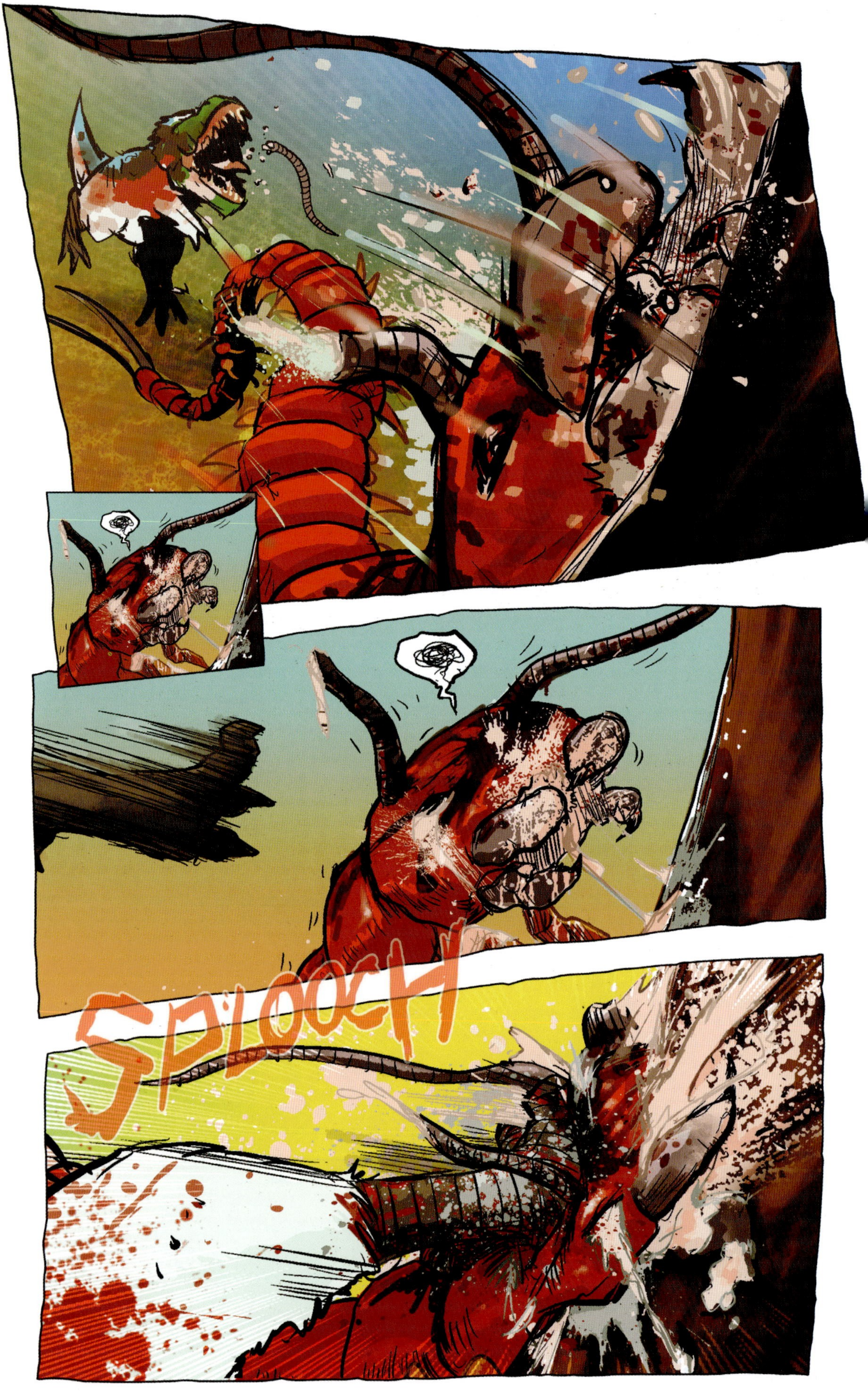
SPLOOCH

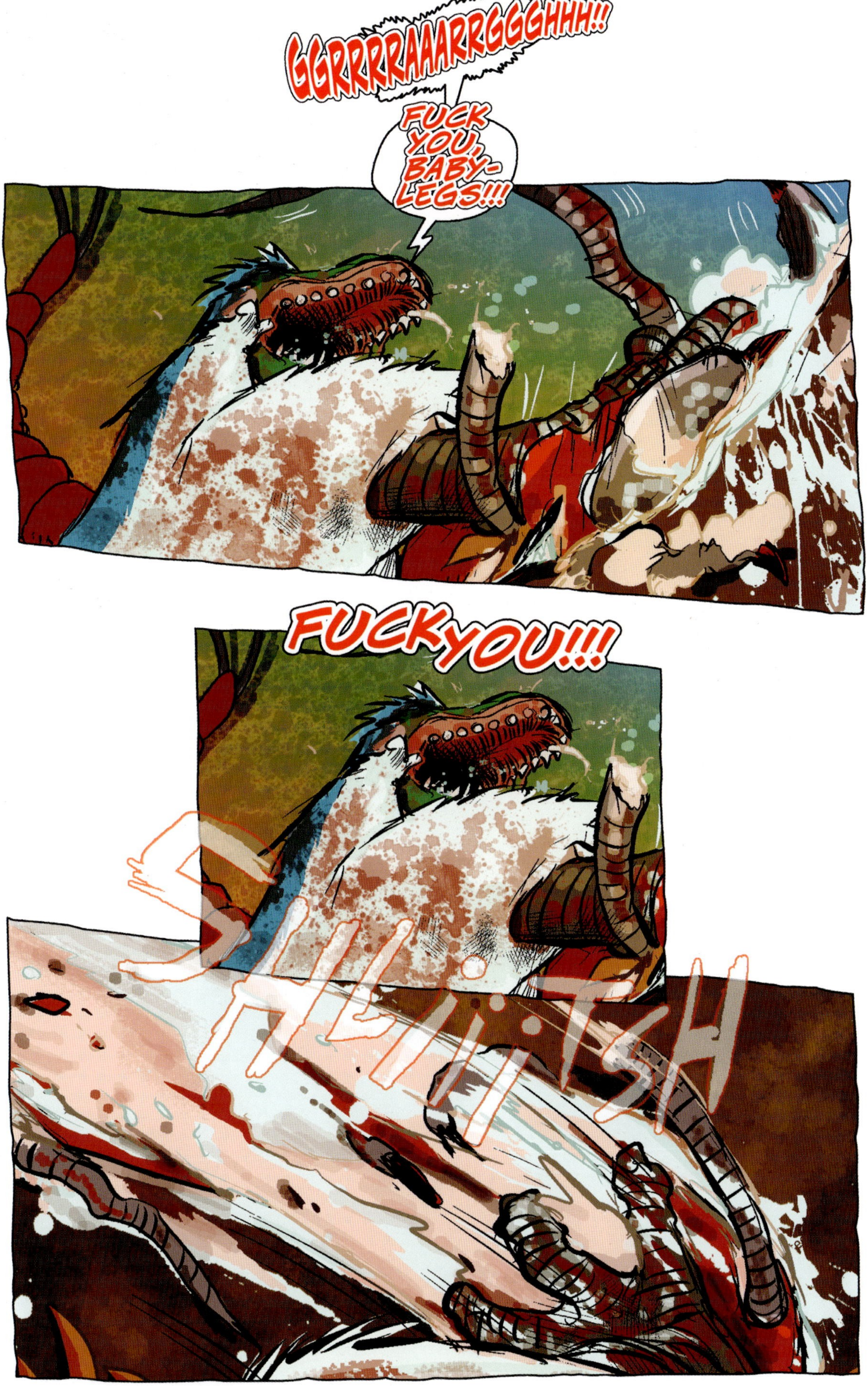
GGRRRRAAARRGGGHHH!!
FUCK YOU, BABY-LEGS!!!
FUCK YOU!!!
SHLLiiTSH

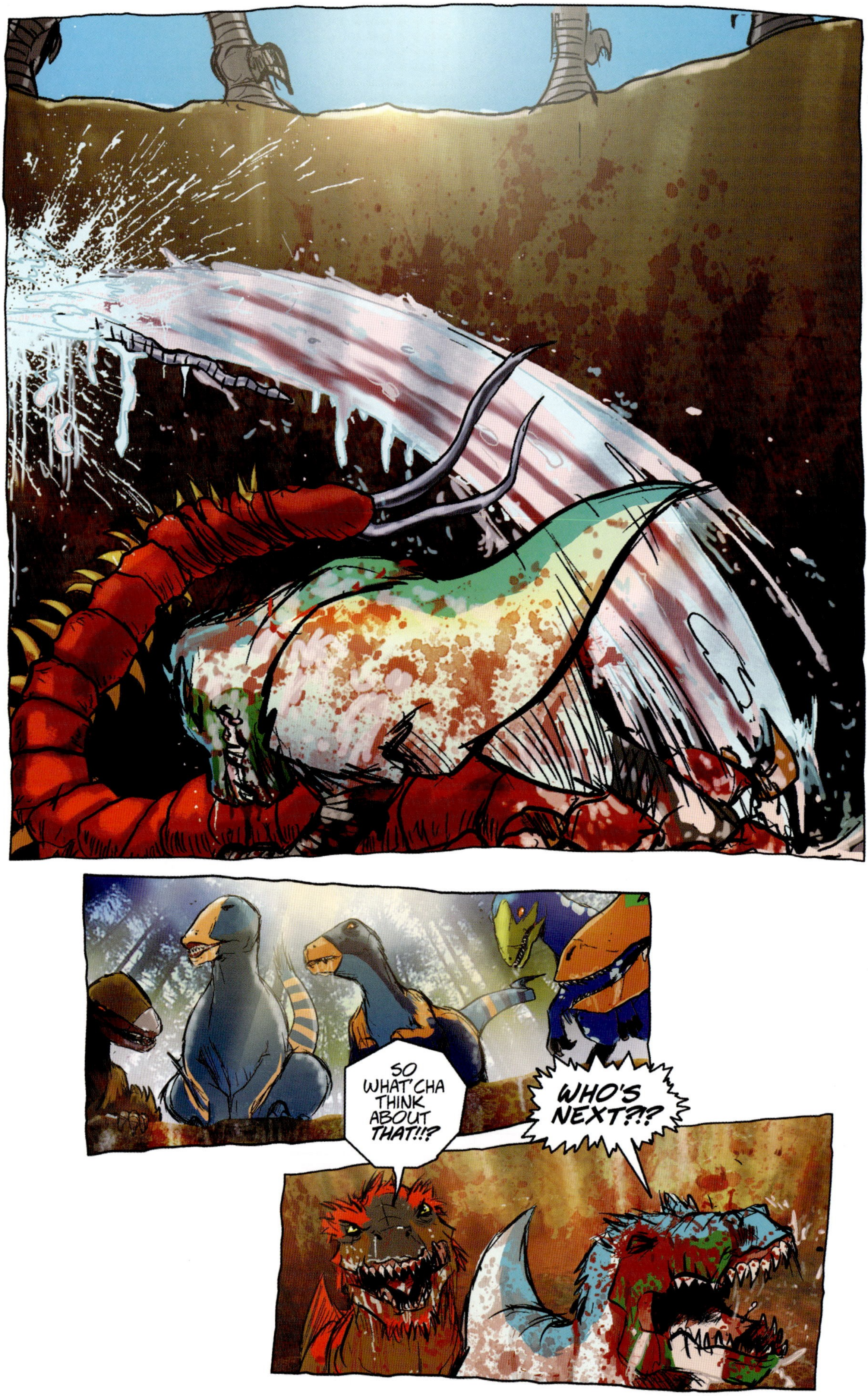
SO WHAT'CHA THINK ABOUT THAT!!?
WHO'S NEXT?!?

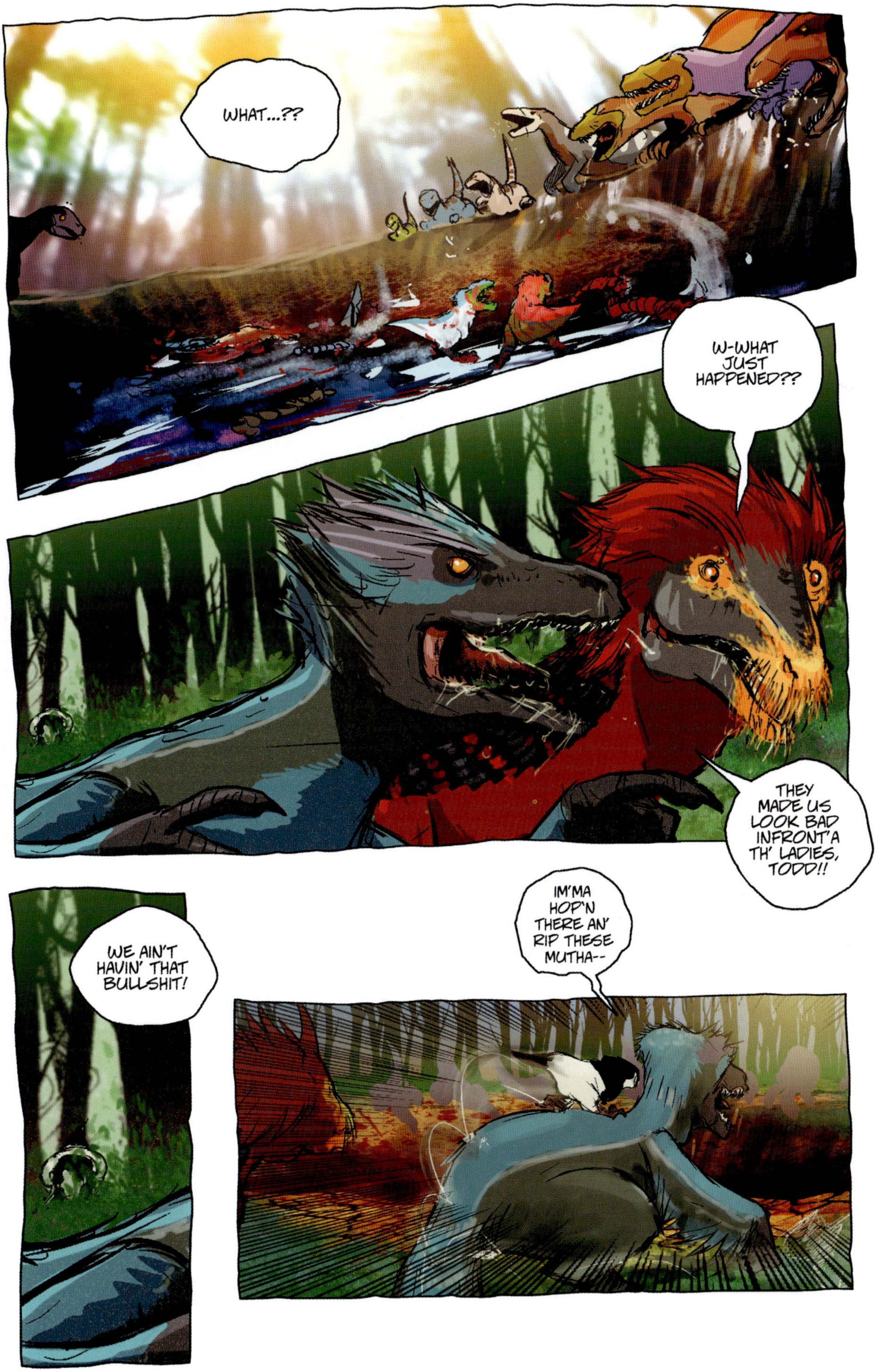
WHAT...??
W-WHAT JUST HAPPENED??
THEY MADE US LOOK BAD INFRONT'A TH' LADIES, TODD!!
WE AIN'T HAVIN' THAT BULLSHIT!
IM'MA HOP'N THERE AN' RIP THESE MUTHA--

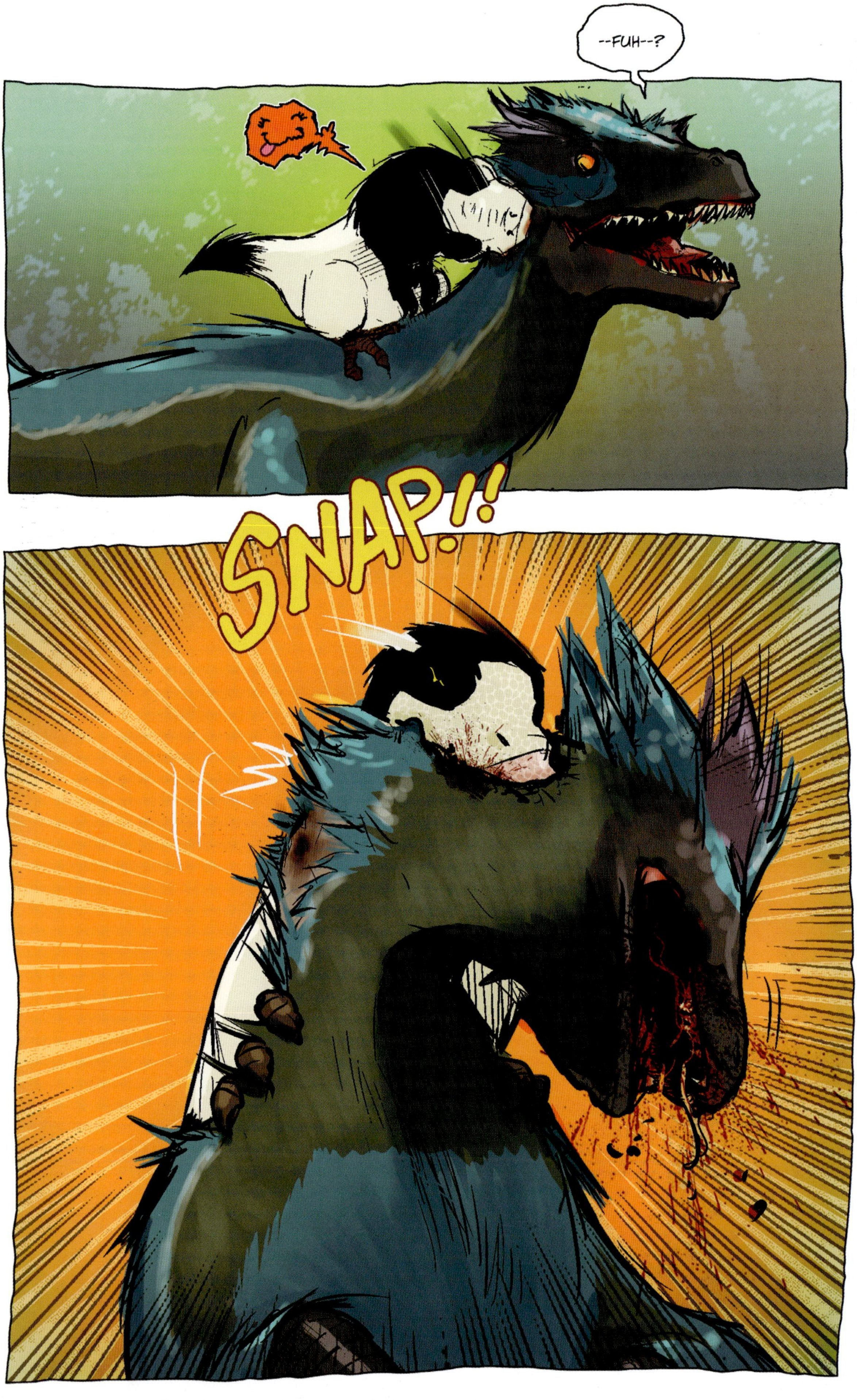
--FUH--?
SNAP!!

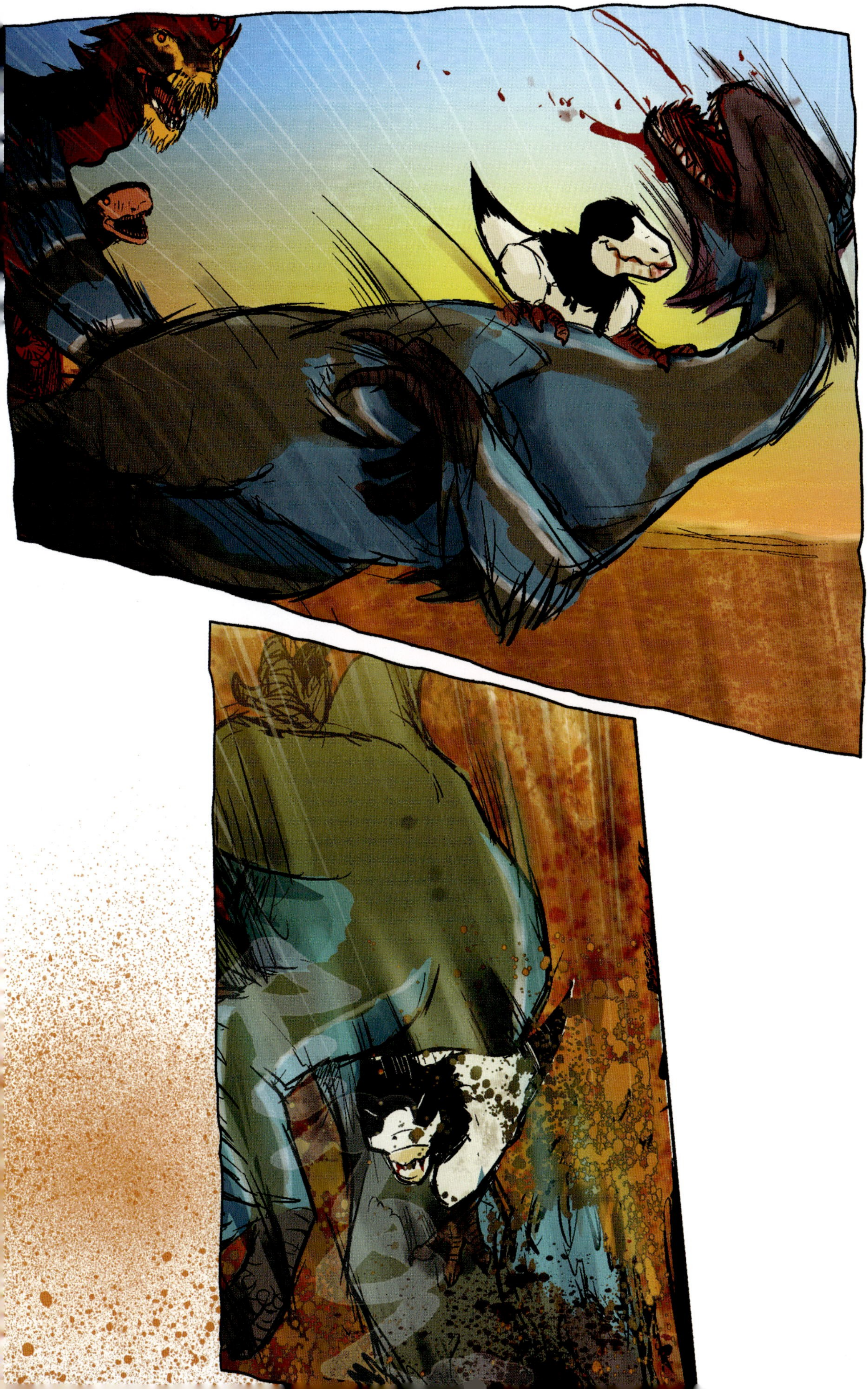

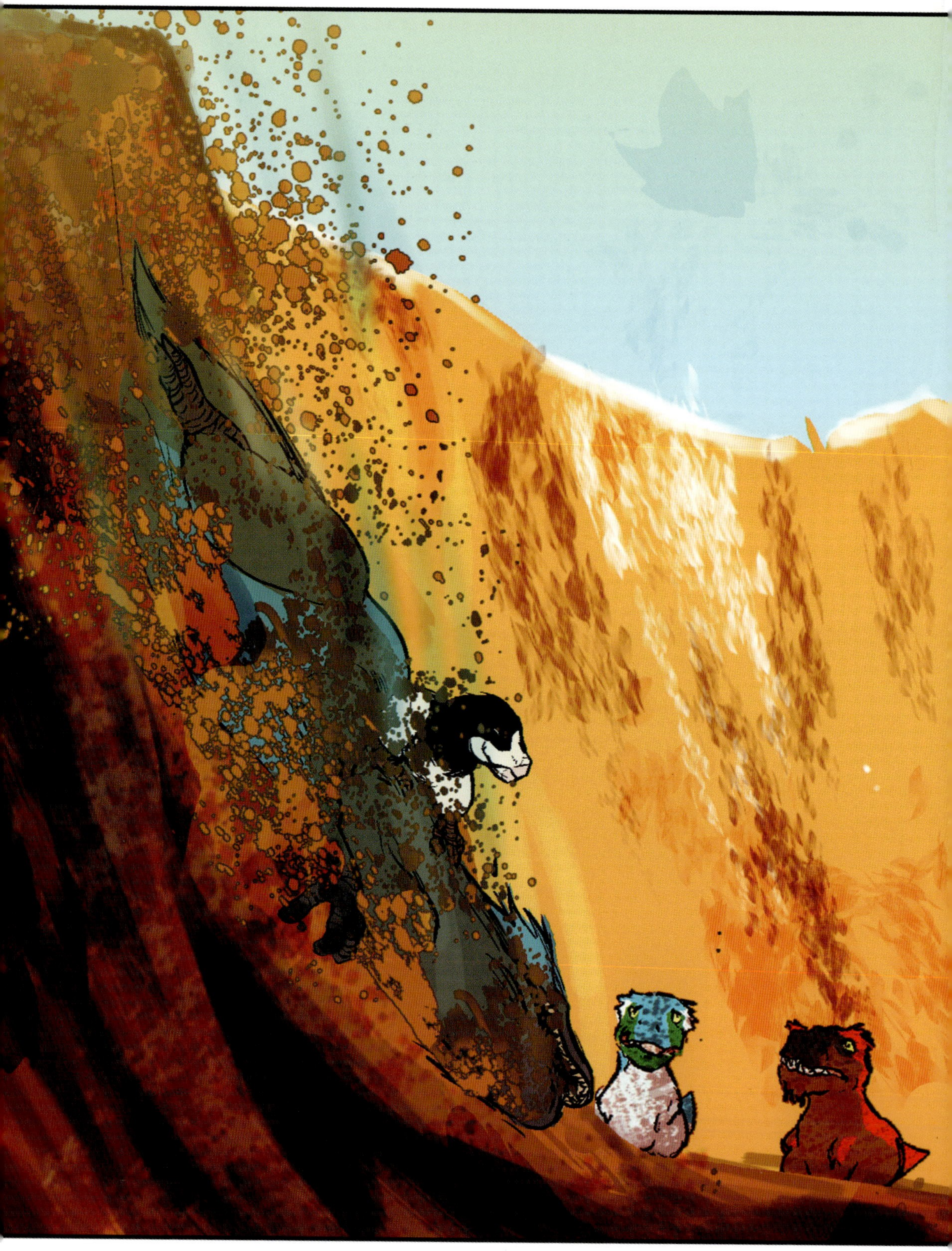

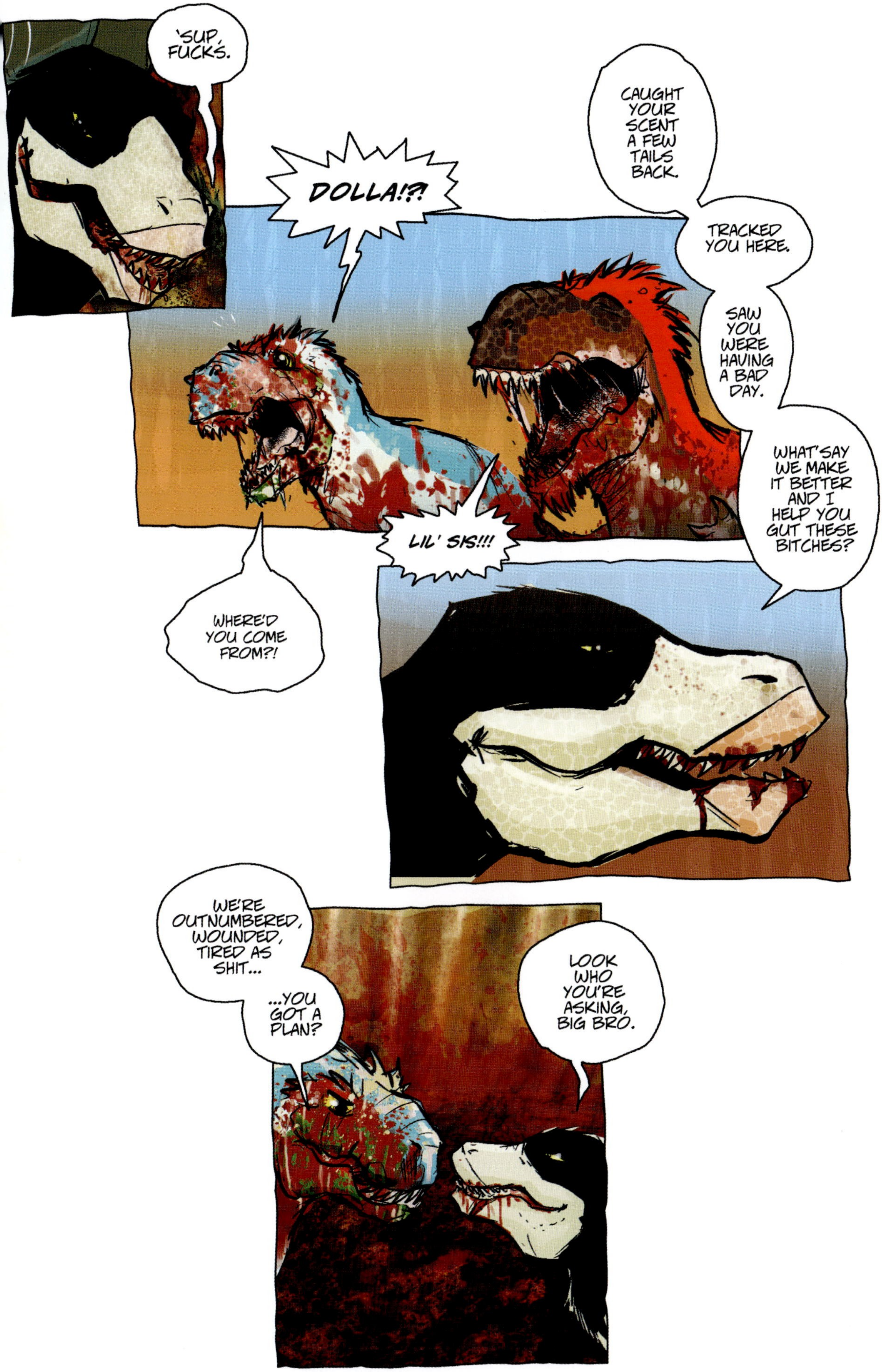
'SUP, FUCKS.
DOLLA!?!
CAUGHT YOUR SCENT A FEW TAILS BACK.
TRACKED YOU HERE.
SAW YOU WERE HAVING A BAD DAY.
WHAT'SAY WE MAKE IT BETTER AND I HELP YOU GUT THESE BITCHES?
WHERE'D YOU COME FROM?!
LIL' SIS!!!
WE'RE OUTNUMBERED, WOUNDED, TIRED AS SHIT...
...YOU GOT A PLAN?
LOOK WHO YOU'RE ASKING, BIG BRO.

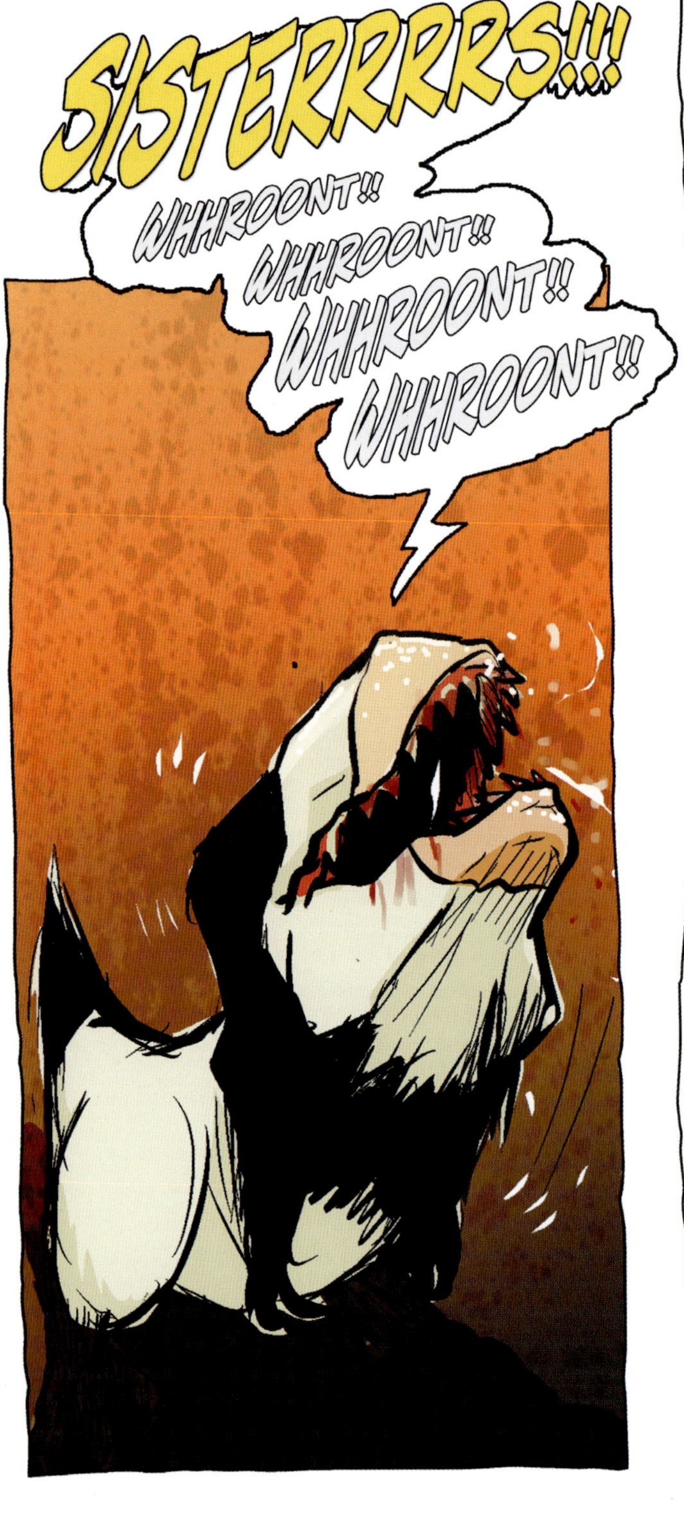
SISTERRRRS!!!
WHHROONT!!
WHHROONT!!
WHHROONT!!
WHHROONT!!

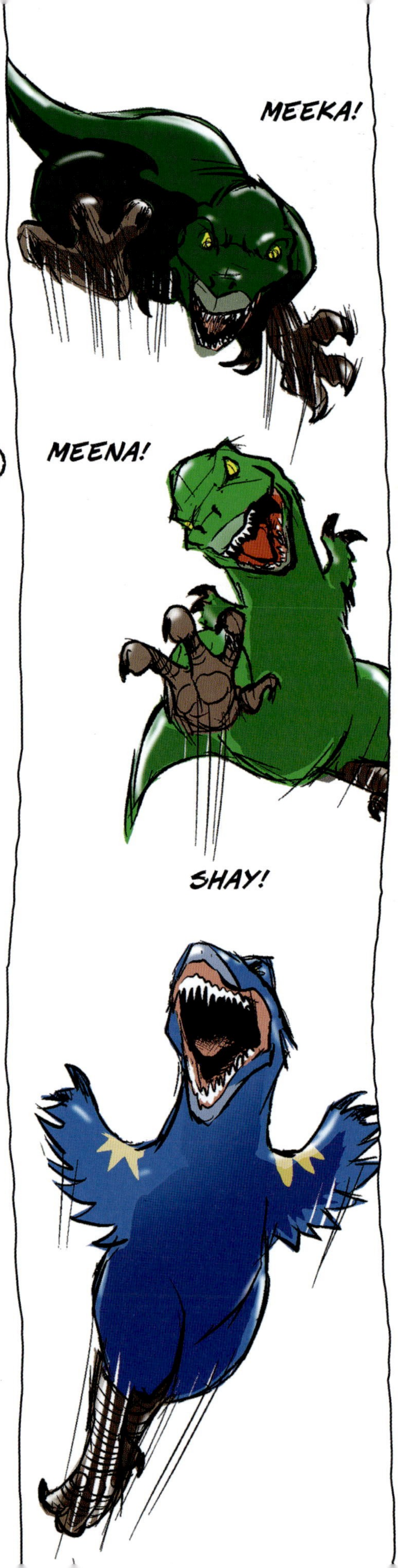
MEEKA!
MEENA!
SHAY!

MY OTHER THREE SISTERS.

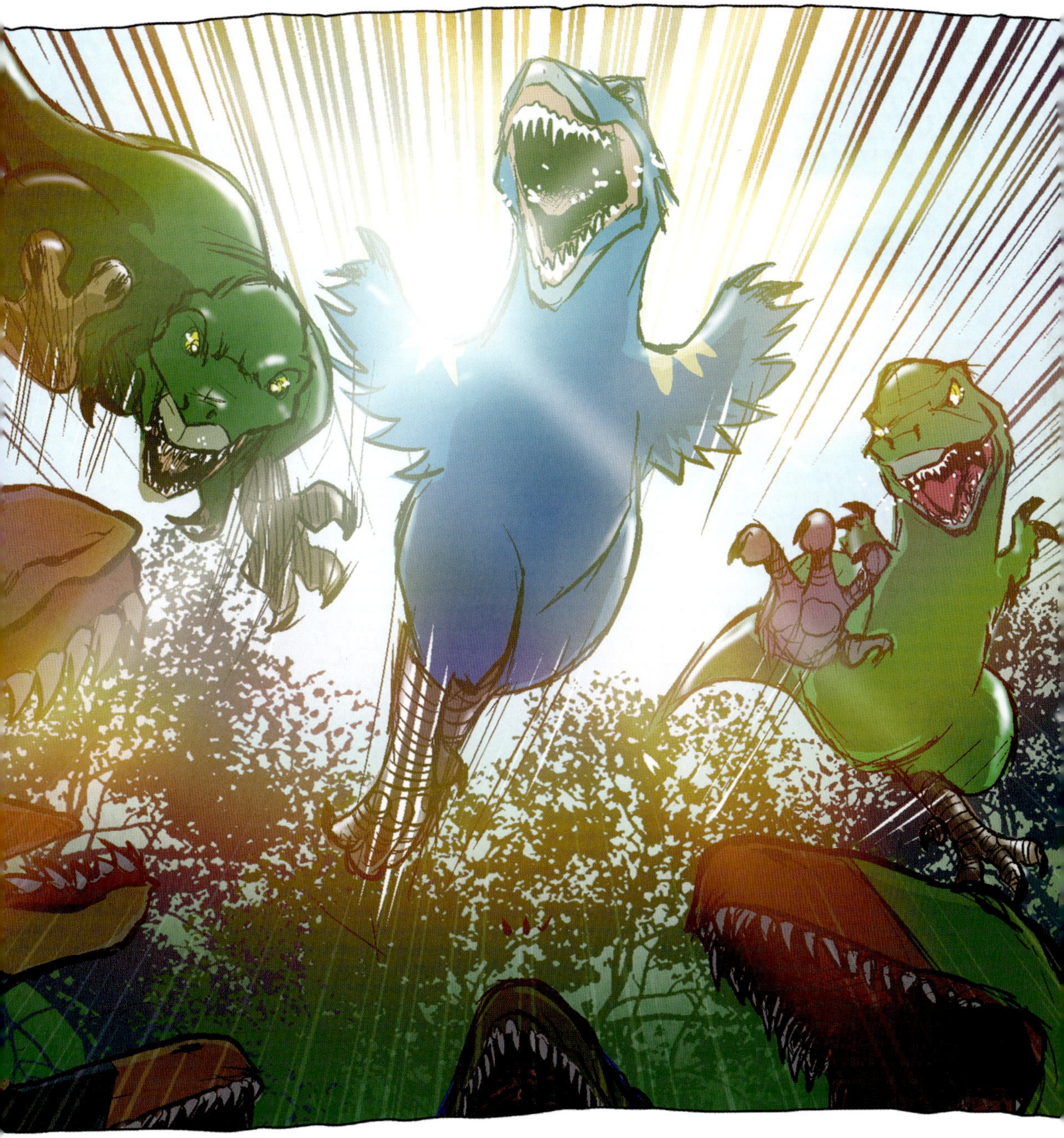

SHIT JUST GOT FIERCE.

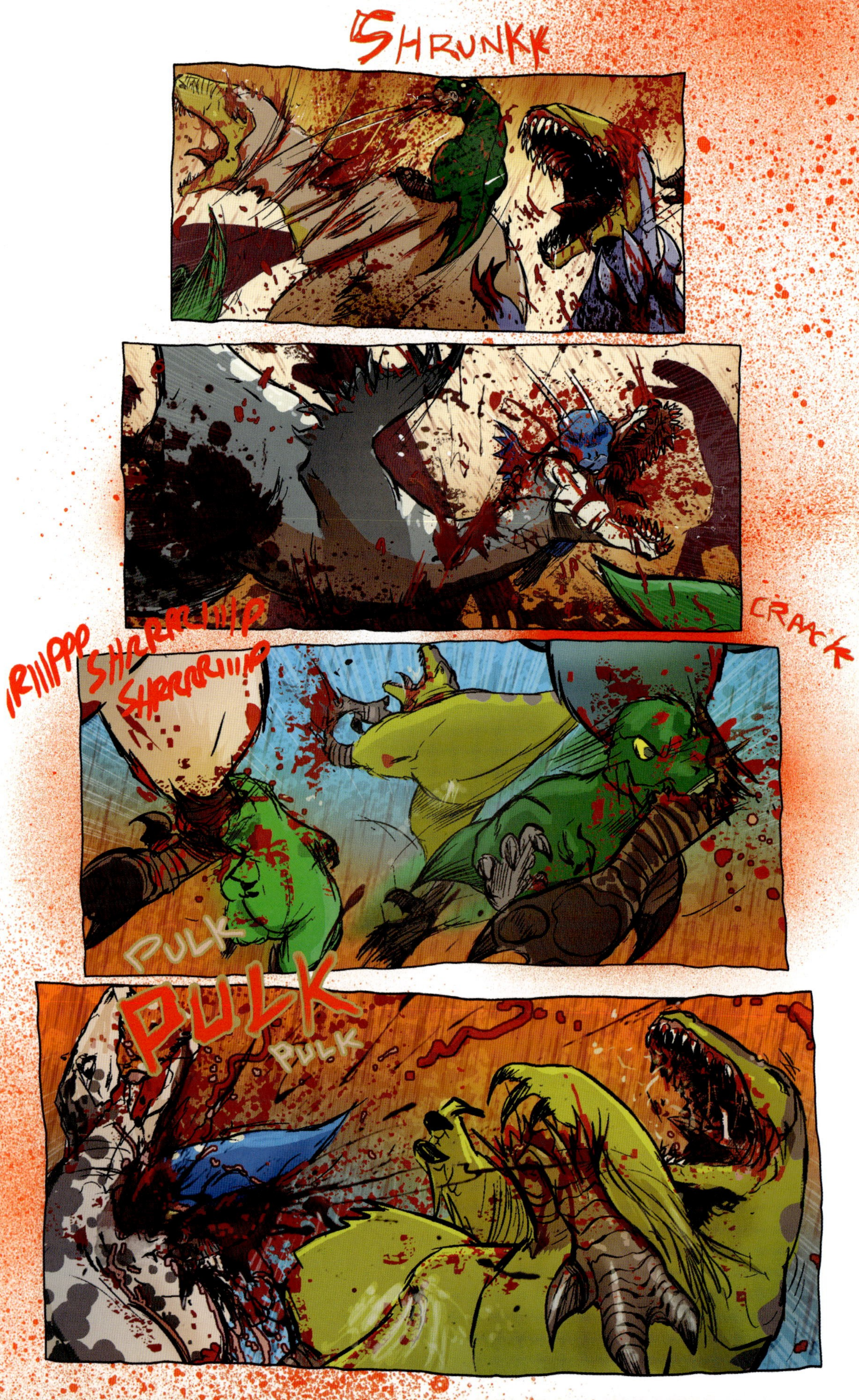
SHRUNKK
SHRRRRIIIP
CRAACK
RIIIPPP
SHRRRRIIIP
PULK
PULK
PULK

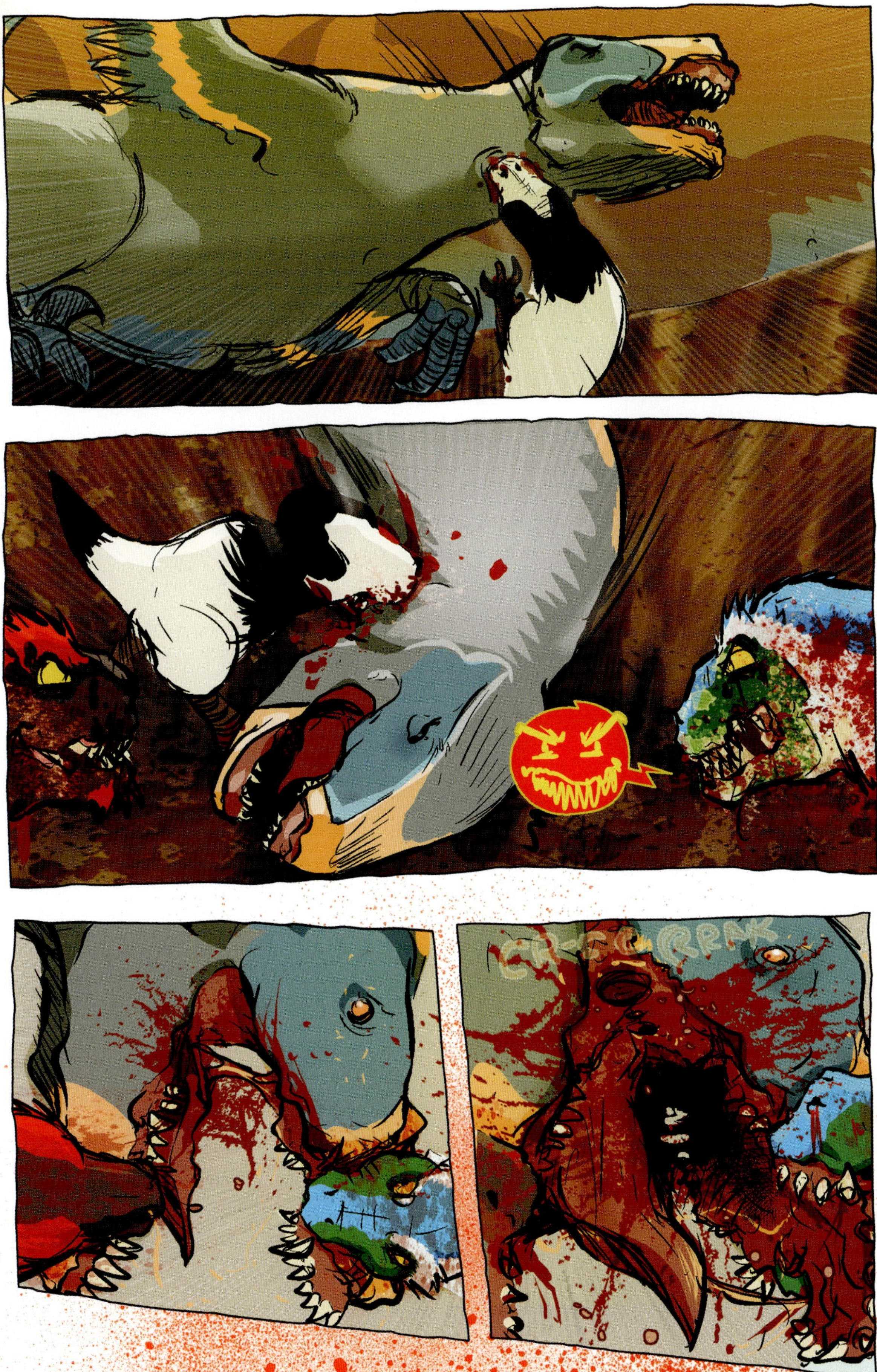

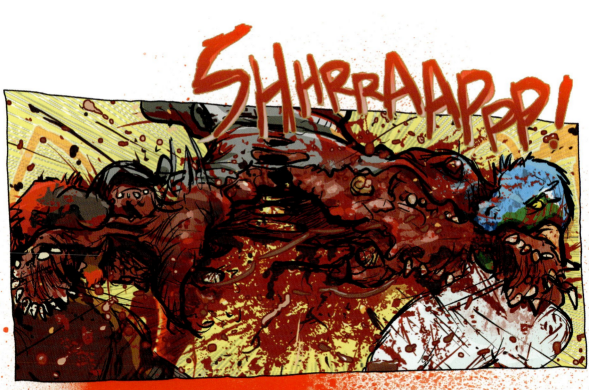

SHHRRAAPPP!

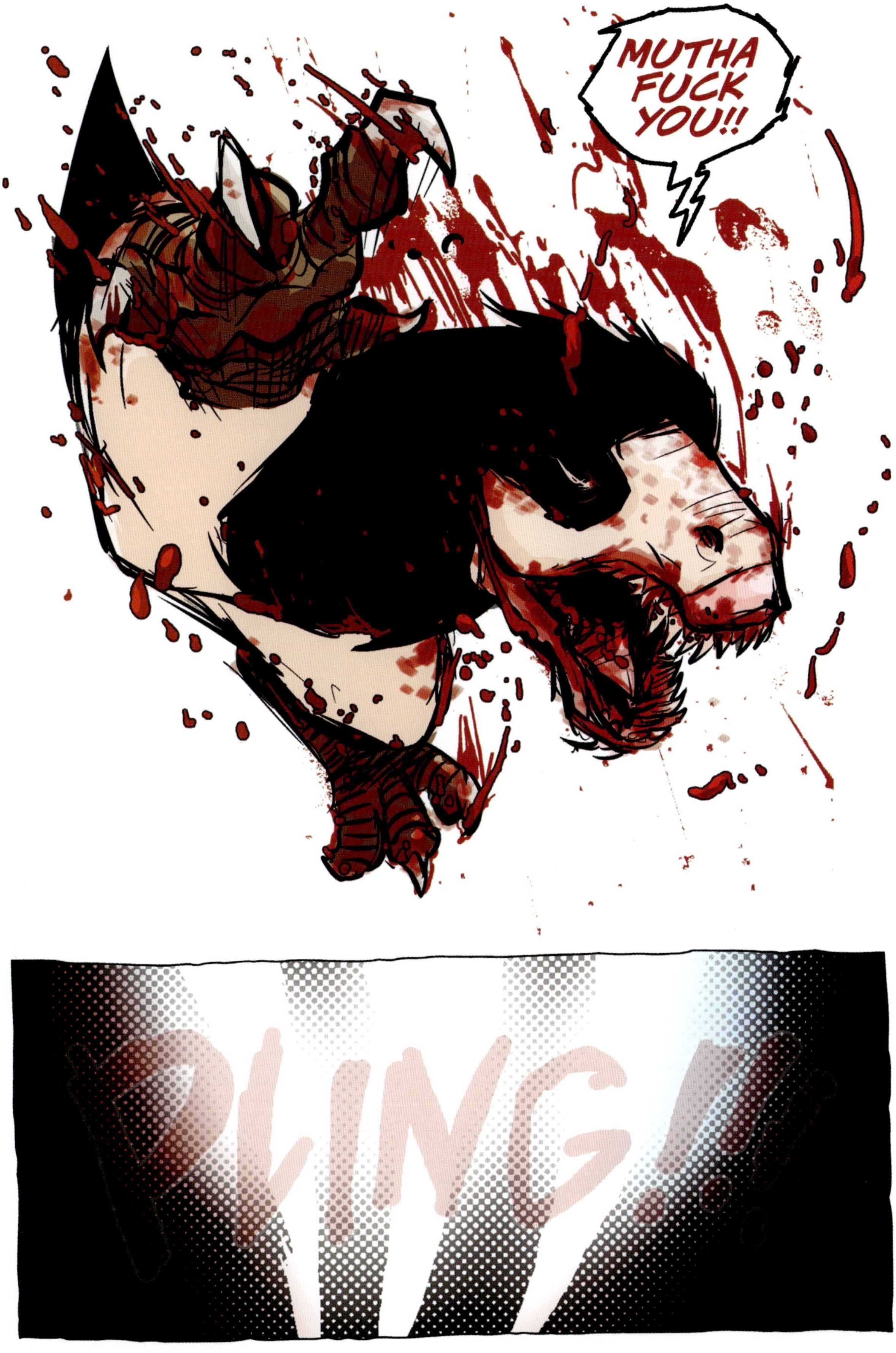
MUTHA FUCK YOU!!
PLING!

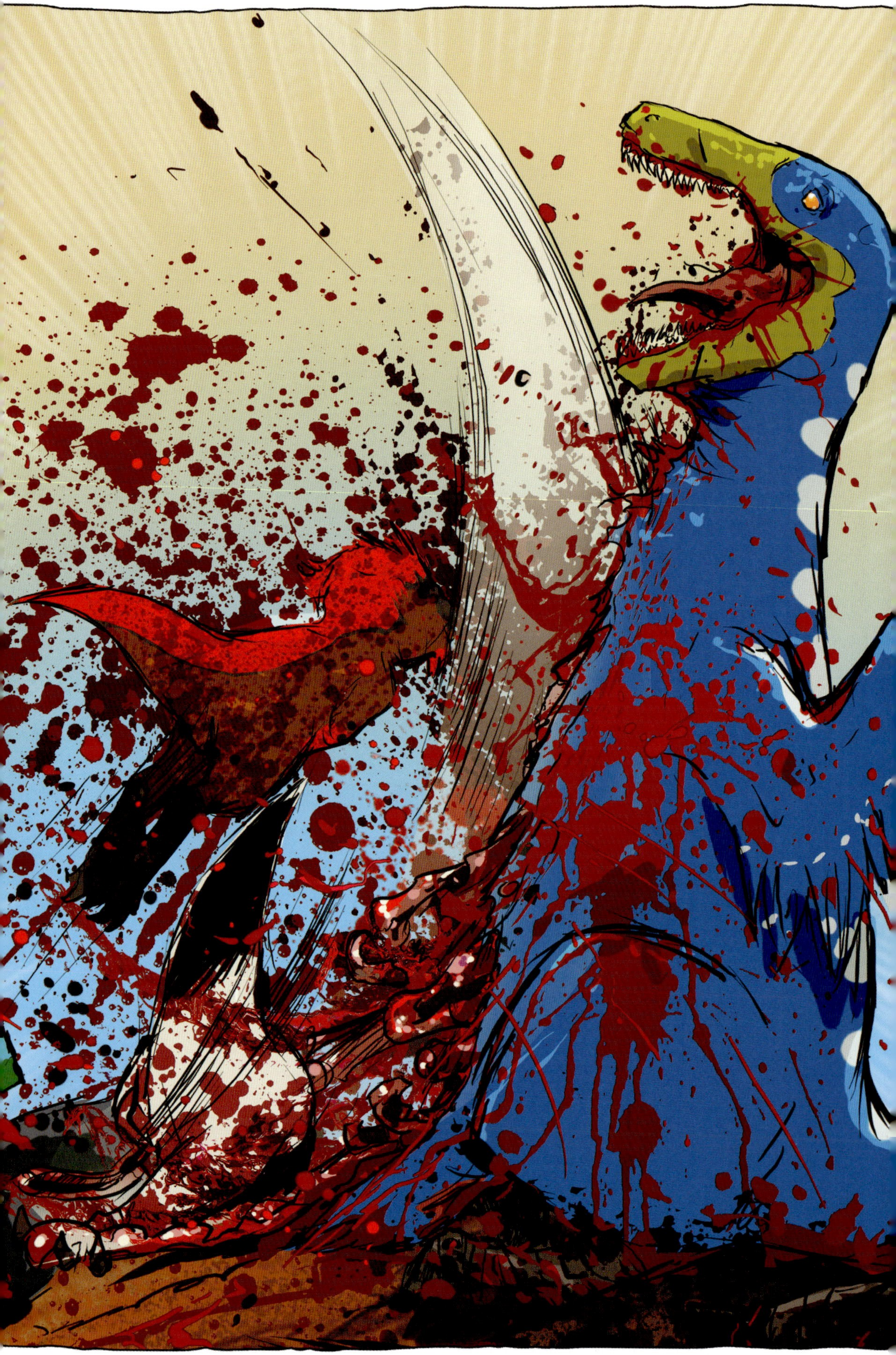

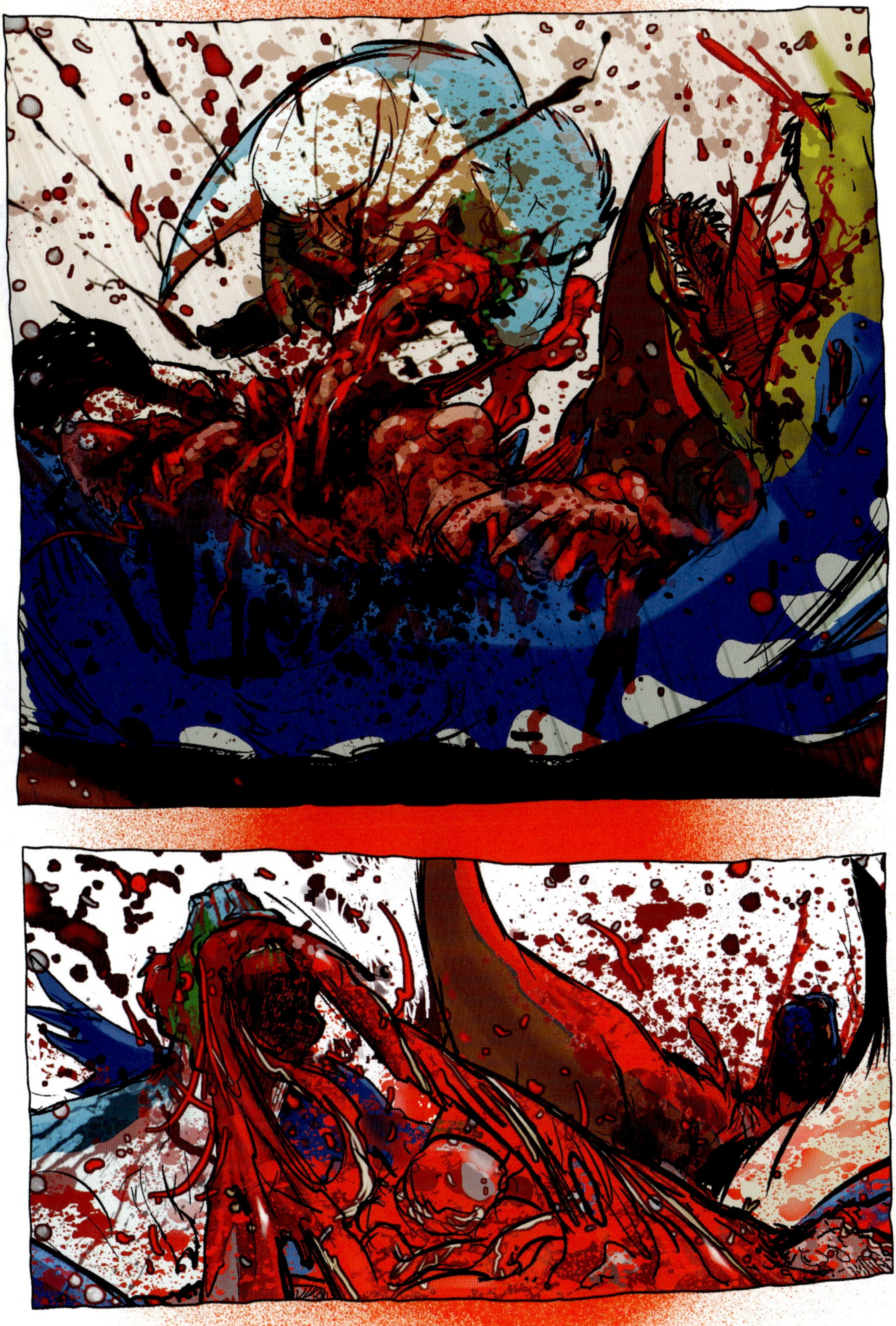

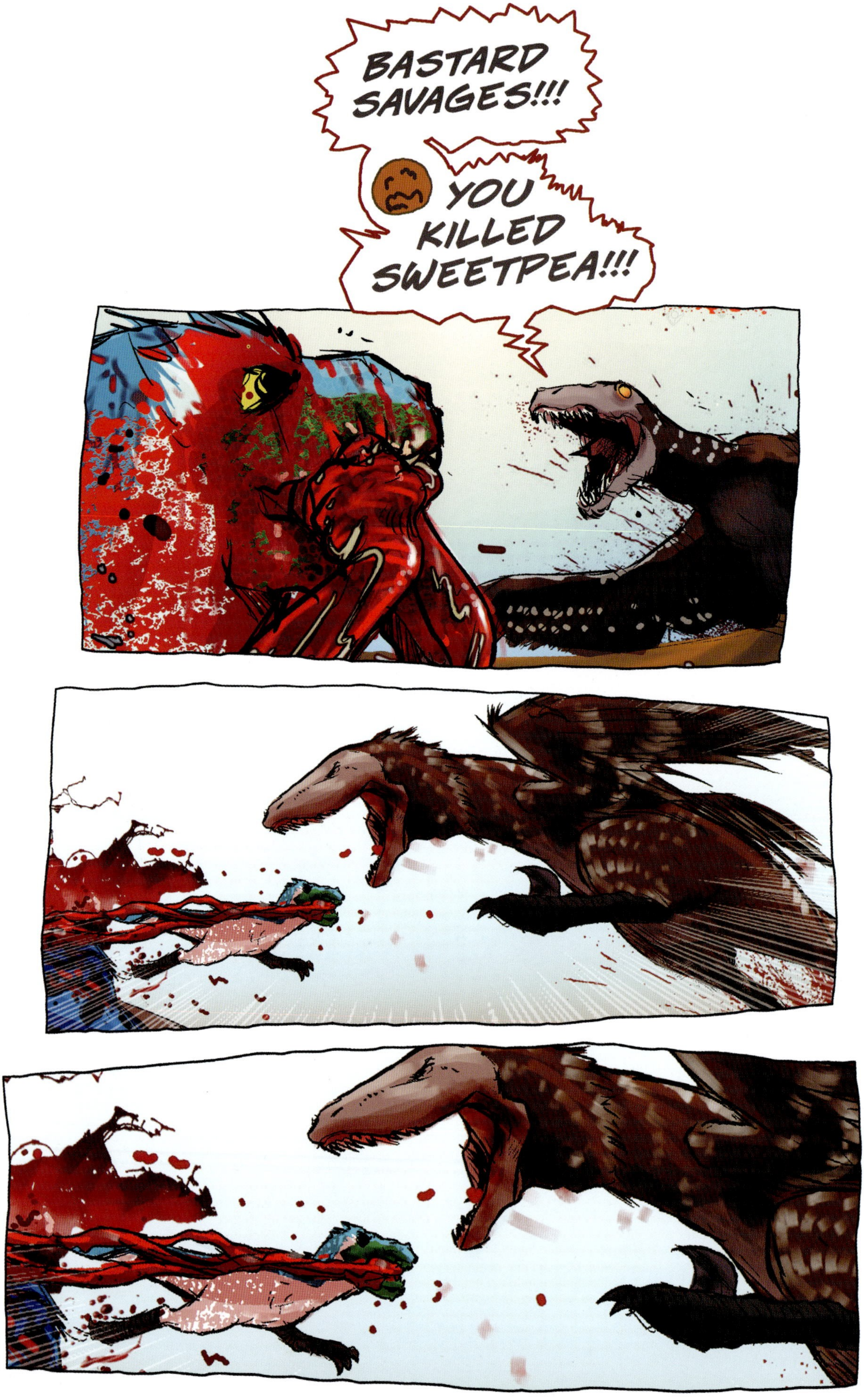
BASTARD SAVAGES!!!
YOU KILLED SWEETPEA!!!

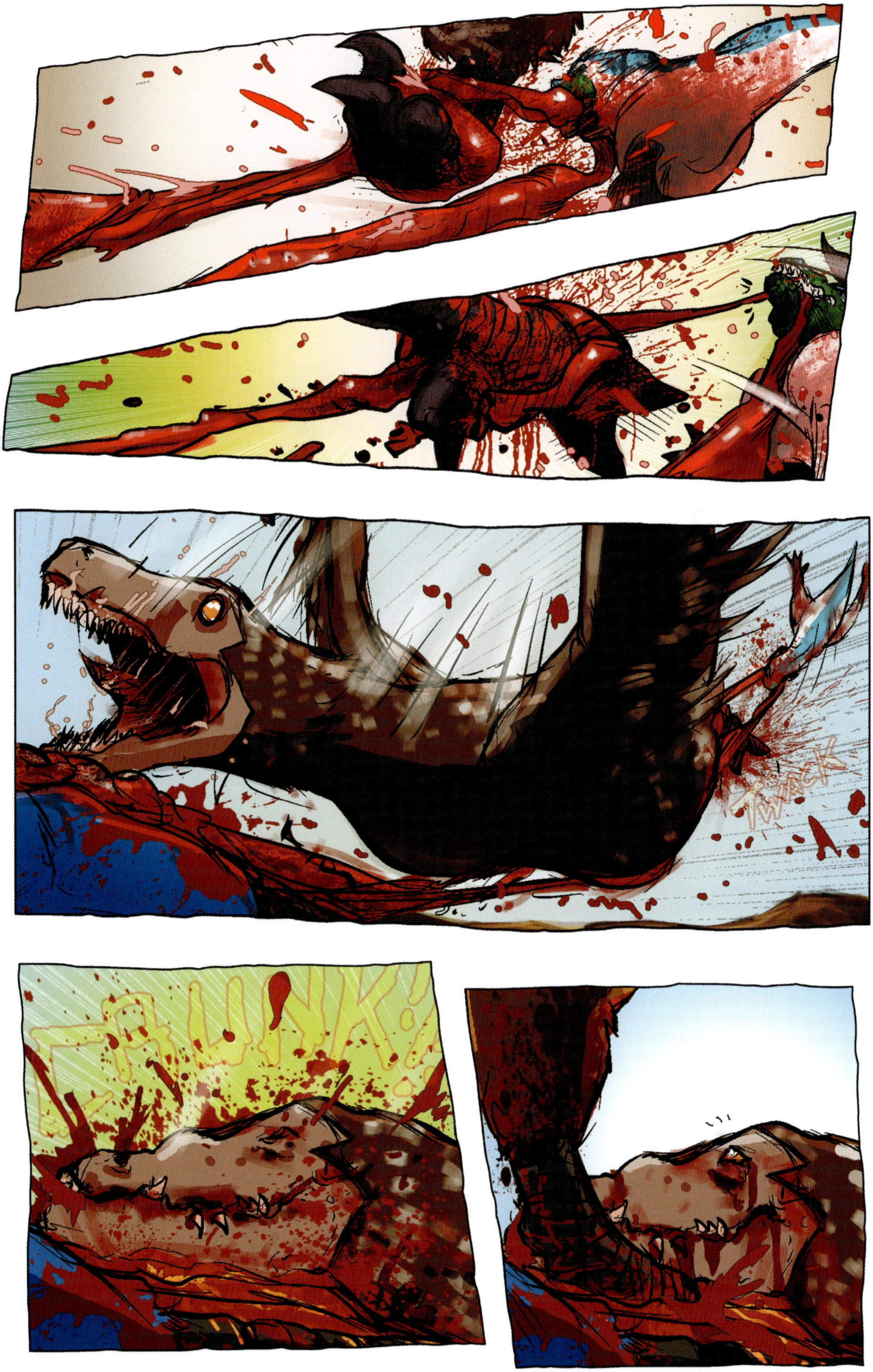
TWACK
CHUNK!

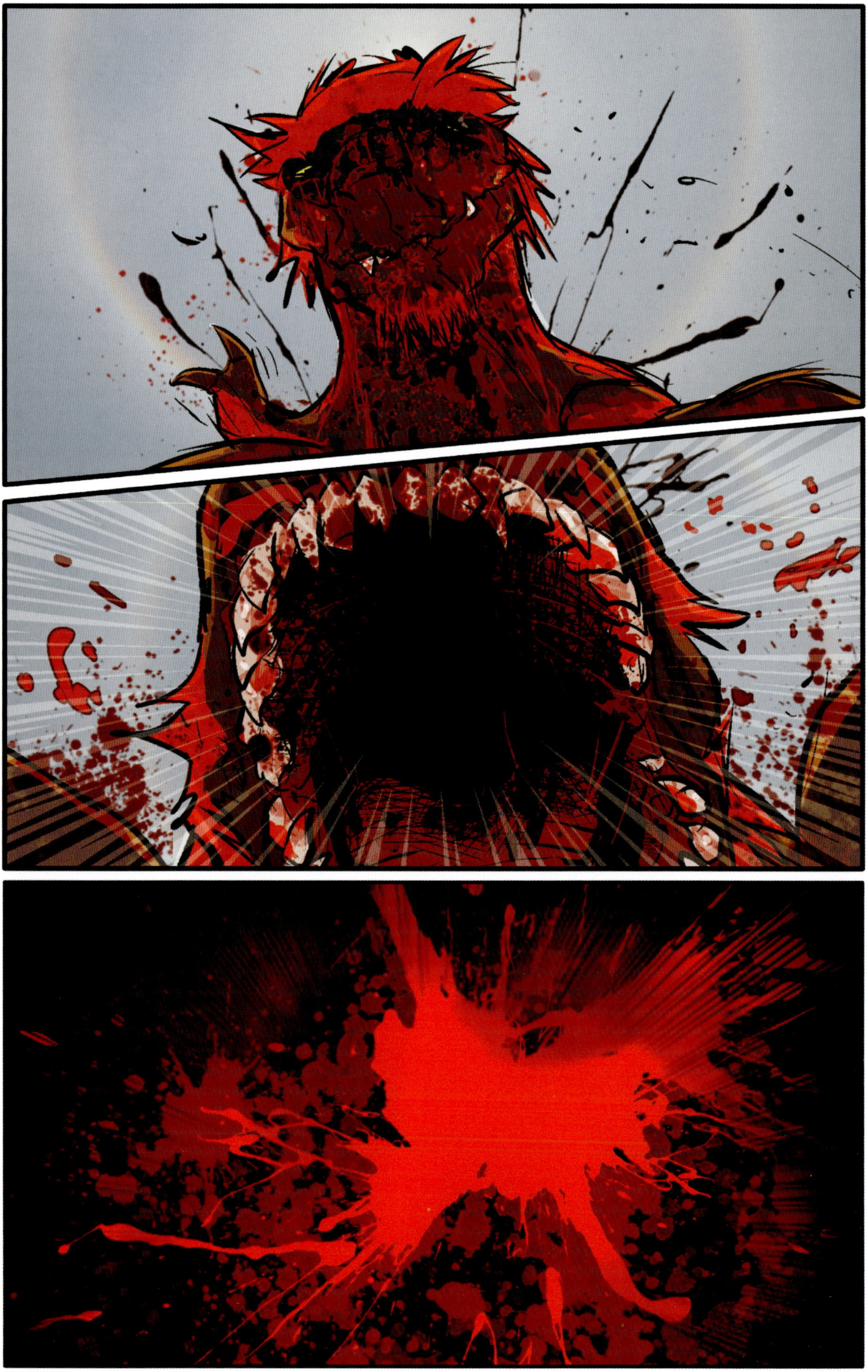

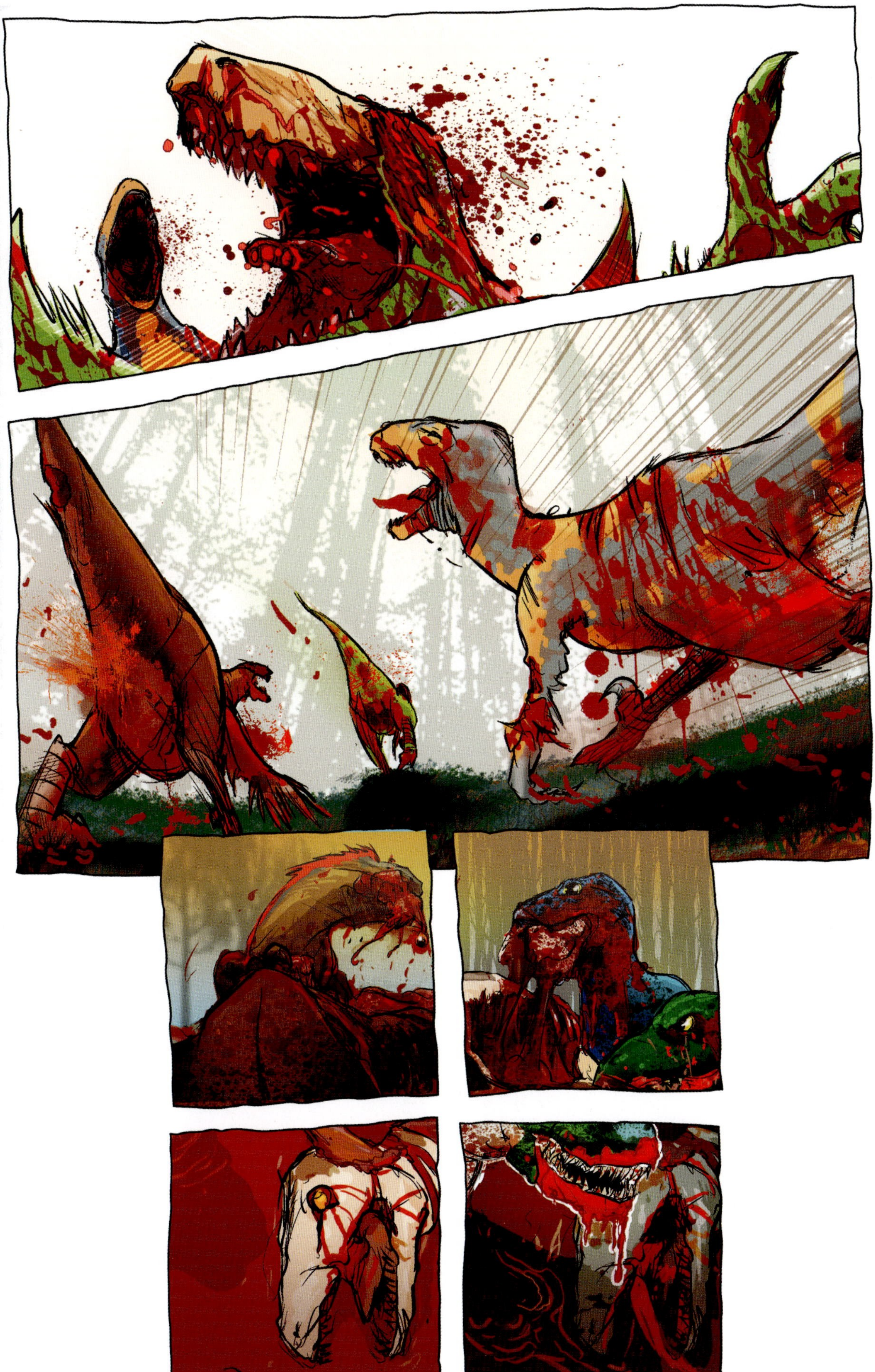

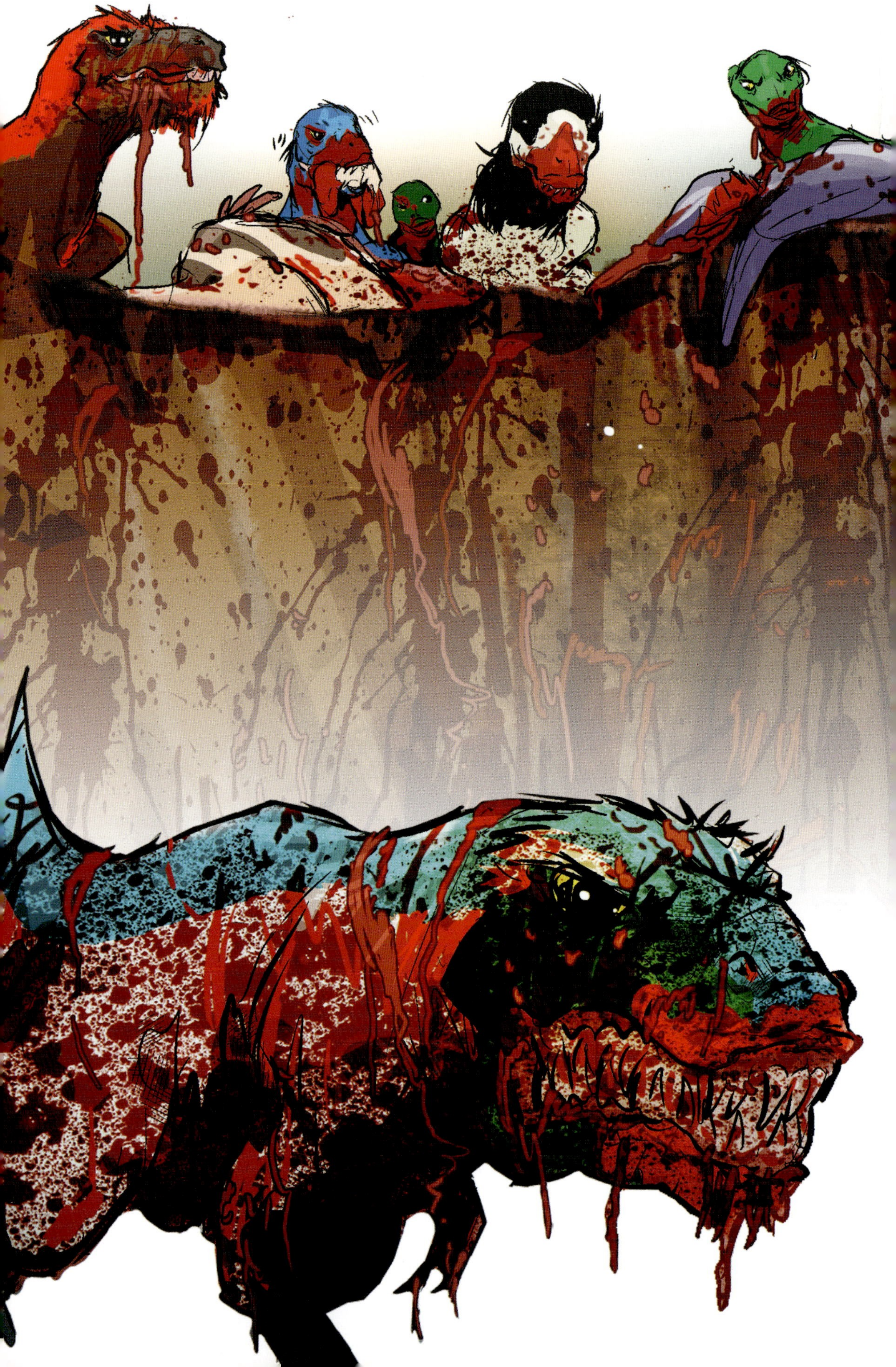

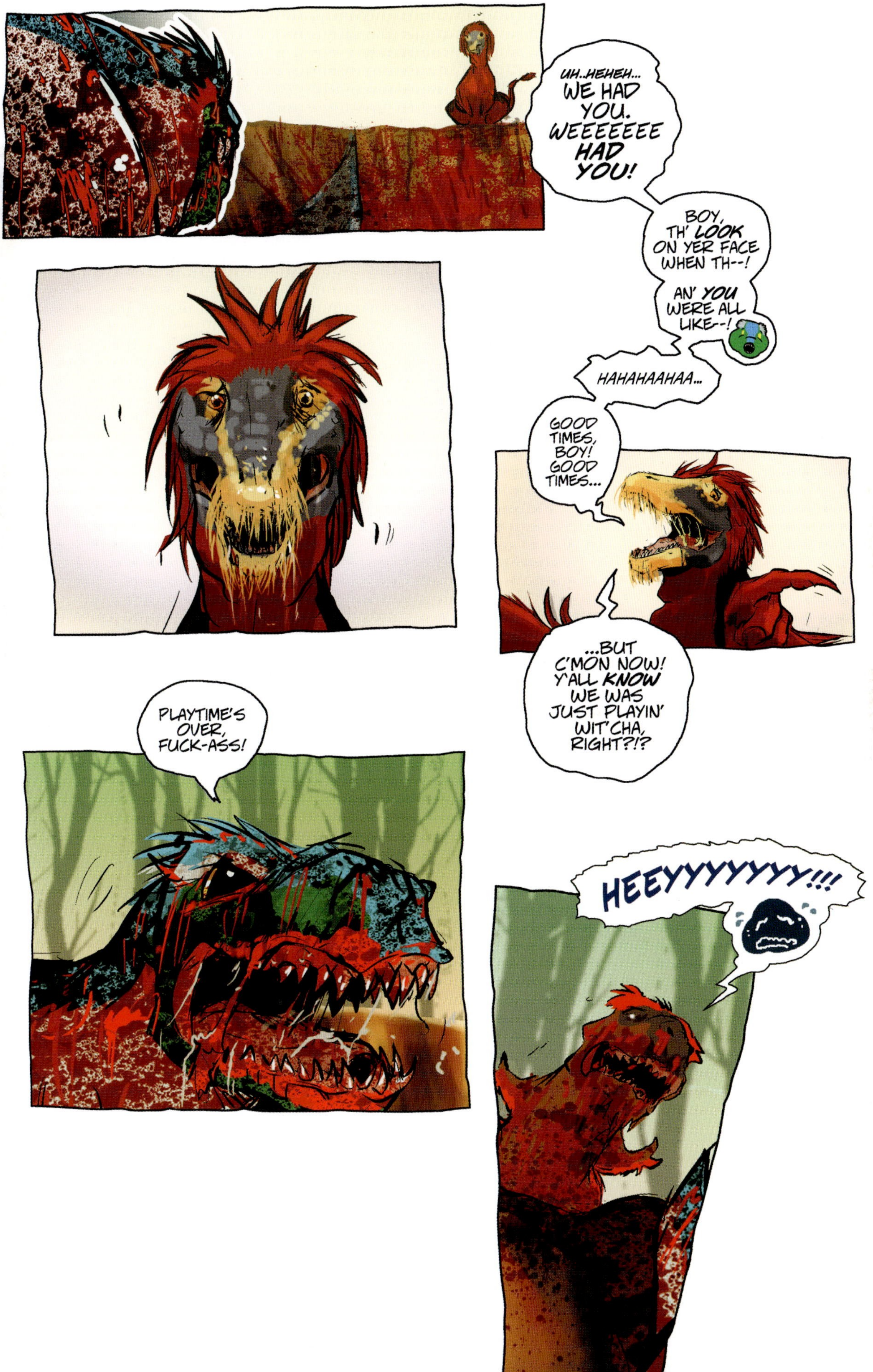
UH..HEHEH... WE HAD YOU. WEEEEEEE HAD YOU!
BOY, TH' LOOK ON YER FACE WHEN TH--!
AN' YOU WERE ALL LIKE--!
HAHAHAAHAA...
GOOD TIMES, BOY! GOOD TIMES...
...BUT C'MON NOW! Y'ALL KNOW WE WAS JUST PLAYIN' WIT'CHA, RIGHT?!?
PLAYTIME'S OVER, FUCK-ASS!
HEEYYYYYYY!!!

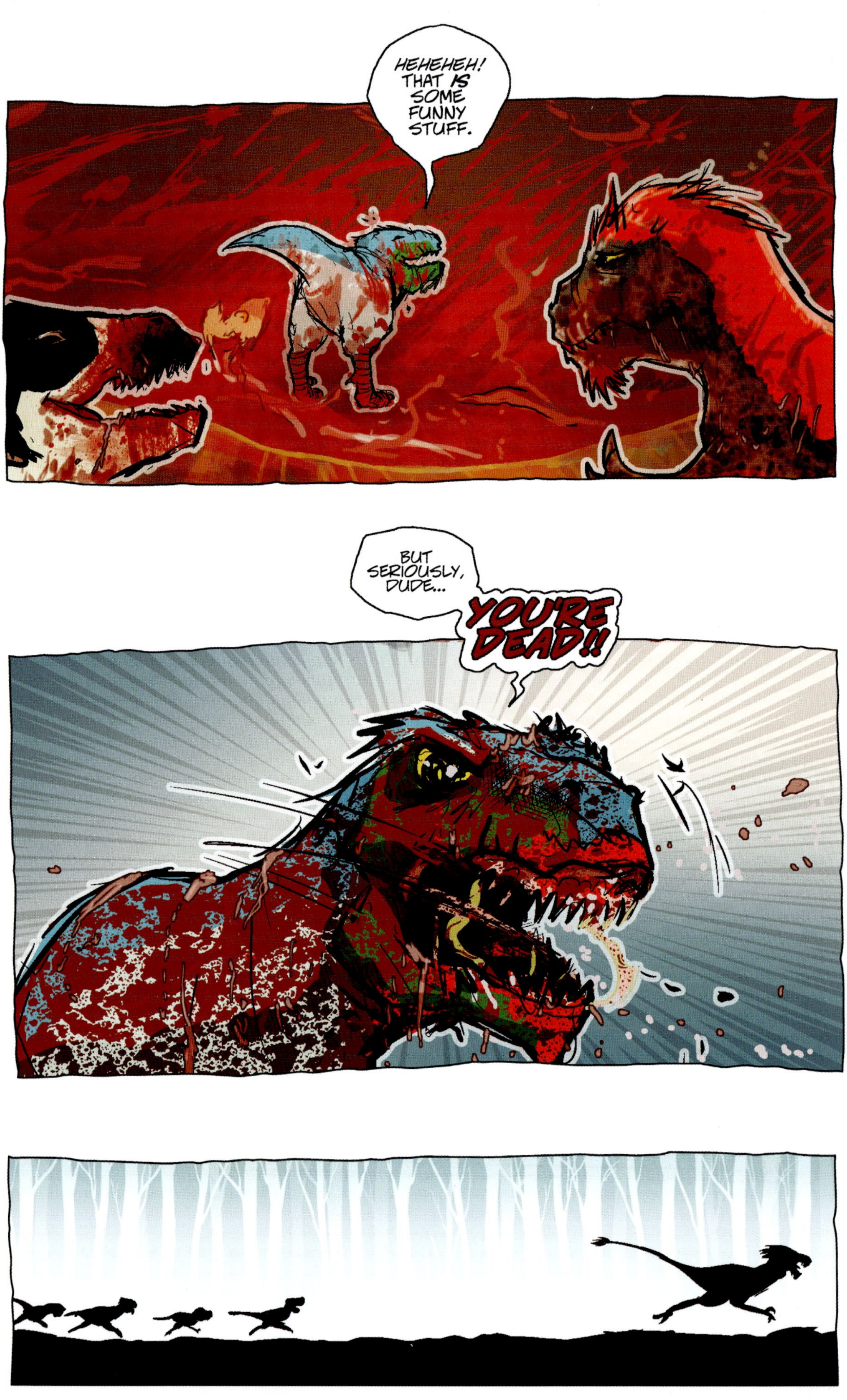
HEHEHEH! THAT IS SOME FUNNY STUFF.
BUT SERIOUSLY, DUDE...
YOU'RE DEAD!!

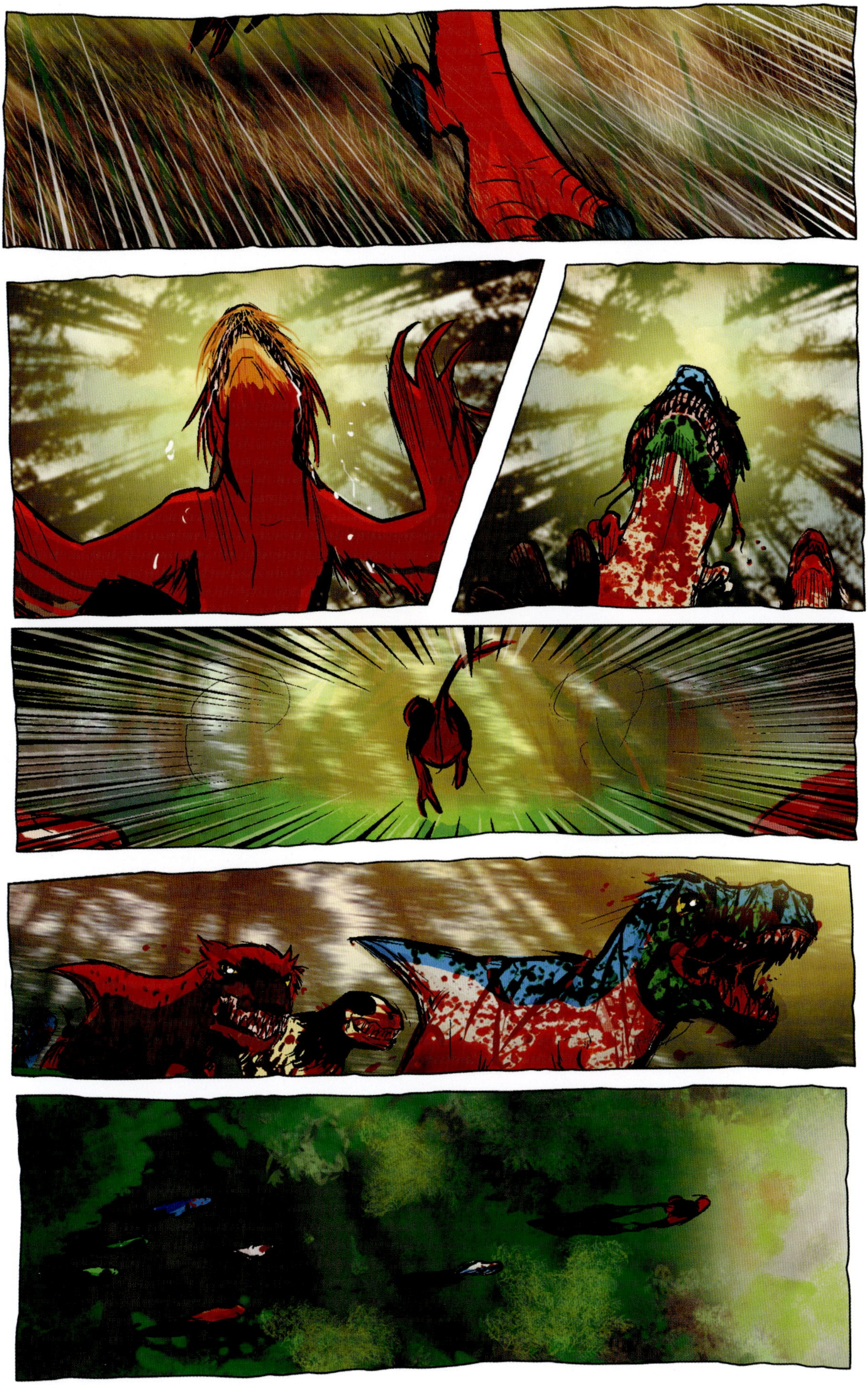

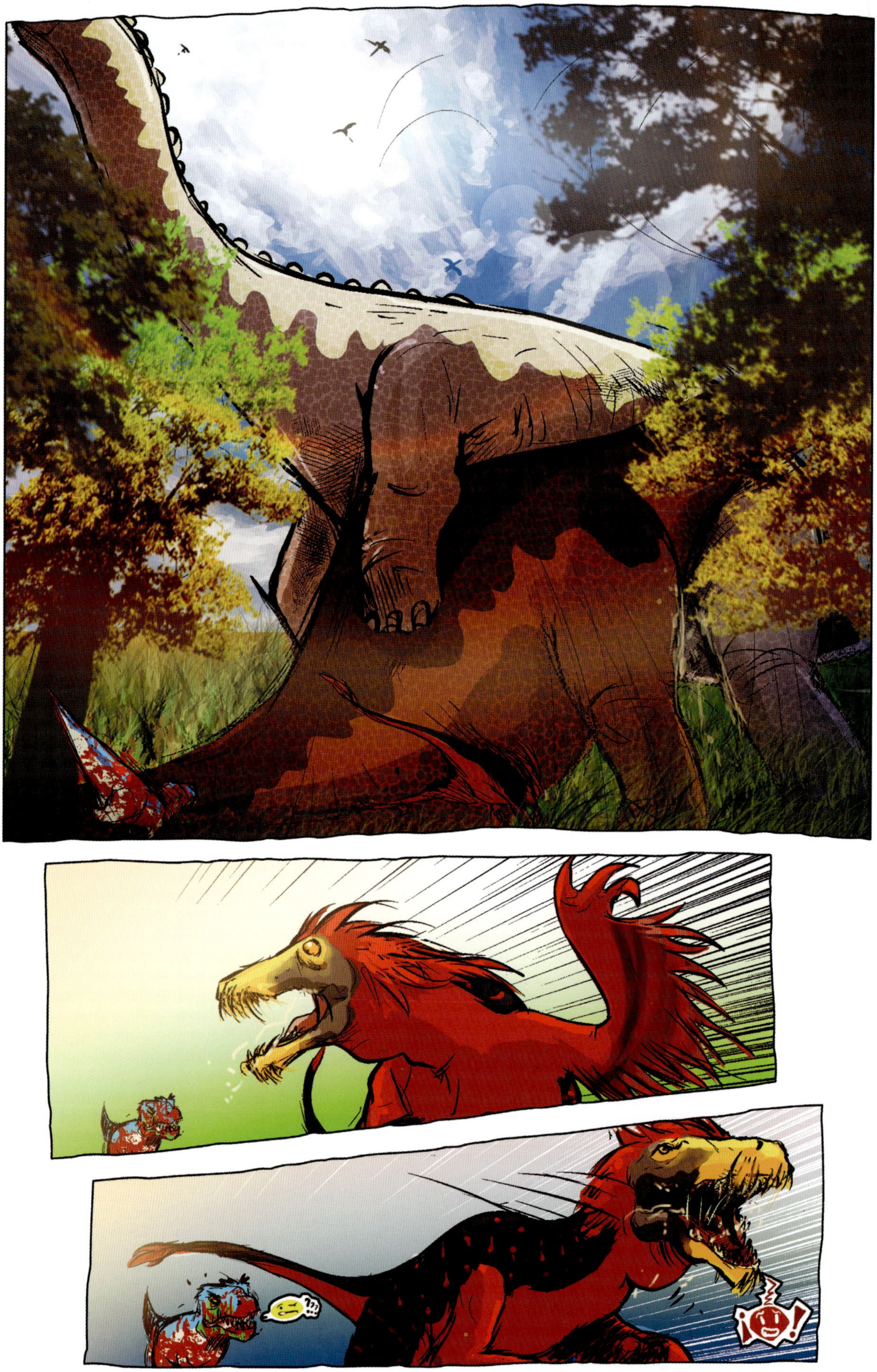

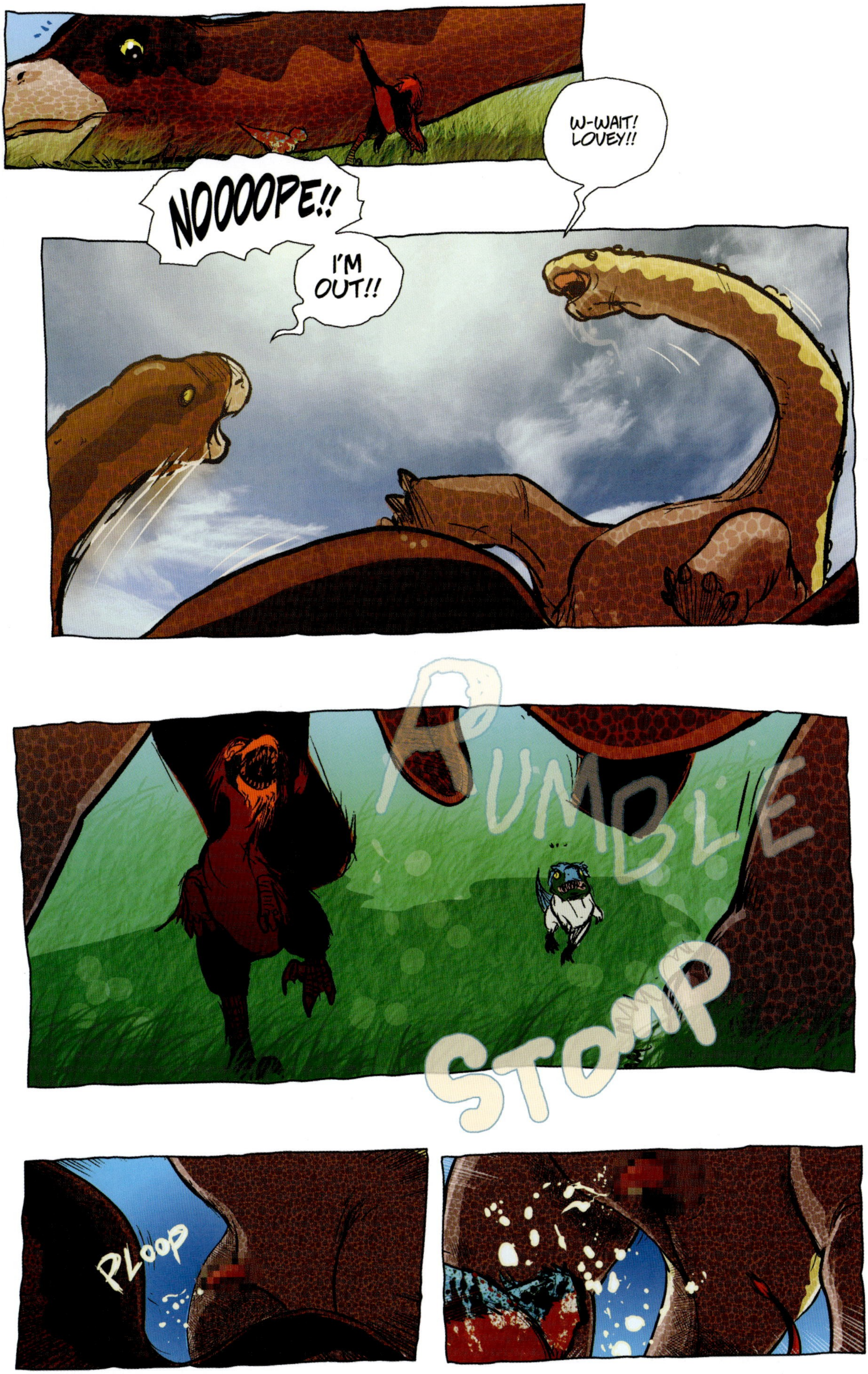
NOOOOPE!!
I'M OUT!!
W-WAIT! LOVEY!!
RUMBLE
STOMP
PLOOP

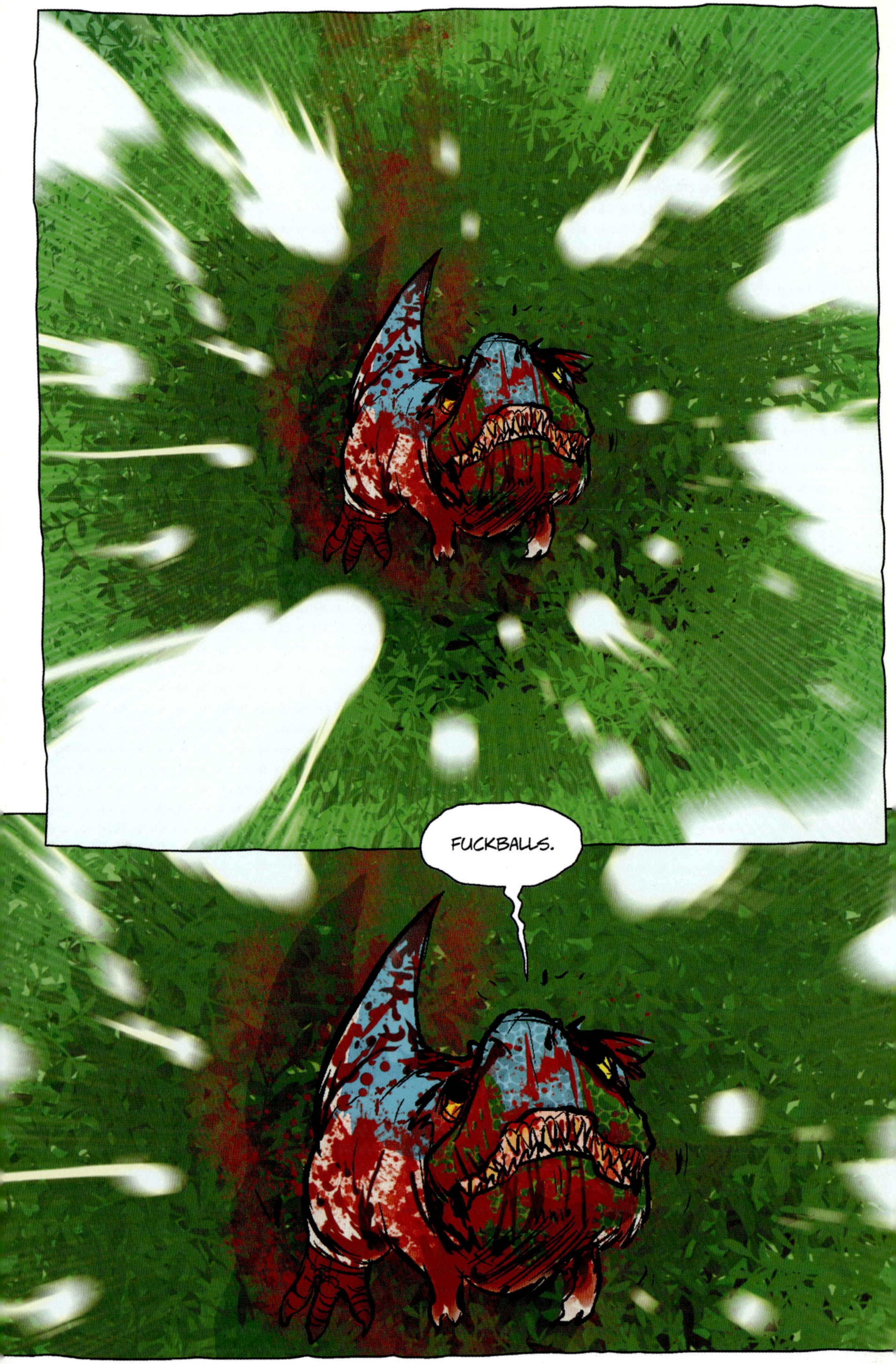
FUCKBALLS.

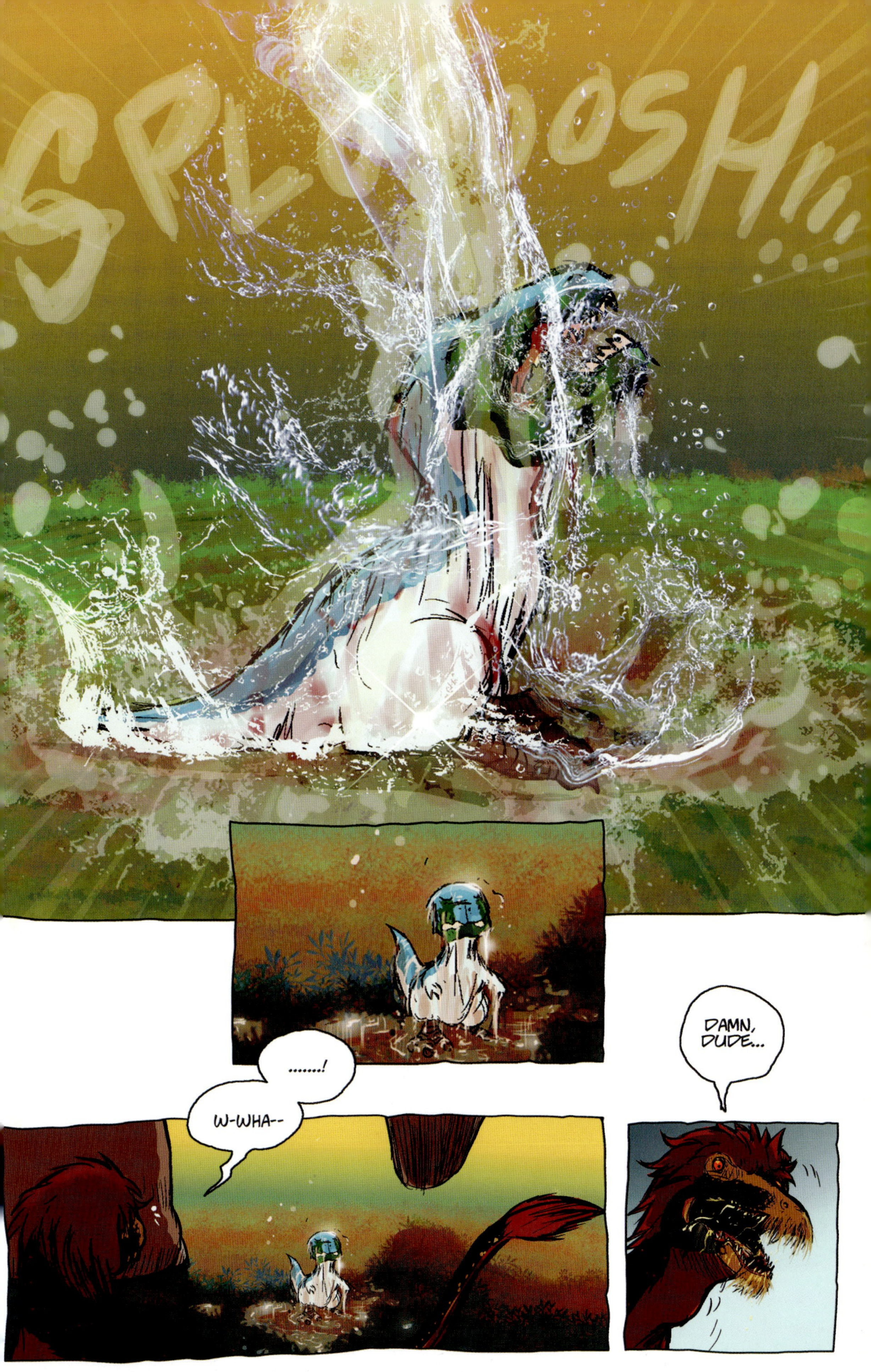
SPLOOOSH!!!
........!
W-WHA--
DAMN, DUDE...

CLUMP

GGHHAAAAHHHH

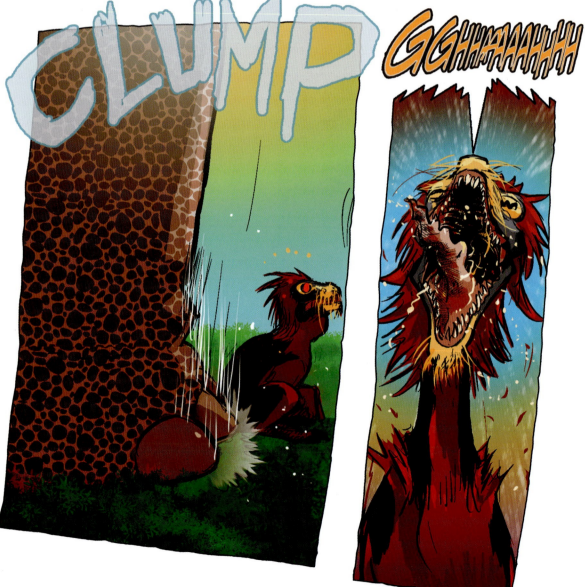

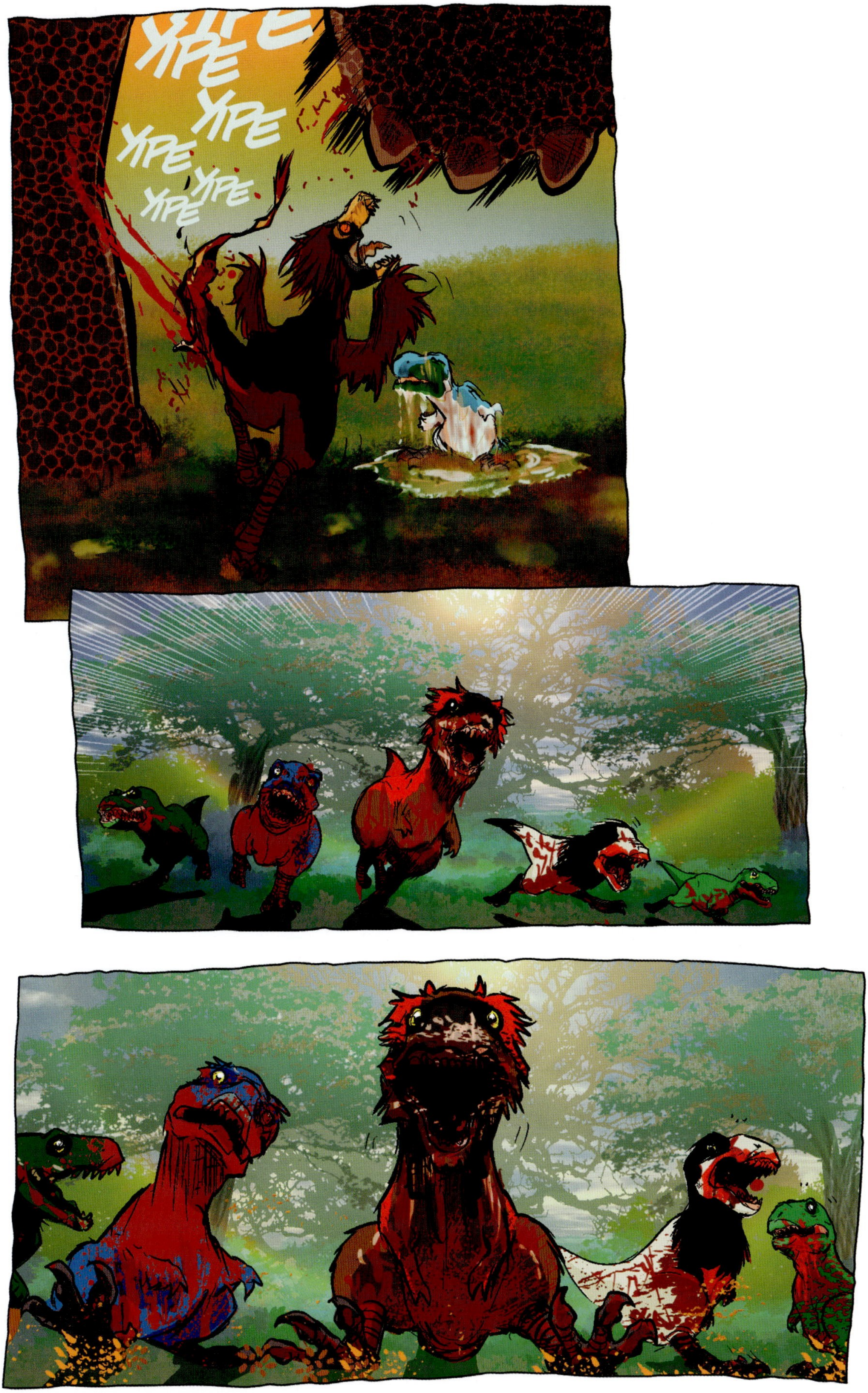

YIPE
YIPE
YIPE
YIPE
YIPE

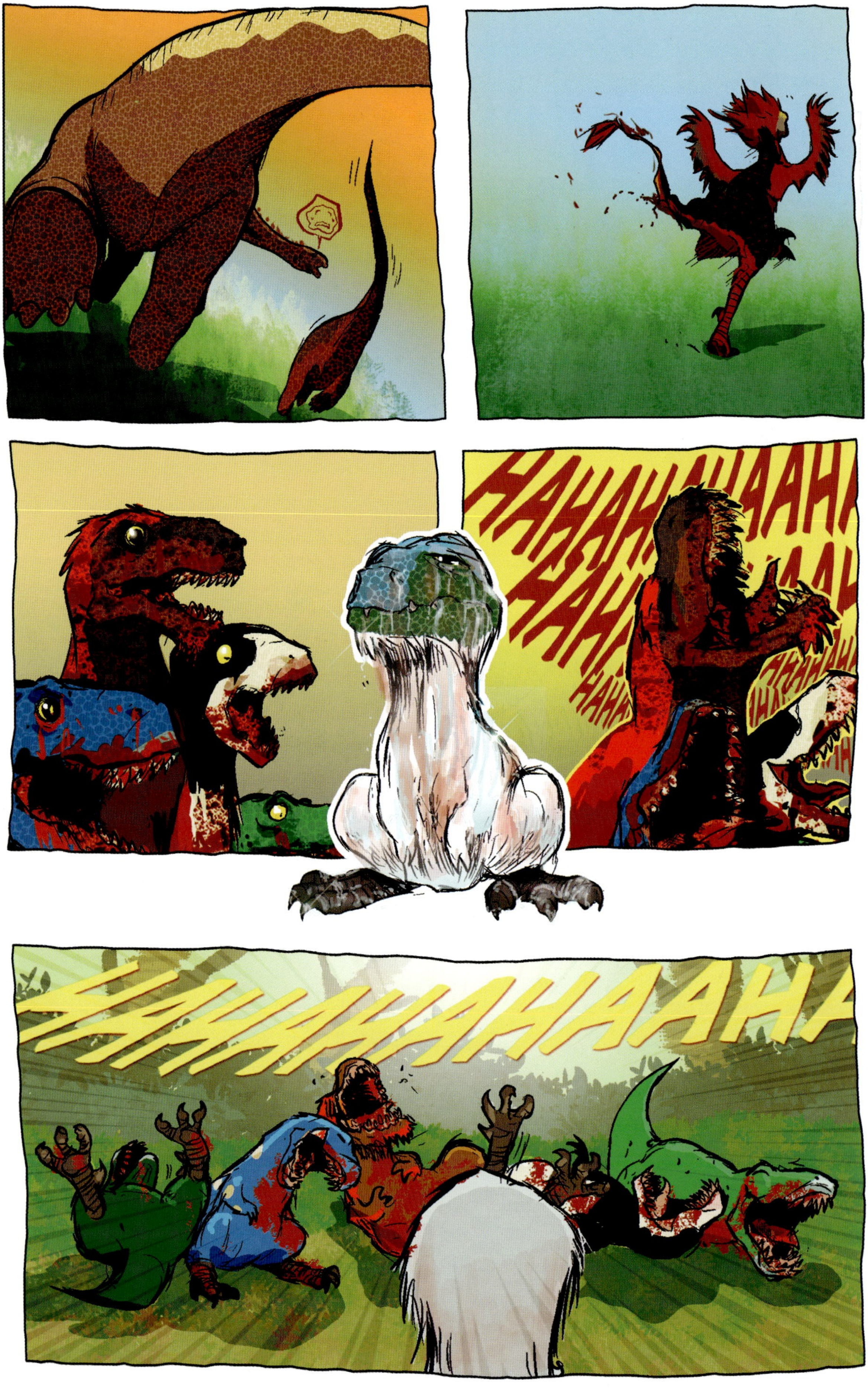
HAHAHAHAAAH
HAHAHAHAHAAAHA

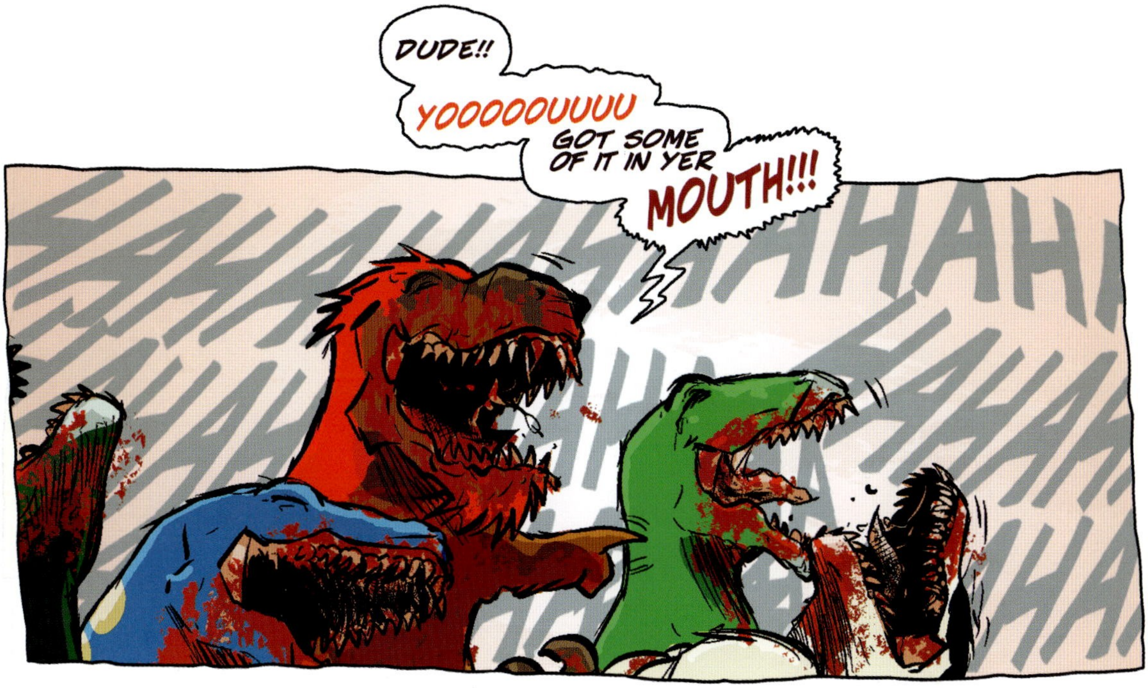
DUDE!!
YOOOOOUUUU GOT SOME OF IT IN YER MOUTH!!!
HAHAHAHAHAHAHAH

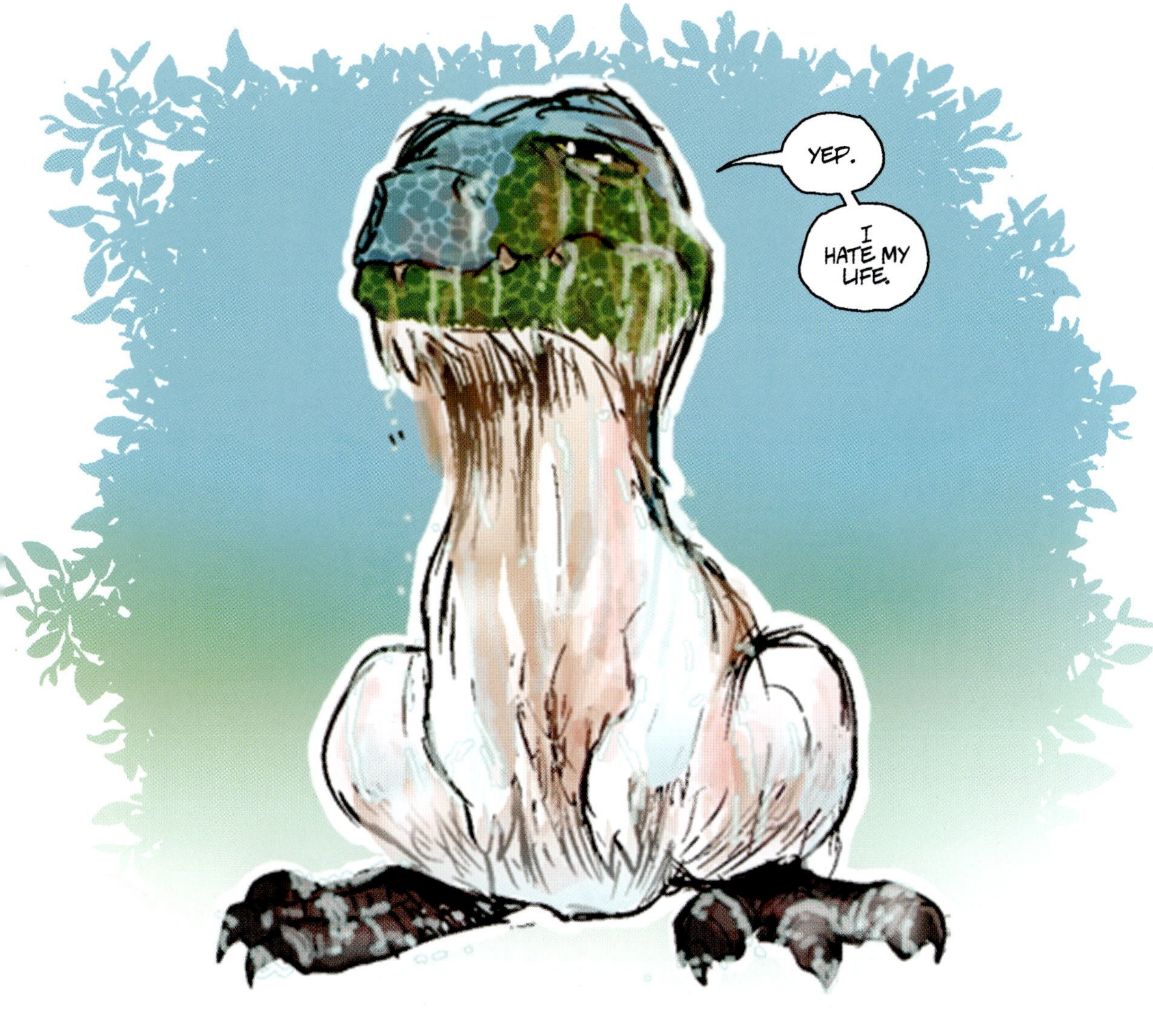
YEP.
I HATE MY LIFE.

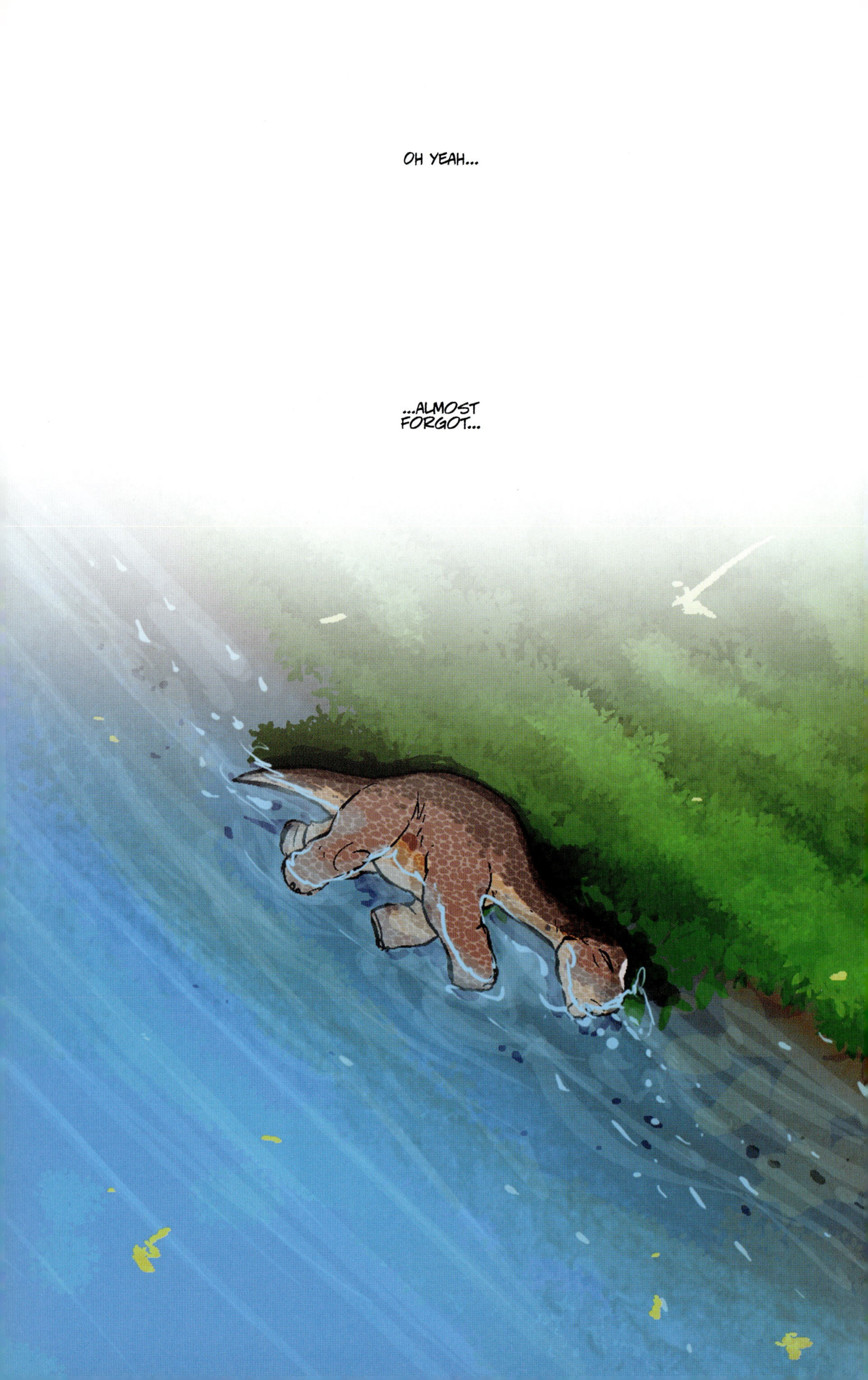
OH YEAH...
...ALMOST FORGOT...

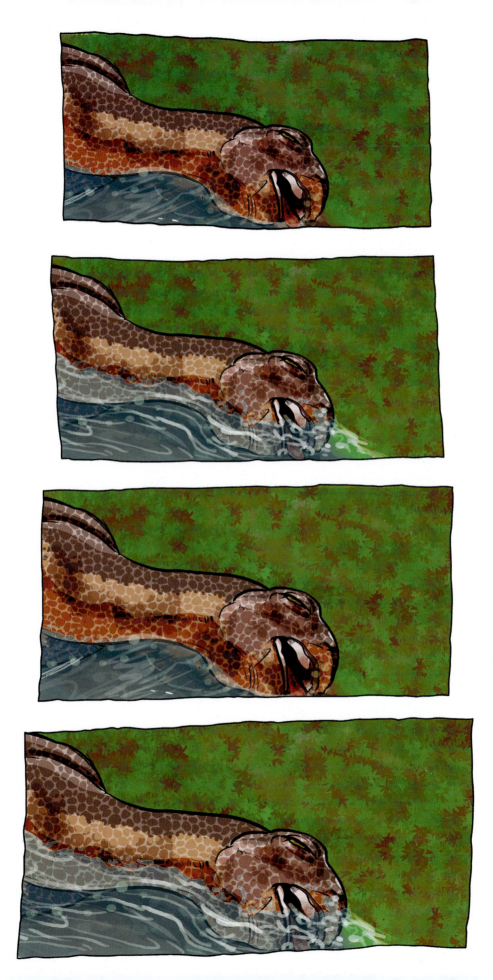

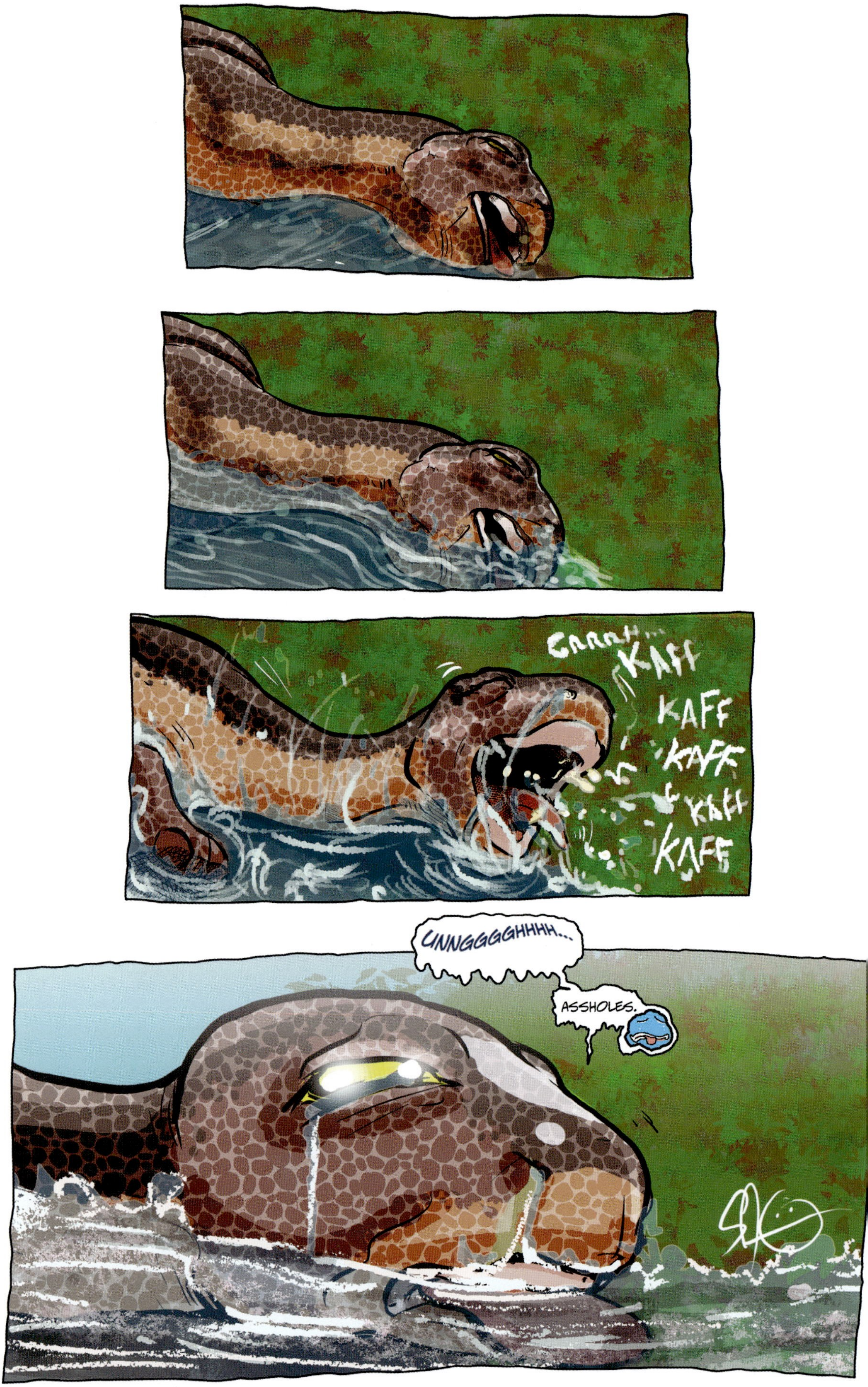
GARRAH...
KAFF
KAFF
KAFF
KAFF
KAFF
UNNGGGGHHHH...
ASSHOLES.

TO BE CONTINUED.

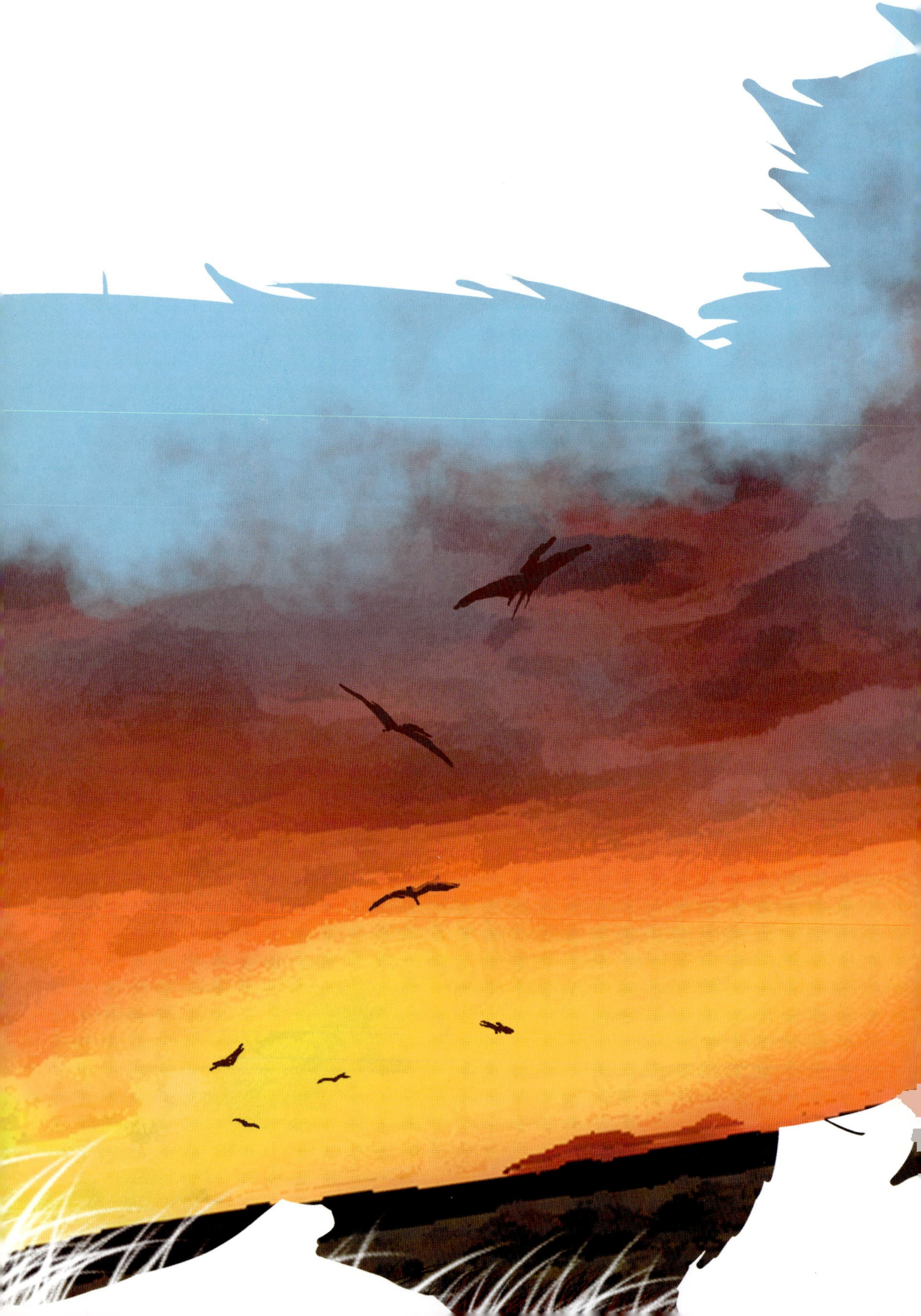

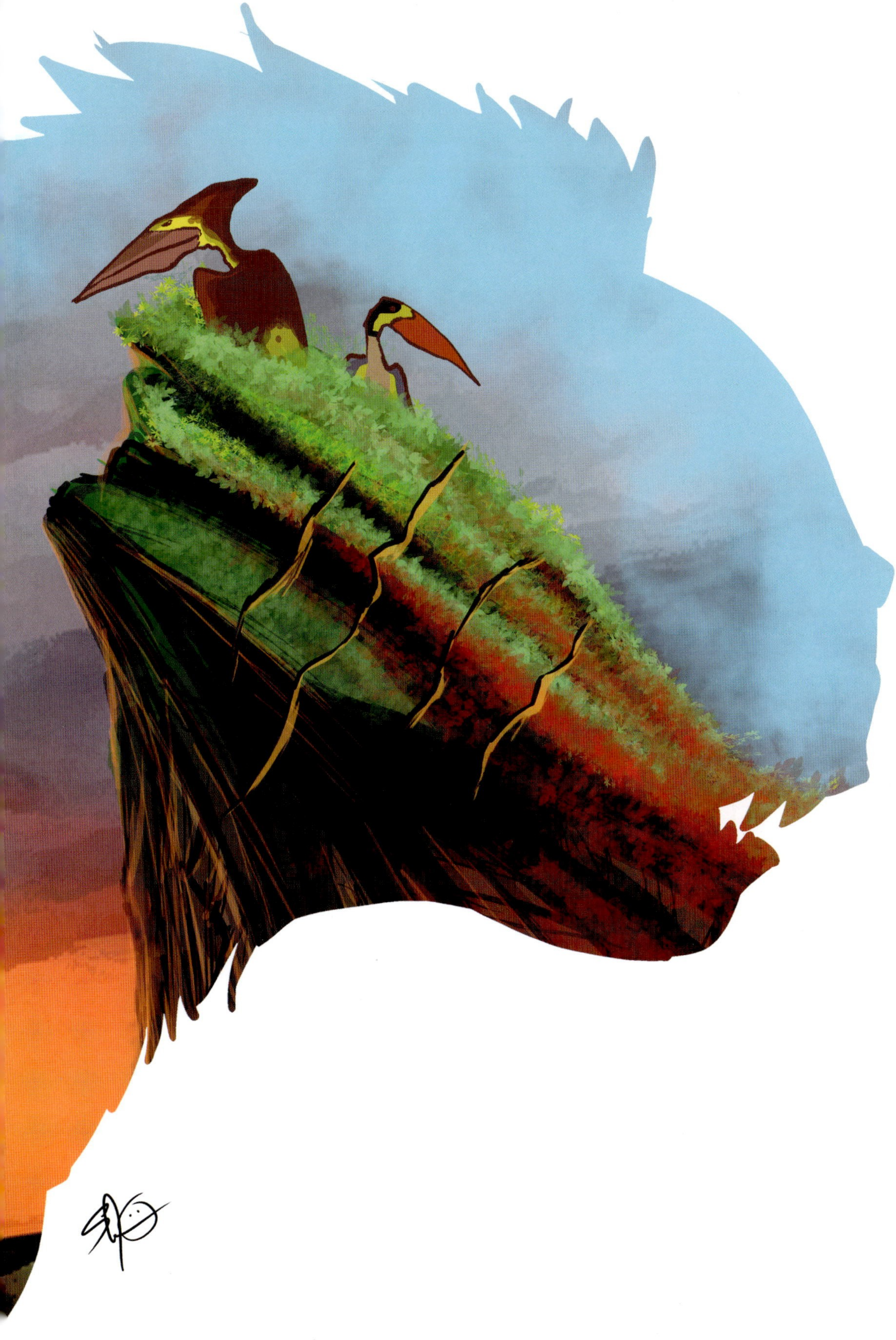